D0037489

Daily Light

As compiled from the

NEW AMERICAN STANDARD BIBLE

Daily Light

As compiled from the
NEW AMERICAN STANDARD BIBLE

by
Vivian Stensland
Morning and Evening Readings

MOODY PRESS
CHICAGO

All Scripture quotations are taken from the New American
Standard Bible,
© THE LOCKMAN FOUNDATION 1960, 1962, 1963, 1968, 1971, 1972,
1973, 1975 and are used by permission.

ISBN: 0-8024-1740-X

11 12 13 14 15 16 17 Printing/EE/Year 87 86 85 84 83 82

Printed in the United States of America

Presented to _____

_____

by _____

_____

on _____

But one thing I do: forgetting what lies behind and reaching forward to what lies ahead, I press on toward the goal for the prize of the upward call of God in Christ Jesus.

Father, I desire that they also whom Thou hast given Me be with Me where I am, in order that they may behold My glory, which Thou hast given me.—I know whom I have believed and I am convinced that He is able to guard what I have entrusted to Him until that day.—He who began a good work in you will perfect it until the day of Christ Jesus.

Do you not know that those who run in a race all run, but only one receives the prize? Run in such a way that you may win. And everyone who competes in the games exercises self-control in all things. They then do it to receive a perishable wreath, but we an imperishable.—Lay aside every encumbrance, and the sin which so easily entangles us, and let us run with endurance the race that is set before us, fixing our eyes on Jesus.

PHIL 3:13,14. Jn 17:24.—2 Ti 1:12.—Phil 1:6. 1 Co 9:24,25.—
Heb 12:1,2.

The Lord is the one who goes ahead of you; He will be with you. He will not fail you.

If Thy presence does not go with us, do not lead us up from here.—I know, O Lord, that a man's way is not in himself; nor is it in a man who walks to direct his steps.

The steps of a man are established by the Lord; and He delights in his way. When he falls, he shall not be hurled headlong; because the Lord is the One who holds his hand.

I am continually with Thee; Thou hast taken hold of my right hand. With Thy counsel Thou wilt guide me, and afterward receive me to glory.—I am convinced that neither death, nor life, nor angels, nor principalities, nor things present, nor things to come, nor powers, nor height, nor depth, nor any other created thing, shall be able to separate us from the love of God, which is in Christ Jesus our Lord.

DEU 31:8. Ex 33:15.—Jer 10:23. Ps 37:23,24. Ps 73:23,24.—
Ro 8:38,39.

Sing to the LORD a new song.

Sing for joy to God our strength; shout joyfully to the God of Jacob. Raise a song, strike the timbrel, the sweet sounding lyre with the harp.—He put a new song in my mouth, a song of praise to our God; many will see and fear, and will trust in the LORD.

Be strong and courageous! Do not tremble or be dismayed, for the LORD your God is with you wherever you go.—The joy of the LORD is your strength.—Paul . . . thanked God and took courage.

Knowing the time, that it is already the hour for you to awaken from sleep; for now salvation is nearer to us than when we believed. The night is almost gone, and the day is at hand. Let us therefore lay aside the deeds of darkness and put on the armor of light. Let us behave properly as in the day, not in carousing and drunkenness, not in sexual promiscuity and sensuality, not in strife and jealousy. But put on the Lord Jesus Christ, and make no provision for the flesh in regard to its lusts.

IS 42:10. Ps 81:1,2—Ps 40:3. Jos 1:9.—Neh 8:10.—Ac 28:15.
Ro 13:11–14.

May my prayer be counted as incense before Thee; the lifting up of my hands as the evening offering.

You shall make an altar as a place for burning incense. . . . And you shall put this altar in front of the veil that is near the ark of the testimony, in front of the mercy seat that is over the ark of the testimony, where I will meet with you. And Aaron shall burn fragrant incense on it; he shall burn it every morning when he trims the lamps. And when Aaron trims the lamps at twilight, he shall burn incense. There shall be perpetual incense before the LORD throughout your generations.

He is able to save forever those who draw near to God through Him, since He always lives to make intercession for them.—The smoke of the incense, with the prayers of the saints, went up before God out of the angel's hand.

You also, as living stones, are being built up as a spiritual house for a holy priesthood, to offer up spiritual sacrifices acceptable to God through Jesus Christ.

Pray without ceasing.

PS 141:2. Ex 30:1,6–8. Heb 7:25.—Rev 8:4. 1 Pe 2:5. 1 Th 5:17.

He led them also by a straight way.

He found (Jacob) in a desert land, and in the howling waste of a wilderness; He encircled him, He cared for him, He guarded him as the pupil of His eye. Like an eagle that stirs up its nest, that hovers over its young, He spread His wings and caught them, He carried them on His pinions. The LORD alone guided him.—Even to your old age, I shall be the same, and even to your graying years I shall bear you! I have done it, and I shall carry you; and I shall bear you, and I shall deliver you.

He restores my soul; He guides me in the paths of righteousness for His name's sake. Even though I walk through the valley of the shadow of death, I fear no evil; for Thou art with me; Thy rod and Thy staff, they comfort me.

And the LORD will continually guide you, and satisfy your desire in scorched places, and give strength to your bones; and you will be like a watered garden, and like a spring of water whose waters do not fail.—For such is God, our God forever and ever; He will guide us until death.—Who is a teacher like Him?

PS 107:7. Deu 32:10–12.—Is 46:4. Ps 23:3,4. Is 58:11.—Ps 48:14.—Job 36:22.

What do you want Me to do for you? . . . Lord, I want to receive my sight!

Open my eyes, that I may behold wonderful things from Thy law.

Then He opened their minds to understand the Scriptures.—The Helper, the Holy Spirit, whom the Father will send in My name, He will teach you all things.—Every good thing bestowed and every perfect gift is from above, coming down from the Father of lights.

The God of our Lord Jesus Christ, the Father of glory, may give to you a spirit of wisdom and of revelation in the knowledge of Him. I pray that the eyes of your heart may be enlightened, so that you may know what is the hope of His calling, what are the riches of the glory of His inheritance in the saints, and what is the surpassing greatness of His power toward us who believe. These are in accordance with the working of the strength of His might.

LK 18:41. Ps 119:18. Lk 24:45.—Jn 14:26.—Ja 1:17. Eph 1:17–19.

You have not as yet come to the resting place and the inheritance which the LORD your God is giving you.

This is no place of rest.—There remains therefore a Sabbath rest for the people of God.—Within the veil, where Jesus has entered as a forerunner for us.

In My Father's house are many dwelling places; if it were not so, I would have told you; for I go to prepare a place for you. And if I go and prepare a place for you, I will come again, and receive you to Myself; that where I am, there you may be also.—With Christ, for that is very much better.

He shall wipe away every tear from their eyes; and there shall no longer be any death; there shall no longer be any mourning, or crying, or pain: the first things have passed away.—There the wicked cease from raging, and there the weary are at rest.

Lay up for yourselves treasures in heaven . . . where your treasure is, there will your heart be also.—Set your mind on the things above, not on the things that are on earth.

DEU 12:9. Mic 2:10.—Heb 4:9.—Heb 6:19,20. Jn 14:2,3.—
Phil 1:23. Rev 21:4.—Job 3:17. Mt 6:20,21.—Col. 3:2.

O Death, where is your victory? O Death, where is your sting?

The sting of death is sin.—But now once at the consummation of the ages He (Jesus) has been manifested to put away sin by the sacrifice of Himself. And inasmuch as it is appointed for men to die once and after this comes the judgment, so Christ also, having been offered once to bear the sins of many, shall appear a second time for salvation without reference to sin, to those who eagerly await Him.

Since then the children share in flesh and blood, He Himself likewise also partook of the same, that through death He might render powerless him who had the power of death, that is, the devil; and might deliver those who through fear of death were subject to slavery all their lives.

For I am already being poured out as a drink offering, and the time of my departure has come. I have fought the good fight, I have finished the course, I have kept the faith; in the future there is laid up for me the crown of righteousness.

1 CO 15:55. 1 Co 15:56.—Heb 9:26–28. Heb 2:14,15. 2 Ti 4:6–8.

We who have believed enter that rest.

They weary themselves committing iniquity.—I see a different law in the members of my body, waging war against the law of my mind, and making me a prisoner of the law of sin which is in my members. Wretched man that I am! Who will set me free from the body of this death?

Come to Me, all who are weary and heavy laden, and I will give you rest.—Having been justified by faith, we have peace with God through our Lord Jesus Christ, through whom also we have obtained our introduction by faith into this grace in which we stand; and we exult in hope of the glory of God.

For the one who has entered His rest has himself also rested from his works.

Not having a righteousness of my own derived from the Law, but that which is through faith in Christ, the righteousness which comes from God on the basis of faith.—Here is rest, give rest to the weary, and here is repose.

HEB 4:3. Jer 9:5.—Ro 7:23,24. Mt 11:28.—Ro 5:1,2. Heb 4:10. Phil 3:9.—Is 28:12.

Set a guard, O LORD, over my mouth; keep watch over the door of my lips.

If Thou, LORD, shouldst mark iniquities, O LORD, who could stand?—Because they were rebellious against His Spirit, he spoke rashly with his lips.

Not what enters into the mouth defiles the man, but what proceeds out of the mouth, this defiles the man.

A slanderer separates intimate friends.—There is one who speaks rashly like the thrusts of a sword, but the tongue of the wise brings healing. Truthful lips will be established forever, but a lying tongue is only for a moment.—No one can tame the tongue; it is a restless evil and full of deadly poison . . . from the same mouth come both blessing and cursing. My brethren, these things ought not to be this way.

Put aside . . . anger, wrath, malice, slander, and abusive speech from your mouth. Do not lie to one another, since you laid aside the old self with its evil practices.—This is the will of God, your sanctification.—No lie was found in their mouth.

PS 141:3. Ps 130:3.—Ps 106:33. Mt 15:11. Pr 16:28.—Pr 12:18,19.— Ja 3:8,10. Col 3:8,9.—1 Th 4:3.—Rev 14:5.

Let the favor of the Lord our God be upon us; and do confirm for us the work of our hands.

Then your fame went forth among the nations on account of your beauty, for it was perfect because of My splendor which I bestowed on you, declares the Lord GOD.—We all, with unveiled face beholding as in a mirror the glory of the Lord, are being transformed into the same image from glory to glory, just as from the Lord, the Spirit.

How blessed is everyone who fears the LORD, who walks in His ways. When you shall eat of the fruit of your hands, you will be happy and it will be well with you.—Commit your works to the LORD, and your plans will be established.

Work out your salvation with fear and trembling; for it is God who is at work in you, both to will and to work for His good pleasure.—May our Lord Jesus Christ Himself and God our Father, who has loved us and given us eternal comfort and good hope by grace, comfort and strengthen your hearts in every good work and word.

PS 90:17. Eze 16:14.—2 Co 3:18. Ps 128:1,2.—Pr 16:3.
Phil 2:12,13.—2 Th 2:16,17.

The apostles gathered together with Jesus; and they reported to Him all that they had done and taught.

There is a friend who sticks closer than a brother.—The LORD used to speak to Moses face to face, just as a man speaks to his friend.—You are My friends, if you do what I command you. No longer do I call you slaves; for the slave does not know what his master is doing; but I have called you friends, for all things that I have heard from My Father I have made known to you.

When you do all the things which are commanded you, say, We are unworthy slaves.

You have not received a spirit of slavery leading to fear again, but you have received a spirit of adoption as sons by which we cry out, Abba! Father!

Be anxious for nothing, but in everything by prayer and supplication with thanksgiving let your requests be made known to God.—The prayer of the upright is His delight.

MK 6:30. Pr 18:24.—Ex 33:11.—Jn 15:14,15. Lk 17:10. Ro 8:15.
Phil 4:6.—Pr 15:8.

Remember me, O my God, for good.

Thus says the LORD, I remember concerning you the devotion of your youth, the love of your betrothals, your following after Me in the wilderness.—I will remember My covenant with you in the days of your youth, and I will establish an everlasting covenant with you.—I will visit you and fulfill My good word to you ... For I know the plans that I have for you, declares the LORD, plans for welfare and not for calamity to give you a future and a hope.

As the heavens are higher than the earth, so are My ways higher than your ways, and My thoughts than your thoughts.— As for me, I would seek God, and I would place my cause before God; who does great and unsearchable things, wonders without number.—Many, O LORD my God, are the wonders which Thou hast done, and Thy thoughts toward us; there is none to compare with Thee; if I would declare and speak of them, they would be too numerous to count.

NEH 5:19. Jer 2:2.—Eze 16:60.—Jer 29:10,11. Is 55:9.—Job 5:8,9.—
Ps 40:5.

I will not fail you or forsake you.

Not one of the good promises which the LORD had made to the house of Israel failed; all came to pass.—God is not a man, that He should lie, nor a son of man, that He should repent; has He said, and will He not do it? or has He spoken, and will He not make it good?

Know therefore that the LORD your God, He is God, the faithful God, who keeps His covenant and His lovingkindness ... with those who love Him and keep His commandments.—He will remember His covenant forever.

Can a woman forget her nursing child, and have no compassion on the son of her womb? Even these may forget, but I will not forget you. Behold, I have inscribed you on the palms of My hands.

The LORD your God is in your midst, a victorious warrior. He will exult over you with joy, He will be quiet in His love, He will rejoice over you with shouts of joy.

JOS 1:5. Jos 21:45.—Num 23:19. Deu 7:9.—Ps 111:5. Is 49:15,16.
Zep 3:17.

Those who know Thy name will put their trust in Thee; for Thou, O LORD, hast not forsaken those who seek Thee.

The name of the LORD is a strong tower; the righteous runs into it and is safe.—God is my salvation, I will trust and not be afraid; for the LORD GOD is my strength and song, and He has become my salvation.

I have been young, and now I am old; yet I have not seen the righteous forsaken or his descendants begging bread.—For the LORD loves justice, and does not forsake His godly ones; they are preserved forever; but the descendants of the wicked will be cut off.—The LORD will not abandon His people on account of His great name, because the LORD has been pleased to make you a people for Himself.—Who delivered us from so great a peril of death, and will deliver us, He on whom we have set our hope. And He will yet deliver us.

Let your character be free from the love of money, being content with what you have; for He Himself has said, I will never desert you, nor will I ever forsake you, so that we confidently say, the LORD is my Helper, I will not be afraid. What shall man do to me?

PS 9:10. Pr 18:10.—Is 12:2. Ps 37:25.—Ps 37:28.—1 Sa 12:22.—
2 Co 1:10. Heb 13:5,6.

They are blameless.

Search will be made for the iniquity of Israel, but there will be none; and for the sins of Judah, but they will not be found; for I shall pardon those whom I leave as a remnant.—Who is a God like Thee, who pardons iniquity and passes over the rebellious act of the remnant of His possession? He does not retain His anger forever, because He delights in unchanging love. He will again have compassion on us; He will tread our iniquities underfoot. Yes, Thou wilt cast all their sins into the depths of the sea.

His grace, which He freely bestowed on us in the Beloved.—To present you before Him holy and blameless and beyond reproach.

Now to Him who is able to keep you from stumbling, and to make you stand in the presence of His glory blameless with great joy, to the only God our Savior, through Jesus Christ our Lord, be glory, majesty, dominion and authority, before all time and now and forever. Amen.

REV 14:5. Jer 50:20.—Mic 7:18,19. Eph 1:6.—Col 1:22. Jude 24,25.

Thou hast given a banner to those who fear Thee, that it may be displayed because of the truth.

The LORD is My Banner.—For He will come like a rushing stream, which the wind of the LORD drives.

We will sing for joy over your victory, and in the name of our God we will set up our banners.—The LORD has brought about our vindication; come and let us recount in Zion the work of the LORD our God.—We overwhelmingly conquer through Him who loved us.—Thanks be to God, who gives us the victory through our Lord Jesus Christ.—The author of their salvation.

Be strong in the Lord, and in the strength of His might.—Truth prevail.—The LORD's battles.—All you people of the land take courage, declares the LORD, and work . . . do not fear!—Lift up your eyes, and look on the fields, that they are white for harvest.—For yet in a very little while, He who is coming will come, and will not delay.

PS 60:4. Ex 17:15.—Is 59:19. Ps 20:5.—Jer 51:10.—Ro 8:37.—
1 Co 15:57.—Heb 2:10. Eph 6:10.—Jer 9:3.—1 Sa 18:17.—
Hag 2:4,5.—Jn 4:35.—Heb 10:37.

Few things are necessary, really only one.

Many are saying, Who will show us any good? Lift up the light of Thy countenance upon us, O LORD! Thou hast put gladness in my heart, more than when their grain and new wine abound.

As the deer pants for the water brooks, so my soul pants for Thee, O God. My soul thirsts for God, for the living God.—O GOD, Thou art my God; I shall seek Thee earnestly; my soul thirsts for Thee, my flesh yearns for Thee, in a dry and weary land where there is no water.

I am the bread of life; he who comes to Me shall not hunger, and he who believes in Me shall never thirst. Lord, evermore give us this bread.—Mary, who moreover was listening to the Lord's word, seated at His feet.—One thing I have asked from the LORD, that I shall seek; that I may dwell in the house of the LORD all the days of my life, to behold the beauty of the LORD, and to meditate in His temple.

LK 10:42. Ps 4:6,7. Ps 42:1,2.—Ps 63:1. Jn 6:35,34.—Lk 10:39.—
Ps 27:4.

May the God of peace Himself sanctify you entirely; and may your spirit and soul and body be preserved complete, without blame at the coming of our Lord Jesus Christ.

Christ also loved the church and gave Himself up for her; that He might present to Himself the church in all her glory, having no spot or wrinkle or any such thing; but that she should be holy and blameless.—We proclaim Him, admonishing every man and teaching every man with all wisdom, that we may present every man complete in Christ.

The peace of God . . . surpasses all comprehension.—Let the peace of Christ rule in your hearts, to which indeed you were called in one body.

Our Lord Jesus Christ Himself and God our Father, who has loved us and given us eternal comfort and good hope by grace, comfort and strengthen your hearts in every good work and word.—Who shall also confirm you to the end, blameless in the day of our Lord Jesus Christ.

1 TH 5:23. Eph 5:25,27.—Col 1:28. Phil 4:7.—Col 3:15.
2 Th 2:16,17.—1 Co 1:8.

But will God indeed dwell with mankind on the earth?

Let them construct a sanctuary for Me, that I may dwell among them.—I will meet there with the sons of Israel, and it shall be consecrated by My glory. And I will dwell among the sons of Israel and will be their God.

Thou hast ascended on high, Thou hast led captive Thy captives; Thou hast received gifts among men, even among the rebellious also, that the LORD God may dwell there.

We are the temple of the living God; just as God said, I will dwell in them and walk among them; and I will be their God, and they shall be My people.—Your body is a temple of the Holy Spirit who is in you.—You also are being built together into a dwelling of God in the Spirit.

The nations will know that I am the LORD who sanctifies Israel, when My sanctuary is in their midst forever.

2 CH 6:18. Ex 25:8.—Ex 29:43,45. Ps 68:18. 2 Co 6:16.—
1 Co 6:19.—Eph 2:22. Eze 37:28.

There will be silence before Thee, and praise ... O God.

There is but one God, the Father, from whom are all things, and we exist for Him; and one Lord, Jesus Christ, through whom are all things, and we exist through Him.—Honor the Son, even as they honor the Father. He who does not honor the Son does not honor the Father who sent Him.—Through Him then let us continually offer up a sacrifice of praise to God, that is, the fruit of lips that give thanks to His name.—He who offers a sacrifice of thanksgiving honors Me; and to him who orders his way aright I shall show the salvation of God.

I looked, and behold, a great multitude, which no one could count, from every nation and all tribes and peoples and tongues, standing before the throne and before the Lamb, clothed in white robes, and palm branches were in their hands; and they cry out with a loud voice, saying, Salvation to our God who sits on the throne, and to the Lamb. Amen, blessing and glory and wisdom and thanksgiving and honor and power and might, be to our God forever and ever. Amen.

PS 65:1. 1 Co 8:6.—Jn 5:23.—Heb 13:15.—Ps 50:23. Rev 7:9,10,12.

Who redeems your life from the pit.

Their Redeemer is strong, the Lord of hosts is His name.—I will ransom them from the power of Sheol; I will redeem them from death. O Death, where are your thorns? O Sheol, where is your sting?

Since then the children share in flesh and blood, He Himself likewise also partook of the same, that through death He might render powerless him who had the power of death, that is, the devil; and might deliver those who through fear of death were subject to slavery all their lives.

He who believes in the Son has eternal life; but he who does not obey the Son shall not see life, but the wrath of God abides on him.

You have died and your life is hidden with Christ in God. When Christ, who is our life, is revealed, then you also will be revealed with Him in glory.—When He comes to be glorified in His saints on that day, and to be marveled at among all who have believed.

PS 103:4. Jer 50:34.—Ho 13:14. Heb 2:14,15. Jn 3:36. Col 3:3,4.—
2 Th 1:10.

The only God our Savior.

By His doing you are in Christ Jesus, who became to us wisdom from God, and righteousness and sanctification, and redemption. —Can you discover the depths of God? Can you discover the limits of the Almighty? They are high as the heavens, what can you do? Deeper than Sheol, what can you know?

We speak God's wisdom in a mystery, the hidden wisdom, which God predestined before the ages to our glory.—To bring to light what is the administration of the mystery which for ages has been hidden in God, who created all things; in order that the manifold wisdom of God might now be made known through the church to the rulers and the authorities in the heavenly places.

If any of you lacks wisdom, let him ask of God, who gives to all men generously and without reproach, and it will be given to him.—The wisdom from above is first pure, then peaceable, gentle, reasonable, full of mercy and good fruits, unwavering, without hypocrisy.

JUDE 25. 1 Co 1:30.—Job 11:7,8. 1 Co 2:7.—Eph 3:9,10. Ja 1:5.—
Ja 3:17.

When shall I arise? But the night continues.

Watchman, how far gone is the night? The watchman says, Morning comes. . . .

For yet in a very little while, He who is coming will come, and will not delay.—Yes, I am coming quickly. Amen. Come, Lord Jesus.

I go to prepare a place for you. I will come again, and receive you to Myself; that where I am, there you may be also. Peace I leave with you; My peace I give to you; not as the world gives, do I give to you. Let not your heart be troubled, nor let it be fearful. You heard that I said to you, I go away, and I will come to you.

Let all Thine enemies perish, O LORD; but let those who love Him be like the rising of the sun in its might.—You are all sons of light and sons of day. We are not of night nor of darkness.

There shall be no night there.

JOB 7:4. Is 21:11,12. Heb 10:37.—Rev 22:20. Jn 14:2,3,27,28.
Judg 5:31.—1 Th 5:5. Rev 21:25.

The steadfast of mind Thou wilt keep in perfect peace, because he trusts in Thee.

Cast your burden upon the Lord, and He will sustain you; He will never allow the righteous to be shaken.—I will trust and not be afraid; for the Lord God is my strength and song, and He has become my salvation.

Why are you timid, you men of little faith?—Be anxious for nothing, but in everything by prayer and supplication with thanksgiving let your requests be made known to God. And the peace of God, which surpasses all comprehension, shall guard your hearts and your minds in Christ Jesus.—In quietness and trust is your strength.

The service of righteousness, quietness and confidence forever.—Peace I leave with you; My peace I give to you; not as the world gives, do I give to you. Let not your heart be troubled, nor let it be fearful.—Peace, from Him who is and who was and who is to come.

IS 26:3. Ps 55:22.—Is 12:2. Mt 8:26.—Phil 4:6,7.—Is 30:15.
Is 32:17.—Jn 14:27.—Rev 1:4.

Do not let the sun go down on your anger.

If your brother sins, go and reprove him in private; if he listens to you, you have won your brother . . . Lord, how often shall my brother sin against me and I forgive him? Up to seven times? Jesus said to him, I do not say to you, up to seven times, but up to seventy times seven.—Whenever you stand praying, forgive, if you have anything against anyone; so that your Father also who is in heaven may forgive you your transgressions.

As those who have been chosen of God, holy and beloved, put on a heart of compassion, kindness, humility, gentleness and patience; bearing with one another, and forgiving each other, whoever has a complaint against any one; just as the Lord forgave you, so also should you.—Be kind one to another, tenderhearted, forgiving each other, just as God in Christ also has forgiven you.

The apostles said to the Lord, Increase our faith!

EPH 4:26. Mt 18:15,21,22.—Mk 11:25. Col 3:12,13.—Eph 4:32.
Lk 17:5.

The Father is greater than I.

When you pray, say: Father, hallowed be Thy name.—My Father and your Father, and My God and your God.

As the Father gave Me commandment, even so I do.—The words that I say to you I do not speak on My own initiative, but the Father abiding in Me does His works.

The Father loves the Son, and has given all things into His hand.—Thou gavest Him authority over all mankind, that to all whom Thou hast given Him, He may give eternal life.

Lord, show us the Father, and it is enough for us. Jesus said to him, Have I been so long with you, and yet you have not come to know Me, Philip? He who has seen Me has seen the Father; how do you say, Show us the Father? Do you not believe that I am in the Father, and the Father is in Me?—I and the Father are one.—As the Father has loved Me, I have also loved you; abide in My love. If you keep My commandments, you will abide in My love; just as I have kept My Father's commandments, and abide in His love.

JN 14:28. Lk 11:2.—Jn 20:17. Jn 14:31.—Jn 14:10. Jn 3:35.—Jn 17:2. Jn 14:8–10.—Jn 10:30.—Jn 15:9,10.

(The woman's seed) shall bruise you on the head, and you shall bruise him on the heel.

His appearance was marred more than any man, and His form more than the sons of men.—He was pierced through for our transgressions, He was crushed for our iniquities; the chastening for our well-being fell upon Him, and by His scourging we are healed.

This hour and the power of darkness are yours.—You would have no authority over Me, unless it had been given you from above.

The Son of God appeared for this purpose, that He might destroy the works of the devil.—He . . . cast out many demons; and He was not permitting the demons to speak, because they knew who He was.

All authority has been given to Me in heaven and on earth.— In My name they will cast out demons.

The God of peace will soon crush Satan under your feet.

GEN 3:15. Is 52:14.—Is 53:5. Lk 22:53.—Jn 19:11. 1 Jn 3:8.— Mk 1:34. Mt 28:18.—Mk 16:17. Ro 16:20.

My soul cleaves to the dust; revive me according to Thy word.

If . . . you have been raised up with Christ, keep seeking the things above, where Christ is, seated at the right hand of God. Set your mind on the things above, not on the things that are on earth. For . . . your life is hidden with Christ in God.—Our citizenship is in heaven, from which also we eagerly wait for a Savior, the Lord Jesus Christ; who will transform the body of our humble state into conformity with the body of His glory, by the exertion of the power that He has even to subject all things to Himself.

For the flesh sets its desire against the Spirit, and the Spirit against the flesh; for these are in opposition to one another, so that you may not do the things that you please.—Brethren, we are under obligation, not to the flesh, to live according to the flesh—for if you are living according to the flesh, you must die; but if by the Spirit you are putting to death the deeds of the body, you will live.—Beloved, I urge you as aliens and strangers to abstain from fleshly lusts, which wage war against the soul.

PS 119:25. Col 3:1-3.—Phil 3:20,21. Gal 5:17.—Ro 8:12,13.—
1 Pe 2:11.

A measure of faith.

One who is weak in faith.—Grew strong in faith, giving glory to God.

O you of little faith, why did you doubt?—Your faith is great; be it done for you as you wish.

Do you believe that I am able to do this? They said to Him, Yes, Lord . . . Be it done to you according to your faith.

Lord, Increase our faith!—Building yourselves up on your most holy faith.—Rooted and now being built up in Him and established in your faith.—He who establishes us with you in Christ and anointed us is God.—After you have suffered for a little while, the God of all grace, who called you to His eternal glory in Christ, will Himself perfect, confirm, strengthen and establish you.

Now we who are strong ought to bear the weaknesses of those without strength and not just please ourselves.—Let us not judge one another any more, but rather determine this—not to put an obstacle or a stumbling block in a brother's way.

RO 12:3. Ro 14:1.—Ro 4:20. Mt 14:31.—Mt 15:28. Mt 9:28,29.
Lk 17:5.—Jude 20.—Col 2:7.—2 Co 1:21.—1 Pe 5:10. Ro 15:1.—
Ro 14:13.

It was the Father's good pleasure for all the fulness to dwell in Him.

The Father loves the Son, and has given all things into His hand.—God highly exalted Him, and bestowed on Him the name which is above every name, that at the name of Jesus every knee should bow, of those who are in heaven, and on earth, and under the earth, and that every tongue should confess that Jesus Christ is Lord, to the glory of God the Father.—Far above all rule and authority and power and dominion, and every name that is named, not only in this age, but also in the one to come.—For in Him all things were created, both in the heavens and on earth, visible and invisible, whether thrones or dominions or rulers or authorities—all things have been created by Him and for Him.

Christ died and lived again, that He might be Lord both of the dead and of the living.—In Him you have been made complete, and He is the head over all rule and authority.—Of His fulness we have all received.

COL 1:19. Jn 3:35.—Phil 2:9–11.—Eph 1:21.—Col 1:16. Ro 14:9.—
Col 2:10.—Jn 1:16.

Write therefore the things which you have seen, and the things which are, and the things which shall take place after these things.

Men moved by the Holy Spirit spoke from God.—What we have seen and heard we proclaim to you also, that you also may have fellowship with us; and indeed our fellowship is with the Father, and with His Son Jesus Christ.

See My hands and My feet, that it is I Myself; touch Me and see, for a spirit does not have flesh and bones as you see that I have.—He who has seen has borne witness, and his witness is true; and he knows that he is telling the truth, so that you also may believe.

We did not follow cleverly devised tales when we made known to you the power and coming of our Lord Jesus Christ, but we are eyewitnesses of His majesty.—That your faith should not rest on the wisdom of men, but on the power of God.

REV 1:19. 2 Pe 1:21.—1 Jn 1:3. Lk 24:39.—Jn 19:35. 2 Pe 1:16.—
1 Co 2:5.

Thou who hast kept my soul from the pit of nothingness.

God has sent His only begotten Son into the world so that we might live through Him. In this is love, not that we loved God, but that He loved us and sent His Son to be the propitiation for our sins.

Who is a God like Thee, who pardons iniquity and passes over the rebellious act of the remnant of His possession? He does not retain His anger forever, because He delights in unchanging love. He will again have compassion on us; He will tread our iniquities underfoot. Yes, Thou wilt cast all their sins into the depths of the sea.—O LORD my God, I cried to Thee for help, and Thou didst heal me. O LORD, Thou hast brought up my soul from Sheol; Thou hast kept me alive, that I should not go down to the pit.—While I was fainting away, I remembered the LORD; and my prayer came to Thee, into Thy holy temple.—I waited patiently for the LORD ... He brought me up out of the pit of destruction, out of the miry clay; and He set my feet upon a rock.

IS 38:17. 1 Jn 4:9,10. Mic 7:18,19.—Ps 30:2,3.—Jon 2:7.—Ps 40:1,2.

The things which are.

Now we see in a mirror dimly.—Thou hast put all things in subjection under His feet.

We have the prophetic word made more sure, to which you do well to pay attention as to a lamp shining in a dark place, until the day dawns and the morning star arises in your hearts.—Thy word is a lamp to my feet, and a light to my path.

You, beloved, ought to remember the words that were spoken beforehand by the apostles of our Lord Jesus Christ; that they were saying to you, In the last time there shall be mockers, following after their own ungodly lusts.—The Spirit explicitly says that in later times some will fall away from the faith, paying attention to deceitful spirits and doctrines of demons.

Children, it is the last hour.—The night is almost gone, and the day is at hand. Let us therefore lay aside the deeds of darkness and put on the armor of light.

REV 1:19. 1 Co 13:12.—Heb 2:8. 2 Pe 1:19.—Ps 119:105.
Jude 17,18.—1 Ti 4:1. Jn 2:18.—Ro 13:12.

Him who was to come.

Him who has been made for a little while lower than the angels, namely, Jesus, because of the suffering of death . . . that by the grace of God He might taste death for every one.—One died for all.—Through the one man's disobedience the many were made sinners, even so through the obedience of the One the many will be made righteous.

The first man, Adam, became a living soul. The last Adam became a life-giving spirit. However, the spiritual is not first, but the natural; then the spiritual.—God said, Let Us make man in Our image, according to Our likeness . . . And God created man in His own image, in the image of God He created him.—God, after He spoke long ago—in these last days has spoken to us in His Son. . . . He is the radiance of His glory and the exact representation of His nature.—Thou gavest Him authority over all mankind.

The first man is from the earth, earthy; the second man is from heaven. As is the earthy, so also are those who are earthy; and as is the heavenly, so also are those who are heavenly.

RO 5:14. Heb 2:9.—2 Co 5:14.—Ro 5:19. 1 Co 15:45,46.—
Gen 1:26,27.—Heb 1:1-3.—Jn 17:2. 1 Co 15:47,48.

The things which shall take place.

It is written, Things which eye has not seen and ear has not heard, and which have not entered the heart of man, all that God has prepared for those who love Him. For to us God revealed them through the Spirit.—The Spirit of truth . . . will disclose to you what is to come.

Behold, He is coming with the clouds, and every eye will see Him, even those who pierced Him; and all the tribes of the earth will mourn over Him. Even so. Amen.

We do not want you to be uninformed, brethren, about those who are asleep, that you may not grieve, as do the rest who have no hope. For if we believe that Jesus died and rose again, even so God will bring with Him those who have fallen asleep in Jesus. For the Lord Himself will descend from heaven with a shout, with the voice of the archangel, and with the trumpet of God; and the dead in Christ shall rise first. Then we who are alive and remain shall be caught up together with them in the clouds to meet the Lord in the air, and thus we shall always be with the Lord.

REV 1:19. 1 Co 2:9,10.—Jn 16:13. Rev 1:7. 1 Th 4:13,14,16,17.

Serving the Lord with all humility.

Whoever wishes to become great among you shall be your servant, and whoever wishes to be first among you shall be your slave; just as the Son of Man did not come to be served, but to serve, and to give His life a ransom for many.

If anyone thinks he is something when he is nothing, he deceives himself.—For through the grace given to me I say to every man among you not to think more highly of himself than he ought to think; but to think so as to have sound judgment, as God has allotted to each a measure of faith.—When you do all the things which are commanded you, say, We are unworthy slaves; we have done only that which we ought to have done.

Our proud confidence is this, the testimony of our conscience that in holiness and godly sincerity, not in fleshly wisdom but in the grace of God, we have conducted ourselves in the world.— We have this treasure in earthen vessels, that the surpassing greatness of the power may be of God and not from ourselves.

AC 20:19. Mt 20:26–28. Gal 6:3.—Ro 12:3.—Lk 17:10. 2 Co 1:12.—
2 Co 4:7.

Each of us has turned to his own way.

Noah . . . planted a vineyard. And he drank of the wine and became drunk.—(Abram) said to Sarai his wife . . . say that you are my sister so that it may go well with me because of you.— Isaac said to Jacob. . . . Are you really my son Esau? And he said, I am.—Moses . . . spoke rashly with his lips.—The men of Israel took some of their provisions, and did not ask for the counsel of the LORD. And Joshua made peace with them.—David did what was right in the sight of the LORD, and had not turned aside from any thing that He commanded him all the days of his life, except in the case of Uriah the Hittite.

All these, having gained approval through their faith.—Being justified as a gift by His grace through the redemption which is in Christ Jesus.—The LORD has caused the iniquity of us all to fall on Him.

I am not doing this for your sake, declares the Lord GOD, let it be known to you. Be ashamed and confounded for your ways.

IS 53:6. Gen 9:20,21.—Gen 12:11,13.—Gen 27:21,24.—
Ps 106:32,33.—Jos 9:14,15.—1 Ki 15:5. Heb 11:39.—Ro 3:24.—
Is 53:6. Eze 36:32.

His name will be called Wonderful.

The Word became flesh, and dwelt among us, and we beheld His glory, glory as of the only begotten from the Father, full of grace and truth.—Thou hast magnified Thy word according to all Thy name.

They shall call His name Immanuel, which translated means, God with us.—Jesus, for it is He who will save His people from their sins.

Honor the Son, even as . . . the Father.

God highly exalted Him, and bestowed on Him the name which is above every name.—Far above all rule and authority and power and dominion, and every name that is named, not only in this age, but also in the one to come. And He put all things in subjection under His feet.—He has a name written upon Him which no one knows except Himself . . . KING OF KINGS, AND LORD OF LORDS.

The Almighty—we cannot find Him; He is exalted in power. —What is His name or His son's name? Surely you know!

IS 9:6. Jn 1:14.—Ps 138:2. Mt 1:23.—Mt 1:21. Jn 5:23. Phil 2:9.—
Eph 1:21,22.—Rev 19:12,16. Job 37:23.—Pr 30:4.

The LORD's portion is His people.

You belong to Christ; and Christ belongs to God.—I am my beloved's, and his desire is for me.—I am his.—Son of God . . . loved me, and delivered Himself up for me.

Your body is a temple of the Holy Spirit who is in you . . . you are not your own. For you have been bought with a price: therefore glorify God in your body.—The LORD has taken you and brought you out of the iron furnace . . . to be a people for His own possession.

You are God's field, God's building.—Christ was faithful as a Son over His house whose house we are, if we hold fast our confidence and the boast of our hope firm until the end.—A spiritual house for a holy priesthood.

They will be Mine, says the LORD of hosts, on the day that I prepare My own possession.—All things that are Mine are Thine, and Thine are Mine; and I have been glorified in them.—The glory of His inheritance in the saints.

DEU 32:9. 1 Co 3:23.—Song 7:10.—Song 2:16.—Gal 2:20.
1 Co 6:19,20.—Deu 4:20. 1 Co 3:9.—Heb 3:6.—1 Pe 2:5.
Mal 3:17.—Jn 17:10.—Eph 1:18.

Every branch that bears fruit, He prunes it.

He is like a refiner's fire and like fullers' soap. And He will sit as a smelter and purifier of silver, and He will purify ... and refine them like gold and silver, so that they may present to the LORD offerings in righteousness.

We also exult in our tribulations; knowing that tribulation brings about perseverance; and perseverance, proven character; and proven character, hope; and hope does not disappoint; because the love of God has been poured out within our hearts through the Holy Spirit who was given to us.—God deals with you as with sons; for what son is there whom his father does not discipline? But if you are without discipline, of which all have become partakers, then you are illegitimate children and not sons. All discipline for the moment seems not to be joyful, but sorrowful; yet to those who have been trained by it, afterwards it yields the peaceful fruit of righteousness. Therefore, strengthen the hands that are weak and the knees that are feeble.

JN 15:2. Mal 3:2,3. Ro 5:3–5.—Heb 12:7,8,11,12.

Now we call the arrogant blessed.

Thus says the high and exalted One who lives forever, whose name is Holy. I dwell on a high and holy place, and also with the contrite and lowly of spirit in order to revive the spirit of the lowly.

It is better to be of a humble spirit with the lowly, than to divide the spoil with the proud.—Blessed are the poor in spirit, for theirs is the kingdom of heaven.

There are six things which the LORD hates, yes, seven which are an abomination to Him: haughty eyes, etc.—Everyone who is proud in heart is an abomination to the LORD.

Search me, O God, and know my heart; try me and know my anxious thoughts; and see if there be any hurtful way in me, and lead me in the everlasting way.

Grace to you and peace from God our Father and the Lord Jesus Christ. I thank my God in all my remembrance of you.— Blessed are the gentle, for they shall inherit the earth.

MAL 3:15. Is 57:15. Pr 16:19.—Mt 5:3. Pr 6:16,17.—Pr 16:5.
Ps 139:23,24. Phil 1:2,3.—Mt 5:5.

For such is God, our God forever and ever; He will guide us until death.

O LORD, Thou art my God; I will exalt Thee, I will give thanks to Thy name; for Thou hast worked wonders, plans formed long ago, with perfect faithfulness.—The LORD is the portion of my inheritance and my cup.

He guides me in the paths of righteousness for His name's sake. Even though I walk through the valley of the shadow of death, I fear no evil; for Thou art with me; Thy rod and Thy staff, they comfort me.—I am continually with Thee; Thou hast taken hold of my right hand. With Thy counsel Thou wilt guide me, and afterward receive me to glory. Whom have I in heaven but Thee? And besides Thee, I desire nothing on earth. My flesh and my heart may fail; but God is the strength of my heart and my portion forever.—Our heart rejoices in Him, because we trust in His holy name.—The LORD will accomplish what concerns me; Thy lovingkindness, O LORD, is everlasting; do not forsake the works of Thy hands.

PS 48:14. Is 25:1.—Ps 16:5. Ps 23:3,4.—Ps 73:23–26.—Ps 33:21.—
Ps 138:8.

When my anxious thoughts multiply within me, Thy consolations delight my soul.

When my heart is faint; lead me to the rock that is higher than I.

O Lord, I am oppressed, be my security.—Cast your burden upon the LORD, and He will sustain you.

I am but a little child: I do not know how to go out or come in.—If any of you lacks wisdom, let him ask of God . . . and it will be given to him.

Who is adequate for these things?—I know that nothing good dwells in me, that is, in my flesh.—My grace is sufficient for you, for power is perfected in weakness.

Take courage, My son, your sins are forgiven. . . . Daughter, take courage; your faith has made you well.

My soul is satisfied as with marrow and fatness . . . When I remember Thee on my bed. I meditate on Thee in the night watches.

PS 94:19. Ps 61:2. Is 38:14.—Ps 55:22. 1 Ki 3:7.—Ja 1:5.
2 Co 2:16.—Ro 7:18.—2 Co 12:9. Mt 9:2,22. Ps 63:5,6.

Hope does not disappoint.

I am the LORD; those who hopefully wait for Me will not be put to shame.—Blessed is the man who trusts in the LORD and whose trust is the LORD.—The steadfast of mind Thou wilt keep in perfect peace, because he trusts in Thee. Trust in the LORD forever. For in God the LORD, we have an everlasting Rock.— My soul, wait in silence for God only, for my hope is from Him. He only is my rock and my salvation, my stronghold; I shall not be shaken.—I am not ashamed; for I know whom I have believed.

God, desiring . . . to show to the heirs of the promise the unchangeableness of His purpose, interposed with an oath, in order that by two unchangeable things, in which it is impossible for God to lie, we may have strong encouragement, we who have fled for refuge in laying hold of the hope set before us. This hope we have as an anchor of the soul, a hope both sure and steadfast and one which enters within the veil, where Jesus has entered as a forerunner for us.

RO 5:5. Is 49:23.—Jer 17:7.—Is 26:3,4.—Ps 62:5,6.—2 Ti 1:12.
Heb 6:17–20.

The stumbling block of the cross.

If any one wishes to come after Me, let him deny himself, and take up his cross, and follow Me.

Do you not know that friendship with the world is hostility toward God? Therefore whoever wishes to be a friend of the world makes himself an enemy of God.—Through many tribulations we must enter the kingdom of God.

He who believes in Him will not be disappointed.—This precious value, then, is for you who believe, but for those who disbelieve, the stone which the builders rejected, this became the very corner stone, and, a stone of stumbling and a rock of offense.

May it never be that I should boast, except in the cross of our Lord Jesus Christ, through which the world has been crucified to me, and I to the world.—I have been crucified with Christ.— Those who belong to Christ Jesus have crucified the flesh with its passions and desires.

If we endure, we shall also reign with Him; if we deny Him, He also will deny us.

GAL 5:11. Mt 16:24. Ja 4:4.—Ac 14:22. Ro 9:33.—1 Pe 2:7,8.
Gal 6:14.—Gal 2:20.—Gal 5:24. 2 Ti 2:12.

The Lord is near.

For the Lord Himself will descend from heaven with a shout, with the voice of the archangel, and with the trumpet of God; and the dead in Christ shall rise first. Then we who are alive and remain shall be caught up together with them in the clouds to meet the Lord in the air, and thus we shall always be with the Lord. Therefore comfort one another with these words.—He who testifies to these things says, Yes, I am coming quickly. Amen. Come, Lord Jesus.

Therefore, beloved, since you look for these things, be diligent to be found by Him in peace, spotless and blameless.—Abstain from every form of evil. Now may the God of peace Himself sanctify you entirely; and may your spirit and soul and body be preserved complete, without blame at the coming of our Lord Jesus Christ. Faithful is He who calls you, and He also will bring it to pass.

You too be patient; strengthen your hearts, for the coming of the Lord is at hand.

PHIL 4:5. 1 Th 4:16–18.—Rev 22:20. 2 Pe 3:14.—1 Th 5:22–24. Ja 5:8.

The choice vine.

My well-beloved had a vineyard on a fertile hill. And he dug it all around, removed its stones, and planted it with the choicest vine ... Then he expected it to produce good grapes, but it produced only worthless ones.—Yet I planted you a choice vine, a completely faithful seed. How then have you turned yourself before Me into the degenerate shoots of a foreign vine?

The deeds of the flesh are evident, which are: immorality, impurity, sensuality, idolatry, sorcery, enmities, strife, jealousy, outbursts of anger, disputes, dissensions, factions, envyings, drunkenness, carousings, and things like these ... but the fruit of the Spirit is love, joy, peace, patience, kindness, goodness, faithfulness, gentleness, self-control.

I am the true vine, and My Father is the vinedresser. Every branch in Me that does not bear fruit, He takes away; and every branch that bears fruit, He prunes it, that it may bear more fruit. Abide in Me, and I in you. By this is My Father glorified, that you bear much fruit, and so prove to be My disciples.

GEN 49:11. Is 5:1,2.—Jer 2:21. Gal 5:19–23. Jn 15:1,2,4,8.

The righteousness of God through faith in Jesus Christ for all those who believe.

He made Him who knew no sin to be sin on our behalf, that we might become the righteousness of God in Him.—Christ redeemed us from the curse of the Law, having become a curse for us.—By His doing you are in Christ Jesus, who became to us wisdom from God, and righteousness and sanctification, and redemption.—Not on the basis of deeds which we have done in righteousness, but according to His mercy, by the washing of regeneration and renewing by the Holy Spirit, whom He poured out upon us richly through Jesus Christ our Savior.

I count all things to be loss in view of the surpassing value of knowing Christ Jesus my Lord, for whom I have suffered the loss of all things, and count them but rubbish in order that I may gain Christ, and may be found in Him, not having a righteousness of my own derived from the Law, but that which is through faith in Christ, the righteousness which comes from God on the basis of faith.

RO 3:22. 2 Co 5:21.—Gal 3:13.—1 Co 1:30.—Titus 3:5,6. Phil 3:8,9.

A spirit of adoption . . . by which we cry out, Abba! Father!

Jesus . . . lifting up His eyes to heaven, He said, Father . . . Holy Father . . . O righteous Father.—He was saying, Abba (Father). —Because you are sons, God has sent forth the Spirit of His Son into our hearts, crying, Abba! Father!—For through Him we both have our access in one Spirit to the Father. So then you are no longer strangers and aliens, but you are fellow-citizens with the saints, and are of God's household.

Thou art our Father . . . Thou, O LORD, art our Father, our Redeemer from of old is Thy name.

I will get up and go to my father, and will say to him, Father, I have sinned against heaven, and in your sight; I am no longer worthy to be called your son; make me as one of your hired men. And he got up and came to his father.

Therefore be imitators of God, as beloved children.

RO 8:15. Jn 17:1,11,25.—Mk 14:36.—Gal 4:6.—Eph 2:18,19.
Is 63:16. Lk 15.18–20. Eph 5:1.

Let us go out to Him outside the camp, bearing His reproach. For here we do not have a lasting city, but we are seeking the city which is to come.

Beloved, do not be surprised at the fiery ordeal among you, which comes upon you for your testing, as though some strange thing were happening to you; but to the degree that you share the sufferings of Christ, keep on rejoicing; so that also at the revelation of His glory, you may rejoice with exultation.—As you are sharers of our sufferings, so also you are sharers of our comfort.

If you are reviled for the name of Christ, you are blessed, because the Spirit of glory and of God rests upon you.

So they went on their way from the presence of the Council, rejoicing that they had been considered worthy to suffer shame for His name.—Choosing rather to endure ill-treatment with the people of God, than to enjoy the passing pleasures of sin; considering the reproach of Christ greater riches than the treasures of Egypt; for he was looking to the reward.

HEB 13:13,14. 1 Pe 4:12,13.—2 Co 1:7. 1 Pe 4:14. Ac 5:41.—
Heb 11:25,26.

The Lord Jesus Christ ... who will transform the body of our humble state into conformity with the body of His glory.

On that which resembled a throne, high up, was a figure with the appearance of a man. Then I noticed from the appearance of his loins and upward something like glowing metal that looked like fire all around within it, and from the appearance of his loins and downward I saw something like fire; and there was a radiance around him. As the appearance of the rainbow in the clouds on a rainy day, so was the appearance of the surrounding radiance. Such was the appearance of the likeness of the glory of the LORD.

We all, with unveiled face beholding as in a mirror the glory of the Lord, are being transformed into the same image from glory to glory, just as from the Lord, the Spirit.—It has not appeared as yet what we shall be. We know that, when He appears, we shall be like Him, because we shall see Him just as He is.

They shall hunger no more, neither thirst any more.—They sang the song of Moses the bond-servant of God and the song of the Lamb.

PHIL 3:20,21. Eze 1:26–28. 2 Co 3:18.—1 Jn 3:2. Rev 7:16.—
Rev 15:3.

You know that He appeared in order to take away sins; and in Him there is no sin.

God . . . in these last days has spoken to us in His Son . . . and He is the radiance of His glory and the exact representation of His nature, and upholds all things by the word of His power. When He had made purification of sins, He sat down at the right hand of the Majesty on high.—He made Him who knew no sin to be sin on our behalf, that we might become the righteousness of God in Him.

Conduct yourselves in fear during the time of your stay upon earth; knowing that you were not redeemed with perishable things like silver or gold . . . but with precious blood, as of a lamb unblemished and spotless, the blood of Christ. For He was foreknown before the foundation of the world, but has appeared in these last times for the sake of you.—For the love of Christ controls us, having concluded this, that one died for all, therefore all died; and He died for all, that they who live should no longer live for themselves, but for Him who died and rose again on their behalf.

1 JN 3:5. Heb 1:1–3.—2 Co 5:21. 1 Pe 1:17–20.—2 Co 5:14,15.

I have set before you life and death, the blessing and the curse. So choose life.

For I have no pleasure in the death of anyone who dies, declares the Lord GOD. Therefore, repent and live.

If I had not come and spoken to them, they would not have sin, but now they have no excuse for their sin.

And that slave who knew his master's will and did not get ready or act in accord with his will, shall receive many lashes.

For the wages of sin is death, but the free gift of God is eternal life in Christ Jesus our Lord.—He who believes in the Son has eternal life; but he who does not obey the Son shall not see life, but the wrath of God abides on him.—Do you not know that when you present yourselves to someone as slaves for obedience, you are slaves of the one whom you obey, either of sin resulting in death, or of obedience resulting in righteousness?

If any one serves Me, let him follow Me; and where I am, there shall My servant also be; if any one serves Me, the Father will honor him.

DEU 30:19. Eze 18:32. Jn 15:22. Lk 12:47. Ro 6:23.—Jn 3:36.—Ro 6:16. Jn 12:26.

According to your days, so shall your leisurely walk be.

When they arrest you and deliver you up, do not be anxious beforehand about what you are to say, but say whatever is given you in that hour; for it is not you who speak, but it is the Holy Spirit.—Therefore do not be anxious for tomorrow; for tomorrow will care for itself. Each day has enough trouble of its own.

The God of Israel Himself gives strength and power to the people. Blessed be God!—He gives strength to the weary, and to him who lacks might He increases power.

My grace is sufficient for you, for power is perfected in weakness. Most gladly, therefore, I will rather boast about my weaknesses, that the power of Christ may dwell in me. Therefore I am well content with weaknesses, with insults, with distresses, with persecutions, with difficulties, for Christ's sake; for when I am weak, then I am strong.—I can do all things through Him who strengthens me.—O my soul, march on with strength.

DEU 33:25. Mk 13:11.—Mt 6:34. Ps 68:35.—Is 40:29.
2 Co 12:9,10.—Phil 4:13.—Judg 5:21.

Awake, O north wind, . . . make my garden breathe out fragrance, let its spices be wafted abroad.

All discipline for the moment seems not to be joyful, but sorrowful; yet to those who have been trained by it, afterwards it yields the peaceful fruit of righteousness.—The fruit of the Spirit.

With His fierce wind He has expelled them on the day of the east wind.

Just as a father has compassion on his children, so the LORD has compassion on those who fear Him.

Though our outer man is decaying, yet our inner man is being renewed day by day. For momentary, light affliction is producing for us an eternal weight of glory far beyond all comparison, while we look not at the things which are seen, but at the things which are not seen.

Although He (Jesus) was a Son, He learned obedience from the things which He suffered.—One who has been tempted in all things as we are, yet without sin.

SONG 4:16. Heb 12:11.—Gal 5:22. Is 27:8. Ps 103:13. 2 Co 4:16–18.
Heb 5:8.—Heb 4:15.

Thou art a God who sees.

O LORD, Thou hast searched me and known me. Thou dost know when I sit down and when I rise up; Thou dost understand my thought from afar. Thou dost scrutinize my path and my lying down, and art intimately acquainted with all my ways. Even before there is a word on my tongue, behold, O LORD, Thou dost know it all. Such knowledge is too wonderful for me; it is too high, I cannot attain to it.

The eyes of the LORD are in every place, watching the evil and the good.—The ways of a man are before the eyes of the LORD, and He watches all his paths.—God knows your hearts; for that which is highly esteemed among men is detestable in the sight of God.—For the eyes of the LORD move to and fro throughout the earth that He may strongly support those whose heart is completely His.

Jesus . . . knew all men, and because He did not need any one to bear witness concerning man for He Himself knew what was in man.—Lord, You know all things; You know that I love You.

GEN 16:13. Ps 139:1-4,6. Pr 15:3.—Pr 5:21.—Lk 16:15.—2 Ch 16:9. Jn 2:24,25.—Jn 21:17.

I will give thanks to Thee, O Lord my God, with all my heart, and will glorify Thy name forever.

He who offers a sacrifice of thanksgiving honors Me.—It is good to give thanks to the LORD, and to sing praises to Thy name, O Most High.

Let everything that has breath praise the LORD.

I urge you therefore, brethren, by the mercies of God, to present your bodies a living and holy sacrifice, acceptable to God, which is your spiritual service of worship.—Jesus . . . that He might sanctify the people through His own blood, suffered outside the gate. Through Him then let us continually offer up a sacrifice of praise to God, that is, the fruit of lips that give thanks to His name.—Always giving thanks for all things in the name of our Lord Jesus Christ to God, even the Father.

Worthy is the Lamb that was slain to receive power and riches and wisdom and might and honor and glory and blessing.

PS 86:12. Ps 50:23.—Ps 92:1,2. Ps 150:6. Ro 12:1.—Heb 13:12,15.— Eph 5:20. Rev 5:12.

Let us run with endurance the race that is set before us, fixing our eyes on Jesus, the author and perfecter of faith.

If anyone wishes to come after Me, let him deny himself, and take up his cross daily, and follow Me.—No one of you can be My disciple who does not give up all his own possessions.—Lay aside the deeds of darkness.

Everyone who competes in the games exercises self-control in all things. They then do it to receive a perishable wreath, but we an imperishable. Therefore I run in such a way, as not without aim; I box in such a way, as not beating the air; but I buffet my body and make it my slave, lest possibly, after I have preached to others, I myself should be disqualified.—Brethren, I do not regard myself as having laid hold of it yet; but one thing I do; forgetting what lies behind and reaching forward to what lies ahead, I press on toward the goal for the prize of the upward call of God in Christ Jesus.—Let us press on to know the LORD.

HEB 12:1,2. Lk 9:23.—Lk 14:33.—Ro 13:12. 1 Co 9:25–27.— Phil 3:13,14.—Ho 6:3.

It is good for a man that he should bear the yoke in his youth.

Train up a child in the way he should go, even when he is old he will not depart from it.

We had earthly fathers to discipline us, and we respected them; shall we not much rather be subject to the Father of spirits, and live? For they disciplined us for a short time as seemed best to them, but He disciplines us for our good, that we may share His holiness.

Before I was afflicted I went astray, but now I keep Thy word. It is good for me that I was afflicted, that I may learn Thy statutes.

For I know the plans that I have for you, declares the LORD, plans for welfare and not for calamity to give you a future and a hope.—Humble yourselves, therefore, under the mighty hand of God, that He may exalt you at the proper time.

LAM 3:27. Pr 22:6. Heb 12:9,10. Ps 119:67,71. Jer 29:11.—1 Pe 5:6.

But if you do not drive out the inhabitants of the land from before you, then it shall come about that those whom you let remain of them will become as pricks in your eyes and as thorns in your sides, and they shall trouble you in the land in which you live.

Fight the good fight of faith.—The weapons of our warfare are not of the flesh, but divinely powerful for the destruction of fortresses. We are destroying ... every lofty thing raised up against the knowledge of God, and we are taking every thought captive to the obedience of Christ.

Brethren, we are under obligation, not to the flesh, to live according to the flesh—for if you are living according to the flesh, you must die; but if by the Spirit you are putting to death the deeds of the body, you will live.

For the flesh sets its desire against the Spirit, and the Spirit against the flesh; for these are in opposition to one another, so that you may not do the things that you please.—I see a different law in the members of my body, waging war against the law of my mind, and making me a prisoner of the law of sin which is in my members.—In all these things we overwhelmingly conquer through Him who loved us.

NUM 33:55. 1 Ti 6:12.—2 Co 10:4,5. Ro 8:12,13. Gal 5:17.—
Ro 7:23.—Ro 8:37.

If a man sins against the LORD, who can intercede for him?

If anyone sins, we have an Advocate with the Father, Jesus Christ the righteous; and He Himself is the propitiation for our sins; and not for ours only, but also for those of the whole world. —Whom God displayed publicly as a propitiation in His blood through faith. This was to demonstrate His righteousness, because in the forbearance of God He passed over the sins previously committed; for the demonstration, I say, of His righteousness at the present time, that He might be just and the justifier of the one who has faith in Jesus.

Then let him be gracious to him, and say, Deliver him from going down to the pit, I have found a ransom.

What then shall we say to these things? If God is for us, who is against us? Who will bring a charge against God's elect? God is the one who justifies; who is the one who condemns? Christ Jesus is He who died, yes, rather who was raised, who is at the right hand of God, who also intercedes for us.

1 SA 2:25. 1 Jn 2:1,2.—Ro 3:25,26. Job 33:24. Ro 8:31,33,34.

Though you have not seen Him, you love Him.

We walk by faith, not by sight.—We love, because He first loved us.—We have come to know and have believed the love which God has for us. God is love, and the one who abides in love abides in God, and God abides in him.—In Him, you also, after listening to the message of truth, the gospel of your salvation—having also believed, you were sealed in Him with the Holy Spirit of promise.—God willed to make known what is the riches of the glory of this mystery among the Gentiles, which is Christ in you, the hope of glory.

If some one says, I love God, and hates his brother, he is a liar; for the one who does not love his brother whom he has seen, cannot love God whom he has not seen.

Jesus said to him (Thomas), Because you have seen Me, have you believed? Blessed are they who did not see, and yet believed. —How blessed are all who take refuge in Him!

1 PE 1:8. 2 Co 5:7.—1 Jn 4:19.—1 Jn 4:16.—Eph 1:13.—Col 1:27.
1 Jn 4:20. Jn 20:29.—Ps 2:12.

The Lord our righteousness.

All of us have become like one who is unclean, and all our righteous deeds are like a filthy garment.

I will come with the mighty deeds of the Lord God; I will make mention of Thy righteousness, Thine alone.—I will rejoice greatly in the Lord, my soul will exult in my God; for He has clothed me with garments of salvation, He has wrapped me with a robe of righteousness, as a bridegroom decks himself with a garland, and as a bride adorns herself with her jewels.

Quickly bring out the best robe and put it on him.—It was given to her to clothe herself in fine linen, bright and clean; for the fine linen is the righteous acts of the saints.

I count all things to be loss in view of the surpassing value of knowing Christ Jesus my Lord, for whom I have suffered the loss of all things, and count them but rubbish in order that I may gain Christ, and may be found in Him, not having a righteousness of my own derived from the Law, but that which is through faith in Christ, the righteousness which comes from God on the basis of faith.

JER 23:6. Is 64:6. Ps 71:16.—Is 61:10. Lk 15:22.—Rev 19:8.
Phil 3:8,9.

Oh that Thou wouldst bless me . . . and keep me from harm.

Why are you sleeping? Rise and pray that you may not enter into temptation.—The spirit is willing, but the flesh is weak.

Two things I asked of Thee, do not refuse me before I die: keep deception and lies far from me, give me neither poverty nor riches, feed me with the food that is my portion, lest I be full and deny Thee and say, Who is the LORD? Or lest I be in want and steal, and profane the name of my God.

The LORD will protect you from all evil; He will keep your soul. —I will deliver you from the hand of the wicked, and I will redeem you from the grasp of the violent.—He (Jesus) who was born of God keeps him and the evil one does not touch him.

Because you have kept the word of My perseverance, I also will keep you from the hour of testing, that hour which is about to come upon the whole world, to test those who dwell upon the earth.—The Lord knows how to rescue the godly from temptation.

1 CH 4:10. Lk 22:46.—Mt. 26:41. Pr 30:7–9. Ps 121:7.—Jer 15:21.—
1 Jn 5:18. Rev 3:10.—2 Pe 2:9.

Star differs from star in glory.

On the way they had discussed with one another which of them was the greatest. And sitting down, He called the twelve and said to them, If any one wants to be first, he shall be last of all, and servant of all.—Clothe yourselves with humility toward one another, for God is opposed to the proud but gives grace to the humble. Humble yourselves, therefore, under the mighty hand of God, that He may exalt you at the proper time.

Have this attitude in yourselves which was also in Christ Jesus, who . . . emptied Himself, taking the form of a bond-servant, and being made in the likeness of men. Therefore also God highly exalted Him, and bestowed on Him the name which is above every name, that at the name of Jesus every knee should bow.

Those who have insight will shine brightly like the brightness of the expanse of heaven, and those who lead the many to righteousness, like the stars forever and ever.

1 CO 15:41. Mk 9:34,35.—1 Pe 5:5,6. Phil 2:5–7,9,10. Dan 12:3.

Take courage ... and work; for I am with you, says the LORD of hosts.

I am the vine, you are the branches; he who abides in Me, and I in him, he bears much fruit; for apart from Me you can do nothing.—I can do all things through Him who strengthens me.—Be strong in the Lord, and in the strength of His might.—The joy of the LORD is your strength.

Thus says the LORD of hosts, Let your hands be strong, you who are listening in these days to these words from the mouth of the prophets.—Encourage the exhausted, and strengthen the feeble. Say to those with anxious heart, Take courage, fear not.—The LORD looked at him and said, Go in this your strength.

If God is for us, who is against us?—Therefore, since we have this ministry, as we received mercy, we do not lose heart.

Let us not lose heart in doing good, for in due time we shall reap if we do not grow weary.—Thanks be to God, who gives us the victory through our Lord Jesus Christ.

HAG 2:4. Jn 15:5.—Phil 4:13.—Eph 6:10.—Neh 8:10. Zec 8:9.—
Is 35:3,4.—Judg 6:14. Ro 8:31.—2 Co 4:1. Gal 6:9.—1 Co 15:57.

Even the darkness is not dark to Thee.

His eyes are upon the ways of a man, and He sees all his steps. There is no darkness or deep shadow, where the workers of iniquity may hide themselves.—Can a man hide himself in hiding places, so I do not see him? ... Do I not fill the heavens and the earth? declares the LORD.

You will not be afraid of the terror by night ... of the pestilence that stalks in darkness ... For you have made the LORD, my refuge, even the Most High, your dwelling place. No evil will befall you, nor will any plague come near your tent.—He who keeps you will not slumber. The LORD is your keeper; the LORD is your shade on your right hand. The sun will not smite you by day, nor the moon by night. The LORD will protect you from all evil.

Even though I walk through the valley of the shadow of death, I fear no evil, for Thou art with me.

PS 139:12. Job 34:21,22.—Jer 23:24. Ps 91:5,6,9,10.—Ps 121:3,5–7.
Ps 23:4.

The LORD has said to you, You shall never again return that way.

Indeed if they had been thinking of that country from which they went out, they would have had opportunity to return. But as it is, they desire a better country, that is a heavenly one. Choosing rather to endure ill-treatment with the people of God, than to enjoy the passing pleasures of sin; considering the reproach of Christ greater riches than the treasures of Egypt.—My righteous one shall live by faith; and if he shrinks back, My soul has no pleasure in him. But we are not of those who shrink back to destruction, but of those who have faith to the preserving of the soul.—No one, after putting his hand to the plow and looking back, is fit for the kingdom of God.

May it never be that I should boast, except in the cross of our Lord Jesus Christ, through which the world has been crucified to me, and I to the world.—Come out from their midst and be separate, says the Lord. And do not touch what is unclean; and I will welcome you.

He who began a good work in you will perfect it until the day of Christ Jesus.

DEU 17:16. Heb 11:15,16,25,26.—Heb 10:38,39.—Lk 9:62.
Gal 6:14.—2 Co 6:17. Phil 1:6.

They tell of the pain of those whom Thou hast wounded.

While I was only a little angry, they furthered the disaster.

Brethren, even if a man is caught in any trespass, you who are spiritual, restore such a one in a spirit of gentleness; each one looking to yourself, lest you too be tempted.

He who turns a sinner from the error of his way will save his soul from death, and will cover a multitude of sins.—Encourage the fainthearted, help the weak, be patient with all men.

Let us not judge one another any more, but rather determine this—not to put an obstacle or a stumbling block in a brother's way.—We who are strong ought to bear the weaknesses of those without strength and not just please ourselves.

Love . . . does not rejoice in unrighteousness.—Let him who thinks he stands take heed lest he fall.

PS 69:26. Zec 1:15. Gal 6:1. Ja 5:20.—1 Th 5:14. Ro 14:13.—
Ro 15:1. 1 Co 13:4,6.—1 Co 10:12.

I came that they might have life, and might have it abundantly.

In the day that you eat from it you shall surely die.—She took from its fruit and ate; and she gave also to her husband with her, and he ate.

The wages of sin is death, but the free gift of God is eternal life in Christ Jesus our Lord.—If by the transgression of the one, death reigned through the one, much more those who receive the abundance of grace and of the gift of righteousness will reign in life through the One, Jesus Christ.—For since by a man came death, by a man also came the resurrection of the dead. For as in Adam all die, so also in Christ all shall be made alive.—Our Savior Christ Jesus ... abolished death, and brought life and immortality to light through the gospel.

God has given us eternal life, and this life is in His Son. He who has the Son has the life; he who does not have the Son of God does not have the life.—For God did not send the Son into the world to judge the world; but that the world should be saved through Him.

JN 10:10. Gen 2:17.—Gen 3:6. Ro 6:23.—Ro 5:17.—
1 Co 15:21,22.—2 Ti 1:10. 1 Jn 5:11,12.—Jn 3:17.

The judgment seat.

We know that the judgment of God rightly falls.—When the Son of Man comes in His glory, and all the angels with Him, then He will sit on His glorious throne. And all the nations will be gathered before Him; and He will separate them from one another, as the shepherd separates the sheep from the goats.

Then the righteous will shine forth as the sun in the kingdom of their Father.—Who will bring a charge against God's elect? God is the one who justifies; who is the one who condemns? Christ Jesus is He who died, yes, rather who was raised, who is at the right hand of God, who also intercedes for us.—There is therefore now no condemnation for those who are in Christ Jesus.

When we are judged, we are disciplined by the Lord in order that we may not be condemned along with the world.

2 CO 5:10. Ro 2:2.—Mt 25:31,32. Mt 13:43.—Ro 8:33,34.—Ro 8:1.
1 Co 11:32.

The grace of our Lord was more than abundant, with the faith and love which are found in Christ Jesus.

For you know the grace of our Lord Jesus Christ, that though He was rich, yet for your sake He became poor, that you through His poverty might become rich.—Where sin increased, grace abounded all the more.

In the ages to come He might show the surpassing riches of His grace in kindness toward us in Christ Jesus. For by grace you have been saved through faith; and that not of yourselves, it is the gift of God; not as a result of works, that no one should boast. —Knowing that a man is not justified by the works of the Law but through faith in Christ Jesus, even we have believed in Christ Jesus, that we may be justified by faith in Christ, and not by the works of the Law; since by the works of the Law shall no flesh be justified.—He saved us, not on the basis of deeds which we have done in righteousness, but according to His mercy, by the washing of regeneration and renewing by the Holy Spirit, whom He poured out upon us richly through Jesus Christ our Savior.

1 TI 1:14. 2 Co 8:9.—Ro 5:20. Eph 2:7–9.—Gal 2:16.—Titus 3:5,6.

I am . . . the bright morning star.

A star shall come forth from Jacob.

The night is almost gone, and the day is at hand. Let us therefore lay aside the deeds of darkness and put on the armor of light. —Until the cool of the day when the shadows flee away, turn, my beloved, and be like a gazelle or a young stag on the mountains of Bether.

Watchman, how far gone is the night? The watchman says, Morning comes but also night. If you would inquire, inquire; come back again.

I am the light of the world.—I will give him the morning star.

Take heed, keep on the alert; for you do not know when the appointed time is. It is like a man, away on a journey, who upon leaving his house and putting his slaves in charge, assigning to each one his task, also commanded the doorkeeper to stay on the alert. Therefore, be on the alert . . . lest he come suddenly and find you asleep. And what I say to you I say to all, Be on the alert!

REV 22:16. Num 24:17. Ro 13:12.—Song 2:17. Is 21:11,12.
Jn 8:12.—Rev 2:28. Mk. 13:33–37.

When you have eaten and are satisfied, you shall bless the LORD your God for the good land which He has given you.

Beware lest you forget the LORD your God.—One of them, when he saw that he had been healed, turned back, glorifying God with a loud voice, and he fell on his face at His feet, giving thanks to Him. And he was a Samaritan. And Jesus answered and said, Were there not ten cleansed? But the nine—where are they? Were none found who turned back to give glory to God, except this foreigner?

For everything created by God is good, and nothing is to be rejected, if it is received with gratitude: for it is sanctified by means of the word of God and prayer.—He who eats, does so for the Lord, for he gives thanks to God.—It is the blessing of the LORD that makes rich, and he adds no sorrow to it.

Bless the LORD, O my soul; and all that is within me, bless His holy name. Bless the LORD, O my soul . . . who pardons all your iniquities; . . . who crowns you with loving kindness and compassion.

DEU 8:10. Deu 8:11.—Lk 17:15–18. 1 Ti 4:4,5.—Ro 14:6.—
Pr 10:22. Ps 103:1–4.

He (Jesus) felt compassion for them.

Jesus Christ is the same yesterday and today, yes and forever. —We do not have a high priest who cannot sympathize with our weaknesses, but one who has been tempted in all things as we are, yet without sin.—He can deal gently with the ignorant and misguided, since he himself also is beset with weakness.—He came and found them sleeping, and said to Peter, Simon, are you asleep? Could you not keep watch for one hour? Keep watching and praying, that you may not come into temptation; the spirit is willing, but the flesh is weak.

Just as a father has compassion on his children, so the LORD has compassion on those who fear Him. For He Himself knows our frame; He is mindful that we are but dust.

But Thou, O LORD, art a God merciful and gracious, slow to anger and abundant in lovingkindness and truth. Turn to me, and be gracious to me; oh grant Thy strength to Thy servant, and save the son of Thy handmaid.

MT 14:14. Heb 13:8.—Heb 4:15.—Heb 5:2.—Mk 14:37,38.
Ps 103:13,14. Ps 86:15,16.

No longer do I call you slaves; for the slave does not know what his master is doing; but I have called you friends.

And the LORD said, Shall I hide from Abraham what I am about to do?—To you it has been granted to know the mysteries of the kingdom of heaven.—For to us God revealed them through the Spirit; for the Spirit searches all things, even the depths of God. —We speak God's wisdom in a mystery, the hidden wisdom, which God predestined before the ages to our glory.

How blessed is the one whom Thou dost choose, and bring near to Thee, to dwell in Thy courts. We will be satisfied with the goodness of Thy house, Thy holy temple.—The secret of the LORD is for those who fear Him, and He will make them know His covenant.—For the words which Thou gavest Me I have given to them; and they received them, and truly understood that I came forth from Thee, and they believed that Thou didst send Me.

JN 15:15. Gen 18:17.—Mt 13:11.—1 Co 2:10.—1 Co 2:7. Ps 65:4.— Ps 25:14.—Jn 17:8.

You will call your walls salvation, and your gates praise.

The wall of the city had twelve foundation stones, and on them were the twelve names of the twelve apostles of the Lamb.

So then you are no longer strangers and aliens, but you are fellow-citizens with the saints, and are of God's household, having been built upon the foundation of the apostles and prophets, Christ Jesus Himself being the cornerstone, in whom the whole building, being fitted together is growing into a holy temple in the Lord; in whom you also are being built together into a dwelling of God in the Spirit.—If you have tasted the kindness of the Lord. And coming to Him as to a living stone, rejected by men, but choice and precious in the sight of God, you also, as living stones, are being built up as a spiritual house for a holy priesthood, to offer up spiritual sacrifices acceptable to God through Jesus Christ.

There will be silence before Thee, and praise in Zion, O God.

IS 60:18. Rev 21:14. Eph 2:19–22.—1 Pe 2:3–5. Ps 65:1.

He is being comforted here.

Your sun will set no more, neither will your moon wane; for you will have the LORD for an everlasting light, and the days of your mourning will be finished.—He will swallow up death for all time, and the Lord GOD will wipe tears away from all faces, and He will remove the reproach of His people from all the earth.—These are the ones who come out of the great tribulation, and they have washed their robes and made them white in the blood of the Lamb. For this reason, they are before the throne of God; and they serve Him day and night in His temple; and He who sits on the throne shall spread His tabernacle over them. They shall hunger no more, neither thirst any more; neither shall the sun beat down on them, nor any heat; for the Lamb in the center of the throne shall be their shepherd, and shall guide them to springs of the water of life—He shall wipe away every tear from their eyes; and there shall no longer be any death; there shall no longer be any mourning, or crying, or pain: the first things have passed away.

LK 16:25. Is 60:20.—Is 25:8.—Rev 7:14–17.—Rev 21:4.

Night is coming, when no man can work.

Blessed are the dead who die in the Lord, . . . they . . . rest from their labors, for their deeds follow with them.—There the wicked cease from raging, and there the weary are at rest.— Samuel said to Saul, Why have you disturbed me by bringing me up?

Whatever your hand finds to do, verily, do it with all your might; for there is no activity or planning or wisdom in Sheol where you are going.—The dead do not praise the LORD, nor do any who go down into silence.

I am already being poured out as a drink offering, and the time of my departure has come. I have fought the good fight, I have finished the course, I have kept the faith; in the future there is laid up for me the crown of righteousness, which the Lord, the righteous Judge, will award to me on that day.

There remains therefore a Sabbath rest for the people of God. For the one who has entered His rest has himself also rested from his works, as God did from His.

JN 9:4. Rev 14:13.—Job 3:17.—1 Sa 28:15. Ec 9:10.—Ps 115:17.
2 Ti 4:6–8. Heb 4:9,10.

The lamp of your body is your eye; when your eye is clear, your whole body also is full of light.

But a natural man does not accept the things of the Spirit of God; for they are foolishness to him, and he cannot understand them, because they are spiritually appraised.—Open my eyes, that I may behold wonderful things from Thy law.

I am the light of the world; he who follows Me shall not walk in the darkness, but shall have the light of life.—We all, with unveiled face beholding as in a mirror the glory of the Lord, are being transformed into the same image . . . just as from the Lord, the Spirit.—God, who said, Light shall shine out of darkness, is the One who has shone in our hearts to give the light of the knowledge of the glory of God in the face of Christ.

The God of our Lord Jesus Christ, the Father of glory, . . . give to you a spirit of wisdom and of revelation in the knowledge of Him . . . that you may know what is the hope of His calling, what are the riches of the glory of His inheritance in the saints.

LK 11:34. 1 Co 2:14.—Ps 119:18. Jn 8:12.—2 Co 3:18.—2 Co 4:6.
Eph 1:17,18.

He struck the rock, so that waters gushed out, and streams were overflowing.

Our fathers were all under the cloud, and all passed through the sea; and all were baptized into Moses in the cloud and in the sea; and all ate the same spiritual food; and all drank the same spiritual drink, for they were drinking from a spiritual rock which followed them; and the rock was Christ.—One of the soldiers pierced His side with a spear, and immediately there came out blood and water.—He was pierced through for our transgressions, He was crushed for our iniquities; the chastening for our well-being fell upon Him, and by His scourging we are healed.

You are unwilling to come to Me, that you may have life.—For My people have committed two evils; they have forsaken Me, the fountain of living waters, to hew for themselves cisterns, broken cisterns, that can hold no water.

If any man is thirsty, let him come to Me and drink.—Let the one who wishes take the water of life without cost.

PS 78:20. 1 Co 10:1–4.—Jn 19:34.—Is 53:5. Jn 5:40.—Jer 2:13.
Jn 7:37.—Rev 22:17.

Those who feared the LORD spoke to one another, and the LORD gave attention and heard it, and a book of remembrance was written before Him for those who fear the LORD and who esteem His name.

And it came about that while they were conversing and discussing, Jesus Himself approached, and began traveling with them.—Where two or three have gathered together in My name, there I am in their midst.—My fellow-workers, whose names are in the book of life.

Let the word of Christ richly dwell within you; with all wisdom teaching and admonishing one another with psalms and hymns and spiritual songs, singing with thankfulness in your hearts to God.—Encourage one another day after day, as long as it is still called Today, lest any one of you be hardened by the deceitfulness of sin.

Every careless word that men shall speak, they shall render account for it in the day of judgment. For by your words you shall be justified, and by your words you shall be condemned.—Behold, it is written before Me.

MAL 3:16. Lk 24:15.—Mt 18:20.—Phil 4:3. Col 3:16.—Heb 3:13. Mt 12:36,37.—Is 65:6.

The trees of the LORD drink their fill.

I will be like the dew to Israel; he will blossom like the lily and he will take root like the cedars of Lebanon. His shoots will sprout, and his beauty will be like the olive tree, and his fragrance like the cedars of Lebanon.—Blessed is the man who trusts in the LORD and whose trust is the LORD. For he will be like a tree planted by the water, that extends its roots by a stream and will not fear when the heat comes; but its leaves will be green, and it will not be anxious in a year of drought nor cease to yield fruit.

I bring down the high tree, exalt the low tree, dry up the green tree, and make the dry tree flourish. I am the LORD.

And he will be like a tree firmly planted by streams of water, which yields its fruit in its season, and its leaf does not wither. Planted in the house of the LORD, they will flourish in the courts of our God. They will still yield fruit in old age; they shall be full of sap and very green.

PS 104:16. Ho 14:5,6.—Jer 17:7,8. Eze 17:24. Ps 1:3.— Ps 92:13–14.

They will be Mine, says the LORD of hosts, on the day that I prepare My own possession.

I manifested Thy name to the men whom Thou gavest Me out of the world; Thine they were, and Thou gavest them to Me, and they have kept Thy word. I ask on their behalf; I do not ask on behalf of the world, but of those whom Thou hast given Me; for they are Thine; and all things that are Mine are Thine, and Thine are Mine; and I have been glorified in them. Father, I desire that they also whom Thou hast given Me be with Me where I am, in order that they may behold My glory, which Thou hast given Me; for Thou didst love Me before the foundation of the world.

I will come again, and receive you to Myself.—When He comes to be glorified in His saints on that day, and to be marveled at among all who have believed.—We who are alive and remain shall be caught up together with them in the clouds to meet the Lord in the air, and thus we shall always be with the Lord.—You will also be a crown of beauty in the hand of the LORD, and a royal diadem in the hand of your God.

MAL 3:17. Jn 17:6,9,10,24. Jn 14:3.—2 Th 1:10.—1 Th 4:17.— Is 62:3.

I pray Thee, show me Thy glory!

God, who said, Light shall shine out of darkness, is the One who has shone in our hearts to give the light of the knowledge of the glory of God in the face of Christ.—The Word became flesh, and dwelt among us, and we beheld His glory, glory as of the only begotten from the Father, full of grace and truth. No man has seen God at any time; the only begotten God, who is in the bosom of the Father, He has explained Him.

My soul thirsts for God, for the living God; when shall I come and appear before God?—When Thou didst say, Seek My face, my heart said to Thee, Thy face, O LORD, I shall seek.

We all, with unveiled face beholding as in a mirror the glory of the Lord, are being transformed into the same image from glory to glory, just as from the Lord, the Spirit.—Father, I desire that they also whom Thou hast given Me be with Me where I am, in order that they may behold My glory, which Thou hast given Me; for Thou didst love Me before the foundation of the world.

EX 33:18. 2 Co 4:6.—Jn 1:14,18. Ps 42:2.—Ps 27:8. 2 Co 3:18.— Jn 17:24.

On that which resembled a throne ... was a figure with the appearance of a man.

The man Christ Jesus.—Emptied Himself, taking the form of a bond-servant, and being made in the likeness of men.—Since then the children share in flesh and blood, He Himself likewise also partook of the same, that through death He might render powerless him who had the power of death.

The living One; and I was dead, and behold, I am alive forevermore.—Christ, having been raised from the dead, is never to die again; death no longer is master over Him. For the death that He died, He died to sin, once for all; but the life that He lives, He lives to God.—What then if you should behold the Son of Man ascending where He was before?—He raised Him from the dead, and seated Him at His right hand in the heavenly places.—In Him all the fulness of Deity dwells in bodily form.

For indeed He was crucified because of weakness, yet He lives because of the power of God. For we also are weak in Him, yet we shall live with Him because of the power of God.

EZE 1:26. 1 Ti 2:5.—Phil 2:7.—Heb 2:14. Rev 1:18.—Ro 6:9,10.—
Jn 6:62.—Eph 1:20.—Col 2:9. 2 Co 13:4.

Thy word has revived me.

The first man, Adam, became a living soul. The last Adam became a life-giving spirit.

For just as the Father has life in Himself, even so He gave to the Son also to have life in Himself.—I am the resurrection and the life; he who believes in Me shall live even if he dies, and everyone who lives and believes in Me shall never die.

In Him was life; and the life was the light of men. As many as received Him, to them He gave the right to become children of God, even to those who believe in His name, who were born not of blood, nor of the will of the flesh, nor of the will of man, but of God.

It is the Spirit who gives life; the flesh profits nothing; the words that I have spoken to you are spirit and are life.—The word of God is living and active and sharper than any two-edged sword, and piercing as far as the division of soul and spirit, of both joints and marrow, and able to judge the thoughts and intentions of the heart.

PS 119:50. 1 Co 15:45. Jn 5:26.—Jn 11:25,26. Jn 1:4,12,13.
Jn 6:63.—Heb 4:12.

Permit it at this time; for in this way it is fitting for us to fulfill all righteousness.

I delight to do Thy will, O my God; Thy Law is within my heart.

Do not think that I came to abolish the Law or the Prophets; I did not come to abolish, but to fulfill. For truly I say to you, until heaven and earth pass away, not the smallest letter or stroke shall pass away from the Law, until all is accomplished.—The LORD was pleased for His righteousness' sake to make the law great and glorious.—Unless your righteousness surpasses that of the scribes and Pharisees, you shall not enter the kingdom of heaven.

For what the Law could not do, weak as it was through the flesh, God did: sending His own Son in the likeness of sinful flesh and as an offering for sin, He condemned sin in the flesh, in order that the requirement of the Law might be fulfilled in us, who do not walk according to the flesh, but according to the Spirit.— Christ is the end of the law for righteousness to everyone who believes.

MT 3:15. Ps 40:8. Mt 5:17,18.—Is 42:21.—Mt 5:20. Ro 8:3,4.—
Ro 10:4.

I am your portion and your inheritance.

Whom have I in heaven but thee? And besides Thee, I desire nothing on earth. My flesh and my heart may fail; but God is the strength of my heart and my portion forever.—The LORD is the portion of my inheritance and my cup; Thou dost support my lot. The lines have fallen to me in pleasant places; indeed, my heritage is beautiful to me.

The LORD is my portion, says my soul, therefore I have hope in Him.

I have inherited Thy testimonies forever, for they are the joy of my heart.

O God, Thou art my God; I shall seek Thee earnestly; my soul thirsts for Thee, my flesh yearns for Thee, in a dry and weary land where there is no water. For Thou hast been my help, and in the shadow of Thy wings I sing for joy.

My beloved is mine, and I am his.

NUM 18:20. Ps 73:25,26.—Ps 16:5,6. Lam 3:24. Ps 119:111.
Ps 63:1,7. Song 2:16.

Who can say, I have cleansed my heart?

The LORD has looked down from heaven upon the sons of men, to see if there are any who understand, who seek after God. They have all turned aside; together have become corrupt; there is no one who does good, not even one.—Those who are in the flesh cannot please God.

The wishing is present in me, but the doing of the good is not. For the good that I wish, I do not do; but I practice the very evil that I do not wish.—All of us have become like one who is unclean, and all our righteous deeds are like a filthy garment; and all of us wither like a leaf, and our iniquities, like the wind, take us away.

The Scripture has shut up all men under sin, that the promise by faith in Jesus Christ might be given to those who believe.— God was in Christ reconciling the world to Himself, not counting their trespasses against them.

If we say that we have no sin, we are deceiving ourselves, and the truth is not in us. If we confess our sins, He is faithful and righteous to forgive us our sins and to cleanse us from all unrighteousness.

PR 20:9. Ps 14:2,3.—Ro 8:8. Ro 7:18,19.—Is 64:6. Gal 3:22.—
2 Co 5:19. 1 Jn 1:8,9.

The floods lift up their pounding waves.

More than the sounds of many waters, than the mighty breakers of the sea, the LORD on high is mighty.—O Lord GOD of hosts, who is like Thee, O mighty LORD? Thy faithfulness also surrounds Thee. Thou dost still them.

Do you not fear Me? declares the LORD. Do you not tremble in My presence? For I have placed the sand as a boundary for the sea, an eternal decree, so it cannot cross over it.

When you pass through the waters, I will be with you; and through the rivers, they will not overflow you.

Peter . . . walked on the water and came toward Jesus. But seeing the wind, he became afraid, and beginning to sink, he cried out, saying, Lord, save me! And immediately Jesus stretched out His hand and took hold of him, and said to him, O you of little faith, why did you doubt?

When I am afraid, I will put my trust in Thee.

PS 93:3. Ps 93:4.—Ps 89:8,9. Jer 5:22. Is 43:2. Mt 14:29–31. Ps 56:3.

Your name is like purified oil.

Christ . . . loved you, and gave Himself up for us, an offering and a sacrifice to God as a fragrant aroma.—This precious value, then, is for you who believe.—Therefore also God highly exalted Him, and bestowed on Him the name which is above every name, that at the name of Jesus every knee should bow.—In Him all the fulness of Deity dwells in bodily form.

If you love Me, you will keep My commandments.—The love of God has been poured out within our hearts through the Holy Spirit who was given to us.—The house was filled with the fragrance of the ointment.—They were marveling, and began to recognize them as having been with Jesus.

O LORD, our Lord, how majestic is Thy name in all the earth, who hast displayed Thy splendor above the heavens!—Immanuel . . . God with us.—His name will be called Wonderful Counselor, Mighty God, Eternal Father, Prince of Peace.—The name of the LORD is a strong tower; the righteous runs into it and is safe.

SONG 1:3. Eph 5:2.—1 Pe 2:7.—Phil 2:9,10.—Col 2:9. Jn 14:15.—
Ro 5:5.—Jn 12:3.—Ac 4:13. Ps 8:1.—Mt 1:23.—Is 9:6.—Pr 18:10.

While we are in this tent, we groan, being burdened.

Lord, all my desire is before Thee; and my sighing is not hidden from Thee. . . . For my iniquities are gone over my head; as a heavy burden they weigh too much for me.—Wretched man that I am! Who will set me free from the body of this death?

The whole creation groans and suffers the pains of childbirth together until now. . . . Also we ourselves, having the first fruits of the Spirit . . . groan within ourselves, waiting eagerly for our adoption as sons, the redemption of our body.—Even though now for a little while, if necessary, you have been distressed by various trials.

Knowing that the laying aside of my earthly dwelling is imminent.—For this perishable must put on the imperishable, and this mortal must put on immortality. But when this perishable will have put on the imperishable, and this mortal will have put on immortality, then will come about the saying that is written, Death is swallowed up in victory.

2 CO 5:4. Ps 38:9,4.—Ro 7:24. Ro 8:22,23.—1 Pe 1:6.—2 Pe 1:14.—
1 Co 15:53,54.

The bull, he is to bring out to a clean place outside the camp where the ashes are poured out, and burn it on wood with fire; where the ashes are poured out it shall be burned.

They took Jesus therefore; and He went out, bearing His own cross, to the place called the Place of a Skull, which is called in Hebrew Golgotha. There they crucified Him.—For the bodies of those animals whose blood is brought into the holy place by the high priest as an offering for sin, are burned outside the camp. Therefore Jesus also, that He might sanctify the people through His own blood, suffered outside the gate. Hence, let us go out to Him outside the camp, bearing His reproach.—The fellowship of His sufferings.

To the degree that you share the sufferings of Christ, keep on rejoicing; so that also at the revelation of His glory, you may rejoice with exultation.—For momentary, light affliction is producing for us an eternal weight of glory far beyond all comparison.

LEV 4:12. Jn 19:17–18.—Heb 13:11–13.—Phil 3:10. 1 Pe 4:13.—
2 Co 4:17.

God created man in His own image.

Being then the offspring of God, we ought not to think that the Divine Nature is like gold or silver or stone, an image formed by the art and thought of man.

But God, being rich in mercy, because of His great love with which He loved us, even when we were dead in our transgressions, made us alive together with Christ. For we are His workmanship, created in Christ Jesus for good works, which God prepared beforehand, that we should walk in them.—For whom He foreknew, He also predestined to become conformed to the image of His Son, that He might be the first-born among many brethren.

We know that, when He appears, we shall be like Him, because we shall see Him just as He is.—I will be satisfied with Thy likeness when I awake.

He who overcomes shall inherit these things, and I will be his God and he will be My son.—If children, heirs also, heirs of God and fellow-heirs with Christ.

GEN 1:27. Ac 17:29. Eph 2:4,5,10.—Ro 8:29. 1 Jn 3:2.—Ps 17:15.
Rev 21:7.—Ro 8:17.

Thou art my refuge in the day of disaster.

Many are saying, Who will show us any good? Lift up the light of Thy countenance upon us, O Lord!—I shall sing of Thy strength; yes, I shall joyfully sing of Thy lovingkindness in the morning, for Thou hast been my stronghold, and a refuge in the day of my distress.

I said in my prosperity, I will never be moved. . . . Thou didst hide Thy face, I was dismayed. To Thee, O Lord, I called, and to the Lord I made supplication; what profit is there in my blood, if I go down to the pit? Will the dust praise Thee? Will it declare Thy faithfulness? Hear, O Lord, and be gracious to me; O Lord, be Thou my helper.

For a brief moment I forsook you, but with great compassion I will gather you. In an outburst of anger I hid My face from you for a moment; but with everlasting lovingkindness I will have compassion on you, says the Lord your Redeemer.—Your sorrow will be turned to joy.—Weeping may last for the night, but a shout of joy comes in the morning.

JER 17:17. Ps 4:6.—Ps 59:16. Ps 30:6–10. Is 54:7,8.—Jn 16:20.—
Ps 30:5.

Adam . . . became the father of a son in his own likeness.

Who can make the clean out of the unclean?—Behold, I was brought forth in iniquity, and in sin my mother conceived me.

You were dead in your trespasses and sins . . . by nature children of wrath, even as the rest.—I am of flesh, sold into bondage to sin. For that which I am doing, I do not understand; for I am not practicing what I would like to do, but I am doing the very thing I hate. For I know that nothing good dwells in me, that is, in my flesh.

Through one man sin entered into the world . . . through the one man's disobedience the many were made sinners.—For if by the transgression of the one the many died, much more did the grace of God and the gift by the grace of the one Man, Jesus Christ, abound to the many.

The law of the Spirit of life in Christ Jesus has set you free from the law of sin and death.

Thanks be to God, who gives us the victory through our Lord Jesus Christ.

GEN 5:3. Job 14:4.—Ps 51:5. Eph 2:1,3.—Ro 7:14,15,18.
Ro 5:12,19.—Ro 5:15. Ro 8:2. 1 Co 15:57.

The LORD gives wisdom; from His mouth come knowledge and understanding.

Trust in the LORD with all your heart, and do not lean on your own understanding.—If any of you lacks wisdom, let him ask of God, who gives to all men generously and without reproach, and it will be given to him.—The foolishness of God is wiser than men, and the weakness of God is stronger than men.—God has chosen the foolish things of the world to shame the wise . . . that no man should boast before God.

The unfolding of Thy words gives light; it gives understanding to the simple.—Thy word I have treasured in my heart, that I may not sin against Thee.

All were speaking well of Him, and wondering at the gracious words which were falling from His lips.—Never did a man speak the way this man speaks.—By His doing you are in Christ Jesus, who became to us wisdom from God, and righteousness and sanctification, and redemption.

PR 2:6. Pr 3:5.—Ja 1:5.—1 Co 1:25.—1 Co 1:27,29. Ps 119:130.—
Ps 119:11. Lk 4:22.—Jn 7:46.—1 Co 1:30.

My year of redemption has come.

You shall consecrate the fiftieth year and proclaim a release through the land to all its inhabitants. It shall be a jubilee for you, and each of you shall return to his own property, and . . . to his family.

Your dead will live; their corpses will rise. You who lie in the dust, awake and shout for joy, for your dew is as the dew of the dawn, and the earth will give birth to the departed spirits.

For the Lord Himself will descend from heaven with a shout, with the voice of the archangel, and with the trumpet of God; and the dead in Christ shall rise first. Then we who are alive and remain shall be caught up together with them in the clouds to meet the Lord in the air, and thus we shall always be with the Lord.

I will ransom them from the power of Sheol; I will redeem them from death. O Death, where are your thorns? O Sheol, where is your sting?

Their Redeemer is strong, the Lord of hosts is His name.

IS 63:4. Lev 25:10. Is 26:19. 1 Th 4:16,17. Ho 13:14. Jer 50:34.

As a result of the anguish of His soul, He will see it and be satisfied.

Jesus . . . said, It is finished! And He bowed His head, and gave up His spirit.—He made Him who knew no sin to be sin on our behalf, that we might become the righteousness of God in Him.

The people whom I formed for Myself, will declare My praise. —In order that the manifold wisdom of God might now be made known through the church to the rulers and the authorities in the heavenly places. This was in accordance with the eternal purpose which He carried out in Christ Jesus our Lord.—In order that in the ages to come He might now show the surpassing riches of His grace in kindness toward us in Christ Jesus.

Having also believed, you were sealed in Him with the Holy Spirit of promise, who is given as a pledge of our inheritance, with a view to the redemption of God's own possession, to the praise of His glory.—You are a chosen race, a royal priesthood, a holy nation, a people for God's own possession, that you may proclaim the excellencies of Him who has called you out of darkness into His marvelous light.

IS 53:11. Jn 19:30.—2 Co 5:21. Is 43:21.—Eph 3:10,11.—Eph 2:7. Eph 1:13,14.—1 Pe 2:9.

The day of trial in the wilderness.

Let no one say when he is tempted, I am being tempted by God; for God cannot be tempted by evil, and He Himself does not tempt any one. But each one is tempted when he is carried away and enticed by his own lust. Then when lust has conceived, it gives birth to sin; and when sin is accomplished, it brings forth death.

(They) craved intensely in the wilderness, and tempted God in the desert.

Jesus, full of the Holy Spirit . . . was led about by the Spirit in the wilderness for forty days, while tempted by the devil. And He ate nothing during those days; and when they had ended, He became hungry. And the devil said to Him, If you are the Son of God, tell this stone to become bread.

For since He Himself was tempted in that which He has suffered, He is able to come to the aid of those who are tempted. —Simon, Simon . . . Satan has demanded permission to sift you like wheat; but I have prayed for you, that your faith may not fail.

HEB 3:8. Ja 1:13–15. Ps 106:14. Lk 4:1–3. Heb 2:18.—Lk 22:31,32.

I am the LORD who sanctifies you.

I am the LORD your God, who has separated you from the peoples. Thus you are to be holy to Me, for I the LORD am holy; and I have set you apart from the peoples to be Mine.

Called, beloved in God the Father.—Sanctify them in the truth; Thy word is truth.—May the God of peace Himself sanctify you entirely; and may your spirit and soul and body be preserved complete, without blame at the coming of our Lord Jesus Christ.

Jesus . . . that He might sanctify the people through His own blood, suffered outside the gate.—Our great God and Savior, Christ Jesus; who gave Himself for us, that He might redeem us from every lawless deed and purify for Himself a people for His own possession, zealous for good deeds.

For both He who sanctifies and those who are sanctified are all from one Father; for which reason He is not ashamed to call them brethren.—For their sakes I sanctify Myself, that they themselves also may be sanctified in truth.—By the sanctifying work of the Spirit, that you may obey Jesus Christ and be sprinkled with His blood.

LEV 20:8. Lev 20:24,26. Jude 1.—Jn 17:17.—1 Th 5:23.
Heb 13:12.—Titus 2:13,14.—Heb 2:11.—Jn 17:19.—1 Pe 1:2.

Light is sown like seed for the righteous, and gladness for the upright in heart.

Those who sow in tears shall reap with joyful shouting. He who goes to and fro weeping, carrying his bag of seed, shall indeed come again with a shout of joy, bringing his sheaves with him.

That which you sow, you do not sow the body which is to be.

Blessed be the God and Father of our Lord Jesus Christ, who according to His great mercy has caused us to be born again to a living hope through the resurrection of Jesus Christ from the dead. In this you greatly rejoice, even though now for a little while, if necessary, you have been distressed by various trials, that the proof of your faith, being more precious than gold which is perishable, even though tested by fire, may be found to result in praise and glory and honor at the revelation of Jesus Christ.

PS 97:11. Ps 126:5,6. 1 Co 15:37. 1 Pe 1:3,6,7.

Who is the man who fears the LORD? He will instruct him in the way he should choose.

The lamp of the body is the eye; if therefore your eye is clear, your whole body will be full of light.

Thy word is a lamp to my feet, and a light to my path.—And your ears will hear a word behind you, This is the way, walk in it, whenever you turn to the right or to the left.—I will instruct you and teach you in the way which you should go; I will counsel you with My eye upon you. Do not be as the horse or as the mule which have no understanding, whose trappings include bit and bridle to hold them in check, otherwise they will not come near to you. Many are the sorrows of the wicked; but he who trusts in the LORD, lovingkindness shall surround him. Be glad in the LORD and rejoice you righteous ones, and shout for joy all you who are upright in heart.

I know, O LORD, that a man's way is not in himself; nor is it in a man who walks to direct his steps.

PS 25:12. Mt 6:22. Ps 119:105.—Is 30:21.—Ps 32:8–11. Jer 10:23.

When you lie down, you will not be afraid; when you lie down, your sleep will be sweet.

There arose a fierce gale of wind, and the waves were breaking over the boat so much that the boat was already filling up. And He Himself was in the stern, asleep on the cushion.

Be anxious for nothing, but in everything by prayer and supplication with thanksgiving let your requests be made known to God. And the peace of God, which surpasses all comprehension, shall guard your hearts and your minds in Christ Jesus.

In peace I will both lie down and sleep, for Thou alone, O LORD, dost make me to dwell in safety.—For He gives to His beloved even in his sleep.

And they went on stoning Stephen as he called upon the Lord and said, Lord Jesus, receive my spirit! And falling on his knees, he cried out with a loud voice, Lord, do not hold this sin against them! And having said this, he fell asleep.—Absent from the body . . . at home with the Lord.

PR 3:24. Mk 4:37,38. Phil 4:6,7. Ps 4:8.—Ps 127:2. Ac 7:59,60.—
2 Co 5:8.

The sprinkled blood, which speaks better than the blood of Abel.

Behold, the Lamb of God who takes away the sin of the world! —The Lamb who has been slain.—For it is impossible for the blood of bulls and goats to take away sins. Therefore, when He comes into the world, He says, Sacrifice and offering Thou hast not desired, but a body Thou hast prepared for Me. By this will we have been sanctified through the offering of the body of Jesus Christ once for all.

Abel, on his part also brought of the firstlings of his flock and of their fat portions. And the LORD had regard for Abel and for his offering.—Christ ... loved you, and gave Himself up for us, an offering and a sacrifice to God as a fragrant aroma.

Let us draw near with a sincere heart in full assurance of faith, having our hearts sprinkled clean from an evil conscience and our body washed with pure water.—Brethren, we have confidence to enter the holy place by the blood of Jesus.

HEB 12:24. Jn 1:29.—Rev 13:8.—Heb 10:4,5,10. Gen 4:4.—Eph 5:2. Heb 10:22.—Heb 10:19.

Who understands the power of Thine anger?

Now from the sixth hour darkness fell upon all the land until the ninth hour. And about the ninth hour Jesus cried out with a loud voice, saying, Eli, Eli lama sabachthani? that is, My God, My God, why hast Thou forsaken Me?—The LORD has caused the iniquity of us all to fall on Him.

There is therefore now no condemnation for those who are in Christ Jesus.—Having been justified by faith, we have peace with God through our Lord Jesus Christ.—Christ redeemed us from the curse of the Law, having become a curse for us.

God has sent His only begotten Son into the world so that we might live through Him. In this is love, not that we loved God, but that He loved us and sent His Son to be the propitiation for our sins.—That He might be just and the justifier of the one who has faith in Jesus.

PS 90:11. Mt 27:45,46.—Is 53:6. Ro 8:1.—Ro 5:1.—Gal 3:13. 1 Jn 4:9,10.—Ro 3:26.

Thus says the Lord God, This also I will let the house of Israel ask Me to do for them.

You do not have because you do not ask.

Ask, and it shall be given to you; seek, and you shall find; knock, and it shall be opened to you. For every one who asks receives; and he who seeks finds; and to him who knocks it shall be opened. —And this is the confidence which we have before Him, that, if we ask anything according to His will, He hears us. And if we know that He hears us in whatever we ask, we know that we have the requests which we have asked from Him.—If any of you lacks wisdom, let him ask of God, who gives to all men generously and without reproach, and it will be given to him.—Open your mouth wide and I will fill it.—At all times (men) ought to pray and not to lose heart.

The eyes of the LORD are toward the righteous, and His ears are open to their cry. The righteous cry and the LORD hears, and delivers them out of all their troubles.—In that day you will ask in My name; and I do not say to you that I will request the Father on your behalf; for the Father Himself loves you, because you have loved Me. In My name; ask, and you will receive, that your joy may be made full.

EZE 36:37. Ja 4:2. Mt 7:7,8.—1 Jn 5:14,15.—Ja 1:5.—Ps 81:10.— Lk 18:1. Ps 34:15,17.—Jn 16:26,27,24.

Shall we indeed accept good from God and not accept adversity?

I know, O LORD, that Thy judgments are righteous, and that in faithfulness Thou hast afflicted me.—O LORD, Thou art our Father, we are the clay, and Thou our potter; and all of us are the work of Thy hand.—It is the LORD: let Him do what seems good to Him.

Righteous art Thou, O LORD, that I would plead my case with Thee; indeed I would discuss matters of justice with Thee.

He will sit as a smelter and purifier of silver.—For those whom the Lord loves He disciplines, and He scourges every son whom He receives.—It is enough for the disciple that he become as his teacher, and the slave as his master.—Although He was a Son, He learned obedience from the things which He suffered.

To the degree that you share the sufferings of Christ, keep on rejoicing; so that also at the revelation of His glory, you may rejoice with exultation.—These are the ones who come out of the great tribulation, and they have washed their robes and made them white in the blood of the Lamb.

JOB 2:10. Ps 119:75.—Is 64:8.—1 Sa 3:18. Jer 12:1. Mal 3:3.— Heb 12:6.—Mt 10:25.—Heb 5:8. 1 Pe 4:13.—Rev 7:14.

Resist the devil and he will flee from you.

For He will come like a rushing stream, which the wind of the LORD drives.—Begone, Satan! For it is written, You shall worship the Lord your God, and serve Him only. Then the devil left Him; and behold, angels came and began to minister to Him.

Be strong in the Lord, and in the strength of His might. Put on the full armor of God, that you may be able to stand firm against the schemes of the devil.—Do not participate in the unfruitful deeds of darkness, but instead even expose them.—That no advantage be taken of us by Satan; for we are not ignorant of his schemes.—Be of sober spirit, be on the alert. Your adversary, the devil, prowls about like a roaring lion, seeking someone to devour. But resist him, firm in your faith, knowing that the same experiences of suffering are being accomplished by your brethren who are in the world.—This is the victory that has overcome the world—our faith.

Who will bring a charge against God's elect? God is the one who justifies.

JA 4:7. Is 59:19.—Mt 4:10,11. Eph 6:10,11.—Eph 5:11.—
2 Co 2:11.—1 Pe 5:8,9.—1 Jn 5:4. Ro 8:33.

Oh that I knew where I might find Him.

Who is among you that fears the LORD, that obeys the voice of His servant, that walks in darkness and has no light? Let him trust in the name of the LORD and rely on his God.

And you will seek Me and find Me, when you search for Me with all your heart.—Seek, and you shall find; knock, and it shall be opened to you. For everyone who asks receives; and he who seeks finds; and to him who knocks it shall be opened.

Indeed our fellowship is with the Father, and with His Son Jesus Christ.—Now in Christ Jesus you who formerly were far off have been brought near by the blood of Christ. For through Him we both have our access in one Spirit to the Father.

If we say that we have fellowship with Him and yet walk in the darkness, we lie and do not practice the truth.

Lo, I am with you always.—I will never desert you, nor will I ever forsake you.—Another Helper . . . the Spirit of truth. . . . He abides with you, and will be in you.

JOB 23:3. Is 50:10. Jer 29:13.—Lk 11:9,10. 1 Jn 1:3.—Eph 2:13,18.
1 Jn 1:6. Mt 28:20.—Heb 13:5.—Jn 14:16,17.

Let us examine and probe our ways, and let us return to the
LORD.

Examine me, O LORD, and try me; test my mind and my heart.
—Behold, Thou dost desire truth in the innermost being, and in
the hidden part Thou wilt make me know wisdom.—I considered my ways, and turned my feet to Thy testimonies. I hastened
and did not delay, to keep Thy commandments.—Let a man
examine himself, and so let him eat of the bread and drink of the
cup.

If we confess our sins, He is faithful and righteous to forgive
us our sins and to cleanse us from all unrighteousness.—We have
an Advocate with the Father, Jesus Christ the righteous; and He
Himself is the propitiation for our sins.—Since therefore, brethren, we have confidence to enter the holy place by the blood of
Jesus, by a new and living way which He inaugurated for us
through the veil, that is, His flesh, and since we have a great
priest over the house of God, let us draw near with a sincere
heart in full assurance of faith, having our hearts sprinkled clean
from an evil conscience and our body washed with pure water.

LAM 3:40. Ps 26:2.—Ps 51:6.—Ps 119:59,60.—1 Co 11:28.
1 Jn 1:9.—1 Jn 2:1,2.—Heb 10:19–22.

There was a rainbow around the throne, like an emerald in
appearance.

This is the sign of the covenant which I am making between
Me and you and every living creature that is with you, for all
successive generations; I set My bow in the cloud. . . . I will look
upon it, to remember the everlasting covenant between God
and every living creature of all flesh that is on the earth.—For
He has made an everlasting covenant with me, ordered in all
things, and secured.—That by two unchangeable things, in
which it is impossible for God to lie, we may have strong encouragement, we who have fled for refuge in laying hold of the hope
set before us.

We preach to you the good news of the promise made to the
fathers, that God has fulfilled this promise to our children in that
He raised up Jesus.

Jesus Christ is the same yesterday and today, yes and forever.

REV 4:3. Gen 9:12,13,16.—2 Sa 23:5.—Heb 6:18. Ac 13:32,33.
Heb 13:8.

Consider yourselves to be dead to sin, but alive to God in Christ Jesus.

He who hears My word, and believes Him who sent Me, has eternal life, and does not come into judgment, but has passed out of death into life.—Through the Law I died to the Law, that I might live to God. I have been crucified with Christ, and it is no longer I who live, but Christ lives in me; and the life which I now live in the flesh I live by faith in the Son of God, who loved me, and delivered Himself up for me.

Because I live, you shall live also.—I give eternal life to them; and they shall never perish, and no one shall snatch them out of My hand. My Father, who has given them to Me, is greater than all; and no one is able to snatch them out of the Father's hand. I and the Father are one.

If then you have been raised up with Christ, keep seeking the things above, where Christ is, seated at the right hand of God. . . . For you have died and your life is hidden with Christ in God.

RO 6:11. Jn 5:24.—Gal 2:19,20. Jn 14:19.—Jn 10:28–30. Col 3:1,3.

God, who gives . . . generously and without reproach.

Woman, where are they? Did no one condemn you? And she said, No one, Lord. And Jesus said, Neither do I condemn you; go your way; from now on sin no more.

The grace of God and the gift by the grace of the one Man, Jesus Christ, abound to the many . . . the free gift arose from many transgressions resulting in justification.

God, being rich in mercy, because of His great love with which He loved us, even when we were dead in our transgressions, made us alive together with Christ (by grace you have been saved), and raised us up with Him, and seated us with Him in the heavenly places, in Christ Jesus, in order that in ages to come He might show the surpassing riches of His grace in kindness toward us in Christ Jesus.

He who did not spare His own Son, but delivered Him up for us all, how will He not also with Him freely give us all things?

JA 1:5. Jn 8:10,11. Ro 5:15,16. Eph 2:4–7. Ro 8:32.

God so loved the world, that He gave His only begotten Son, that whoever believes in Him should not perish, but have eternal life.

God, who reconciled us to Himself through Christ, and gave us the ministry of reconciliation, namely, that God was in Christ reconciling the world to Himself, not counting their trespasses against them, and He has committed to us the word of reconciliation. Therefore, we are ambassadors for Christ, as though God were entreating through us; we beg you on behalf of Christ, be reconciled to God. He made Him who knew no sin to be sin on our behalf, that we might become the righteousness of God in Him.—God is love. By this the love of God was manifested in us, that God has sent His only begotten Son into the world so that we might live through Him. In this is love, not that we loved God, but that He loved us and sent His Son to be the propitiation for our sins.

JN 3:16. 2 Co 5:18–21.—1 Jn 4:8–11.

The spirit of man is the lamp of the Lord.

He who is without sin among you, let him be the first to throw a stone at her. . . . And when they heard it, they began to go out one by one, beginning with the older ones.

Who told you that you were naked? Have you eaten from the tree of which I commanded you not to eat?

One who knows the right thing to do, and does not do it, to him it is sin.—In whatever our heart condemns us; for God is greater than our heart, and knows all things. Beloved, if our heart does not condemn us, we have confidence before God.

All things indeed are clean, but they are evil for the man who eats and gives offense. Happy is he who does not condemn himself in what he approves.

Search me, O God, and know my heart; try me and know my anxious thoughts; and see if there be any hurtful way in me, and lead me in the everlasting way.

PR 20:27. Jn 8:7,9. Gen 3:11. Ja 4:17.—1 Jn 3:20,21. Ro 14:20,22.
Ps 139:23,24.

Do not boast about tomorrow, for you do not know what a day may bring forth.

Behold, now is the acceptable time, behold, now is the day of salvation.—For a little while longer the light is among you. Walk while you have the light, that darkness may not overtake you; he who walks in the darkness does not know where he goes. While you have the light, believe in the light, in order that you may become sons of light.

Whatever your hand finds to do, verily, do it with all your might; for there is no activity or planning or wisdom in Sheol where you are going.

Soul, you have many goods laid up for many years to come; take your ease, eat, drink and be merry. . . . You fool! This very night your soul is required of you; and now who will own what you have prepared? So is the man who lays up treasure for himself, and is not rich toward God.

You do not know what your life will be like tomorrow. You are just a vapor that appears for a little while and then vanishes away.—The world is passing away, and also its lusts; but the one who does the will of God abides forever.

PR 27:1. 2 Co 6:2.—Jn 12:35,36. Ec 9:10. Lk 12:19–21. Ja 4:14.—
1 Jn 2:17.

Thou art the same, and Thy years will not come to an end.

Before the mountains were born, or Thou didst give birth to the earth and the world, even from everlasting to everlasting, Thou art God.

I, the LORD, do not change; therefore you, O sons of Jacob, are not consumed.—Jesus Christ is the same yesterday and today, yes and forever.

Every good thing bestowed and every perfect gift is from above, coming down from the Father of lights, with whom there is no variation, or shifting shadow.—For the gifts and the calling of God are irrevocable.

God is not a man, that He should lie, nor a son of man, that He should repent.—The LORD's lovingkindnesses indeed never cease, for His compassions never fail.

Because He abides forever, holds His priesthood permanently. Hence also He is able to save forever those who draw near to God through Him, since He always lives to make intercession for them.—Do not be afraid; I am the first and the last.

PS 102:27. Ps 90:2. Mal 3:6.—Heb 13:8. Ja 1:17.—Ro 11:29.
Num 23:19.—Lam 3:22. Heb 7:24,25.—Rev: 1:17.

The fruit of the Spirit is love.

God is love, and the one who abides in love abides in God, and God abides in him.—The love of God has been poured out within our hearts through the Holy Spirit who was given to us.—Precious value . . . for you who believe.—We love, because He first loved us.—For the love of Christ controls us, having concluded this, that one died for all, therefore all died; and He died for all, that they who live should no longer live for themselves, but for Him who died and rose again on their behalf.

You yourselves are taught by God to love one another.—This is My commandment, that you love one another, just as I have loved you.—Above all, keep fervent in your love for one another, because love covers a multitude of sins.—Walk in love, just as Christ also loved you and gave Himself up for us, an offering and a sacrifice to God as a fragrant aroma.

GAL 5:22. 1 Jn 4:16.—Ro 5:5.—1 Pe 2:7.—1 Jn 4:19.—2 Co 5:14,15. 1 Th 4:9.—Jn 15:12.—1 Pe 4:8.—Eph 5:2.

The LORD is My Banner.

If God is for us, who is against us?—The LORD is for me; I will not fear; what can man do to me?

Thou hast given a banner to those who fear Thee.

The LORD is my light and my salvation; whom shall I fear? The LORD is the defense of my life; whom shall I dread? Though a host encamp against me, my heart will not fear; though war arise against me, in spite of this I shall be confident.

God is with us at our head.—The LORD of hosts is with us; the God of Jacob is our stronghold.

These will wage war against the Lamb, and the Lamb will overcome them.

Why are the nations in an uproar, and the peoples devising a vain thing? He who sits in the heavens laughs, the Lord scoffs at them.—Devise a plan but it will be thwarted; state a proposal, but it will not stand, for God is with us.

EX 17:15. Ro 8:31.—Ps 118:6. Ps 60:4. Ps 27:1,3. 2 Ch 13:12.— Ps 46:7. Rev 17:14. Ps 2:1,4.—Is 8:10.

God has made me fruitful in the land of my affliction.

Blessed be the God and Father of our Lord Jesus Christ, the Father of mercies and God of all comfort; who comforts us in all our affliction so that we may be able to comfort those who are in any affliction with the comfort with which we ourselves are comforted by God. For just as the sufferings of Christ are ours in abundance, so also our comfort is abundant through Christ.

Now for a little while, if necessary, you have been distressed by various trials, that the proof of your faith, being more precious than gold which is perishable, even though tested by fire, may be found to result in praise and glory and honor at the revelation of Jesus Christ.—But the Lord stood with me, and strengthened me.

Let those also who suffer according to the will of God entrust their souls to a faithful Creator in doing what is right.

GEN 41:52. 2 Co 1:3–5. 1 Pe 1:6,7.—2 Ti 4:17. 1 Pe 4:19.

There remains therefore a Sabbath rest for the people of God.

There the wicked cease from raging, and there the weary are at rest. The prisoners are at ease together; they do not hear the voice of the taskmaster.

Blessed are the dead who die in the Lord from now on! . . . they may rest from their labors, for their deeds follow with them.

Our friend Lazarus has fallen asleep. . . . Now Jesus had spoken of his death; but they thought that He was speaking of literal sleep.

For indeed while we are in this tent, we groan, being burdened.—We ourselves, having the first fruits of the Spirit, even we ourselves groan within ourselves, waiting eagerly for our adoption as sons, the redemption of our body. For in hope we have been saved, but hope that is seen is not hope; for why does one also hope for that he sees? But if we hope for what we do not see, with perseverance we wait eagerly for it.

HEB 4:9. Job 3:17,18. Rev 14:13. Jn 11:11,13. 2 Co 5:4.—
Ro 8:23,25.

Trust in the LORD with all your heart, and do not lean on your own understanding. In all your ways acknowledge Him, and He will make your paths straight.

Trust in Him at all times, O people; pour out your heart before Him; God is a refuge for us.

I will instruct you and teach you in the way which you should go; I will counsel you with My eye upon you. Do not be as the horse or as the mule which have no understanding; whose trappings include bit and bridle to hold them in check, otherwise they will not come near to you. Many are the sorrows of the wicked; but he who trusts in the LORD, lovingkindness shall surround him.—And your ears will hear a word behind you, This is the way, walk in it, whenever you turn to the right or to the left.

If Thy presence does not go with us, do not lead us up from here. For how then can it be known that I have found favor in Thy sight, I and Thy people? Is it not by Thy going with us, so that we, I and Thy people, may be distinguished from all the other people who are upon the face of the earth?

PR 3:5,6. Ps 62:8. Ps 32:8–10.—Is 30:21. Ex 33:15,16.

I press on toward the goal for the prize of the upward call of God in Christ Jesus.

You shall have treasure in heaven; . . . come, follow Me.—I am a shield to you; your reward shall be very great.

Well done, good and faithful slave; you were faithful with a few things, I will put you in charge of many things, enter into the joy of your master.—They shall reign forever and ever.

You will receive the unfading crown of glory.—The crown of life.—The crown of righteousness.—A . . . wreath . . . imperishable.

Father, I desire that they also whom Thou hast given Me be with Me where I am, in order that they may behold My glory, which Thou hast given Me.—Thus we shall always be with the Lord.

For I consider that the sufferings of this present time are not worthy to be compared with the glory that is to be revealed to us.

PHIL 3:14. Mt 19:21.—Gen 15:1. Mt 25:21.—Rev 22:5. 1 Pe 5:4.— Ja 1:12.—2 Ti 4:8.—1 Co 9:25.— Jn 17:24.—1 Th 4:17. Ro 8:18.

Set your mind on the things above, not on the things that are on earth.

Do not love the world, nor the things in the world. If any one loves the world, the love of the Father is not in him.—Do not lay up for yourselves treasures upon earth, where moth and rust destroy, and where thieves break in and steal; but lay up for yourselves treasures in heaven, where neither moth nor rust destroys, and where thieves do not break in or steal; for where your treasure is, there will your heart be also.

We walk by faith, not by sight.—We do not lose heart, but though our outer man is decaying, yet our inner man is being renewed day by day. For momentary, light affliction is producing for us an eternal weight of glory far beyond all comparison, while we look not at the things which are seen, but at the things which are not seen; for the things which are seen are temporal, but the things which are not seen are eternal.—An inheritance which is imperishable and undefiled and will not fade away, reserved in heaven for you.

COL 3:2. 1 Jn 2:15.—Mt 6:19-21. 2 Co 5:7.—2 Co 4:16-18.—1 Pe 1:4.

He bowed his shoulder to bear burdens.

As an example, brethren, of suffering and patience, take the prophets who spoke in the name of the Lord.—Now these things happened to them as an example, and they were written for our instruction, upon whom the ends of the ages have come.

Shall we indeed accept good from God and not accept adversity? In all this Job did not sin with his lips.—Aaron, therefore, kept silent.—It is the Lord; let Him do what seems good to Him.

Cast your burden upon the Lord, and He will sustain you.—Surely our griefs He Himself bore, and our sorrows He carried.

Come to Me, all who are weary and heavy laden, and I will give you rest. Take My yoke upon you, and learn from Me, for I am gentle and humble in heart; and you shall find rest for your souls. For My yoke is easy, and My load is light.

GEN 49:15. Ja 5:10.—1 Co 10:11. Job 2:10.—Lev 10:3.—I Sa 3:18. Ps 55:22.—Is 53:4. Mt 11:28-30.

O Lord, I am oppressed, be my security.

To Thee I lift up my eyes, O Thou who art enthroned in the heavens! Behold, as the eyes of servants look to the hand of their master, as the eyes of a maid to the hand of her mistress; so our eyes look to the LORD our God.—Hear my cry, O God; give heed to my prayer. From the end of the earth I call to Thee, when my heart is faint; lead me to the rock that is higher than I. For Thou hast been a refuge for me, a tower of strength against the enemy. Let me dwell in Thy tent forever; let me take refuge in the shelter of Thy wings.—For Thou hast been a defense for the helpless. A defense for the needy in his distress, a refuge from the storm.

Christ also suffered for you, leaving you an example for you to follow in His steps, who committed no sin, nor was any deceit found in His mouth; and while being reviled, He did not revile in return; while suffering, He uttered no threats, but kept entrusting Himself to Him who judges righteously.

IS 38:14. Ps 123:1,2.—Ps 61:1–4.—Is 25:4. 1 Pe 2:21–23.

Fight the good fight of faith.

We were afflicted on every side: conflicts without, fears within. —Do not fear, for those who are with us are more than those who are with them.—Be strong in the Lord, and in the strength of His might.

You come to me with a sword, a spear, and a javelin, but I come to you in the name of the LORD of hosts, the God of the armies of Israel, whom you have taunted.—God is my strong fortress. . . . He trains my hands for battle, so that my arms can bend a bow of bronze.—Our adequacy is from God.

The angel of the LORD encamps around those who fear Him, and rescues them.—The mountain was full of horses and chariots of fire all around Elisha.

Time will fail me if I tell of . . . (those) . . . who by faith conquered kingdoms . . . from weakness were made strong, became mighty in war, put foreign armies to flight.

1 TI 6:12. 2 Co 7:5.—2 Ki 6:16.—Eph 6:10. 1 Sa 17:45.—
2 Sa 22:33,35.—2 Co 3:5. Ps 34:7.—2 Ki 6:17. Heb 11:32–34.

He preserves the way of His godly ones.

The LORD your God, who goes before you on your way, to seek out a place for you to encamp, in fire by night and cloud by day, to show you the way in which you should go.—Like an eagle that stirs up its nest, that hovers over its young, He spread His wings and caught them, He carried them on His pinions. The LORD alone guided him.—The steps of a man are established by the LORD; and He delights in his way. When he falls, he shall not be hurled headlong; because the LORD is the One who holds his hand.—Many are the afflictions of the righteous; but the LORD delivers him out of them all.—For the LORD knows the way of the righteous, but the way of the wicked will perish.—We know that God causes all things to work together for good to those who love God, to those who are called according to His purpose.—With us is the LORD our God to help us and to fight our battles.

The LORD your God is in your midst, a victorious warrior. . . . He will rejoice over you with shouts of joy.

PR 2:8. Deu 1:32,33.—Deu 32:11,12.—Ps 37:23,24.—Ps 34:19.—
Ps 1:6.—Ro 8:28.—2 Ch 32:8. Zep 3:17.

My God, My God, why hast Thou forsaken Me?

He was pierced through for our transgressions, He was crushed for our iniquities; the chastening for our well-being fell upon Him . . . the LORD has caused the iniquity of us all to fall on Him. . . . For the transgression of my people to whom the stroke was due? But the LORD was pleased to crush Him, putting Him to grief.

Jesus our Lord . . . was delivered up because of our transgressions.—Christ . . . died for sins once for all, the just for the unjust, in order that He might bring us to God.—He Himself bore our sins in His body on the cross, that we might die to sin and live to righteousness; for by His wounds you were healed.

He made Him who knew no sin to be sin on our behalf, that we might become the righteousness of God in Him.

Christ redeemed us from the curse of the Law, having become a curse for us.

MT 27:46. Is 53:5,6,8,10. Ro 4:24,25.—1 Pe 3:18.—1 Pe 2:24.
2 Co 5:21. Gal 3:13.

For your husband is your Maker, whose name is the LORD of hosts.

This mystery is great; but I am speaking with reference to Christ and the church.

It will no longer be said to you, Forsaken ... but you will be called, My delight is in her. ... For the LORD delights in you ... and as the bridegroom rejoices over the bride, so your God will rejoice over you.—He has sent me ... to comfort all who mourn, to grant those who mourn in Zion, giving them a garland instead of ashes, the oil of gladness instead of mourning, the mantle of praise instead of a spirit of fainting.

I will rejoice greatly in the LORD, my soul will exult in my God; for He has clothed me with garments of salvation ... as a bridegroom decks himself with a garland, and as a bride adorns herself with her jewels.

I will betroth you to Me forever; yes, I will betroth you to Me in righteousness and in justice, in lovingkindness and in compassion.

Who shall separate us from the love of Christ?

IS 54:5. Eph 5:32. Is 62:4,5.—Is 61:1–3. Is 61:10. Ho 2:19. Ro 8:35.

My times are in Thy hand.

All Thy holy ones are in Thy hand.—The word of the LORD came to (Elijah), saying, Go away from here and turn eastward, and hide yourself by the brook Cherith, which is east of the Jordan. And it shall be that you shall drink of the brook, and I have commanded the ravens to provide for you there. Then the word of the LORD came to him, saying, Arise, go to Zarephath, which belongs to Sidon, and stay there; behold, I have commanded a widow there to provide for you.

Do not be anxious for your life, as to what you shall eat, or what you shall drink; nor for your body, as to what you shall put on. Your heavenly Father knows that you need all these things.

Trust in the LORD with all your heart, and do not lean on your own understanding. In all your ways acknowledge Him, and He will make your paths straight.—Casting all your anxiety upon Him, because He cares for you.

Ps 31:15. Deu 33:3.—1 Ki 17:2–4,8,9. Mt 6:25,32. Pr 3:5,6.—
1 Pe 5:7.

Thou hast cast all my sins behind Thy back.

Who is a God like Thee, who pardons iniquity and passes over the rebellious act of the remnant of His possession? He does not retain His anger forever, because He delights in unchanging love. He will again have compassion on us; He will tread our iniquities underfoot. Yes, Thou wilt cast all their sins into the depths of the sea.

For a brief moment I forsook you, but with great compassion I will gather you. In an outburst of anger I hid My face from you for a moment; but with everlasting lovingkindness I will have compassion on you, says the LORD your Redeemer.—I will forgive their iniquity, and their sin I will remember no more.

How blessed is he whose transgression is forgiven, whose sin is covered! How blessed is the man to whom the LORD does not impute iniquity, and in whose spirit there is no deceit!—The blood of Jesus His Son cleanses us from all sin.

IS 38:17. Mic 7:18,19. Is 54:7,8.—Jer 31:34. Ps 32:1,2.—1 Jn 1:7.

For I know whom I have believed and I am convinced that He is able.

Able to do exceeding abundantly beyond all that we ask or think.

Able to make all grace abound to you, that always having all sufficiency in everything, you may have an abundance for every good deed.

Able to come to the aid of those who are tempted.

Able to save forever those who draw near to God through Him, since He always lives to make intercession for them.

Able to keep you from stumbling, and to make you stand in the presence of His glory blameless with great joy.

Able to guard what I have entrusted to Him until that day.

(The Lord Jesus Christ); who will transform the body of our humble state into conformity with the body of His glory, by the exertion of the power that He has even to subject all things to Himself.

Do you believe that I am able to do this? . . . Yes, Lord. . . . Be it done to you according to your faith.

2 Ti 1:12. Eph 3:20. 2 Co 9:8. Heb 2:18. Heb 7:25. Jude 24.
2 Ti 1:12. Phil 3:21. Mt 9:28,29.

God, who richly supplies us with all things to enjoy.

Beware lest you forget the LORD your God by not keeping His commandments and His ordinances and His statutes which I am commanding you today; lest, when you have eaten and are satisfied, and have built good houses and lived in them . . . then your heart becomes proud, and you forget the LORD your God . . . for it is He who is giving you power to make wealth.

Unless the LORD builds the house, they labor in vain who build it; unless the LORD guards the city, the watchman keeps awake in vain. It is vain for you to rise up early, to retire late, to eat the bread of painful labors; for He gives to His beloved even in his sleep.—For by their own sword they did not possess the land; and their own arm did not save them; but Thy right hand, and Thine arm, and the light of Thy presence, for Thou didst favor them. —Many are saying, Who will show us any good? Lift up the light of Thy countenance upon us, O LORD!

1 TI 6:17. Deu 8:11,12,14,18. Ps 127:1,2.—Ps 44:3.—Ps 4:6.

They sang a new song.

A new and living way which He inaugurated for us.—Not on the basis of deeds which we have done in righteousness, but according to His mercy, by the washing of regeneration and renewing by the Holy Spirit, whom He poured out upon us richly through Jesus Christ our Savior.—By grace you have been saved through faith; and that not of yourselves, it is the gift of God; not as a result of works, that no one should boast.

Not to us, O LORD, not to us, but to Thy name give glory.—To Him who loves us, and released us from our sins by His blood, and He has made us to be a kingdom, priests to His God and Father; to Him be the glory and the dominion forever and ever. Amen. —Thou wast slain, and didst purchase for God with Thy blood men from every tribe and tongue and people and nation.—I looked, and behold, a great multitude, which no one could count . . . cry . . . saying, Salvation to our God who sits on the throne, and to the Lamb.

REV 14:3. Heb 10:20.—Titus 3:5,6.—Eph 2:8,9. Ps 115:1.— Rev 1:5,6.—Rev 5:9.—Rev 7:9,10.

The LORD Will Provide.

God will provide for Himself the lamb for the burnt offering.
Behold, the LORD's hand is not so short that it cannot save;
neither is His ear so dull that it cannot hear.—The Deliverer will
come from Zion, He will remove ungodliness from Jacob.

How blessed is he whose help is the God of Jacob, whose hope
is in the LORD his God.—Behold, the eye of the LORD is on those
who fear Him, on those who hope for His lovingkindness; to
deliver their soul from death.

My God shall supply all your needs according to His riches in
glory in Christ Jesus.—He Himself has said, I will never desert
you, nor will I ever forsake you, so that we confidently say, the
Lord is my helper, I will not be afraid. What shall man do to me?
—The LORD is my strength and my shield; my heart trusts in
Him, and I am helped; therefore my heart exults, and with my
song I shall thank Him.

GEN 22:14. Gen 22:8. Is 59:1.—Ro 11:26. Ps 146:5.—Ps 33:18,19.
Phil 4:19.—Heb 13:5,6.—Ps 28:7.

He pastures his flock among the lilies.

Where two or three have gathered together in My name, there
I am in their midst.—If anyone loves Me, he will keep My word;
and My Father will love him, and We will come to him, and make
Our abode with him.

If you keep My commandments, you will abide in My love; just
as I have kept My Father's commandments, and abide in His
love.

May my beloved come into his garden and eat its choice fruits!
—I have come into my garden, my sister, my bride; I have gathered my myrrh along with my balsam. I have eaten my honeycomb and my honey.—The fruit of the Spirit is love, joy, peace,
patience, kindness, goodness, faithfulness, gentleness, self-control.

By this is My Father glorified, that you bear much fruit, and
so prove to be My disciples.—Every branch that bears fruit, He
prunes it, that it may bear more fruit.—Having been filled with
the fruit of righteousness which comes through Jesus Christ, to
the glory and praise of God.

SONG 2:16. Mt 18:20.—Jn 14:23. Jn 15:10. Song 4:16.—Song 5:1.—
Gal 5:22,23. Jn 15:8.—Jn 15:2.—Phil 1:11.

The LORD bless you, and keep you.

It is the blessing of the LORD that makes rich, and He adds no sorrow to it.—Thou who dost bless the righteous man, O LORD, Thou dost surround him with favor as with a shield.

He will not allow your foot to slip; He who keeps you will not slumber. Behold, He who keeps Israel will neither slumber nor sleep. The LORD is your keeper; the LORD is your shade on your right hand. The LORD will protect you from all evil; He will keep your soul. The LORD will guard your going out and your coming in from this time forth and forever.—I the LORD am its keeper; I water it every moment. Lest anyone damage it, I guard it night and day.

Holy Father, keep them in Thy name, the name which Thou hast given Me. . . . While I was with them, I was keeping them in Thy name which Thou hast given Me; and I guarded them.

The Lord will deliver me from every evil deed, and will bring me safely to His heavenly kingdom; to Him be the glory forever and ever. Amen.

NUM 6:24. Pr 10:22.—Ps 5:12. Ps 121:3–5,7,8.—Is 27:3. Jn 17:11,12.
2 Ti 4:18.

Jesus wept.

A man of sorrows, and acquainted with grief.—We do not have a high priest who cannot sympathize with our weaknesses.—It was fitting for Him, for whom are all things, and through whom are all things, in bringing many sons to glory, to perfect the author of their salvation through sufferings.—Although He was a Son, He learned obedience from the things which He suffered.

I was not disobedient, nor did I turn back. I gave My back to those who strike Me, and My cheeks to those who pluck out the beard; I did not cover My face from humiliation and spitting.

Behold how He loved.—Assuredly He does not give help to angels, but He gives help to the seed of Abraham. Therefore, He had to be made like His brethren in all things, that He might become a merciful and faithful high priest in things pertaining to God, to make propitiation for the sins of the people.

JN 11:35. Is 53:3.—Heb 4:15.—Heb 2:10.—Heb 5:8. Is 50:5,6.
Jn 11:36.—Heb 2:16,17.

The LORD make His face shine on you, and be gracious to you; the LORD lift up His countenance on you, and give you peace.

No man has seen God at any time; the only begotten God, who is in the bosom of the Father, He has explained Him.—He is the radiance of His glory and the exact representation of His nature. —The god of this world has blinded the minds of the unbelieving, that they might not see the light of the gospel of the glory of Christ, who is the image of God.

Make Thy face to shine upon Thy servant; save me in Thy lovingkindness. Let me not be put to shame, O LORD, for I call upon Thee.—O LORD, by Thy favor Thou hast made my mountain to stand strong; Thou didst hide Thy face, I was dismayed. — How blessed are the people who know the joyful sound! O LORD, they walk in the light of Thy countenance.

The LORD will give strength to His people; the LORD will bless His people with peace.

Take courage, it is I; do not be afraid.

NUM 6:25,26. Jn 1:18.—Heb 1:3.—2 Co 4:4. Ps 31:16,17.— Ps 30:7.—Ps 89:15. Ps 29:11. Mt 14:27.

Things that are pleasing in His sight.

Without faith it is impossible to please Him.—Those who are in the flesh cannot please God.—The LORD takes pleasure in His people.

This finds favor, if for the sake of conscience toward God a man bears up under sorrows when suffering unjustly. If when you do what is right and suffer for it you patiently endure it, this finds favor with God.—A gentle and quiet spirit, which is precious in the sight of God.

He who offers a sacrifice of thanksgiving honors Me; and to him who orders his way aright I shall show the salvation of God.—I will praise the name of God with song, and shall magnify Him with thanksgiving. And it will please the LORD better than an ox or a young bull with horns and hoofs.

I urge you therefore, brethren, by the mercies of God, to present your bodies a living and holy sacrifice, acceptable to God, which is your spiritual service of worship.

1 JN 3:22. Heb 11:6.—Ro 8:8.—Ps 149:4. 1 Pe 2:19,20.—1 Pe 3:4. Ps 50:23.—Ps 69:30,31. Ro 12:1.

There is one God, and one mediator also between God and men, the man Christ Jesus.

Since ... the children share in flesh and blood, He Himself likewise also partook of the same.

Turn to Me, and be saved, all the ends of the earth; for I am God, and there is no other.

We have an advocate with the Father, Jesus Christ the righteous.—Now in Christ Jesus you who formerly were far off have been brought near by the blood of Christ. For He Himself is our peace.—Through His own blood, He entered the holy place once for all, having obtained eternal redemption. For this reason He is the mediator of a new covenant, in order that since a death has taken place for the redemption of the transgressions that were committed under the first covenant, those who have been called may receive the promise of the eternal inheritance.—He is able to save forever those who draw near to God through Him, since He always lives to make intercession for them.

1 TI 2:5. Heb 2:14. Is 45:22. 1 Jn 2:1.—Eph 2:13,14.—
Heb 9:12,15.—Heb 7:25.

Oh my God, my soul is in despair within me.

The steadfast of mind Thou wilt keep in perfect peace, because he trusts in Thee. Trust in the LORD forever, for in GOD the LORD, we have an everlasting Rock.

Cast your burden upon the LORD, and He will sustain you.—He has not despised nor abhorred the affliction of the afflicted; neither has He hidden His face from him; but when he cried to Him for help, He heard.—Is anyone among you suffering? Let him pray.

Let not your heart be troubled, nor let it be fearful.—Do not be anxious for your life, as to what you shall eat, or what you shall drink; nor for your body, as to what you shall put on. Is not life more than food, and the body than clothing? Look at the birds of the air, that they do not sow, neither do they reap, nor gather into barns; and yet your heavenly Father feeds them. Are you not worth much more than they?—Be not unbelieving, but believing.—Lo, I am with you always.

PS 42:6. Is 26:3,4. Ps 55:22.—Ps 22:24.—Ja 5:13. Jn 14:27.—
Mt 6:25,26.—Jn 20:27.—Mt 28:20.

Adorn the doctrine of God our Savior in every respect.

Conduct yourselves in a manner worthy of the gospel of Christ.—Abstain from every form of evil.—If you are reviled for the name of Christ, you are blessed. . . . By no means let any of you suffer as a murderer, or thief, or evil-doer, or a troublesome meddler.—Be blameless and innocent, children of God above reproach in the midst of a crooked and perverse generation, among whom you appear as lights in the world.—Let your light shine before men in such a way that they may see your good works, and glorify your Father who is in heaven.

Do not let kindness and truth leave you; bind them around your neck, write them on the tablet of your heart. So you will find favor and good repute in the sight of God and man.—Brethren, whatever is true, whatever is honorable, whatever is right, whatever is pure, whatever is lovely, whatever is of good repute; if there is any excellence and if anything worthy of praise, let your mind dwell on these things.

TITUS 2:10. Phil 1:27.—1 Th 5:22.—1 Pe 4:14,15.—Phil 2:15.—
Mt 5:16. Pr 3:3,4.—Phil 4:8.

The words that I have spoken to you are spirit and are life.

Of His will He brought us forth by the word of truth.—The letter kills, but the Spirit gives life.

Christ . . . loved the church and gave Himself up for her; that He might sanctify her, having cleansed her by the washing of water with the word, that He might present to Himself the church in all her glory, having no spot or wrinkle or any such thing.

How can a young man keep his way pure? By keeping it according to Thy word. Thy word has revived me. Thy word I have treasured in my heart, that I may not sin against Thee. I shall not forget Thy word. I trust in Thy word. The law of Thy mouth is better to me than thousands of gold and silver pieces. I will never forget Thy precepts, for by them Thou hast revived me. How sweet are Thy words to my taste! Yes, sweeter than honey to my mouth! From Thy precepts I get understanding; therefore I hate every false way.

JN 6:63. Ja 1:18.—2 Co 3:6. Eph 5:25–27.
Ps 119:9,50,11,16,42,72,93,103,104.

Salvation through sufferings.

My soul is deeply grieved, to the point of death; remain here and keep watch with Me. And He went a little beyond them, and fell on His face and prayed, saying, My Father, if it is possible, let this cup pass from Me; yet not as I will, but as Thou wilt.— And being in agony He was praying very fervently; and His sweat became like drops of blood, falling down upon the ground.

The cords of death encompassed me, and the terrors of Sheol came upon me; I found distress and sorrow.—Reproach has broken my heart, and I am so sick. And I looked for sympathy, but there was none; and for comforters, but I found none.—Look to the right and see; for there is no one who regards me; there is no escape for me; no one cares for my soul.

He was despised and forsaken of men, a man of sorrows, and acquainted with grief; and like one from whom men hide their face. He was despised, and we did not esteem Him.

HEB 2:10. Mt 26:38,39.—Lk 22:44. Ps 116:3.—Ps 69:20.—Ps 142:4.
Is 53:3.

The LORD made the heavens and the earth, the sea and all that is in them.

The heavens are telling of the glory of God; and the firmament is declaring the work of His hands.—By the word of the LORD the heavens were made, and by the breath of His mouth all their host. For He spoke, and it was done; He commanded, and it stood fast.—Behold, the nations are like a drop from a bucket, and are regarded as a speck of dust on the scales; behold, He lifts up the islands like fine dust.

By faith we understand that the worlds were prepared by the word of God, so that what is seen was not made out of things which are visible.

When I consider Thy heavens, the work of Thy fingers, the moon and the stars, which Thou hast ordained; what is man, that Thou dost take thought of him? And the son of man, that Thou dost care for him?

EX 20:11. Ps 19:1.—Ps 33:6,9.—Is 40:15. Heb 11:3. Ps 8:3,4.

You do not know what your life will be like tomorrow. You are just a vapor that appears for a little while and then vanishes away.

Now my days are swifter than a runner; they flee away, they see no good. They slip by like reed boats, like an eagle that swoops on its prey.—Thou hast swept them away like a flood, they fall asleep; in the morning they are like grass which sprouts anew. In the morning it flourishes, and sprouts anew; towards evening it fades, and withers away.—Man, who is born of woman, is short-lived and full of turmoil. Like a flower he comes forth and withers.

The world is passing away, and also its lusts; but the one who does the will of God abides forever.—Even they will perish, but Thou dost endure; and all of them will wear out like a garment; like clothing Thou wilt change them, and they will be changed. But Thou art the same, and Thy years will not come to an end. —Jesus Christ is the same yesterday and today, yes and forever.

JA 4:14. Job 9:25,26.—Ps 90:5,6.—Job 14:1,2. 1 Jn 2:17.—
Ps 102:26,27.—Heb 13:8.

I shall sing with the spirit and I shall sing with the mind also.

Be filled with the Spirit, speaking to one another in psalms and hymns and spiritual songs, singing and making melody with your heart to the Lord.—Let the word of Christ richly dwell within you; with all wisdom teaching and admonishing one another with psalms and hymns and spiritual songs, singing with thankfulness in your hearts to God.

My mouth will speak the praise of the LORD; and all flesh will bless His holy name forever and ever.

Praise the LORD! For it is good to sing praises to our God; for it is pleasant and praise is becoming. Sing to the LORD with thanksgiving; sing praises to our God on the lyre.

I heard a voice from heaven, like the sound of many waters and like the sound of loud thunder, and the voice which I heard was like the sound of harpists playing on their harps.

1 CO 14:15. Eph 5:18,19.—Col 3:16. Ps 145:21. Ps 147:1,7.
Rev 14:2.

And he shall lay his hand on the head of the burnt offering, that it may be accepted for him to make atonement on his behalf.

Knowing that you were not redeemed with perishable things like silver or gold from your futile way of life inherited from your forefathers, but with precious blood, as of a lamb unblemished and spotless, the blood of Christ.—He Himself bore our sins in His body on the cross.

His grace, which He freely bestowed on us in the Beloved.

As living stones ... built up as a spiritual house for a holy priesthood, to offer up spiritual sacrifices acceptable to God through Jesus Christ.—I urge you therefore, brethren, by the mercies of God, to present your bodies a living and holy sacrifice, acceptable to God, which is your spiritual service of worship.

Now to Him who is able to keep you from stumbling, and to make you stand in the presence of His glory blameless with great joy, to the only God our Savior, through Jesus Christ our Lord, be glory, majesty, dominion and authority, before all time and now and forever.

LEV 1:4. 1 Pe 1:18,19.—1 Pe 2:24. Eph 1:6. 1 Pe 2:5.—Ro 12:1.
Jude 24,25.

Tempted in all things as we are, yet without sin.

When the woman saw that the tree was good for food (the lust of the flesh), and that it was a delight to the eyes (the lust of the eyes), and that the tree was desirable to make one wise (the pride of life), she took from its fruit and ate; and she gave also to her husband with her, and he ate.

The tempter came and said to Him (Jesus), If You are the Son of God, command that these stones become bread (the lust of the flesh). But He answered. ... Man shall not live on bread alone, but on every word that proceeds out of the mouth of God. The devil ... showed Him all the kingdoms of the world, and their glory (the lust of the eyes, and the pride of life). Then Jesus said to him, Begone, Satan!

Since He Himself was tempted in that which He has suffered, He is able to come to the aid of those who are tempted.

Blessed is a man who perseveres under trial.

HEB 4:15. Gen 3:6. Mt 4:3,4,8,10. Heb 2:18. Ja 1:12.

My eyes look wistfully to the heights.

Be gracious to me, O LORD, for I am pining away; heal me, O LORD, for my bones are dismayed. And my soul is greatly dismayed; but Thou, O LORD—how long? Return, O LORD, rescue my soul; save me because of Thy lovingkindness.—My heart is in anguish within me, and the terrors of death have fallen upon me. Fear and trembling come upon me; and horror has overwhelmed me. And I said, O that I had wings like a dove! I would fly away and be at rest.

You have need of endurance.

As they were gazing intently into the sky while He was departing, behold, two men in white clothing stood beside them; and they also said, Men of Galilee, why do you stand looking into the sky? This Jesus, who has been taken up from you into heaven, will come in just the same way as you have watched Him go into heaven.—Our citizenship is in heaven, from which also we eagerly wait for a Savior, the Lord Jesus Christ.—The blessed hope and the appearing of the glory of our great God and Savior, Christ Jesus.

IS 38:14. Ps 6:2–4.—Ps 55:4–6. Heb 10:36. Ac 1:10,11.—Phil 3:20.—
Titus 2:13.

His name shall be on their foreheads.

I am the good shepherd; and I know My own.—The firm foundation of God stands, having this seal, The Lord knows those who are His, and, Let every one who names the name of the Lord abstain from wickedness.

The LORD is good, a stronghold in the day of trouble, and He knows those who take refuge in Him.—Do not harm the earth or the sea or the trees, until we have sealed the bond-servants of our God on their foreheads.

Having . . . believed, you were sealed in Him with the Holy Spirit of promise, who is given as a pledge of our inheritance.—Now He who establishes us with you in Christ and anointed us is God, who also sealed us and gave us the Spirit in our hearts as a pledge.

I will write upon him the name of My God, and the name of the city of My God, the new Jerusalem, which comes down out of heaven from My God, and My new name.—This is the name by which she shall be called: the LORD is our righteousness.

REV 22:4. Jn 10:14.—2 Ti 2:19. Nah 1:7.—Rev 7:3. Eph 1:13,14.—
2 Co 1:21,22. Rev 3:12.—Jer 33:16.

God raised up His Servant, and sent Him to bless you by turn-ing every one of you from your wicked ways.

Blessed be the God and Father of our Lord Jesus Christ, who according to His great mercy has caused us to be born again to a living hope through the resurrection of Jesus Christ from the dead.—Saved by His life.

Our great God and Savior, Christ Jesus; who gave Himself for us, that He might redeem us from every lawless deed and purify for Himself a people for His own possession, zealous for good deeds.—Like the Holy One who called you, be holy yourselves also in all your behavior; because it is written, You shall be holy, for I am holy.

The God and Father of our Lord Jesus Christ, who has blessed us with every spiritual blessing in the heavenly places in Christ. —In Him all the fulness of Deity dwells in bodily form, and in Him you have been made complete.—Of His fulness we have all received, and grace upon grace.

He who did not spare His own Son, but delivered Him up for us all, how will He not also with Him freely give us all things?

AC 3:26. 1 Pe 1:3.—Ro 5:10. Titus 2:13,14.—1 Pe 1:15,16.
Eph 1:3.—Col 2:9,10.—Jn 1:16. Ro 8:32.

Strengthen me according to Thy word.

Remember the word to Thy servant, in which Thou hast made me hope.—O Lord, I am oppressed, be my security.

Heaven and earth will pass away, but My words will not pass away.—You know in all your hearts and in all your souls that not one word of all the good words which the LORD your God spoke concerning you has failed; all have been fulfilled for you, not one of them has failed.

Do not be afraid. Peace be with you; take courage and be courageous! Now as soon as he spoke to me, I received strength and said, May my lord speak, for you have strengthened me.— Take courage . . . and work; for I am with you, says the LORD of hosts.—Not by might nor by power, but by My Spirit, says the LORD of hosts.

Be strong in the Lord, and in the strength of His might.

PS 119:28. Ps 119:49.—Is 38:14. Lk 21:33.—Jos 23:14. Dan 10:19.—
Hag 2:4.—Zec 4:6. Eph 6:10.

The unfolding of Thy words gives light.

This is the message we have heard from Him . . . God is light, and in Him there is no darkness at all.—God, who said, Light shall shine out of darkness, is the One who has shone in our hearts to give the light of the knowledge of the glory of God in the face of Christ.—The Word was God. In Him was life; and the life was the light of men.—If we walk in the light as He Himself is in the light, we have fellowship with one another, and the blood of Jesus His Son cleanses us from all sin.

Thy word I have treasured in my heart, that I may not sin against Thee.—You are already clean because of the word which I have spoken to you.

You were formerly darkness, but now you are light in the Lord; walk as children of light.—You are a chosen race, a royal priesthood, a holy nation, a people for God's own possession, that you may proclaim the excellencies of Him who has called you out of darkness into His marvelous light.

PS 119:130. 1 Jn 1:5.—2 Co 4:6.—Jn 1:1,4.—1 Jn 1:7. Ps 119:11.—
Jn 15:3. Eph 5:8.—1 Pe 2:9.

Noah was a righteous man.

The righteous man shall live by faith.—Noah built an altar to the LORD, and took of every clean animal and of every clean bird and offered burnt offerings on the altar. And the LORD smelled the soothing aroma.—From the foundation of the world . . . the Lamb who has been slain.

Having been justified by faith, we have peace with God through our Lord Jesus Christ.

By the works of the Law no flesh will be justified in His sight; for through the Law comes the knowledge of sin. But now apart from the Law the righteousness of God has been manifested, being witnessed by the Law and the Prophets; even the righteousness of God through faith in Jesus Christ for all those who believe; for there is no distinction.

We . . . exult in God through our Lord Jesus Christ, through whom we have now received the reconciliation.

Who will bring a charge against God's elect? God is the one who justifies.—Whom He predestined, these He also called; and whom He called, these He also justified.

GEN 6:9. Gal 3:11.—Gen 8:20,21.—Rev 13:8. Ro 5:1. Ro 3:20–22.
Ro 5:11. Ro 8:33.—Ro 8:30.

Wake up, and strengthen the things that remain, which were about to die.

The end of all things is at hand; therefore, be of sound judgment and sober spirit for the purpose of prayer.—Be of sober spirit, be on the alert. Your adversary, the devil, prowls about like a roaring lion, seeking someone to devour.—Give heed to yourself and keep your soul diligently, lest you forget the things which your eyes have seen, and lest they depart from your heart all the days of your life.—But My righteous one shall live by faith; and if he shrinks back, My soul has no pleasure in him. But we are not of those who shrink back to destruction, but of those who have faith to the preserving of the soul.

What I say to you I say to all, Be on the alert!

Do not fear, for I am with you; do not anxiously look about you, for I am your God. I will strengthen you, surely I will help you, surely, I will uphold you with My righteous right hand. For I am the LORD your God, who upholds your right hand.

REV 3:2. 1 Pe 4:7.—1 Pe 5:8.—Deu 4:9.—Heb 10:38,39. Mk 13:37. Is 41:10,13.

Has His lovingkindness ceased forever?

His lovingkindness is everlasting.—The LORD is slow to anger and abundant in lovingkindness.—Who is a God like Thee, who pardons iniquity? . . . He does not retain His anger forever, because He delights in unchanging love. He will again have compassion on us; He will tread our iniquities underfoot. Yes, Thou wilt cast all their sins into the depths of the sea.—He saved us, not on the basis of deeds which we have done in righteousness, but according to His mercy.

Blessed be the God and Father of our Lord Jesus Christ, the Father of mercies and God of all comfort; who comforts us in all our affliction so that we may be able to comfort those who are in any affliction with the comfort with which we ourselves are comforted by God.

A merciful and faithful high priest in things pertaining to God, to make propitiation for the sins of the people. For since He Himself was tempted in that which He has suffered, He is able to come to the aid of those who are tempted.

PS 77:8. Ps 136:23.—Num 14:18.—Mic 7:18,19.—Titus 3:5. 2 Co 1:3,4. Heb 2:17,18.

Lot lifted up his eyes and saw all the valley of the Jordan, that it was well watered everywhere—this was before the LORD destroyed Sodom and Gomorrah—like the garden of the LORD. . . .
So Lot chose for himself all the valley of the Jordan.

Righteous Lot . . . that righteous man.
Do not be deceived, God is not mocked; for whatever a man sows, this he will also reap.—Remember Lot's wife.
Do not be bound together with unbelievers; for what partnership have righteousness and lawlessness, or what fellowship has light with darkness? Therefore, come out from their midst and be separate, says the Lord. And do not touch what is unclean.—Do not be partakers with them; for you were formerly darkness, but now you are light in the Lord; walk as children of light . . . trying to learn what is pleasing to the Lord. And do not participate in the unfruitful deeds of darkness, but instead even expose them.

GEN 13:10,11. 2 Pe 2:7,8. Gal 6:7.—Lk 17:32. 2 Co 6:14,17.—
Eph 5:7,8,10,11.

The LORD will be with me, and I shall drive them out as the LORD has spoken.

He Himself has said, I will never desert you, nor will I ever forsake you . . . so that we confidently say, The LORD is my helper, I will not be afraid. What shall man do to me?—I will come with the mighty deeds of the Lord GOD; I will make mention of Thy righteousness, Thine alone.
The work of righteousness will be peace, and the service of righteousness, quietness and confidence forever.
Stand firm . . . having girded your loins with truth, and having put on the breastplate of righteousness. For our struggle is not against flesh and blood, but against the rulers, against the powers, against the world-forces of this darkness, against the spiritual forces of wickedness in the heavenly places. Therefore, take up the full armor of God, that you may be able to resist in the evil day, and having done everything, to stand firm.—The LORD is with you. . . . Go in this your strength.

JOS 14:12. Heb 13:5,6.—Ps 71:16. Is 32:17. Eph 6:14,12,13.—
Judg 6:12,14.

Holy, holy, holy, is the Lord God, the Almighty.

Thou art holy, O Thou who art enthroned upon the praises of Israel.—Do not come near here; remove your sandals from your feet, for the place on which you are standing is holy ground. . . . I am the God of your father, the God of Abraham, the God of Isaac, and the God of Jacob. Then Moses hid his face, for he was afraid to look at God.—To whom then will you liken Me that I should be his equal? says the Holy One.—I am the Lord your God, the Holy One of Israel, your Savior. I, even I, am the Lord; and there is no savior besides Me.

Like the Holy One who called you, be holy yourselves also in all your behavior; because it is written, You shall be holy, for I am holy.—Do you not know that your body is a temple of the Holy Spirit who is in you, whom you have from God, and that you are not your own?—For we are the temple of the living God; just as God said, I will dwell in them and walk among them; and I will be their God, and they shall be My people.—Do two men walk together unless they have made an appointment?

REV 4:8. Ps 22:3.—Ex 3:5,6.—Is 40:25.—Is 43:3,11. 1 Pe 1:15,16.—
1 Co 6:19.—2 Co 6:16.—Amos 3:3.

They urged Him, saying, Stay with us.

Behold, I stand at the door and knock; if any one hears My voice and opens the door, I will come in to him, and will dine with him, and he with Me.—Tell me, O you whom my soul loves, where do you pasture your flock, where do you make it lie down at noon? For why should I be like one who veils herself beside the flocks of your companions?—I found him whom my soul loves; I held on to him and would not let him go.

May my beloved come into his garden and eat its choice fruits! —I have come into my garden.—I did not say to the offspring of Jacob, Seek me in a waste place.

Lo, I am with you always, even to the end of the age.—I will never desert you, nor will I ever forsake you.—Where two or three have gathered together in My name, there I am in their midst.—The world will behold Me no more; but you will behold Me.

LK 24:29. Rev 3:20.—Song 1:7.—Song 3:4. Song 4:16.—Song 5:1.—
Is 45:19. Mt 28:20.—Heb 13:5.—Mt 18:20.—Jn 14:19.

(Abraham) believed in the LORD; and He reckoned it to him as righteousness.

He did not waver in unbelief, but grew strong in faith, giving glory to God, and being fully assured that what He had promised, He was able also to perform. Therefore also it was reckoned to Him as righteousness. Now not for his sake only was it written, that it was reckoned to him, but for our sake also, to whom it will be reckoned, as those who believe in Him who raised Jesus our Lord from the dead.

The promise to Abraham or to his descendants that he would be heir of the world was not through the Law, but through the righteousness of faith.

The righteous man shall live by faith.—Let us hold fast the confession of our hope without wavering, for He who promised is faithful.—Our God is in the heavens; He does whatever He pleases.—For nothing will be impossible with God. Blessed is she who believed that there would be a fulfillment of what had been spoken to her by the Lord.

GEN 15:6. Ro 4:20–24. Ro 4:13. Ro 1:17.—Heb 10:23.—Ps 115:3.—Lk 1:37,45.

God who calls you into His own kingdom and glory.

My kingdom is not of this world. If My kingdom were of this world, then My servants would be fighting. . . . My kingdom is not of this realm.—Waiting . . . until His enemies be made a footstool for His feet.

The kingdom of the world has become the kingdom of our Lord, and of His Christ; and He will reign forever and ever.—Thou hast made them to be a kingdom and priests to our God; and they will reign upon the earth.—And I saw thrones, and they sat upon them, and judgment was given to them . . . and reigned with Christ for a thousand years.—Then the righteous will shine forth as the sun in the kingdom of their Father.—Do not be afraid, little flock, for your Father has chosen gladly to give you the kingdom.

Just as My Father has granted Me a kingdom, I grant you that you may eat and drink at My table in My kingdom, and you will sit on thrones judging the twelve tribes of Israel.

Thy kingdom come.

1 TH 2:12. Jn 18:36.—Heb 10:13. Rev 11:15.—Rev 5:10.—Rev 20:4.—Mt 13:43.—Lk 12:32. Lk 22:29,30. Mt 6:10.

I will never desert you, nor will I ever forsake you.

So that we confidently say, the Lord is my helper, I will not be afraid. What shall man do to me?

Behold, I am with you, and will keep you wherever you go, and will bring you back to this land; for I will not leave you until I have done what I have promised you.—Be strong and courageous, do not be afraid or tremble at them, for the LORD your God is the one who goes with you. He will not fail you or forsake you.

Demas, having loved this present world, has deserted me. At my first defense no one supported me, but all deserted me; may it not be counted against them. But the Lord stood with me, and strengthened me.—My father and my mother have forsaken me, but the LORD will take me up.

Lo, I am with you always, even to the end of the age.—The living One; and I was dead, and behold, I am alive forevermore. —I will not leave you as orphans; I will come to you.—My peace I give to you.

HEB 13:5. Heb 13:6. Gen 28:15.—Deu 31:6. 2 Ti 4:10,16,17.—
Ps 27:10. Mt 28:20.—Rev 1:18.—Jn 14:18.—Jn 14:27.

Master, we worked hard all night and caught nothing, but at Your bidding I will let down the nets.

All authority has been given to Me in heaven and on earth. Go therefore and make disciples of all the nations, baptizing them in the name of the Father and the Son and the Holy Spirit . . . lo, I am with you always, even to the end of the age.

The kingdom of heaven is like a drag net cast into the sea.

For if I preach the gospel, I have nothing to boast of, for I am under compulsion; for woe is me if I do not preach the gospel. I have become all things to all men, that I may by all means save some.

Let us not lose heart in doing good, for in due time we shall reap if we do not grow weary.—My word . . . shall not return to Me empty, without accomplishing what I desire.—So then neither the one who plants nor the one who waters is anything, but God who causes the growth.

LK 5:5. Mt 28:18–20. Mt 13:47. 1 Co 9:16,22. Gal 6:9.—Is 55:11.—
1 Co 3:7.

Just like a man about to go on a journey, who called his own slaves, and entrusted his possessions to them ... each according to his own ability.

Do you not know that when you present yourselves to someone as slaves for obedience, you are slaves of the one whom you obey?

But one and the same Spirit works all these things, distributing to each one individually just as He wills. But to each one is given the manifestation of the Spirit for the common good.—As each one has received a special gift, employ it in serving one another, as good stewards of the manifold grace of God.—It is required of stewards that one be found trustworthy.—From everyone who has been given much shall much be required; and to whom they entrusted much, of him they will ask all the more.

Who is adequate for these things?—I can do all things through Him who strengthens me.

MT 25:14,15. Ro 6:16. 1 Co 12:11,7.—1 Pe 4:10.—1 Co 4:2.—
Lk 12:48. 2 Co 2:16.—Phil 4:13.

Contributing to the needs of the saints.

David said, Is there yet anyone left of the house of Saul, that I may show him kindness for Jonathan's sake?

Come, you who are blessed of My Father, inherit the kingdom prepared for you from the foundation of the world. For I was hungry, and you gave Me something to eat; I was thirsty, and you gave Me drink; I was a stranger, and you invited Me in; naked, and you clothed Me; I was sick, and you visited Me; I was in prison, and you came to Me. To the extent that you did it to one of these brothers of Mine, even the least of them, you did it to Me.—Whoever in the name of a disciple gives to one of these little ones even a cup of cold water to drink, truly I say to you he shall not lose his reward.

Do not neglect doing good and sharing; for with such sacrifices God is pleased.—God is not unjust so as to forget your work and the love which you have shown toward His name, in having ministered and in still ministering to the saints.

RO 12:13. 2 Sa 9:1. Mt 25:34-36,40.—Mt 10:42. Heb 13:16.—
Heb 6:10.

He who sows righteousness gets a true reward.

After a long time the master of those slaves came and settled accounts with them. And the one who had received the five talents came up and brought five more talents, saying, Master, you entrusted five talents to me; see, I have gained five more talents. His master said to him, Well done, good and faithful slave; you were faithful with a few things, I will put you in charge of many things, enter into the joy of your master.

For we must all appear before the judgment seat of Christ, that each one may be recompensed for his deeds in the body, according to what he has done, whether good or bad.

I have fought the good fight, I have finished the course, I have kept the faith; in the future there is laid up for me the crown of righteousness, which the Lord, the righteous Judge, will award to me on that day; and not only to me, but also to all who have loved His appearing.

I am coming quickly; hold fast what you have, in order that no one take your crown.

PR 11:18. Mt 25:19–21. 2 Co 5:10. 2 Ti 4:7,8. Rev 3:11.

God is faithful.

God is not a man, that He should lie, nor a son of man, that He should repent; has He said, and will He not do it? Or has He spoken, and will He not make it good?—The LORD has sworn and will not change His mind.

God, desiring even more to show to the heirs of the promise the unchangeableness of His purpose, interposed with an oath, in order that by two unchangeable things, in which it is impossible for God to lie, we may have strong encouragement, we who have fled for refuge in laying hold of the hope set before us.— Therefore, let those also who suffer according to the will of God entrust their souls to a faithful Creator in doing what is right.

I know whom I have believed and I am convinced that He is able to guard what I have entrusted to Him until that day.— Faithful is He who calls you, and He also will bring it to pass.— For as many as may be the promises of God, in Him they are yes; wherefore also by Him is our Amen to the glory of God through us.

1 CO 10:13. Num 23:19.—Heb 7:21. Heb 6:17,18.—1 Pe 4:19.
2 Ti 1:12.—1 Th 5:24.—2 Co 1:20.

Be strong and courageous.

The LORD is my light and my salvation; whom shall I fear? The LORD is the defense of my life; whom shall I dread?—He gives strength to the weary, and to him who lacks might He increases power. Though youths grow weary and tired, and vigorous young men stumble badly, yet those who wait for the LORD will gain new strength; they will mount up with wings like eagles, they will run and not get tired, they will walk and not become weary.—My flesh and my heart may fail; but God is the strength of my heart and my portion forever.

If God is for us, who is against us?—The LORD is for me; I will not fear; what can man do to me?—Through Thee we will push back our adversaries; through Thy name we will trample down those who rise up against us.—We overwhelmingly conquer through Him who loved us.

Arise and work, and may the LORD be with you.

JOS 1:18. Ps 27:1.—Is 40:29–31.—Ps 73:26. Ro 8:31.—Ps 118:6.—
Ps 44:5.—Ro 8:37. 1 Ch 22:16.

Our friend ... has fallen asleep.

We do not want you to be uninformed, brethren, about those who are asleep, that you may not grieve, as do the rest who have no hope. For if we believe that Jesus died and rose again, even so God will bring with Him those who have fallen asleep in Jesus.

For if the dead are not raised, not even Christ has been raised; and if Christ has not been raised, your faith is worthless; you are still in your sins. Then those also who have fallen asleep in Christ have perished. But now Christ has been raised from the dead, the first fruits of those who are asleep.

Now it came about when all the nation had finished crossing the Jordan, that the LORD spoke to Joshua, saying. ... Take up for yourselves twelve stones from here out of the middle of the Jordan, from the place where the priests' feet are standing firm. ... So these stones shall become a memorial to the sons of Israel forever.—This Jesus God raised up again, to which we are all witnesses.—Witnesses who were chosen beforehand by God ... who ate and drank with Him after He arose from the dead.

JN 11:11. 1 Th 4:13,14. 1 Co 15:16–18,20. Jos 4:1,3,7.—Ac 2:32.—
Ac 10:41.

Come, you who are blessed of My Father, inherit the kingdom prepared for you from the foundation of the world.

Do not be afraid, little flock, for your Father has chosen gladly to give you the kingdom.—Did not God choose the poor of this world to be rich in faith and heirs of the kingdom which He promised to those who love Him?—Heirs of God and fellow-heirs with Christ, if indeed we suffer with Him in order that we may also be glorified with him.

The Father Himself loves you, because you have loved Me.— God is not ashamed to be called their God; for He has prepared a city for them.

He who overcomes shall inherit these things, and I will be his God and he will be My son.—There is laid up for me the crown of righteousness, which the Lord, the righteous Judge, will award to me on that day; and not only to me, but also to all who have loved His appearing.—He who began a good work in you will perfect it until the day of Christ Jesus.

MT 25:34. Lk 12:32.—Ja 2:5.—Ro 8:17. Jn 16:27.—Heb 11:16.
Rev 21:7.—2 Ti 4:8.—Phil 1:6.

For riches are not forever, nor does a crown endure to all generations.

Surely every man walks about as a phantom; surely they make an uproar for nothing; he amasses riches, and does not know who will gather them.—Set your mind on the things above, not on the things that are on earth.—Do not lay up for yourselves treasures upon earth, where moth and rust destroy, and where thieves break in and steal; but lay up for yourselves treasures in heaven, where neither moth nor rust destroys, and where thieves do not break in or steal; for where your treasure is, there will your heart be also.

They then do it to receive a perishable wreath, but we an imperishable.—We look not at the things which are seen, but at the things which are not seen.—He who sows righteousness gets a true reward.—There is laid up for me the crown of righteousness, which the Lord, the righteous Judge, will award to me on that day; and not only to me, but also to all who have loved His appearing.—You will receive the unfading crown of glory.

PR 27:24. Ps 39:6.—Col 3:2.—Mt 6:19–21. 1 Co 9:25.—
2 Co 4:18.—Pr 11:18.—2 Ti 4:8.—1 Pe 5:4.

Isaac went out to meditate in the field toward evening.

Let the words of my mouth and the meditation of my heart be acceptable in Thy sight, O LORD, my rock and my redeemer.

When I consider Thy heavens, the work of Thy fingers, the moon and the stars, which Thou hast ordained; what is man, that Thou dost take thought of him? And the son of man, that Thou dost care for him?—Great are the works of the LORD; they are studied by all who delight in them.

How blessed is the man who does not walk in the counsel of the wicked, nor stand in the path of sinners, nor sit in the seat of scoffers! But his delight is in the law of the LORD, and in His law he meditates day and night.—This book of the law shall not depart from your mouth, but you shall meditate on it day and night.—My soul is satisfied as with marrow and fatness. And my mouth offers praises with joyful lips; when I remember Thee on my bed. I meditate on Thee in the night watches.

GEN 24:63. Ps 19:14. Ps 8:3,4.—Ps 111:2. Ps 1:1,2.—Jos 1:8.—
Ps 63:5,6.

How long, O LORD? Wilt Thou forget me forever? How long wilt Thou hide Thy face from me?

Every good thing bestowed and every perfect gift is from above, coming down from the Father of lights, with whom there is no variation, or shifting shadow.—But Zion said, The LORD has forsaken me, and the Lord has forgotten me. Can a woman forget her nursing child, and have no compassion on the son of her womb? Even these may forget, but I will not forget you.

You will not be forgotten by Me. I have wiped out your transgressions like a thick cloud, and your sins like a heavy mist.

Now Jesus loved Martha, and her sister, and Lazarus. When therefore He heard that he was sick, He stayed then two days longer in the place where He was.—A ... woman ... began to cry out, saying, Have mercy on me, O Lord, Son of David; ... but He did not answer her a word.

The proof of your faith, being more precious than gold which is perishable.

PS 13:1. Ja 1:17.—Is 49:14,15. Is 44:21,22. Jn 11:5,6.—Mt 15:22,23.
1 Pe 1:7.

My God shall supply all your needs according to His riches in glory in Christ Jesus.

Seek first His kingdom, and His righteousness; and all these things shall be added to you.—He who did not spare His own Son, but delivered Him up for us all, how will He not also with Him freely give us all things?—All things belong to you, whether Paul or Apollos or Cephas or the world or life or death or things present or things to come; all things belong to you, and you belong to Christ; and Christ belongs to God.—As having nothing yet possessing all things.

The LORD is my shepherd, I shall not want.—The LORD God is a sun and shield; the LORD gives grace and glory; no good thing does He withhold from those who walk uprightly.—God, who richly supplies us with all things to enjoy.—God is able to make all grace abound to you, that always having all sufficiency in everything, you may have an abundance for every good deed.

PHIL 4:19. Mt 6:33.—Ro 8:32.—1 Co 3:21-23.—2 Co 6:10.
Ps 23:1.—Ps 84:11.—1 Ti 6:17.—2 Co 9:8.

What fellowship has light with darkness?

Men loved the darkness rather than the light; for their deeds were evil.—You are all sons of light and sons of day. We are not of night nor of darkness.

Darkness has blinded his eyes.—Thy word is a lamp to my feet, and a light to my path.

The dark places of the land are full of the habitations of violence.—Love is from God; and every one who loves is born of God and knows God. The one who does not love does not know God, for God is love.

The way of the wicked is like darkness; they do not know over what they stumble. But the path of the righteous is like the light of dawn, that shines brighter and brighter until the full day.

I have come as light into the world, that everyone who believes in Me may not remain in darkness.

You were formerly darkness, but now you are light in the Lord; walk as children of light.

2 Co 6:14. Jn 3:19.—1 Th 5:5. 1 Jn 2:11.—Ps 119:105. Ps 74:20.—
1 Jn 4:7,8. Pr 4:19,18. Jn 12:46. Eph 5:8.

The fruit of the Spirit is love.

Joy in the Holy Spirit.—Joy inexpressible and full of glory.

Sorrowful yet always rejoicing.—Overflowing with joy in all our affliction.—We also exult in our tribulations.

Jesus, the author and perfecter of faith, who for the joy set before Him endured the cross, despising the shame.—These things I have spoken to you, that My joy may be in you, and that your joy may be made full.—Just as the sufferings of Christ are ours in abundance, so also our comfort is abundant through Christ.

Rejoice in the Lord always; again I will say, rejoice!—The joy of the LORD is your strength.

In Thy presence is fulness of joy; in Thy right hand there are pleasures forever.—For the Lamb in the center of the throne shall be their shepherd, and shall guide them to springs of the water of life; and God shall wipe every tear from their eyes.

GAL 5:22. Ro 14:17.—1 Pe 1:8. 2 Co 6:10;—7:4.—Ro 5:3.
Heb 12:2.—Jn 15:11.—2 Co 1:5. Phil 4:4.—Neh 8:10. Ps 16:11.—
Rev 7:17.

The LORD is peace. (Jehova-shalom)

Behold, a son shall be born to you, who shall be a man of rest; and I will give him rest from all his enemies on every side; for his name shall be Solomon, and I will give peace and quiet to Israel in his days.

Something greater than Solomon is here.—For a child will be born to us, a son will be given to us; and the government will rest on His shoulders; and His name will be called Wonderful Counselor, Mighty God, Eternal Father, Prince of Peace.—My people will live in a peaceful habitation, and in secure dwellings and in undisturbed resting places; and it will hail when the forest comes down. And the city will be utterly laid low.

He Himself is our peace.—This One will be our peace. When the Assyrian invades our land.

These will wage war against the Lamb, and the Lamb will overcome them, because He is Lord of lords and King of kings.

Peace I leave with you; My peace I give to you.

JUDG 6:24. 1 Ch 22:9. Mt. 12:42.—Is 9:6.—Is 32:18,19. Eph 2:14.—
Mic 5:5. Re 17:14. Jn 14:27.

If you return to the LORD with all your heart, remove the foreign gods and the Ashtaroth from among you and direct your hearts to the LORD and serve Him alone.

Little children, guard yourselves from idols.—Come out from their midst and be separate, says the Lord. And do not touch what is unclean; and I will welcome you. And I will be a Father to you, and you shall be sons and daughters to Me, says the Lord Almighty.—You cannot serve God and Mammon.

For you shall not worship any other god, for the LORD, whose name is Jealous, is a jealous God.—Serve Him with a whole heart and a willing mind; for the LORD searches all hearts, and understands every intent of the thoughts.

Thou dost desire truth in the innermost being, and in the hidden part Thou wilt make me know wisdom.—God sees not as man sees, for man looks at the outward appearance, but the LORD looks at the heart.—Beloved, if our heart does not condemn us, we have confidence before God.

1 SA 7:3. 1 Jn 5:21.—2 Co 6:17,18.—Mt 6:24. Ex 34:14.—1 Ch 28:9. Ps 51:6.—1 Sa 16:7.—1 Jn 3:21.

When the Son of Man comes, will He find faith on the earth?

He came to His own, and those who were His own did not receive Him.—The Spirit explicitly says that in later times some will fall away from the faith.

Preach the word; be ready in season and out of season; reprove, rebuke, exhort, with great patience and instruction. For the time will come when they will not endure sound doctrine; but wanting to have their ears tickled, they will accumulate for themselves teachers in accordance to their own desires; and will turn away their ears from the truth, and will turn aside to myths.

But of that day or hour no one knows, not even the angels in heaven, nor the Son, but the Father alone. Take heed, keep on the alert; for you do not know when the appointed time is.— Blessed are those slaves whom the master shall find on the alert when he comes.—Looking for the blessed hope and the appearing of the glory of our great God and Savior, Christ Jesus.

LK 18:8. Jn 1:11.—1 Ti 4:1. 2 Ti 4:2-4. Mk 13:32,33.—Lk 12:37.— Titus 2:13.

Do not let this one fact escape your notice, beloved, that with the Lord one day is as a thousand years, and a thousand years as one day. The Lord is not slow about His promise, as some count slowness.

For My thoughts are not your thoughts, neither are your ways My ways, declares the LORD. For as the heavens are higher than the earth, so are My ways higher than your ways, and My thoughts than your thoughts. For as the rain and the snow come down from heaven, and do not return there without watering the earth ... so shall My word be which goes forth from My mouth; it shall not return to Me empty, without accomplishing what I desire, and without succeeding in the matter for which I sent it.

For God has shut up all in disobedience that He might show mercy to all. Oh the depth of the riches both of the wisdom and knowledge of God! How unsearchable are His judgments and unfathomable His ways!

2 PE 3:8,9. Is 55:8–11. Ro 11:32,33.

You were like a firebrand snatched from a blaze.

Sinners in Zion are terrified; trembling has seized the godless. Who among us can live with the consuming fire? Who among us can live with continual burning?—We had the sentence of death within ourselves in order that we should not trust in ourselves, but in God who raises the dead; who delivered us from so great a peril of death, and will deliver us.—For the wages of sin is death, but the free gift of God is eternal life in Christ Jesus our Lord.

It is a terrifying thing to fall into the hands of the living God. —Knowing the fear of the Lord, we persuade men.

Be ready in season and out of season.—Save others, snatching them out of the fire.

Not by might nor by power, but by My Spirit, says the LORD of hosts.—Who desires all men to be saved and to come to the knowledge of the truth.

AMOS 4:11. Is 33:14.—2 Co 1:9,10.—Ro 6:23. Heb 10:31.—
2 Co 5:11. 2 Ti 4:2.—Jude 23. Zec 4:6.—1 Ti 2:4.

Do not be afraid; I am the first and the last.

You have not come to a mountain that may be touched and to a blazing fire, and to darkness and gloom and whirlwind . . . but you have come to Mount Zion . . . to God, the Judge of all, and to the spirits of righteous men made perfect, and to Jesus the mediator of a new covenant.—Jesus, the author and perfecter of faith.—We do not have a high priest who cannot sympathize with our weaknesses, but one who has been tempted in all things as we are, yet without sin. Let us therefore draw near with confidence to the throne of grace, that we may receive mercy and may find grace to help in time of need.

Thus says the LORD, the King of Israel and his Redeemer, the LORD of hosts: I am the first and I am the last, and there is no God besides Me.—Mighty God, Eternal Father, Prince of Peace.

Art Thou not from everlasting, O LORD, my God, my Holy One?—Who is God, besides the LORD? And who is a rock, besides our God?

REV 1:17. Heb 12:18,22–24.—Heb 12:2.—Heb 4:15,16. Is 44:6.—
Is 9:6. Hab 1:12.—2 Sa 22:32.

Lead me to the rock that is higher than I.

Be anxious for nothing, but in everything by prayer and supplication with thanksgiving let your requests be made known to God. And the peace of God, which surpasses all comprehension, shall guard your hearts and your minds in Christ Jesus.

When my spirit was overwhelmed within me; Thou didst know my path.—He knows the way I take; when He has tried me, I shall come forth as gold.—LORD, Thou hast been our dwelling place in all generations.—Thou hast been a defense for the helpless. A defense for the needy in his distress, a refuge from the storm, a shade from the heat.

Who is a rock, except our God?—They shall never perish, and no one shall snatch them out of My hand.—Sustain me according to Thy word, that I may live; and do not let me be ashamed of my hope.—This hope we have as an anchor of the soul, a hope both sure and steadfast and one which enters within the veil.

PS 61:2. Phil 4:6,7. Ps 142:3.—Job 23:10.—Ps 90:1.—Is 25:4.
Ps 18:31.—Jn 10:28.—Ps 119:116.—Heb 6:19.

I will not let you go unless you bless me.

Let him rely on My protection, let him make peace with Me, let him make peace with Me.

O woman, your faith is great; be it done for you as you wish. —Be it done to you according to your faith.—Let him ask in faith without any doubting, for the one who doubts is like the surf of the sea driven and tossed by the wind. For let not that man expect that he will receive anything from the Lord.

They approached the village where they were going, and He acted as though He would go farther. And they urged Him, saying, Stay with us. . . . He vanished from their sight. And they said to one another, Were not our hearts burning within us while He was speaking to us on the road, while He was explaining the Scriptures to us?—I pray Thee, if I have found favor in Thy sight, let me know Thy ways, that I may know Thee, so that I may find favor in Thy sight. . . . My presence shall go with you, and I will give you rest.

GEN 32:26. Is 27:5. Mt 15:28.—Mt 9:29.—Ja 1:6,7.
Lk 24:28,29,31,32.—Ex 33:13,14.

Jesus, the author and perfecter of faith.

I am the Alpha and the Omega, says the Lord God, who is and who was and who is to come, the Almighty.—Who has performed and accomplished it, calling forth the generations from the beginning? I, the LORD, am the first, and with the last. I am He.

Called, beloved in God the Father, and kept for Jesus Christ.

May the God of peace Himself sanctify you entirely; and may your spirit and soul and body be preserved complete, without blame at the coming of our Lord Jesus Christ. Faithful is He who calls you, and He also will bring it to pass.—He who began a good work in you will perfect it until the day of Christ Jesus.—Are you so foolish? Having begun by the Spirit, are you now being perfected by the flesh?—The LORD will accomplish what concerns me.

It is God who is at work in you, both to will and to work for His good pleasure.

HEB 12:2. Rev 1:8.—Is 41:4. Jude 1. 1 Th 5:23,24.—Phil 1:6.—
Gal 3:3.—Ps 138.8. Phil 2:13.

He always lives to make intercession for them.

Who is the one who condemns? Christ Jesus is He who died
. . . who also intercedes for us.—Christ did not enter a holy place
made with hands, a mere copy of the true one, but into heaven
itself, now to appear in the presence of God for us.

If anyone sins, we have an Advocate with the Father, Jesus
Christ the righteous.—There is one God, and one mediator also
between God and men, the man Christ Jesus.

Since then we have a great high priest who has passed through
the heavens, Jesus the Son of God, let us hold fast our confession.
For we do not have a high priest who cannot sympathize with
our weaknesses, but one who has been tempted in all things as
we are, yet without sin. Let us therefore draw near with confidence to the throne of grace, that we may receive mercy and
may find grace to help in time of need.—Through Him we . . .
have our access in one Spirit to the Father.

HEB 7:25. Ro 8:34.—Heb 9:24. 1 Jn 2:1.—1 Ti 2:5. Heb 4:14–16.—
Eph 2:18.

Those who know Thy name will put their trust in Thee.

This is His name by which He will be called, The LORD our
righteousness.—I will come with the mighty deeds of the Lord
GOD; I will make mention of Thy righteousness, Thine alone.

His name shall be called Wonderful Counselor.—I know, O
LORD, that a man's way is not in himself; nor is it in a man who
walks to direct his steps.

Mighty God, Eternal Father.—I know whom I have believed
and I am convinced that He is able to guard what I have entrusted to Him until that day.

Prince of Peace.—He Himself is our peace.—Having been justified by faith, we have peace with God through our Lord Jesus
Christ.

The name of the LORD is a strong tower; the righteous runs
into it and is safe.—Woe to those who go down to Egypt for help.
—Like flying birds so the LORD of hosts will protect Jerusalem.
He will protect and deliver it; He will pass over and rescue it.

PS 9:10. Jer 23:6.—Ps 71:16. Is 9:6.—Jer 10:23. Is 9:6.—2 Ti 1:12.
Is 9:6.—Eph 2:14.—Ro 5:1. Pr 18:10.—Is 31:1.—Is 31:5.

As sorrowful yet always rejoicing, as poor yet making many rich, as having nothing yet possessing all things.

We exult in hope of the glory of God. And not only this, but we also exult in our tribulations.—I am filled with comfort. I am overflowing with joy in all our affliction.—Believe in Him, you greatly rejoice with joy inexpressible and full of glory.

In a great ordeal of affliction their abundance of joy and their deep poverty overflowed in the wealth of their liberality.—To me, the very least of all saints, this grace was given, to preach to the Gentiles the unfathomable riches of Christ, and to bring to light what is the administration of the mystery which for ages has been hidden in God, who created all things.

Did not God choose the poor of this world to be rich in faith and heirs of the kingdom which He promised to those who love Him?—God is able to make all grace abound to you, that always having all sufficiency in everything, you may have an abundance for every good deed.

2 CO 6:10. Ro 5:2,3.—2 Co 7:4.—1 Pe 1:8. 2 Co 8:2.—Eph 3:8,9.
Ja 2:5—2 Co 9:8.

The LORD will sustain him upon his sickbed; in his illness, Thou dost restore him to health.

In all their affliction He was afflicted, and the angel of His presence saved them; in His love and in His mercy He redeemed them; and He lifted them and carried them all the days of old. —He whom You love is sick.—My grace is sufficient for you, for power is perfected in weakness. Most gladly, therefore, I will rather boast about my weaknesses, that the power of Christ may dwell in me.—I can do all things through Him who strengthens me.

We do not lose heart, but though our outer man is decaying, yet our inner man is being renewed day by day.

In Him we live and move and exist.—He gives strength to the weary, and to him who lacks might He increases power. Though youths grow weary and tired, and vigorous young men stumble badly, yet those who wait for the LORD will gain new strength. —The eternal God is a dwelling place, and underneath are the everlasting arms.

PS 41:3. Is 63:9.—Jn 11:3.—2 Co 12:9.—Phil 4:13. 2 Co 4:16.
Ac 17:28.—Is 40:29–31.—Deu 33:27.

In everything you were enriched in Him.

While we were still helpless, at the right time Christ died for the ungodly.—He who did not spare His own Son, but delivered Him up for us all, how will He not also with Him freely give us all things?

In Him all the fulness of Deity dwells in bodily form, and in Him you have been made complete, and He is head over all rule and authority.

Abide in Me, and I in you. As the branch cannot bear fruit of itself, unless it abides in the vine, so neither can you, unless you abide in Me. I am the vine, you are the branches; he who abides in Me, and I in him, he bears much fruit; for apart from Me you can do nothing.—The wishing is present in me, but the doing of the good is not.—To each one of us grace was given according to the measure of Christ's gift.

If you abide in Me, and My words abide in you, ask whatever you wish, and it shall be done for you.—Let the word of Christ richly dwell within you.

1 CO 1:5. Ro 5:6.—Ro 8:32. Col 2:9,10. Jn 15:4,5.—Ro 7:18.—
Eph 4:7. Jn 15:7.—Col 3:16.

They shall see His face.

I pray Thee, show me Thy glory! But He said, You cannot see My face, for no man can see Me and live!—No man has seen God at any time; the only begotten God, who is in the bosom of the Father, He has explained Him.

Every eye will see Him, even those who pierced Him; and all the tribes of the earth will mourn over Him.—I see him, but not now; I behold him, but not near.

I know that my Redeemer lives, and at the last He will take His stand on the earth. Even after my skin is destroyed, yet from my flesh I shall see God.—I shall behold Thy face in righteousness; I will be satisfied with Thy likeness when I awake.—We shall be like Him, because we shall see Him just as He is.—The Lord Himself will descend from heaven . . . the dead in Christ shall rise first. Then we who are alive and remain shall be caught up together with them in the clouds to meet the Lord in the air, and thus we shall always be with the Lord.

REV 22:4. Ex 33:18,20.—Jn 1:18. Rev 1:7.—Num 24:17.
Job 19:25,26.—Ps 17:15.—1 Jn 3:2.—1 Th 4:16,17.

Do not fear, for I have redeemed you.

Fear not for you will not be put to shame; neither feel humili-ated, for you will not be disgraced; but you will forget the shame of your youth, and the reproach of your widowhood you will remember no more. For your husband is your Maker, whose name is the LORD of hosts; and your Redeemer is the Holy One of Israel.—I have wiped out your transgressions like a thick cloud, and your sins like a heavy mist. Return to Me, for I have redeemed you.—With precious blood, as of a lamb unblemished and spotless, the blood of Christ.

Their Redeemer is strong, the Lord of hosts is His name; He will vigorously plead their case.—My Father, who has given them to Me, is greater than all; and no one is able to snatch them out of the Father's hand.

Grace to you and peace from God our Father, and the Lord Jesus Christ, who gave Himself for our sins, that He might deliver us out of this present evil age, according to the will of our God and Father, to whom be the glory forevermore. Amen.

IS 43:1. Is 54:4,5.—44:22.—1 Pe 1:19. Jer 50:34.—Jn 10:29.
Gal 1:3–5.

I shall make mention of the lovingkindnesses of the LORD, the praises of the LORD, according to all that the LORD has granted us.

He brought me up out of the pit of destruction, out of the miry clay; and He set my feet upon a rock making my footsteps firm. —The Son of God . . . loved me, and delivered Himself up for me. —He who did not spare His own Son, but delivered Him up for us all, how will He not also with Him freely give us all things?— God demonstrates His own love toward us, in that while we were yet sinners, Christ died for us.

Who also sealed us and gave us the Spirit in our hearts as a pledge.—Who is given as a pledge of our inheritance, with a view to the redemption of God's own possession, to the praise of His glory.

God, being rich in mercy, because of His great love with which He loved us, even when we were dead in transgressions, made us alive together with Christ (by grace you have been saved), and raised us up with Him, and seated us with Him in the heavenly places, in Christ Jesus.

IS 63:7. Ps 40:2.—Gal 2:20.—Ro 8:32.—Ro 5:8. 2 Co 1:22.—
Eph 1:14. Eph 2:4–6.

I am black but lovely.

Behold, I was brought forth in iniquity, and in sin my mother conceived me.—Your fame went forth among the nations on account of your beauty, for it was perfect because of My splendor which I bestowed on you, declares the Lord GOD.

I am a sinful man, O Lord!—How beautiful you are, my darling, how beautiful you are!

I retract, and I repent in dust and ashes.—You are altogether beautiful, my darling, and there is no blemish in you.

Evil is present in me, the one who wishes to do good.—Take courage, My son, your sins are forgiven.

I know that nothing good dwells in me, that is, in my flesh.—In Him you have been made complete.—Complete in Christ.

You were washed . . . you were sanctified . . . you were justified in the name of the Lord Jesus Christ, and in the Spirit of our God.—That you may proclaim the excellencies of Him who has called you out of darkness into His marvelous light.

SONG 1:5. Ps 51:5.—Eze 16:14. Lk 5:8.—Song 4:1. Job 42:6.—Song 4:7. Ro 7:21.—Mt. 9:2. Ro 7:18.—Col 2:10.—1:28. 1 Co 6:11.—1 Pe 2:9.

All who desire to live godly in Christ Jesus will be persecuted.

I came to set a man against his father, and a daughter against her mother, and a daughter-in-law against her mother-in-law.—Whoever wishes to be a friend of the world makes himself an enemy of God.—Do not love the world, nor the things in the world. If any one loves the world, the love of the Father is not in him. For all that is in the world, the lust of the flesh and the lust of the eyes and the boastful pride of life, is not from the Father, but is from the world.

If the world hates you, you know that it has hated Me before it hated you. If you were of the world, the world would love its own; but because you are not of the world, but I chose you out of the world, therefore the world hates you. . . . A slave is not greater than his master.—I have given them Thy word; and the world has hated them, because they are not of the world, even as I am not of the world.

2 TI 3:12. Mt 10:35,36.—Ja 4:4.—1 Jn 2:15,16. Jn 15:18–20.—Jn 17:14.

When there are many words, transgression is unavoidable, but he who restrains his lips is wise.

Beloved brethren . . . let every one be quick to hear, slow to speak and slow to anger.—He who is slow to anger is better than the mighty, and he who rules his spirit, than he who captures a city.—If any one does not stumble in what he says, he is a perfect man, able to bridle the whole body as well.—By your words you shall be justified, and by your words you shall be condemned.—Set a guard, O LORD, over my mouth; keep watch over the door of my lips.

Christ . . . suffered for you, leaving you an example for you to follow in His steps, who committed no sin, nor was any deceit found in His mouth; and while being reviled, He did not revile in return; while suffering, He uttered no threats, but kept entrusting Himself to Him who judges righteously.—Consider Him who has endured such hostility by sinners against Himself, so that you may not grow weary and lose heart.

No lie was found in their mouth; they are blameless.

PR 10:19. Ja 1:19.—Pr 16:32.—Ja 3:2.—Mt 12:37.—Ps 141:3.
1 Pe 2:21–23.—Heb 12:3. Rev 14:5.

Teach me Thy way, O LORD.

I will instruct you and teach you in the way which you should go; I will counsel you with My eye upon you.—Good and upright is the LORD; therefore He instructs sinners in the way. He leads the humble in justice, and He teaches the humble His way.

I am the door; if anyone enters through Me, he shall be saved, and shall go in and out, and find pasture.

Jesus said to him, I am the way, and the truth, and the life; no one comes to the Father, but through Me.—We have confidence to enter the holy place by the blood of Jesus, by a new and living way which He inaugurated for us through the veil, that is, His flesh, and since we have a great priest over the house of God, let us draw near with a sincere heart in full assurance of faith.

Let us press on to know the LORD.—All the paths of the LORD are lovingkindness and truth to those who keep His covenant and His testimonies.

PS 27:11. Ps 32:8.—Ps 25:8,9. Jn 10:9. Jn 14:6.—Heb 10:19–22.
Ho 6:3.—Ps 25:10.

What the Law could not do, weak as it was through the flesh, God did: sending His own Son in the likeness of sinful flesh and as an offering for sin, He condemned sin in the flesh.

The Law, since it has only a shadow of the good things to come and not the very form of things, can never by the same sacrifices year by year, which they offer continually, make perfect those who draw near. Otherwise, would they not have ceased to be offered?—Through Him everyone who believes is freed from all things, from which you could not be freed through the Law of Moses.

Since ... the children share in flesh and blood, He Himself likewise also partook of the same, that through death He might render powerless him who had the power of death, that is, the devil; and might deliver those who through fear of death were subject to slavery all their lives. For assuredly He does not give help to angels, but He gives help to the seed of Abraham. Therefore, He had to be made like His brethren in all things.

RO 8:3. Heb 10:1,2.—Ac 13:39. Heb 2:14–17.

All have sinned and fall short of the glory of God.

There is none righteous, not even one; ... there is none who does good, there is not even one.—There is not a righteous man on earth who continually does good and who never sins.—How can he be clean who is born of woman?

Therefore, let us fear lest, while a promise remains of entering His rest, any one of you should seem to have come short of it.

I know my transgressions, and my sin is ever before me. Behold, I was brought forth in iniquity, and in sin my mother conceived me.

The LORD ... has taken away your sin; you shall not die.—Whom He justified, these He also glorified.—We all, with unveiled face beholding as in a mirror the glory of the LORD, are being transformed into the same image from glory to glory, just as from the Lord, the Spirit.—If indeed you continue in the faith firmly established and steadfast, and not moved away from the hope of the gospel that you have heard.

Walk in a manner worthy of the God who calls you into His own kingdom and glory.

Ro 3:23. Ro 3:10,12.—Ec 7:20.—Job 25:4. Heb 4:1. Ps 51:3,5.
2 Sa 12:13.—Ro 8:30.—2 Co 3:18.—Col 1:23. 1 Th 2:12.

Honor the LORD from your wealth, and from the first of all your produce.

He who sows sparingly shall also reap sparingly; and he who sows bountifully shall also reap bountifully.—On the first day of every week let one of you put aside and save, as he may prosper.

God is not unjust so as to forget your work and the love which you have shown toward His name, in having ministered and in still ministering to the saints.

I urge you . . . brethren, by the mercies of God, to present your bodies a living and holy sacrifice, acceptable to God, which is your spiritual service of worship.—For the love of Christ controls us, having concluded this, that one died for all, therefore all died; and He died for all, that they who live should no longer live for themselves, but for Him who died and rose again on their behalf. —Whether, then, you eat or drink or whatever you do, do all to the glory of God.

PR 3:9. 2 Co 9:6.—1 Co 16:2. Heb 6:10. Ro 12:1.—2 Co 5:14,15.— 1 Co 10:31.

There shall be no night there.

You will have the LORD for an everlasting light, and your God for your glory.

The city has no need of the sun or of the moon to shine upon it, for the glory of God has illumined it, and its lamp is the Lamb. —They shall not have need of the light of a lamp nor the light of the sun, because the Lord God shall illumine them.

You are a chosen race, a royal priesthood, a holy nation, a people for God's own possession, that you may proclaim the excellencies of Him who has called you out of darkness into His marvelous light.—Giving thanks to the Father, who has qualified us to share in the inheritance of the saints in light. For He delivered us from the domain of darkness, and transferred us to the kingdom of His beloved Son.—You were formerly darkness, but now you are light in the Lord; walk as children of light.

We are not of night nor of darkness.

The path of the righteous is like the light of dawn, that shines brighter and brighter until the full day.

REV 21:25. Is 60:19. Rev 21:23.—Rev 22:5. 1 Pe 2:9.— Col 1:12,13.—Eph 5:8. 1 Th 5:5. Pr 4:18.

My soul is satisfied as with marrow and fatness. And my mouth offers praises with joyful lips; when I remember Thee on my bed. I meditate on Thee in the night watches.

How precious also are Thy thoughts to me, O God! How vast is the sum of them! If I should count them, they would outnumber the sand. When I awake, I am still with Thee.—How sweet are Thy words to my taste! Yes, sweeter than honey to my mouth! —Your love is better than wine.

Whom have I in heaven but Thee? And besides Thee, I desire nothing on earth.—Thou art fairer than the sons of men.

Like an apple tree among the trees of the forest, so is my beloved among the young men. In his shade I took great delight and sat down, and his fruit was sweet to my taste. He has brought me to his banquet hall, and his banner over me is love.—His appearance is like Lebanon, choice as the cedars. His mouth is full of sweetness. And he is wholly desirable. This is my beloved and this is my friend.

PS 63:5,6. Ps 139:17,18.—Ps 119:103.—Song 1:2. Ps 73:25.—Ps 45:2.
Song 2:3,4.—Song 5:15,16.

Restore to me the joy of Thy salvation.

I have seen his ways, but I will heal him; I will lead him and restore comfort to him and to his mourners.

Come now, and let us reason together, says the LORD, though your sins are as scarlet, they will be as white as snow; though they are red like crimson, they will be like wool.—Return, O faithless sons, I will heal your faithlessness. Behold, we come to Thee; for Thou art the LORD our God.—I will hear what God the LORD will say; for He will speak peace to His people, to His godly ones; but let them not turn back to folly.

Bless the LORD, O my soul, and forget none of His benefits; who pardons all your iniquities; who heals all your diseases.—He restores my soul.—I will give thanks to Thee, O LORD; for although Thou wast angry with me, thine anger is turned away, and Thou dost comfort me.

Uphold me that I may be safe.

I, even I, am the one who wipes out your transgressions for My own sake; and I will not remember your sins.

PS 51:12. Is 57:18. Is 1:18.—Jer 3:22.—Ps 85:8. Ps 103:2,3.—
Ps 23:3.—Is 12:1. Ps 119:117. Is 43:25.

Their Redeemer is strong.

I know your transgressions are many and your sins are great. —I have given help to one who is mighty.—The LORD . . . your Savior, and your Redeemer, the Mighty One of Jacob.—Greatness of His strength.—Able to keep you from stumbling.—Where sin increased, grace abounded all the more.

He who believes in Him is not judged; he who does not believe has been judged already, because he has not believed in the name of the only begotten Son of God.—He is able to save forever those who draw near to God through Him.

Is My hand so short that it cannot ransom?

Who shall separate us from the love of Christ? I am convinced that neither death, nor life, nor angels, nor principalities, nor things present, nor things to come, nor powers, nor height, nor depth, nor any other created thing, shall be able to separate us from the love of God, which is in Christ Jesus our Lord.

JER 50:34. Amos 5:12.—Ps 89:19.—Is 49:26.—Is 63:1.—Jude 24.— Ro 5:20. Jn 3:18.—Heb 7:25. Is 50:2. Ro 8:35,38,39.

Are you seeking great things for yourself? Do not seek them.

Take My yoke upon you, and learn from Me, for I am gentle and humble in heart; and you shall find rest for your souls.—Have this attitude in yourselves which was also in Christ Jesus, who, although He existed in the form of God, did not regard equality with God a thing to be grasped, but emptied Himself, taking the form of a bond-servant, and being made in the likeness of men. And being found in appearance as a man, He humbled Himself by becoming obedient to the point of death, even death on a cross.

He who does not take his cross and follow after Me is not worthy of Me.—Christ also suffered for you, leaving you an example for you to follow in His steps.

Godliness actually is a means of great gain, when accompanied by contentment. For we have brought nothing into the world, so we cannot take anything out of it either. And if we have food and covering, with these we shall be content.

I have learned to be content in whatever circumstances I am.

JER 45:5. Mt 11:29.—Phil 2:5–8. Mt. 10:38.—1 Pe 2:21. 1 Ti 6:6–8. Phil 4:11.

As for me, I said in my alarm, I am cut off from before Thine eyes; nevertheless Thou didst hear the voice of my supplications when I cried to Thee.

I have sunk in deep mire, and there is no foothold; I have come into deep waters, and a flood overflows me.—Waters flowed over my head; I said, I am cut off! I called on Thy name, O LORD, out of the lowest pit. Thou hast heard my voice, Do not hide Thine ear from my prayer for relief, from my cry for help. Thou didst draw near when I called on Thee; Thou didst say, Do not fear!

Will the Lord reject forever? And will He never be favorable again? Has His lovingkindness ceased forever? Has His promise come to an end forever? Has God forgotten to be gracious? Or has He in anger withdrawn His compassion? Then I said, It is my grief, that the right hand of the Most High has changed. I shall remember the deeds of the LORD; surely I will remember Thy wonders of old.—I would have despaired unless I had believed that I would see the goodness of the LORD in the land of the living.

PS 31:22. Ps 69:2.—Lam 3:54–57. Ps 77:7–11.—Ps 27:13.

He will call upon Me, and I will answer him; I will be with him in trouble; I will rescue him.

Jabez called on the God of Israel, saying, Oh that Thou wouldst bless me indeed, and enlarge my border, and that Thy hand might be with me, and that Thou wouldst keep me from harm, that it may not pain me! And God granted him what he requested.—Ask what I shall give you. And Solomon said to God. . . . Give me now wisdom and knowledge, that I may go out and come in before this people.—God gave Solomon wisdom and very great discernment and breadth of mind, like the sand that is on the seashore.

Asa called to the LORD his God, and said, Lord, there is no one besides Thee to help in the battle between the powerful and those who have no strength . . . O LORD, Thou art our God; let not man prevail against Thee. So the LORD routed the Ethiopians before Asa.

O Thou who dost hear prayer, to Thee all men come.

PS 91:15. 1 Ch 4:10.—2 Ch 1:7,8,10.—1 Ki 4:29. 2 Ch 14:11,12. Ps 65:2.

He who offers a sacrifice of thanksgiving honors Me.

Let the word of Christ richly dwell within you; with all wisdom teaching and admonishing one another with psalms and hymns and spiritual songs, singing with thankfulness in your hearts to God. And whatever you do in word or deed, do all in the name of the Lord Jesus, giving thanks through Him to God the Father. —Glorify God in your body.

You are a . . . royal priesthood . . . that you may proclaim the excellencies of Him who has called you out of darkness into His marvelous light.—You . . . as living stones, are being built up as a spiritual house for a holy priesthood, to offer up spiritual sacrifices acceptable to God through Jesus Christ.—Through Him then let us continually offer up a sacrifice of praise to God, that is, the fruit of lips that give thanks to His name.

My soul shall make its boast in the LORD; the humble shall hear it and rejoice. O magnify the LORD with me, and let us exalt His name together.

PS 50:23. Col 3:16,17.—1 Co 6:20. 1 Pe 2:9.—1 Pe 2:5.—Heb 13:15.
Ps 34:2,3.

Draw me after you and let us run together!

I have loved you with an everlasting love; therefore I have drawn you with lovingkindness.—I led them with cords of a man, with bonds of love.—I, if I be lifted up from the earth, will draw all men to Myself.—Behold, the Lamb of God!—As Moses lifted up the serpent in the wilderness, even so must the Son of Man be lifted up; that whoever believes may in Him have eternal life.

Whom have I in heaven but Thee? And besides Thee, I desire nothing on earth.—We love, because He first loved us.

My beloved responded and said to me, Arise, my darling, my beautiful one, and come along. For behold, the winter is past, the rain is over and gone. The flowers have already appeared in the land; . . . the voice of the turtledove has been heard in our land. The fig tree has ripened its figs, and the vines in blossom have given forth their fragrance. Arise, my darling, my beautiful one, and come along!

SONG 1:4. Jer 31:3.—Ho 11:4.—Jn 12:32.—Jn 1:36.—Jn 3:14,15.
Ps 73:25.—1 Jn 4:19. Song 2:10-13.

I will raise up a prophet from among their countrymen like you.

I (Moses) was standing between the LORD and you at that time, to declare to you the word of the LORD; for you were afraid.— There is one God, and one mediator also between God and men, the man Christ Jesus.

(Now the man Moses was very humble, more than any man who was on the face of the earth.)—Take My yoke upon you, and learn from Me, for I am gentle and humble in heart; and you shall find rest for your souls.—Have this attitude in yourselves which was also in Christ Jesus, who, although He existed in the form of God, did not regard equality with God a thing to be grasped, but emptied Himself, taking the form of a bond-servant, and being made in the likeness of men.

Now Moses was faithful in all His house as a servant, for a testimony of those things which were to be spoken later; but Christ was faithful as a Son over His house whose house we are, if we hold fast our confidence and the boast of our hope firm until the end.

DEU 18:18. Deu 5:5.—1 Ti 2:5. Num 12:3.—Mt 11:29.—Phil 2:5-7. Heb 3:5,6.

Eternal comfort.

I will remember My covenant with you in the days of your youth, and I will establish an everlasting covenant with you.

By one offering He has perfected for all time those who are sanctified.—He is able to save forever those who draw near to God through Him, since He always lives to make intercession for them.—I know whom I have believed and I am convinced that He is able to guard what I have entrusted to Him until that day.

The gifts and the calling of God are irrevocable.—Who shall separate us from the love of Christ?—The Lamb in the center of the throne shall be their shepherd, and shall guide them to springs of the water of life; and God shall wipe every tear from their eyes.—Thus we shall always be with the Lord. Therefore comfort one another with these words.

This is no place of rest.—Here we do not have a lasting city, but we are seeking the city which is to come.

2 TH 2:16. Eze 16:60. Heb 10:14.—Heb 7:25.—2 Ti 1:12. Ro 11:29.—Ro 8:35.—Rev 7:17.—1 Th 4:17,18. Mic 2:10.— Heb 13:14.

Truly, truly, I say to you, I am the door of the sheep.

The veil of the temple was torn in two from top to bottom.—Christ also died for sins once for all, the just for the unjust, in order that He might bring us to God.—The way into the holy place has not yet been disclosed, while the outer tabernacle is still standing.

I am the door; if anyone enters through Me, he shall be saved, and shall go in and out, and find pasture.

No one comes to the Father, but through Me.—For through Him we both have our access in one Spirit to the Father. So then you are no longer strangers and aliens, but you are fellow-citizens with the saints, and are of God's household.—We have confidence to enter the holy place by the blood of Jesus, by a new and living way which He inaugurated for us through the veil, that is, His flesh.—We have peace with God through our Lord Jesus Christ, through whom also we have obtained our introduction by faith into this grace in which we stand; and we exult in hope of the glory of God.

JN 10:7. Mt 27:51.—1 Pe 3:18.—Heb 9:8. Jn 10:9. Jn 14:6.—
Eph 2:18,19.—Heb 10:19,20.—Ro 5:1,2.

In my heart it (the word of the LORD) becomes like a burning fire shut up in my bones; and I am weary of holding it in.

I am under compulsion; for woe is me if I do not preach the gospel. What then is my reward? That, when I preach the gospel, I may offer the gospel without charge, so as not to make full use of my right in the gospel.—They commanded them not to speak or teach at all in the name of Jesus. But Peter and John answered and said to them . . . we cannot stop speaking what we have seen and heard.—The love of Christ controls us.

I was afraid, and went away and hid your talent in the ground. . . . You wicked, lazy slave . . . you ought to have put my money in the bank, and on my arrival I would have received my money back with interest.

Go home to your people and report to them what great things the Lord has done for you.

JER 20:9. 1 Co 9:16,18.—Ac 4:18–20.—2 Co 5:14. Mt 25:25–27.
Mk 5:19.

Nothing from that which is put under the ban shall cling to your hand.

Come out from their midst and be separate, says the Lord. And do not touch what is unclean.—Beloved, I urge you as aliens and strangers to abstain from fleshly lusts, which wage war against the soul.—Hating even the garment polluted by the flesh.

Beloved, now we are children of God, and it has not appeared as yet what we shall be. We know that, when He appears, we shall be like Him, because we shall see Him just as He is. And every one who has this hope fixed on Him purifies himself, just as He is pure.—The grace of God has appeared, bringing salvation to all men, instructing us to deny ungodliness and worldly desires and to live sensibly, righteously and godly in the present age, looking for the blessed hope and the appearing of the glory of our great God and Savior, Christ Jesus; who gave Himself for us, that He might redeem us from every lawless deed and purify for Himself a people for His own possession, zealous for good deeds.

DEU 13:17. 2 Co 6:17.—1 Pe 2:11.—Jude 23. Jn 3:2,3.—
Titus 2:11–14.

Who art Thou, Lord? I am Jesus.

It is I; do not be afraid.—When you pass through the waters, I will be with you; and through the rivers, they will not overflow you. When you walk through the fire, you will not be scorched, nor will the flame burn you. For I am the LORD your God . . . your Savior.

Though I walk through the valley of the shadow of death, I fear no evil; for Thou art with me; Thy rod and Thy staff, they comfort me.—Immanuel, . . . God with us.

You shall call His name Jesus, for it is He who will save His people from their sins.—If anyone sins, we have an Advocate with the Father, Jesus Christ the righteous.—Who is the one who condemns? Christ Jesus is He who died, yes, rather who was raised, who is at the right hand of God, who also intercedes for us. Who shall separate us from the love of Christ? Shall tribulation, or distress, or persecution, or famine, or nakedness, or peril, or sword?

AC 26:15. Mt 14:27.—Is 43:2,3. Ps 23:4.—Mt 1:23. Mt 1:21.—
1 Jn 2:1.—Ro 8:34,35.

Stand firm in the Lord.

My foot has held fast to His path; I have kept His way and not turned aside.

For the LORD loves justice, and does not forsake His godly ones; they are preserved forever.—The LORD will protect you from all evil; He will keep your soul.

My righteous one shall live by faith; and if he shrinks back, My soul has no pleasure in him. But we are not of those who shrink back to destruction, but of those who have faith to the preserving of the soul.—If they had been of us, they would have remained with us; but they went out, in order that it might be shown that they all are not of us.

If you abide in My word, then you are truly disciples of Mine. —The one who endures to the end, it is he who shall be saved. —Be on the alert, stand firm in the faith, act like men, be strong. —Hold fast what you have, in order that no one take your crown. —He who overcomes shall thus be clothed in white garments; and I will not erase his name from the book of life.

PHIL 4:1. Job 23:11. Ps 37:28.—Ps 121:7. Heb 10:38,39.—1 Jn 2:19. Jn 8:31.—Mt 24:13.—1 Co 16:13.—Rev 3:11.—Rev 3:5.

Enoch walked with God.

Do two men walk together unless they have made an appointment?

Having made peace through the blood of His cross ... although you were formerly alienated and hostile in mind, engaged in evil deeds, yet He has now reconciled you in His fleshly body through death, in order to present you before Him holy and blameless and beyond reproach.—Now in Christ Jesus you who formerly were far off have been brought near by the blood of Christ.

If while we were enemies, we were reconciled to God through the death of His Son, much more, having been reconciled, we shall be saved by His life. And not only this, but we also exult in God through our Lord Jesus Christ.

Our fellowship is with the Father, and with His Son Jesus Christ.

The grace of the Lord Jesus Christ, and the love of God, and the fellowship of the Holy Spirit, be with you all.

GEN 5:22. Amos 3:3. Col 1:20–22.—Eph 2:13. Ro 5:10,11. 1 Jn 1:3. 2 Co 13:14.

If his offering is a burnt offering from the herd, he shall offer it a male without defect; he shall offer it at the doorway of the tent of meeting, that he may be accepted before the LORD. And he shall lay his hand on the head of the burnt offering, that it may be accepted for him to make atonement on his behalf.

God will provide for Himself the lamb for the burnt offering. —Behold, the Lamb of God who takes away the sin of the world! —We have been sanctified through the offering of the body of Jesus Christ once for all.—His life a ransom for many.

No one has taken it away from Me, but I lay it down on My own initiative. I have authority to lay it down, and I have authority to take it up again.—I will love them freely.—The Son of God, who loved me, and delivered Himself up for me.

He made Him who knew no sin to be sin on our behalf, that we might become the righteousness of God in Him.—His grace, which He freely bestowed on us in the Beloved.

LEV 1:3,4. Gen 22:8.—Jn 1:29.—Heb 10:10.—Mt 20:28. Jn 10:18.— Ho 14:4.—Gal 2:20. 2 Co 5:21.—Eph 1:6.

For Thy lovingkindness toward me is great, and Thou hast delivered my soul from the depths of Sheol.

Fear Him who is able to destroy both soul and body in hell.

Do not fear, for I have redeemed you; I have called you by name; you are Mine! I, even I, am the LORD; and there is no savior besides Me. I, even I, am the one who wipes out your transgressions for My own sake; and I will not remember your sins.—Even those who trust in their wealth, and boast in the abundance of their riches? No man can by any means redeem his brother, or give to God a ransom for him—for the redemption of his soul is costly.—I have found a ransom.—God, being rich in mercy, because of His great love with which He loved us, even when we were dead in our transgressions, made us alive together with Christ.

And there is salvation in no one else; for there is no other name under heaven that has been given among men, by which we must be saved.

PS 86:13. Mt 10:28. Is 43:1,11,25.—Ps 49:6–8.—Job 33:24.— Eph 2:4,5. Ac 4:12.

The LORD was my stay.

Surely, the hills are a deception, a tumult on the mountains. Surely, in the LORD our God is the salvation of Israel.—The LORD is my rock and my fortress and my deliverer, my God, my rock, in whom I take refuge; my shield and the horn of my salvation, my stronghold.—Cry aloud and shout for joy, O inhabitant of Zion, for great in your midst is the Holy One of Israel.

The angel of the LORD encamps around those who fear Him, and rescues them. The righteous cry and the LORD hears, and delivers them out of all their troubles.—The eternal God is a dwelling place, and underneath are the everlasting arms.—So that we confidently say, the Lord is my helper, I will not be afraid. What shall man do to me?—For who is God, but the LORD? And who is a rock, except our God, the God who girds me with strength, and makes my way blameless?

By the grace of God I am what I am.

PS 18:18. Jer 3:23.—Ps 18:2.—Is 12:6. Ps 34:7,17.—Deu 33:27.—
Heb 13:6.—Ps 18:31,32. 1 Co 15:10.

All of us like sheep have gone astray.

If we say that we have no sin, we are deceiving ourselves, and the truth is not in us.—There is none righteous, not even one; there is none who understands, . . . all have turned aside, together they have become useless.

You were continually straying like sheep, but now you have returned to the Shepherd and Guardian of your souls.—I have gone astray like a lost sheep; seek Thy servant, for I do not forget Thy commandments.

He restores my soul; He guides me in the paths of righteousness for His name's sake.

My sheep hear My voice, and I know them, and they follow Me; and I give eternal life to them; and they shall never perish; and no one shall snatch them out of My hand.

What man among you, if he has a hundred sheep and has lost one of them, does not leave the ninety-nine in the open pasture, and go after the one which is lost, until he finds it?

IS 53:6. 1 Jn 1:8.—Ro 3:10–12. 1 Pe 2:25.—Ps 119:176. Ps 23.3.
Jn 10:27,28. Lk 15:4.

The LORD took note of Sarah as He had said, and the LORD did for Sarah as He had promised.

Trust in Him at all times, O people; pour out your heart before Him; God is a refuge for us.—David strengthened himself in the LORD his God.—God will surely take care of you, and bring you up from this land to the land which He promised on oath to Abraham, to Isaac and to Jacob.—I have certainly seen the oppression of My people in Egypt, and have heard their groans, and I have come down to deliver them. . . . This man (Moses) led them out, performing wonders and signs in the land of Egypt and in the Red Sea and in the wilderness for forty years.—Not one of the good promises which the LORD had made to the house of Israel failed; all came to pass.

He who promised is faithful.—Has He said, and will He not do it? Or has He spoken, and will He not make it good?—Heaven and earth will pass away, but My words shall not pass away.—The grass withers, the flower fades, but the word of our God stands forever.

GEN 21:1. Ps 62:8.—1 Sa 30:6.—Gen 50:24.—Ac 7:34,36.—
Jos 21:45. Heb 10:23.—Num 23:19.—Mt 24:35.—Is 40:8.

The eyes of all look to Thee.

He Himself gives to all life and breath and all things.—The LORD is good to all, and His mercies are over all His works.—Look at the birds of the air, that they do not sow, neither do they reap, nor gather into barns; and yet your heavenly Father feeds them.

The same Lord is Lord of all, abounding in riches for all who call upon Him.

I will lift up my eyes to the mountains; from whence shall my help come?—Behold, as the eyes of servants look to the hand of their master, as the eyes of a maid to the hand of her mistress; so our eyes look to the LORD our God.

For the LORD is a God of justice; how blessed are all those who long for Him.—And it will be said in that day, Behold, this is our God for whom we have waited that He might save us. This is the LORD for whom we have waited; let us rejoice and be glad in His salvation.—If we hope for what we do not see, with perseverance we wait eagerly for it.

PS 145:15. Ac 17:25.—Ps 145:9.—Mt 6:26. Ro 10:12. Ps 121:1.—
Ps 123:2. Is 30:18.—Is 25:9.—Ro 8:25.

You shall call His name Jesus, for it is He who will save His people from their sins.

You know that He appeared in order to take away sins.—That we might die to sin and live to righteousness.—He is able to save forever those who draw near to God through Him.

He was pierced through for our transgressions, He was crushed for our iniquities; the chastening for our well-being fell upon Him, and by His scourging we are healed. . . . But the LORD has caused the iniquity of us all to fall on Him.—Christ should suffer . . . that repentance for forgiveness of sins should be proclaimed in His name to all the nations.—He has been manifested to put away sin by the sacrifice of Himself.

He is the one whom God exalted to His right hand as a Prince and a Savior, to grant repentance.—Through Him forgiveness of sins is proclaimed to you, and through Him everyone who believes is freed from all things, from which you could not be freed through the Law of Moses.—Your sins are forgiven you for His name's sake.

MT 1:21. 1 Jn 3:5.—1 Pe 2:24.—Heb 7:25. Is 53:5,6.—
Lk 24:46,47.—Heb 9:26. Ac 5:31.—Ac 13:38,39.—1 Jn 2:12.

Our Lord Jesus Christ, that though He was rich, yet for your sake He became poor, that you through His poverty might become rich.

It was the Father's good pleasure for all the fulness to dwell in Him.—The radiance of His glory and the exact representation of His nature, and upholds all things by the word of His power. When He had made purification of sins, He sat down at the right hand of the Majesty on high; having become so much better than the angels, as He has inherited a more excellent name than they. —Although He existed in the form of God, did not regard equality with God a thing to be grasped, but emptied Himself.

The foxes have holes, and the birds of the air have nests; but the Son of Man has nowhere to lay His head.

All things belong to you, whether Paul or Apollos or Cephas or the world or life or death or things present or things to come; all things belong to you, and you belong to Christ; and Christ belongs to God.

2 CO 8:9. Col 1:19.—Heb 1:3,4.—Phil 2:6,7. Mt 8:20. 1 Co 3:21–23.

Let his left hand be under my head and his right hand embrace me.

The eternal God is a dwelling place, and underneath are the everlasting arms.—Seeing the wind, (Peter) became afraid, and beginning to sink, he cried out, saying, Lord, save me! And immediately Jesus stretched out His hand and took hold of him, and said to him, O you of little faith, why did you doubt?—The steps of a man are established by the LORD; and He delights in his way. When he falls, he shall not be hurled headlong; because the LORD is the One who holds his hand.

The beloved of the LORD dwell in security by Him, who shields him all the day, and he dwells between His shoulders.—Casting all your anxiety upon Him, because He cares for you.—He who touches you, touches the apple of His eye.

They shall never perish, and no one shall snatch them out of My hand. My Father, who has given them to Me, is greater than all.

SONG 2:6. Deu 33:27.—Mt 14:30,31.—Ps 37:23,24. Deu 33:12.—
1 Pe 5:7.—Zec 2:8. Jn 10:28,29.

Who is this that grows like the dawn, as beautiful as the full moon, as pure as the sun, as awesome as an army with banners?

The church of God which He purchased with His own blood.

Christ also loved the church and gave Himself up for her; that He might sanctify her, having cleansed her by the washing of water with the word, that He might present to Himself the church in all her glory, having no spot or wrinkle or any such thing; but that she should be holy and blameless.

A great sign appeared in heaven: a woman clothed with the sun.—The marriage of the Lamb has come and His bride has made herself ready. And it was given to her to clothe herself in fine linen, bright and clean; for the fine linen is the righteous acts of the saints.—The righteousness of God through faith in Jesus Christ for all those who believe.

The glory which Thou hast given Me I have given to them.

SONG 6:10. Ac 20:28. Eph 5:25–27. Rev 12:1.—Rev 19:7,8.—
Ro 3:22. Jn 17:22.

Brethren, the time has been shortened.

Man, who is born of woman, is short-lived and full of turmoil. Like a flower he comes forth and withers. He also flees like a shadow and does not remain.—The world is passing away, and also its lusts; but the one who does the will of God abides forever. —As in Adam all die, so also in Christ all shall be made alive. Death is swallowed up in victory.—If we live, we live for the Lord, or if we die, we die for the Lord; therefore whether we live or die, we are the Lord's.—To live is Christ, and to die is gain.

Do not throw away your confidence, which has a great reward. For you have need of endurance, so that when you have done the will of God, you may receive what was promised. For yet in a very little while, He who is coming will come, and will not delay. —The night is almost gone, and the day is at hand. Let us therefore lay aside the deeds of darkness and put on the armor of light. —The end of all things is at hand; therefore, be of sound judgment and sober spirit for the purpose of prayer.

1 CO 7:29. Job 14:1,2.—1 Jn 2:17.—1 Co 15:22,54.—Ro 14:8.—
Phil 1:21. Heb 10:35–37.—Ro 13:12.—1 Pe 4:7.

A new name.

The disciples were first called Christians in Antioch.—Let every one who names the name of the Lord abstain from wickedness.—Those who belong to Christ Jesus have crucified the flesh with its passions and desires.—You have been bought with a price: therefore glorify God in your body.

May it never be that I should boast, except in the cross of our Lord Jesus Christ, through which the world has been crucified to me, and I to the world. For neither is circumcision anything, nor uncircumcision, but a new creation.

Be imitators of God, as beloved children; and walk in love, just as Christ also loved you, and gave Himself up for us, an offering and a sacrifice to God as a fragrant aroma. But do not let immorality or any impurity or greed even be named among you, as is proper among saints. Now you are light in the Lord; walk as children of light.

REV 2:17. Ac 11:26.—2 Ti 2:19.—Gal 5:24.—1 Co 6:20. Gal 6:14,15.
Eph 5:1–3,8.

Behold, the Lamb of God.

It is impossible for the blood of bulls and goats to take away sins. Therefore, when He comes into the world, He says, Sacrifice and offering Thou hast not desired, but a body Thou hast prepared for Me; in whole burnt offerings and sacrifices for sin Thou hast taken no pleasure. Then I said, Behold, I have come (in the roll of the book it is written of Me) to do Thy will, O God.—He was oppressed and He was afflicted, yet He did not open His mouth; like a lamb that is led to slaughter, and like a sheep that is silent before its shearers, so He did not open His mouth.

You were not redeemed with perishable things like silver or gold . . . but with precious blood, as of a lamb unblemished and spotless, the blood of Christ. . . . He . . . has appeared in these last times for the sake of you who through Him are believers in God . . . so that your faith and hope are in God.

Worthy is the Lamb that was slain to receive power and riches and wisdom and might and honor and glory and blessing.

JN 1:29. Heb 10:4–7.—Is 53:7. 1 Pe 1:18–21. Rev 5:12.

I will hope continually, and will praise Thee yet more and more.

Not that I have already obtained it, or have already become perfect.—Leaving the elementary teaching about the Christ, let us press on to maturity, not laying again a foundation of repentance from dead works and of faith toward God.—The path of the righteous is like the light of dawn, that shines brighter and brighter until the full day.

I love the LORD, because He hears my voice and my supplications. Because He has inclined His ear to me, therefore I shall call upon Him as long as I live.—I will bless the LORD at all times; His praise shall continually be in my mouth.

There will be silence before Thee, and praise in Zion, O God. —Day and night they do not cease to say, Holy, holy, holy, is the Lord God, the Almighty.—He who offers a sacrifice of thanksgiving honors Me.—Rejoice always; pray without ceasing; in everything give thanks; for this is God's will for you in Christ Jesus.— Rejoice in the Lord always; again I will say, rejoice!

PS 71:14. Phil 3:12.—Heb 6:1.—Pr 4:18. Ps 116:1,2.—Ps 34:1.
Ps 65:1.—Rev 4:8.—Ps 50:23.—1 Th 5:16–18.—Phil 4:4.

Consider what great things He has done for you.

You shall remember all the way which the LORD your God has led you in the wilderness these forty years, that He might humble you, testing you, to know what was in your heart, whether you would keep His commandments or not. Thus you are to know in your heart that the LORD your God was disciplining you just as a man disciplines his son.

I know, O LORD, that Thy judgments are righteous, and that in faithfulness Thou hast afflicted me. It is good for me that I was afflicted, that I may learn Thy statutes. Before I was afflicted I went astray, but now I keep Thy word.—The LORD has disciplined me severely, but He has not given me over to death.—He has not dealt with us according to our sins, nor rewarded us according to our iniquities. For as high as the heavens are above the earth, so great is His lovingkindness toward those who fear Him. For He Himself knows our frame; He is mindful that we are but dust.

1 SA 12:24. Deu 8:2,5. Ps 119:75,71,67.—Ps 118:18.—
Ps 103:10,11,14.

The blessed hope and the appearing of the glory of our great God and Savior, Christ Jesus.

This hope we have as an anchor of the soul, a hope both sure and steadfast and one which enters within the veil, where Jesus has entered as a forerunner for us.—Whom heaven must receive until the period of restoration of all things.—When He comes to be glorified in His saints . . . and to be marveled at among all who have believed.

The whole creation groans and suffers the pains of childbirth together until now. And not only this, but also we ourselves . . . groan within ourselves, waiting eagerly for our adoption as sons, the redemption of our body.—Beloved, now we are children of God, and it has not appeared as yet what we shall be. We know that, when He appears, we shall be like Him, because we shall see Him just as He is.—When Christ, who is our life, is revealed, then you also will be revealed with Him in glory.

Yes, I am coming quickly. Amen. Come, Lord Jesus.

TITUS 2:13. Heb 6:19,20.—Ac 3:21.—2 Th 1:10. Ro 8:22,23.—
1 Jn 3:2.—Col 3:4. Rev 22:20.

Whoever keeps His word, in him the love of God has truly been perfected.

The God of peace, who brought up from the dead the great Shepherd of the sheep through the blood of the eternal covenant, even Jesus our Lord, equip you in every good thing to do His will, working in us that which is pleasing in His sight, through Jesus Christ; to whom be the glory forever and ever. Amen.

By this we know that we have come to know Him, if we keep His commandments.—If anyone loves Me, he will keep My word; and My Father will love him, and We will come in to him, and make Our abode with him.—No one who abides in Him sins; no one who sins has seen Him or knows Him. Little children, let no one deceive you; the one who practices righteousness is righteous, just as He is righteous.—By this, love is perfected with us, that we may have confidence in the day of judgment; because as He is, so also are we in this world.

1 JN 2:5. Heb 13:20,21. 1 Jn 2:3.—Jn 14:23.—1 Jn 3:6,7.—1 Jn 4:17.

He who is slow to anger has great understanding.

The LORD passed by in front of him and proclaimed, The LORD, the LORD God, compassionate and gracious, slow to anger, and abounding in lovingkindness and truth.—The Lord is not slow about His promise, as some count slowness, but is patient toward you, not wishing for any to perish but for all to come to repentance.

Be imitators of God, as beloved children; and walk in love.— The fruit of the Spirit is love, joy, peace, patience, kindness, goodness, faithfulness, gentleness, self-control; against such things there is no law.—This finds favor, if for the sake of conscience toward God a man bears up under sorrows when suffering unjustly. . . . If when you do what is right and suffer for it you patiently endure it, this finds favor with God. . . . Christ also suffered for you, leaving you an example for you to follow in His steps, . . . and while being reviled, He did not revile in return; while suffering, He uttered no threats, but kept entrusting Himself to Him who judges righteously.

Be angry, and yet do not sin.

PR 14:29. Ex 34:6.—2 Pe 3:9. Eph 5:1,2.—Gal 5:22,23.—
1 Pe 2:19–21,23. Eph 4:26.

The fruit of the Spirit is . . . peace.

The mind set on the Spirit is life and peace.

God has called us to peace.—Peace I leave with you; My peace I give to you; not as the world gives, do I give to you. Let not your heart be troubled, nor let it be fearful.—May the God of hope fill you with all joy and peace in believing, that you may abound in hope by the power of the Holy Spirit.

I know whom I have believed and I am convinced that He is able to guard what I have entrusted to Him until that day.—The steadfast of mind Thou wilt keep in perfect peace, because he trusts in Thee.

The work of righteousness will be peace, and the service of righteousness, quietness and confidence forever. Then my people will live in a peaceful habitation, and in secure dwellings and in undisturbed resting places.—He who listens to me shall live securely, and shall be at ease from the dread of evil.

Those who love Thy law have great peace.

GAL 5:22. Ro 8:6. 1 Co 7:15.—Jn 14:27.—Ro 15:13. 2 Ti 1:12.— Is 26:3. Is 32:17,18.—Pr 1:33. Ps 119:165.

The LORD is there.

Behold, the tabernacle of God is among men, and He shall dwell among them, and they shall be His people, and God Himself shall be among them.

I saw no temple in it, for the Lord God, the Almighty, and the Lamb, are its temple. And the city has no need of the sun or of the moon to shine upon it, for the glory of God has illumined it, and its lamp is the Lamb.

I will be satisfied with Thy likeness when I awake.—Whom have I in heaven but Thee? And besides Thee, I desire nothing on earth.

Judah will be inhabited forever, and Jerusalem for all generations. And I will avenge their blood which I have not avenged, for the LORD dwells in Zion.—Sing for joy and be glad, O daughter of Zion; for behold I am coming and I will dwell in your midst, declares the LORD.—There shall no longer be any curse; and the throne of God and of the Lamb shall be in it, and His bondservants shall serve Him.

EZE 48:35. Rev 21:3. Rev 21:22,23. Ps 17:15.—Ps 73:25. Joel 3:20,21.—Zec 2:10.—Rev 22:3.

Surely the LORD is in this place, and I did not know it.

Where two or three have gathered together in My name, there I am in their midst.—Lo, I am with you always, even to the end of the age.—My presence shall go with you, and I will give you rest.

Where can I go from Thy Spirit? Or where can I flee from Thy presence? If I ascend to heaven, Thou art there; if I make my bed in Sheol, behold, Thou art there.—Am I a God who is near, declares the LORD, and not a God far off? Can a man hide himself in hiding places, so I do not see him? declares the LORD. Do I not fill the heavens and the earth? declares the LORD.

Behold, heaven and the highest heaven cannot contain Thee, how much less this house which I have built!—Thus says the high and exalted One who lives forever, whose name is Holy, I dwell on a high and holy place, and also with the contrite and lowly of spirit in order to revive the spirit of the lowly and to revive the heart of the contrite.—We are the temple of the living God.

GEN 28:16. Mt 18:20.—Mt 28:20.—Ex 33:14. Ps 139:7,8.—
Jer 23:23,24. 1 Ki 8:27.—Is 57:15.—2 Co 6:16.

Guard yourselves from idols.

Give me your heart, my son.—Set your mind on the things above, not on the things that are on earth.

Son of man, these men have set up their idols in their hearts, and have put right before their faces the stumbling block of their iniquity. Should I be consulted by them at all?—Consider the members of your earthly body as dead to immorality, impurity, passion, evil desire, and greed, which amounts to idolatry.—But those who want to get rich fall into temptation and a snare and many foolish and harmful desires which plunge men into ruin and destruction. For the love of money is a root of all sorts of evil, and some by longing for it have wandered away from the faith, and pierced themselves with many a pang. But flee from these things, you man of God.

If riches increase, do not set your heart upon them.—My fruit is better than gold, even pure gold, and my yield than choicest silver.

Where your treasure is, there will your heart be also.—The LORD looks at the heart.

1 JN 5:21. Pr 23:26.—Col 3:2. Eze 14:3.—Col 3:5.—1 Ti 6:9–11.
Ps 62:10.—Pr 8:19. Mt 6:21.—1 Sa 16:7.

You are to be perfect, as your heavenly Father is perfect.

I am God Almighty; walk before Me, and be blameless.—You are to be holy to Me, for I the Lord am holy; and I have set you apart from the peoples to be Mine.

You have been bought with a price: therefore glorify God in your body.

In Him you have been made complete, and He is the head over all rule and authority.—Who gave Himself for us, that He might redeem us from every lawless deed.—Be diligent to be found by Him in peace, spotless and blameless.

How blessed are those whose way is blameless, who walk in the law of the Lord.—One who looks intently at the perfect law, the law of liberty, and abides by it, not having become a forgetful hearer but an effectual doer, this man shall be blessed in what he does.—Search me, O God, and know my heart; try me and know my anxious thoughts; and see if there be any hurtful way in me, and lead me in the everlasting way.

MT 5:48. Gen 17:1.—Lev 20:26. 1 Co 6:20. Col 2:10.—Titus 2:14.—
2 Pe 3:14. Ps 119:1.—Ja 1:25. Ps 139:23,24.

Perfecting holiness in the fear of God.

Let us cleanse ourselves from all defilement of flesh and spirit. Behold, Thou dost desire truth in the innermost being, and in the hidden part Thou wilt make me know wisdom.—Instructing us to deny ungodliness and worldly desires and to live sensibly, righteously and godly in the present age.—Let your light shine before men in such a way that they may see your good works, and glorify your Father who is in heaven.—Not that I have already obtained it, or have already become perfect.

Every one who has this hope fixed on Him purifies himself, just as He is pure.

Now He who prepared us for this very purpose is God, who gave to us the Spirit as a pledge.—For the equipping of the saints for the work of service, to the building up of the body of Christ; until we all attain to the unity of the faith, and of the knowledge of the Son of God, to a mature man, to the measure of the stature which belongs to the fulness of Christ.

2 CO 7:1. 2 Co 7:1. Ps 51:6.—Titus 2:12.—Mt 5:16.—Phil 3:12.
1 Jn 3:3. 2 Co 5:5.—Eph 4:12,13.

Behold, the LORD'S hand is not so short that it cannot save; neither is His ear so dull that it cannot hear.

On the day I called Thou didst answer me; Thou didst make me bold with strength in my soul.—While I was still speaking in prayer, then the man Gabriel, whom I had seen in the vision previously, came to me in my extreme weariness about the time of the evening offering.

Do not hide Thy face from me, do not turn Thy servant away in anger; Thou hast been my help; do not abandon me nor forsake me, O God of my salvation!—But Thou, O LORD, be not far off; O Thou my help, hasten to my assistance.

Ah Lord GOD! Behold, Thou hast made the heavens and the earth by Thy great power and by Thine outstretched arm! Nothing is too difficult for Thee.—Who delivered us from so great a peril of death, and will deliver us, He on whom we have set our hope. And he will yet deliver us.—Now shall not God bring about justice for His elect, who cry to Him day and night, and will He delay long over them? I tell you that He will bring about justice for them speedily.

IS 59:1. Ps 138:3.—Dan 9:21. Ps 27:9.—Ps 22:19. Jer 32:17.—
2 Co 1:10.—Lk 18:7,8.

I glorified Thee on the earth.

My food is to do the will of Him who sent Me, and to accomplish His work.—We must work the works of Him who sent Me, as long as it is day; night is coming, when no man can work.

Did you not know that I had to be in My Father's house? And they did not understand the statement which He had made to them.—This sickness is not unto death, but for the glory of God, that the Son of God may be glorified by it. Did I not say to you, if you believe, you will see the glory of God?

Jesus kept increasing in wisdom and stature, and in favor with God and men.—Thou art My beloved Son, in Thee I am well pleased.—All were speaking well of Him, and wondering at the gracious words which were falling from His lips.

Worthy art Thou ... Thou wast slain, and didst purchase for God with Thy blood men from every tribe and tongue and people and nation. And Thou hast made them to be a kingdom and priests to our God; and they will reign upon the earth.

JN 17:4. Jn 4:34.—Jn 9:4. Lk 2:49,50.—Jn 11:4,40. Lk 2:52.—
Lk 3:22.—Lk 4:22. Rev 5:9,10.

Do not be anxious then, saying, What shall we eat? or, What shall we drink? or, With what shall we clothe ourselves? ... for your heavenly Father knows that you need all these things.

O fear the LORD, you His saints; for to those who fear Him, there is no want. The young lions do lack and suffer hunger; but they who seek the LORD shall not be in want of any good thing. —No good thing does He withhold from those who walk uprightly. O LORD of hosts, how blessed is the man who trusts in Thee!

I want you to be free from concern.—Be anxious for nothing, but in everything by prayer and supplication with thanksgiving let your requests be made known to God.

Are not two sparrows sold for a cent? And yet not one of them will fall to the ground apart from your Father. But the very hairs of your head are all numbered. Therefore do not fear; you are of more value than many sparrows.—Why are you so timid? How is it that you have no faith?—Have faith in God.

MT 6:31,32. Ps 34:9,10.—Ps 84:11,12. 1 Co 7:32.—Phil 4:6. Mt
10:29–31.—Mk 4:40.—Mk 11:22.

He spread a cloud for a covering, and fire to illumine by night.

Just as a father has compassion on his children, so the LORD has compassion on those who fear Him. For He Himself knows our frame; He is mindful that we are but dust.

The sun will not smite you by day, nor the moon by night.— There will be a shelter to give shade from the heat by day, and refuge and protection from the storm and the rain.

The LORD is your keeper; the LORD is your shade on your right hand. The LORD will guard your going out and your coming in from this time forth and forever.—The LORD was going before them in a pillar of cloud by day to lead them on the way, and in a pillar of fire by night to give them light, that they might travel by day and by night. He did not take away the pillar of cloud by day, nor the pillar of fire by night, from before the people.

Jesus Christ is the same yesterday and today, yes and forever.

PS 105:39. Ps 103:13,14. Ps 121:6.—Is 4:6. Ps 121:5,8.—Ex 13:21,22.
Heb 13:8.

Lovingkindness and truth have met together; righteousness and peace have kissed each other.

A righteous God and a Savior.

The LORD was pleased for His righteousness' sake to make the law great and glorious.

God was in Christ reconciling the world to Himself, not counting their trespasses against them.—Whom God displayed publicly as a propitiation in His blood through faith. This was to demonstrate His righteousness, because in the forbearance of God He passed over the sins previously committed; for the demonstration, I say, of His righteousness at the present time, that He might be just and the justifier of the one who has faith in Jesus. —He was pierced through for our transgressions, He was crushed for our iniquities; the chastening for our well-being fell upon Him, and by His scourging we are healed.—Who will bring a charge against God's elect? God is the one who justifies.—To the one who does not work, but believes in Him who justifies the ungodly, his faith is reckoned as righteousness.

PS 85:10. Is 45:21. Is 42:21. 2 Co 5:19.—Ro 3:25,26.—Is 53:5.—
Ro 8:33.—Ro 4:5.

How are the dead raised? And with what kind of body do they come?

Beloved, now we are children of God, and it has not appeared as yet what we shall be. We know that, when He appears, we shall be like Him, because we shall see Him just as He is.—Just as we have borne the image of the earthy, we shall also bear the image of the heavenly.

A Savior, the Lord Jesus Christ; who will transform the body of our humble state into conformity with the body of His glory, by the exertion of the power that He has even to subject all things to Himself.

He Himself stood in their midst. But they were startled and frightened and thought that they were seeing a spirit.—He appeared to Cephas, then to the twelve. After that He appeared to more than five hundred brethren at one time.

If the Spirit of Him who raised Jesus from the dead dwells in you, He who raised Christ Jesus from the dead will also give life to your mortal bodies through His Spirit who indwells you.

1 CO 15:35. 1 Jn 3:2.—1 Co 15:49. Phil 3:20,21. Lk 24:36,37.—
1 Co 15:5,6. Ro 8:11.

You will be hearing of wars and rumors of wars; see that you are not frightened.

God is our refuge and strength, a very present help in trouble. Therefore we will not fear, though the earth should change, and though the mountains slip into the heart of the sea; though its waters roar and foam, though the mountains quake at its swelling pride.—Come, my people, enter into your rooms, and close your doors behind you; hide for a little while, until indignation runs its course. For behold, the Lord is about to come out from His place to punish the inhabitants of the earth for their iniquity.—In the shadow of Thy wings I will take refuge, until destruction passes by.—Your life is hidden with Christ in God.

He will not fear evil tidings; his heart is steadfast, trusting in the Lord.

These things I have spoken to you, that in Me you may have peace. In the world you have tribulation, but take courage; I have overcome the world.

MT 24:6. Ps 46:1–3.—Is 26:20,21.—Ps 57:1.—Col 3:3. Ps 112:7.
Jn 16:33.

They have persecuted him whom Thou Thyself hast smitten.

It is inevitable that stumbling blocks should come, but woe to him through whom they come!—This Man, delivered up by the predetermined plan and foreknowledge of God, you nailed to a cross by the hands of godless men and put Him to death.—They spat in His face and beat Him with their fists, and others slapped Him, and said, Prophesy to us, You Christ; who is the one who hit You?—In the same way the chief priests, along with the scribes and elders, were mocking Him, and saying, He saved others; He cannot save Himself. He is the King of Israel; let Him now come down from the cross.—For truly in this city there were gathered together against Thy holy Servant Jesus, whom Thou didst anoint, both Herod and Pontius Pilate, along with the Gentiles and the peoples of Israel, to do whatever Thy hand and Thy purpose predestined to occur.

Surely our griefs He Himself bore, and our sorrows He carried; yet we ourselves esteemed Him stricken, smitten of God, and afflicted.

PS 69:26. Lk 17:1.—Ac 2:23.—Mt 26:67,68.—Mt 27:41,42.—
Ac 4:27,28. Is 53:4.

The LORD was pleased to crush Him, putting Him to grief.

My soul has become troubled; and what shall I say, Father, save
Me from this hour? But for this purpose I came to this hour.
Father, glorify Thy name. There came therefore a voice out of
heaven: I have both glorified it, and will glorify it again.—Father,
if Thou art willing, remove this cup from Me; yet not My will, but
Thine be done. Now an angel from heaven appeared to Him,
strengthening Him.

Being found in appearance as a man, He humbled Himself by
becoming obedient to the point of death, even death on a cross.
—For this reason the Father loves Me, because I lay down My life
that I may take it again.—For I have come down from heaven,
not to do My own will, but the will of Him who sent Me.—The
cup which the Father has given Me, shall I not drink it?

He has not left Me alone, for I always do the things that are
pleasing to Him.—My beloved Son, in whom I am well pleased.
—My chosen one in whom My soul delights.

IS 53:10. Jn 12:27,28.—Lk 22:42,43. Phil 2:8.—Jn 10:17.—Jn 6:38.—
Jn 18:11. Jn 8:29.—Mt 3:17.—Is 42:1.

You who remind the LORD, take no rest for yourselves.

Thou has made them to be a kingdom and priests.—The
priestly sons of Aaron . . . shall blow the trumpets; and this shall
be for you a perpetual statute throughout your generations. And
when you go to war in your land against the adversary who
attacks you, then you shall sound an alarm with the trumpets,
that you may be remembered before the LORD your God, and
be saved from your enemies.

I did not say to the offspring of Jacob, Seek Me in a waste place.
—Their voice was heard and their prayer came to His holy dwelling place, to heaven.—The eyes of the LORD are toward the
righteous, and His ears are open to their cry.—Pray for one
another. . . . The effective prayer of a righteous man can accomplish much.

Come, Lord Jesus.—Do not delay, O my God.—Looking for
and hastening the coming of the day of God.

IS 62:6. Rev 5:10.—Num 10:8,9. Is 45:19.—2 Ch 30:27.—Ps 34:15.—
Ja 5:16. Rev 22:20.—Ps 40:17.—2 Pe 3:12.

Faith is the assurance of things hoped for, the conviction of things not seen.

If we have only hoped in Christ in this life, we are of all men most to be pitied.

Things which eye has not seen and ear has not heard, and which have not entered the heart of man, all that God has prepared for those who love him. For to us God revealed them through the Spirit.—Having also believed, you were sealed in Him with the Holy Spirit of promise, who is given as a pledge of our inheritance, with a view to the redemption of God's own possession.

Jesus said to him (Thomas), Because you have seen Me, have you believed? Blessed are they who did not see, and yet believed. —Though you have not seen Him, you love Him, and though you do not see Him now, but believe in Him, you greatly rejoice with joy inexpressible and full of glory, obtaining as the outcome of your faith the salvation of your souls.

We walk by faith, not by sight.—Do not throw away your confidence, which has a great reward.

HEB 11:1. 1 Co 15:19. 1 Co 2:9,10.—Eph 1:13,14. Jn 20:29.—
1 Pe 1:8,9. 2 Co 5,7.—Heb 10:35.

It is I; do not be afraid.

When I saw Him, I fell at His feet as a dead man. And He laid His right hand upon me, saying, Do not be afraid; I am the first and the last, and the living One; and I was dead, and behold, I am alive forevermore, and I have the keys of death and of Hades. —I, even I, am the one who wipes out your transgressions for My own sake; and I will not remember your sins.

Woe is me, for I am ruined! . . . my eyes have seen the King, the LORD of hosts. Then one of the seraphim flew to me, with a burning coal in his hand which he had taken from the altar with tongs. And he touched my mouth with it and said, Behold, this has touched your lips; and your iniquity is taken away, and your sin is forgiven.—I have wiped out your transgressions like a thick cloud, and your sins like a heavy mist. Return to Me, for I have redeemed you.

If anyone sins, we have an Advocate with the Father, Jesus Christ the righteous.

JN 6:20. Rev 1:17,18.—Is 43:25. Is 6:5–7.—Is 44:22. 1 Jn 2:1.

The Son of God appeared for this purpose, that He might destroy the works of the devil.

Our struggle is not against flesh and blood, but against the rulers, against the powers, against the world-forces of this darkness, against the spiritual forces of wickedness in the heavenly places.—Since then the children share in flesh and blood, He Himself likewise also partook of the same, that through death He might render powerless him who had the power of death, that is, the devil.—When He had disarmed the rulers and authorities, He made a public display of them, having triumphed over them through Him.—And I heard a loud voice in heaven, saying, Now the salvation, and the power, and the kingdom of our God and the authority of His Christ have come, for the accuser of our brethren has been thrown down, who accuses them before our God day and night. And they overcame him because of the blood of the Lamb and because of the word of their testimony, and they did not love their life even to death.

Thanks be to God, who gives us the victory through our Lord Jesus Christ.

1 JN 3:8. Eph 6:12.—Heb 2:14.—Col 2:15.—Rev 12:10,11.
1 Co 15:57.

Vanity of vanities! All is vanity.

We have finished our years like a sigh. As for the days of our life, they contain seventy years, or if due to strength, eighty years, yet their pride is but labor and sorrow; for soon it is gone and we fly away.

If we have only hoped in Christ in this life, we are of all men most to be pitied.—Here we do not have a lasting city, but we are seeking the city which is to come.—I, the LORD, do not change.—Our citizenship is in heaven, from which also we eagerly wait for a Savior, the Lord Jesus Christ; who will transform the body of our humble state into conformity with the body of His glory, by the exertion of the power that He has even to subject all things to Himself.—The creation was subjected to futility, not of its own will, but because of Him who subjected it, in hope.

Jesus Christ is the same yesterday and today, yes and forever. —Holy, holy, holy, is the Lord God, the Almighty, who was and who is and who is to come.

EC 1:2. Ps 90:9,10. 1 Co 15:19.—Heb 13:14.—Mal 3:6.—
Phil 3:20,21.—Ro 8:20. Heb 13:8.—Rev 4:8.

Become sober-minded as you ought, and stop sinning.

You are all sons of light and sons of day. We are not of night nor of darkness; so then let us not sleep as others do, but let us be alert and sober.

It is already the hour for you to awaken from sleep; for now salvation is nearer to us than when we believed. The night is almost gone, and the day is at hand. Let us therefore lay aside the deeds of darkness and put on the armor of light.—Therefore take up the full armor of God, that you may be able to resist in the evil day, and having done everything, to stand firm.—Cast away from you all your transgressions which you have committed, and make yourselves a new heart and a new spirit!

Therefore putting aside all filthiness and all that remains of wickedness, in humility receive the word implanted, which is able to save your souls.—Little children, abide in Him, so that when He appears, we may have confidence and not shrink away from Him in shame at His coming. If you know that He is righteous, you know that every one also who practices righteousness is born of Him.

1 CO 15:34. 1 Th 5:5,6. Ro 13:11,12.—Eph 6:13.—Eze 18:31.
Ja 1:21.—1 Jn 2:28,29.

My sheep hear My voice.

Behold, I stand at the door and knock; if any one hears My voice and opens the door, I will come in to him, and will dine with him, and he with Me.

I was asleep, but my heart was awake. A voice! My beloved was knocking: Open to me, my sister, my darling, my dove, my perfect one! I opened to my beloved, but my beloved had turned away and had gone! My heart went out to him as he spoke. I searched for him, but I did not find him; I called him, but he did not answer me.

Speak, for Thy servant is listening.—When Jesus came to the place, He looked up and said to him, Zaccheus, hurry and come down, for today I must stay at your house. And he hurried and came down, and received Him gladly.—I will hear what God the LORD will say; for He will speak peace to His people, to His godly ones; but let them not turn back to folly.

JN 10:27. Rev 3:20. Song 5:2,6. 1 Sa 3:10.—Lk 19:5,6.—Ps 85:8.

Beloved, let us love one another, for love is from God; and every one who loves is born of God and knows God.

The love of God has been poured out within our hearts through the Holy Spirit who was given to us.—You have not received a spirit of slavery leading to fear again, but you have received a spirit of adoption as sons by which we cry out, Abba! Father! The Spirit Himself bears witness with our spirit that we are children of God.—The one who believes in the Son of God has the witness in himself.

By this the love of God was manifested in us, that God has sent His only begotten Son into the world so that we might live through Him.—In Him we have redemption through His blood, the forgiveness of our trespasses, according to the riches of His grace.—That in the ages to come He might show the surpassing riches of His grace in kindness toward us in Christ Jesus.

Beloved, if God so loved us, we also ought to love one another.

1 JN 4:7. Ro 5:5.—Ro 8:15,16.—1 Jn 5:10. 1 Jn 4:9.—Eph 1:7.—
Eph 2:7. 1 Jn 4:11.

Reproach has broken my heart.

Is not this the carpenter's son?—Can any good thing come out of Nazareth?—Do we not say rightly that You are a Samaritan and have a demon?—He casts out the demons by the ruler of the demons.—We know that this man is a sinner.—He leads the multitude astray.—This fellow blasphemes.—Behold, a gluttonous man and a drunkard, a friend of tax-gatherers and sinners!

It is enough for the disciple that he become as his teacher, and the slave as his master.—For this finds favor, if for the sake of conscience toward God a man bears up under sorrows when suffering unjustly. For you have been called for this purpose, since Christ also suffered for you, leaving you an example for you to follow in His steps, who committed no sin, nor was any deceit found in His mouth; and while being reviled, He did not revile in return; while suffering, He uttered no threats, but kept entrusting Himself to Him who judges righteously.—If you are reviled for the name of Christ, you are blessed.

PS 69:20. Mt 13:55.—Jn 1:46.—Jn 8:48.—Mt 9:34.—Jn 9:24.—
Jn 7:12.—Mt 9:3.—Mt 11:19. Mt 10:25.—1 Pe 2:19,21–23.—
1 Pe 4:14.

**I want the men in every place to pray, lifting up holy hands,
without wrath and dissension.**

True worshipers shall worship the Father in spirit and truth;
for such people the Father seeks to be His worshipers. God is
spirit; and those who worship Him must worship in spirit and
truth.—Then you will call, and the LORD will answer; you will
cry, and He will say, Here I am.—Whenever you stand praying,
forgive, if you have anything against anyone.

Without faith it is impossible to please Him, for He who comes
to God must believe that He is, and that He is a rewarder of those
who seek Him.—Let him ask in faith without any doubting, for
the one who doubts is like the surf of the sea driven and tossed
by the wind. For let not that man expect that he will receive
anything from the Lord.

If I regard wickedness in my heart, the Lord will not hear.—
My little children, I am writing these things to you that you may
not sin. And if anyone sins, we have an Advocate with the Father,
Jesus Christ the righteous; and He Himself is the propitiation for
our sins.

1 TI 2:8. Jn 4:23,24.—Is 58:9.—Mk 11:25. Heb 11:6.—Ja 1:6,7.
Ps 66:18.—1 Jn 2:1,2.

My heart throbs, my strength fails me.

Hear my cry, O God; give heed to my prayer. From the end
of the earth I call to Thee, when my heart is faint; lead me to the
rock that is higher than I.

He has said to me, My grace is sufficient for you, for power is
perfected in weakness. Most gladly, therefore, I will rather boast
about my weaknesses, that the power of Christ may dwell in me
. . . for when I am weak, then I am strong.

Seeing the wind, he (Peter) became afraid, and beginning to
sink, he cried out, saying, Lord, save me! And immediately Jesus
stretched out His hand and took hold of him, and said to him, O
you of little faith, why did you doubt?—If you are slack in the day
of distress, your strength is limited.—He gives strength to the
weary, and to him who lacks might He increases power.—The
eternal God is a dwelling place, and underneath are the everlasting arms.—Strengthened with all power, according to His glorious might.

PS 38:10. Ps 61:1,2. 2 Co 12:9,10. Mt 14:30,31.—Pr 24:10.—
Is 40:29.—Deu 33:27.—Col 1:11.

The fellowship of His sufferings.

It is enough for the disciple that he become as his teacher, and the slave as his master.

He was despised and forsaken of men, a man of sorrows, and acquainted with grief; and like one from whom men hide their face, He was despised, and we did not esteem Him.—In the world you have tribulation.—You are not of the world, but I chose you out of the world, therefore the world hates you.

I looked for sympathy, but there was none.—At my first defense no one supported me, but all deserted me.

The foxes have holes, and the birds of the air have nests; but the Son of Man has nowhere to lay His head.—Here we do not have a lasting city, but we are seeking the city which is to come.

Let us lay aside every encumbrance, and the sin which so easily entangles us, and let us run with endurance the race that is set before us, fixing our eyes on Jesus, the author and perfecter of faith, who for the joy set before Him endured the cross, despising the shame, and has sat down at the right hand of the throne of God.

PHIL 3:10. Mt 10:25. Is 53:3.—Jn 16:33.—Jn 15:19. Ps 69:20.—
2 Ti 4:16. Mt 8:20.—Heb 13:14. Heb 12:1,2.

They overcame . . . because of the blood of the Lamb.

Who will bring a charge against God's elect? God is the one who justifies; who is the one who condemns? Christ Jesus is He who died.—It is the blood . . . that makes atonement.—I am the LORD. And the blood shall be a sign for you on the houses where you live; and when I see the blood I will pass over you.

There is therefore now no condemnation for those who are in Christ Jesus.

These who are clothed in the white robes, who are they, and from where have they come? These are the ones who come out of the great tribulation, and they have washed their robes and made them white in the blood of the Lamb.

To Him who loves us, and released us from our sins by His blood, and He has made us to be a kingdom, priests to His God and Father; to Him be the glory and the dominion forever and ever. Amen.

REV 12:11. Ro 8:33,34.—Lev 17:11.—Ex 12:12,13. Ro 8:1.
Rev 7:13,14. Rev 1:5,6.

He shall wipe away every tear . . . there shall no longer be any death . . . any mourning, or crying, or pain; the first things have passed away.

He will swallow up death for all time, and the Lord GOD will wipe tears away from all faces, and He will remove the reproach of His people from all the earth; for the LORD has spoken.—Your sun will set no more, neither will your moon wane; for you will have the LORD for an everlasting light, and the days of your mourning will be finished.—No resident will say, I am sick; the people who dwell there will be forgiven their iniquity.—There will no longer be heard in her the voice of weeping and the sound of crying.—Sorrow and sighing will flee away.

I will ransom them from the power of Sheol; I will redeem them from death. O Death, where are your thorns? O Sheol, where is your sting?—The last enemy that will be abolished is death. Then will come about the saying that is written, Death is swallowed up in victory.

The things which are not seen are eternal.

REV 21:4. Is 25:8.—Is 60:20.—Is 33:24.—Is 65:19.—Is 35:10.
Ho 13:14.—1 Co 15:26,54. 2 Co 4:18.

Raised us up with Him . . . in Christ Jesus.

Do not be afraid; . . . I am alive forevermore.—Father, I desire that they also whom Thou hast given Me be with Me where I am.

We are members of His body.—He is also head of the body, the church; and He is the beginning, the first-born from the dead.—In Him you have been made complete, and He is the head.

Since . . . the children share in flesh and blood, He Himself likewise also partook of the same, that through death He might render powerless him who had the power of death, that is, the devil; and might deliver those who through fear of death were subject to slavery all their lives.

For this perishable must put on the imperishable, and this mortal must put on immortality. But when this perishable will have put on the imperishable, and this mortal will have put on immortality, then will come about the saying that is written, Death is swallowed up in victory.

EPH 2:6. Rev 1:17,18.—Jn 17:24. Eph 5:30.—Col 1:18.—Col 2:10.
Heb 2:14,15. 1 Co 15:53,54.

A bond-servant of Christ Jesus.

You call Me Teacher, and Lord; and you are right; for so I am.
—If any one serves Me, let him follow Me; and where I am, there
shall My servant also be; if any one serves Me, the Father will
honor him.—Take My yoke upon you, and learn from Me, for I
am gentle and humble in heart; and you shall find rest for your
souls. For My yoke is easy, and My load is light.

Whatever things were gain to me, those things I have counted
as loss for the sake of Christ.—Having been freed from sin and
enslaved to God, you derive your benefit, resulting in sanctification, and the outcome, eternal life.

No longer do I call you slaves; for the slave does not know what
his master is doing; but I have called you friends, for all things
that I have heard from My Father I have made known to you.
—You are no longer a slave, but a son.

It was for freedom that Christ set us free; therefore keep standing firm and do not be subject again to a yoke of slavery. You
were called to freedom, brethren; only do not turn your freedom
into an opportunity for the flesh.

RO 1:1. Jn 13:13.—Jn 12:26.—Mt 11:29,30. Phil 3:7.—Ro 6:22.
Jn 15:15.—Gal 4:7. Gal 5:1,13.

I will bless the LORD who has counseled me.

His name will be called Wonderful Counselor.—Counsel is
mine and sound wisdom; I am understanding, power is mine.—
Thy word is a lamp to my feet, and a light to my path.—Trust in
the LORD with all your heart, and do not lean on your own
understanding. In all your ways acknowledge Him, and He will
make your paths straight.

I know, O LORD, that a man's way is not in himself; nor is it
in a man who walks to direct his steps.—Your ears will hear a
word behind you, This is the way, walk in it, whenever you turn
to the right or to the left.—Commit your works to the LORD, and
your plans will be established.—He knows the way I take.—
Man's steps are ordained by the LORD, how then can man understand his way?

With Thy counsel Thou wilt guide me, and afterward receive
me to glory.—Such is God, our God forever and ever; He will
guide us until death.

PS 16:7. Is 9:6.—Pr 8:14.—Ps 119:105.—Pr 3:5,6. Jer 10:23.—
Is 30:21.—Pr 16:3.—Job 23:10.—Pr 20:24. Ps 73:24.—Ps 48:14.

I am the Lord your God; walk in My statutes, and keep My ordinances, and observe them.

Like the Holy One who called you, be holy yourselves also in all your behavior.—The one who says he abides in Him ought himself to walk in the same manner as He walked. If you know that He is righteous, you know that every one also who practices righteousness is born of Him.—Circumcision is nothing, and uncircumcision is nothing, but what matters is the keeping of the commandments of God.—Whoever keeps the whole law and yet stumbles in one point, he has become guilty of all.

Not that we are adequate in ourselves to consider anything as coming from ourselves, but our adequacy is from God.—Teach me, O Lord, the way of Thy statutes.

Work out your salvation with fear and trembling; for it is God who is at work in you, both to will and to work for His good pleasure.—The God of peace . . . equip you in every good thing to do His will, working in us that which is pleasing in His sight, through Jesus Christ.

EZE 20:19. 1 Pe 1:15.—1 Jn 2:6,29.—1 Co 7:19.—Ja 2:10. 2 Co 3:5.—Ps 119:33. Phil 2:12,13.—Heb 13:20,21.

I have exalted one chosen from the people.

For assuredly He does not give help to angels, but He gives help to the seed of Abraham. Therefore, He had to be made like His brethren in all things.—On that which resembled a throne, high up, was a figure with the appearance of a man.—He who descended from heaven, even the Son of Man.—See My hands and My feet, that it is I Myself; touch Me and see, for a spirit does not have flesh and bones as you see that I have.

But emptied Himself, taking the form of a bond-servant, and being made in the likeness of men. And being found in appearance as a man, He humbled Himself by becoming obedient to the point of death, even death on a cross. Therefore also God highly exalted Him, and bestowed on Him the name which is above every name, that at the name of Jesus every knee should bow.—Wake up, and strengthen the things that remain, which were about to die; for I have not found your deeds completed in the sight of My God.

PS 89:19. Heb 2:16,17.—Eze 1:26.—Jn 3:13.—Lk 24:39. Phil 2:7–10.—Rev 3:2.

For just as the Father has life in Himself, even so He gave to the Son also to have life in Himself.

Our Savior Christ Jesus, who abolished death, and brought life and immortality to light through the gospel.—I am the resurrection, and the life.—Because I live, you shall live also.—We have become partakers of Christ.—Partakers of the Holy Spirit.—Partakers of the divine nature.—The first man, Adam, became a living soul. The last Adam became a life-giving spirit. Behold, I tell you a mystery; we shall not all sleep, but we shall all be changed, in a moment, in the twinkling of an eye, at the last trumpet; for the trumpet will sound, and the dead will be raised imperishable, and we shall be changed.

Holy, holy, holy, is the Lord God, the Almighty, who was and who is and who is to come . . . to Him who lives forever and ever. —He who is the blessed and only Sovereign, the King of kings, and Lord of lords; who alone possesses immortality.—Now to the King eternal, immortal . . . be honor and glory forever and ever. Amen.

JN 5:26. 2 TI 1:10.—Jn 11:25.—Jn 14:19.—Heb 3:14.—Heb 6:4.—
2 Pe 1:4.—1 Co 15:45,51,52. Rev 4:8,9.—1 Ti 6:15,16.—1 Ti 1:17.

Let us not become boastful.

Gideon said to them, I would request of you, that each of you give me an earring from his spoil. (For they had gold earrings, because they were Ishmaelites.) And they said, We will surely give them. So they spread out a garment, and every one of them threw an earring there from his spoil. And Gideon made it into an ephod, and placed it in his city, Ophrah, and all Israel played the harlot with it there, so that it became a snare to Gideon and his household.

Are you seeking great things for yourself? Do not seek them. —Because of the surpassing greatness of the revelations . . . to keep me from exalting myself, there was given me a thorn in the flesh.

Do nothing from selfishness or empty conceit, but with humility of mind let each of you regard one another as more important than himself.—Love . . . is not jealous; love does not brag and is not arrogant, does not act unbecomingly; it does not seek its own.

Take My yoke upon you, and learn from Me.

GAL 5:26. Judg 8:24,25,27. Jer 45:5.—2 Co 12:7. Phil 2:3.—
1 Co 13:4,5. Mt 11:29.

Wash me thoroughly from my iniquity.

I will cleanse them from all their iniquity by which they have sinned against Me, and I will pardon all their iniquities by which they have sinned against Me, and by which they have transgressed against Me.—I will sprinkle clean water on you, and you will be clean; I will cleanse you from all your filthiness and from all your idols.

Unless one is born of water and the Spirit, he cannot enter into the kingdom of God.—If the blood of goats and bulls and the ashes of a heifer sprinkling those who have been defiled, sanctify for the cleansing of the flesh, how much more will the blood of Christ, who through the eternal Spirit offered Himself without blemish to God, cleanse your conscience from dead works to serve the living God?

He saved them for the sake of His name, that He might make His power known.—Not to us, O LORD, not to us, but to Thy name give glory because of Thy lovingkindness, because of Thy truth.

PS 51:2. Jer 33:8.—Eze 36:25. Jn 3:5.—Heb 9:13,14. Ps 106:8.—
Ps 115:1.

Participation in the gospel.

For even as the body is one and yet has many members, and all the members of the body, though they are many, are one body, so also is Christ. For by one Spirit we were all baptized into one body, whether Jews or Greeks, whether slaves or free, and we were all made to drink of one Spirit.

God is faithful, through whom you were called into fellowship with His Son, Jesus Christ our Lord.—What we have seen and heard we proclaim to you also, that you also may have fellowship with us; and indeed our fellowship is with the Father, and with His Son Jesus Christ.

If we walk in the light as He Himself is in the light, we have fellowship with one another, and the blood of Jesus His Son cleanses us from all sin.—These things Jesus spoke . . . I do not ask in behalf of these alone, but for those also who believe in Me through their word; that they may all be one; even as Thou, Father, art in Me, and I in Thee, that they also may be in Us.

PHIL 1:5. 1 Co 12:12,13. 1 Co 1:9.—1 Jn 1:3. 1 Jn 1:7.—
Jn 17:1,20,21.

Pay close attention to yourself.

Everyone who competes in the games exercises self-control in all things. They then do it to receive a perishable wreath, but we an imperishable. Therefore I run in such a way, as not without aim; I box in such a way, as not beating the air; but I buffet my body and make it my slave, lest possibly, after I have preached to others, I myself should be disqualified.—Put on the full armor of God, that you may be able to stand firm against the schemes of the devil. For our struggle is not against flesh and blood, but against the rulers, against the powers, against the world-forces of this darkness, against the spiritual forces of wickedness in the heavenly places.

Those who belong to Christ Jesus have crucified the flesh with its passions and desires. If we live by the Spirit, let us also walk by the Spirit.—For all who are being led by the Spirit of God, these are sons of God.—Take pains with these things; be absorbed in them, so that your progress may be evident to all.

1 TI 4:16. 1 Co 9:25–27.—Eph 6:11,12. Gal 5:24,25.—Ro 8:14.— 1 Ti 4:15.

Jesus said to her, Mary!

Do not fear, for I have redeemed you; I have called you by name; you are Mine!—He calls his own sheep by name. . . . The sheep follow him because they know his voice.

Behold, I have inscribed you on the palms of My hands; your walls are continually before Me.

The firm foundation of God stands, having this seal, The Lord knows those who are His.—We have a great high priest who has passed through the heavens, Jesus the Son of God.

You shall take two onyx stones and engrave on them the names of the sons of Israel. . . . And Aaron shall bear their names before the LORD on his two shoulders for a memorial. And you shall make a breastpiece of judgment. . . . And you shall mount on it four rows of stones. . . . And the stones shall be according to the names of the sons of Israel. . . . And they shall be over Aaron's heart when he goes in before the LORD.

JN 20:16. Is 43:1.—Jn 10:3,4. Is 49:16. 2 Ti 2:19.—Heb 4:14. Ex 28:9,12,15,17,21,30.

Be strong in the Lord, and in the strength of His might.

My grace is sufficient for you, for power is perfected in weakness. Most gladly, therefore, I will rather boast about my weaknesses, that the power of Christ may dwell in me. Therefore I am well content with weaknesses, with insults, with distresses, with persecutions, with difficulties, for Christ's sake; for when I am weak, then I am strong.—I will come with the mighty deeds of the Lord GOD; I will make mention of Thy righteousness, Thine alone.—The gospel . . . it is the power of God for salvation.

I can do all things through Him who strengthens me.—For this purpose also I labor, striving according to His power, which mightily works within me.—We have this treasure in earthen vessels, that the surpassing greatness of the power may be of God and not from ourselves.

The joy of the LORD is your strength.—Strengthened with all power, according to His glorious might, for the attaining of all steadfastness and patience, joyously.

EPH 6:10. 2 Co 12:9,10.—Ps 71:16.—Ro 1:16. Phil 4:13.—
Col 1:29.—2 Co 4:7. Neh 8:10.—Col 1:11.

Jesus Christ our Lord.

Jesus, for it is He who will save His people from their sins.—He humbled Himself by becoming obedient to the point of death, even death on a cross. Therefore also God highly exalted Him, and bestowed on Him the name which is above every name, that at the name of Jesus every knee should bow, of those who are in heaven, and on earth, and under the earth.

Messiah . . . (He who is called Christ).—The LORD has anointed me to bring good news to the afflicted; He has sent me to bind up the brokenhearted, to proclaim liberty to captives.

The last Adam became a life-giving spirit . . . the second man is from heaven.—My Lord and my God!—You call Me Teacher, and Lord; and you are right; for so I am. If I then, the Lord and the Teacher, washed your feet, you also ought to wash one another's feet. For I gave you an example that you also should do as I did to you.

1 CO 1:9. Mt 1:21.—Phil 2:8–10. Jn 4:25.—Is 61:1. 1 Co 15:45,47.—
Jn 20:28.—Jn 13:13–15.

Peace I leave with you; My peace I give to you; not as the world gives, do I give to you.

The world is passing away, and also its lusts.—Surely every man walks about as a phantom; surely they make an uproar for nothing; he amasses riches, and does not know who will gather them.—Therefore what benefit were you then deriving from the things of which you are now ashamed? For the outcome of those things is death.

Martha, Martha, you are worried and bothered about so many things; but only a few things are necessary, really only one: for Mary has chosen the good part, which shall not be taken away from her.—I want you to be free from concern.

These things I have spoken to you, that in Me you may have peace. In the world you have tribulation, but take courage; I have overcome the world.—May the Lord of peace Himself continually grant you peace in every circumstance.—The LORD bless you, and keep you; the LORD make His face shine on you, and be gracious to you; the LORD lift up His countenance on you, and give you peace.

JN 14:27. 1 Jn 2:17.—Ps 39:6.—Ro 6:21. Lk 10:41,42.—1 Co 7:32. Jn 16:33.—2 Th 3:16.—Num 6:24–26.

The Spirit also helps our weakness.

The Helper, the Holy Spirit.—Do you not know that your body is a temple of the Holy Spirit who is in you, whom you have from God?—It is God who is at work in you.

We do not know how to pray as we should, but the Spirit Himself intercedes for us with groanings too deep for words; and He who searches the hearts knows what the mind of the Spirit is, because He intercedes for the saints according to the will of God.

He Himself knows our frame; He is mindful that we are but dust.—A bruised reed He will not break, and a dimly burning wick He will not extinguish.

The spirit is willing, but the flesh is weak.

The LORD is my shepherd, I shall not want. He makes me lie down in green pastures; He leads me beside quiet waters.

RO 8:26. Jn 14:26.—1 Co 6:19.—Phil 2:13. Ro 8:26,27. Ps 103:14.— Is 42:3. Mt 26:41. Ps 23:1,2.

**And you shall put the two stones on the shoulder pieces of the
ephod, as stones of memorial for the sons of Israel, and Aaron
shall bear their names before the LORD.**

He (Jesus) . . . because He abides forever, holds His priesthood
permanently. Hence . . . He is able to save forever those who
draw near to God through Him, since He always lives to make
intercession for them.—Him who is able to keep you from stumbling, and to make you stand in the presence of His glory blameless.

Since then we have a great high priest who has passed through
the heavens, Jesus the Son of God, let us hold fast our confession.
For we do not have a high priest who cannot sympathize with
our weaknesses, but one who has been tempted in all things as
we are, yet without sin. Let us therefore draw near with confidence to the throne of grace.

The beloved of the LORD dwell in security by Him, who shields
him all the day, and he dwells between His shoulders.

EX 28:12. Heb 7:24,25.—Jude 24. Heb 4:14–16. Deu 33:12.

The king could not sleep.

Thou hast held my eyelids open.—Who is like the LORD our
God . . . who humbles Himself to behold the things that are in
heaven and in the earth?

He does according to His will in the host of heaven and among
the inhabitants of earth.—Thy way was in the sea, and Thy paths
in the mighty waters, and Thy footprints may not be known.—
For the wrath of man shall praise Thee; with a remnant of wrath
Thou shalt gird Thyself.

The eyes of the LORD move to and fro throughout the earth
that He may strongly support those whose heart is completely
His.—We know that God causes all things to work together for
good to those who love God.

Are not two sparrows sold for a cent? And yet not one of them
will fall to the ground apart from your Father. But the very hairs
of your head are all numbered.

EST 6:1. Ps 77:4.—Ps 113:5,6. Dan 4:35.—Ps 77:19.—Ps 76:10.
2 Ch 16:9.—Ro 8:28. Mt 10:29,30.

**Do not grieve the Holy Spirit of God, by whom you were
sealed for the day of redemption.**

The love of the Spirit.—The Helper, the Holy Spirit.—In all
their affliction He was afflicted, and the angel of His presence
saved them; in His love and in His mercy He redeemed them;
and He lifted them and carried them all the days of old. But they
rebelled and grieved His Holy Spirit; therefore, He turned Himself to become their enemy.

By this we know that we abide in Him and He in us, because
He has given us of His Spirit.—Having also believed, you were
sealed in Him with the Holy Spirit of promise, who is given as
a pledge of our inheritance, with a view to the redemption of
God's own possession.—But I say, walk by the Spirit, and you will
not carry out the desire of the flesh. For the flesh sets its desire
against the Spirit, and the Spirit against the flesh; for these are
in opposition to one another, so that you may not do the things
that you please.

The Spirit also helps our weakness.

EPH 4:30. Ro 15:30.—Jn 14:26.—Is 63:9,10. 1 Jn 4:13.—
Eph 1:13,14.—Gal 5:16,17. Ro 8:26.

**I will go away and return to My place until they acknowledge
their guilt and seek My face.**

Your iniquities have made a separation between you and your
God, and your sins have hidden His face from you.—My beloved
had turned away and had gone! . . . I searched for him, but I did
not find him; I called him, but he did not answer me.—I hid My
face and was angry, and he went on turning away, in the way of
his heart. I have seen his ways, but I will heal him.—Have you
not done this to yourself, by your forsaking the LORD your God,
when He led you in the way?

He got up and came to his father. But while he was still a long
way off, his father saw him, and felt compassion for him, and ran
and embraced him, and kissed him.—I will heal their apostasy,
I will love them freely, for My anger has turned away from them.

If we confess our sins, He is faithful and righteous to forgive
us our sins and to cleanse us from all unrighteousness.

HO 5:15. Is 59:2.—Song 5:6.—Is 57:17,18.—Jer 2:17. Lk 15:20.—
Ho 14:4. 1 Jn 1:9.

How great is Thy goodness, which Thou hast stored up for those who fear Thee.

For from of old they have not heard nor perceived by ear, neither has the eye seen a God besides Thee, who acts in behalf of the one who waits for Him.—Eye has not seen and ear has not heard, and which have not entered the heart of man, all that God has prepared for those who love Him. For to us God revealed them through the Spirit.—Thou wilt make known to me the path of life; in Thy presence is fulness of joy; in Thy right hand there are pleasures forever.

How precious is Thy lovingkindness, O God! And the children of men take refuge in the shadow of Thy wings. They drink their fill of the abundance of Thy house; and Thou dost give them to drink of the river of Thy delights. For with Thee is the fountain of life; in Thy light we see light.

Godliness is profitable for all things, since it holds promise for the present life and also for the life to come.

PS 31:19. Is 64:4.—1 Co 2:9,10.—Ps 16:11. Ps 36:7–9. 1 Ti 4:8.

The Son of God, who has eyes like a flame of fire.

The heart is more deceitful than all else and is desperately sick; who can understand it? I the LORD, search the heart, I test the mind, even to give to each man according to his ways, according to the results of his deeds.—Thou hast placed our iniquities before Thee, our secret sins in the light of Thy presence.—The Lord turned and looked at Peter . . . and he went outside and wept bitterly.

Jesus, on His part, was not entrusting Himself to them, for He knew all men, and because He did not need any one to bear witness concerning man for He Himself knew what was in man. —He Himself knows our frame; He is mindful that we are but dust.—A bruised reed He will not break, and a dimly burning wick He will not extinguish.

The Lord knows those who are His.—I am the good shepherd; and I know My own. My sheep hear My voice, and I know them, and they follow Me; and I give eternal life to them; and they shall never perish, and no one shall snatch them out of My hand.

REV 2:18. Jer 17:9,10.—Ps 90:8.—Lk 22:61,62. Jn 2:24,25.—
Ps 103:14.—Is 42:3. 2 Ti 2:19.—Jn 10:14,27,28.

The great Shepherd of the sheep.

The Chief Shepherd.—I am the good shepherd; and I know My own, and My own know Me. My sheep hear My voice, and I know them, and they follow Me; and I give eternal life to them; and they shall never perish, and no one shall snatch them out of My hand.

The LORD is my shepherd, I shall not want. He makes me lie down in green pastures; He leads me beside quiet waters. He restores my soul; He guides me in the paths of righteousness for His name's sake.

All of us like sheep have gone astray, each of us has turned to his own way; but the LORD has caused the iniquity of us all to fall on Him.—I am the good shepherd; the good shepherd lays down His life for the sheep.—I will seek the lost, bring back the scattered, bind up the broken, and strengthen the sick.—You were continually straying like sheep, but now you have returned to the Shepherd and Guardian of your souls.

HEB 13:20. 1 Pe 5:4.—Jn 10:14,27,28. Ps 23:1–3. Is 53:6.—
Jn 10:11.—Eze 34:16.—1 Pe 2:25.

The city has no need of the sun or of the moon to shine upon it, for the glory of God has illumined it, and its lamp is the Lamb.

I saw on the way a light from heaven, brighter than the sun, shining all around me. And I said, Who art Thou, Lord? And the Lord said, I am Jesus whom you are persecuting.—Jesus took with Him Peter and James and John his brother, and brought them up to a high mountain by themselves. And he was transfigured before them; and His face shone like the sun, and His garments became as white as light.—No longer will you have the sun for light by day, nor for brightness will the moon give you light; but you will have the LORD for an everlasting light, and your God for your glory. Your sun will set no more, neither will your moon wane; for you will have the LORD for an everlasting light, and the days of your mourning will be finished.

The God of all grace, who called you to His eternal glory in Christ.

REV 21:23. Ac 26:13,15.—Mt 17:1,2.—Is 60:19,20. 1 Pe 5:10.

The LORD is good, a stronghold in the day of trouble, and He
knows those who take refuge in Him.

Give thanks to the LORD of hosts, for the LORD is good, for His
lovingkindness is everlasting.—God is our refuge and strength,
a very present help in trouble.—I will say to the LORD, My refuge
and my fortress, my God, in whom I trust!—Who is like you, a
people saved by the LORD, who is the shield of your help, and the
sword of your majesty!—As for God, His way is blameless; the
word of the LORD is tested; He is a shield to all who take refuge
in Him. For who is God, besides the LORD? And who is a rock,
besides our God?

If any one loves God, he is known by Him.—The firm foundation of God stands, having this seal, The Lord knows those who
are His, and, Let every one who names the name of the Lord
abstain from wickedness.—For the LORD knows the way of the
righteous, but the way of the wicked will perish.—You have
found favor in My sight, and I have known you by name.

NAH 1:7. Jer 33:11.—Ps 46:1.—Ps 91:2.—Deu 33:29.—
2 Sa 22:31,32. 1 Co 8:3.—2 Ti 2:19.—Ps 1:6.—Ex 33:17.

I want you to be free from concern.

He cares for you.—The eyes of the LORD move to and fro
throughout the earth that He may strongly support those whose
heart is completely His.

O taste and see that the LORD is good; how blessed is the man
who takes refuge in Him! The young lions do lack and suffer
hunger; but they who seek the LORD shall not be in want of any
good thing.—I say to you, do not be anxious for your life, as to
what you shall eat, or what you shall drink; nor for your body, as
to what you shall put on. Is not life more than food, and the body
than clothing? Look at the birds of the air, that they do not sow,
neither do they reap, nor gather into barns; and yet your heavenly Father feeds them. Are you not worth much more than
they?—Be anxious for nothing, but in everything by prayer and
supplication with thanksgiving let your requests be made known
to God. And the peace of God, which surpasses all comprehension, shall guard your hearts and your minds in Christ Jesus.

1 CO 7:32. 1 Pe 5:7.—2 Ch 16:9. Ps 34:8,10.—Mt 6:25.26.—
Phil 4:6,7.

We eagerly wait for a Savior.

For the grace of God has appeared, bringing salvation to all men, instructing us to deny ungodliness and worldly desires and to live sensibly, righteously and godly in the present age, looking for the blessed hope and the appearing of the glory of our great God and Savior, Christ Jesus; who gave Himself for us, that He might redeem us from every lawless deed and purify for Himself a people for His own possession, zealous for good deeds.—According to His promise we are looking for new heavens and a new earth, in which righteousness dwells. Therefore, beloved, since you look for these things, be diligent to be found by Him in peace, spotless and blameless.

Christ also having been offered once to bear the sins of many, shall appear a second time for salvation without reference to sin, to those who eagerly await him.—And it will be said in that day, Behold, this is our God for whom we have waited that He might save us. This is the LORD for whom we have waited; let us rejoice and be glad in His salvation.

PHIL 3:20. Titus 2:11–14.—2 Pe 3:13,14. Heb 9:28.—Is 25:9.

Run in such a way that you may win.

The sluggard says, There is a lion outside.—Let us also lay aside every encumbrance, and the sin which so easily entangles us, and let us run with endurance the race that is set before us, fixing our eyes on Jesus, the author and perfecter of faith.

Let us cleanse ourselves from all defilement of flesh and spirit, perfecting holiness in the fear of God.

I press on toward the goal.—I run in such a way . . . I buffet my body and make it my slave, lest possibly . . . I myself should be disqualified.

The form of this world is passing away.

According to His promise we are looking for new heavens and a new earth, in which righteousness dwells. Therefore, beloved, since you look for these things, be diligent.—Gird your minds for action, keep sober in spirit, fix your hope completely on the grace to be brought to you at the revelation of Jesus Christ.

1 CO 9:24. Pr 22:13.—Heb 12:1,2. 2 Co 7:1. Phil 3:14.—
1 Co 9:26,27. 1 Co 7:31. 2 Pe 3:13,14.—1 Pe 1:13.

For the life of the flesh is in the blood, and I have given it to you on the altar to make atonement for your souls; for it is the blood by reason of the life that makes atonement.

Behold, the Lamb of God who takes away the sin of the world! —The blood of the Lamb.—Precious blood, as of a lamb unblemished and spotless.—Without shedding of blood there is no forgiveness.—The blood of Jesus His Son cleanses us from all sin.

Through His own blood, He entered the holy place once for all, having obtained eternal redemption.—We have confidence to enter the holy place by the blood of Jesus, by a new and living way which He inaugurated for us through the veil, that is, His flesh ... let us draw near with a sincere heart in full assurance of faith.

You have been bought with a price: therefore glorify God in your body.

LEV 17:11. Jn 1:29.—Rev 7:14.—1 Pe 1:19.—Heb 9:22.—1 Jn 1:7. Heb 9:12.—Heb 10:19,20,22. 1 Co 6:20.

O that I had wings like a dove! I would fly away and be at rest.

It came about when the sun came up that God appointed a scorching east wind, and the sun beat down on Jonah's head so that he became faint and begged with all his soul to die, saying, Death is better to me than life.

Job said: Why is light given to him who suffers, and life to the bitter of soul; who long for death, but there is none, and dig for it more than for hidden treasures?—Many are the afflictions of the righteous; but the LORD delivers him out of them all.

Now My soul has become troubled; and what shall I say, Father, save Me from this hour?—He had to be made like His brethren in all things, that He might become a merciful and faithful high priest in things pertaining to God, to make propitiation for the sins of the people. For since He Himself was tempted in that which He has suffered, He is able to come to the aid of those who are tempted.

PS 55:6. Jon 4:8. Job 3:2,20,21.—Ps 34:19. Jn 12:27.—Heb 2:17,18.

Let us therefore be diligent to enter that rest.

Enter by the narrow gate; for the gate is wide, and the way is broad that leads to destruction . . . the gate is small, and the way is narrow that leads to life, and few are those who find it.—The kingdom of heaven suffers violence, and violent men take it by force.—Do not work for the food which perishes, but for the food which endures to eternal life, which the Son of Man shall give to you.—Be all the more diligent to make certain about His calling and choosing you . . . the entrace into the eternal kingdom of our Lord and Savior Jesus Christ will be abundantly supplied to you. —Run in such a way that you may win. And everyone who competes in the games exercises self-control in all things. They then do it to receive a perishable wreath, but we an imperishable.

For the one who has entered His rest has himself also rested from his works, as God did from His.—You will have the LORD for an everlasting light, and your God for your glory.

HEB 4:11. Mt 7:13,14.—Mt 11:12.—Jn 6:27.—2 Pe 1:10,11.—
1 Co 9:24,25. Heb 4:10.—Is 60:19.

Thou hearest Me always.

Jesus raised His eyes, and said, Father, I thank Thee that Thou heardest me.—Father, glorify Thy name. There came therefore a voice out of heaven: I have both glorified it, and will glorify it again.—I have come . . . to do Thy will, O God.—Not My will, but Thine be done.

As He is, so also are we in this world.—This is the confidence which we have before Him, that, if we ask anything according to His will, He hears us.

Whatever we ask we receive from Him, because we keep His commandments and do the things that are pleasing in His sight.

Without faith it is impossible to please Him, for he who comes to God must believe that He is, and that He is a rewarder of those who seek Him.

He always lives to make intercession for them.—We have an Advocate with the Father, Jesus Christ the righteous.

JN 11:42. Jn 11:41.—Jn 12:28.—Heb 10:7.—Lk 22:42. 1 Jn 4:17.—
1 Jn 5:14. 1 Jn 3:22. Heb 11:6. Heb 7:25.—1 Jn 2:1.

Your name shall . . . be . . . Israel; for you have striven with God and with me and have prevailed.

In his maturity he contended with God. Yes, he wrestled with the angel and prevailed; he wept and sought His favor.—With respect to the promise of God, (Abraham) did not waver in unbelief, but grew strong in faith, giving glory to God.

Have faith in God. Truly I say to you, whoever says to this mountain, Be taken up and cast into the sea, and does not doubt in his heart, but believes that what he says is going to happen; it shall be granted him. Therefore I say to you, all things for which you pray and ask, believe that you have received them, and they shall be granted you.—If You can! All things are possible to him who believes.—Blessed is she who believed that there would be a fulfillment of what had been spoken to her by the Lord.

Lord, Increase our faith!

GEN 32:28. Ho 12:3,4.—Ro 4:20. Mk 11:22–24.—Mk 9:23.—
Lk 1:45. Lk 17:5.

Little children, abide in Him.

One who doubts is like the surf of the sea driven and tossed by the wind. For let not that man expect that he will receive anything from the Lord, being a double-minded man, unstable in all his ways.

I am amazed that you are so quickly deserting Him who called you by the grace of Christ, for a different gospel; which is really not another. . . . But even though we, or an angel from heaven, should preach to you a gospel contrary to that which we have preached to you, let him be accursed.

You have been severed from Christ, you who are seeking to be justified by law; you have fallen from grace. You were running well; who hindered you?

As the branch cannot bear fruit of itself, unless it abides in the vine, so neither can you, unless you abide in Me. If you abide in Me, and My words abide in you, ask whatever you wish, and it shall be done for you.—The promises of God, in Him they are yes; wherefore also by Him is our Amen to the glory of God through us.

1 JN 2:28. Ja 1:6–8. Gal 1:6–8. Gal 5:4,7. Jn 15:4,7.—2 Co 1:20.

The fruit of the Spirit is ... patience, kindness.

The LORD, the LORD God, compassionate and gracious, slow to anger, and abounding in lovingkindness and truth.

Walk in a manner worthy of the calling with which you have been called, with all humility and gentleness, with patience, showing forbearance to one another in love.—Be kind to one another, tender-hearted, forgiving each other, just as God in Christ also has forgiven you.—The wisdom from above is first pure, then peaceable, gentle, reasonable, full of mercy and good fruits, unwavering, without hypocrisy.—Love is patient, love is kind.

In due time we shall reap if we do not grow weary.—Be patient, therefore, brethren, until the coming of the Lord. Behold, the farmer waits for the precious produce of the soil, being patient about it, until it gets the early and late rains. You too be patient; strengthen your hearts, for the coming of the Lord is at hand.

GAL 5:22. Ex 34:6. Eph 4:1,2.—Eph 4:32.—Ja 3:17.—1 Co 13:4.
Gal 6:9.—Ja 5:7,8.

Immanuel ... God with us.

Will God indeed dwell with mankind on the earth? Behold, heaven and the highest heaven cannot contain Thee.—The Word became flesh, and dwelt among us, and we beheld His glory, glory as of the only begotten from the Father, full of grace and truth.—Great is the mystery of godliness: He who was revealed in the flesh.

God ... in these last days has spoken to us in His Son, whom He appointed heir of all things, through whom also He made the world.

The first day of the week, and when the doors were shut where the disciples were ... Jesus came and stood in their midst.... The disciples therefore rejoiced when they saw the Lord. ... After eight days again His disciples were inside, and Thomas with them. ... Then He (Jesus) said to Thomas, Reach here your finger, and see My hands; and reach here your hand, and put it into My side; and be not unbelieving, but believing. Thomas answered and said to Him, My Lord and my God!—A son will be given to us; ... His name will be called ... Mighty God, Eternal Father.

MT 1:23. 2 Ch 6:18—Jn 1:14.—1 Ti 3:16. Heb 1:2.
Jn 20:19,20,26–28.—Is 9:6.

Eat it ... with your loins girded ... you shall eat it in haste— it is the LORD'S Passover.

Arise and go, for this is no place of rest.—Here we do not have a lasting city, but we are seeking the city which is to come.— There remains therefore a Sabbath rest for the people of God.

Be dressed in readiness, and keep your lamps alight. And be like men who are waiting for their master when he returns from the wedding feast, so that they may immediately open the door to him when he comes and knocks. Blessed are those slaves whom the master shall find on the alert when he comes.—Gird your minds for action, keep sober in spirit, fix your hope completely on the grace to be brought to you at the revelation of Jesus Christ.—One thing I do: forgetting what lies behind ... I press on toward the goal for the prize of the upward call of God in Christ Jesus. Let us therefore, as many as are perfect, have this attitude.

EX 12:11. Mic 2:10.—Heb 13:14.—Heb 4:9. Lk 12:35–37.—
1 Pe 1:13.—Phil 3:13–15.

The LORD is the portion of my inheritance and my cup.

Heirs of God and fellow-heirs with Christ.—All things belong to you.—My beloved is mine.—The Son of God ... loved me, and delivered Himself up for me.

The LORD said to Aaron, You shall have no inheritance in their land, now own any portion among them; I am your portion and your inheritance among the sons of Israel.

Whom have I in heaven but Thee? And besides Thee, I desire nothing on earth. My flesh and my heart may fail; but God is the strength of my heart and my portion forever.

Though I walk through the valley of the shadow of death, I fear no evil; for Thou art with me; Thy rod and Thy staff, they comfort me.—I know whom I have believed and I am convinced that He is able to guard what I have entrusted to Him until that day.

O GOD, Thou art my God; I shall seek Thee earnestly; my soul thirsts for Thee, my flesh yearns for Thee, in a dry and weary land where there is no water.

PS 16:5. Ro 8:17.—1 Co 3:21.—Song 2:16.—Gal 2:20. Num 18:20.
Ps 73:25,26. Ps 23:4.—2 Ti 1:12. Ps 63:1.

Be on the alert then, for you do not know the day nor the hour.

Be on guard, that your hearts may not be weighted down with dissipation and drunkenness and the worries of life, and that day come on you suddenly like a trap; for it will come upon all those who dwell on the face of all the earth. But keep on the alert at all times, praying in order that you may have strength to escape all these things that are about to take place, and to stand before the Son of Man.

The day of the Lord will come just like a thief in the night. While they are saying, Peace and safety! then destruction will come upon them suddenly like birth pangs upon a woman with child; and they shall not escape. But you, brethren, are not in darkness, that the day should overtake you like a thief; for you are all sons of light and sons of day. We are not of night nor of darkness; so then let us not sleep as others do, but let us be alert and sober.

MT 25:13. Lk 21:34–36. 1 Th 5:2–6.

I am God Almighty; walk before Me, and be blameless.

Not that I have already obtained it, or have already become perfect. . . . Brethren, I do not regard myself as having laid hold of it yet; but one thing I do: forgetting what lies behind and reaching forward to what lies ahead, I press on toward the goal for the prize of the upward call of God in Christ Jesus.

Enoch walked with God; and he was not, for God took him.

Grow in the grace and knowledge of our Lord and Savior Jesus Christ.—We all, with unveiled face beholding as in a mirror the glory of the Lord, are being transformed into the same image from glory to glory, just as from the Lord, the Spirit.

These things Jesus spoke . . . I do not ask Thee to take them out of the world, but to keep them from the evil one. I in them, and Thou in Me, that they may be perfected.

GEN 17:1. Phil 3:12–14. Gen 5:24. 2 Pe 3:18.—2 Co 3:18.
Jn 17:1,15,23.

**The latter glory of this house will be greater than the former,
. . . and in this place I shall give peace.**

The house that is to be built for the LORD shall be exceedingly magnificent, famous and glorious throughout all lands.—The glory of the LORD filled the LORD's house.

Destroy this temple, and in three days I will raise it up. He was speaking of the temple of His body.—Indeed what had glory, in this case has no glory on account of the glory that surpasses it.— The Word became flesh, and dwelt among us, and we beheld His glory, glory as of the only begotten from the Father, full of grace and truth.—God . . . in these last days has spoken to us in His Son, whom He appointed heir of all things, through whom also He made the world.

Glory to God in the highest, and on earth peace among men with whom He is pleased.—Prince of Peace.—He Himself is our peace.—The peace of God, which surpasses all comprehension, shall guard your hearts and your minds in Christ Jesus.

HAG 2:9. 1 Ch 22:5.—2 Ch 7:2. Jn 2:19,21.—2 Co 3:10.—Jn 1:14.—
Heb 1:1,2. Lk 2:14.—Is 9:6.—Eph 2:14.—Phil 4:7.

Put on the armor of light.

Put on the Lord Jesus Christ.—That I may gain Christ, and may be found in Him, not having a righteousness of my own derived from the Law, but that which is through faith in Christ, the righteousness which comes from God on the basis of faith.— The righteousness of God through faith in Jesus Christ for all those who believe.

He has wrapped me with a robe of righteousness.—I will come with the mighty deeds of the Lord GOD; I will make mention of Thy righteousness, Thine alone.

You were formerly darkness, but now you are light in the Lord; walk as children of light. . . . Do not participate in the unfruitful deeds of darkness, but instead even expose them. All things become visible when they are exposed by the light, for everything that becomes visible is light. . . . Awake, sleeper, and arise from the dead, and Christ will shine on you. Therefore be careful how you walk.

RO 13:12. Ro 13:14.—Phil 3:8,9.—Ro 3:22. Is 61:10.—Ps 71:16.
Eph 5:8,11,13–15.

**When you do all the things which are commanded you, say,
We are unworthy slaves.**

Where then is boasting? It is excluded. By what kind of law?
Of works? No, but by a law of faith.—What do you have that you
did not receive? But if you did receive it, why do you boast as if
you had not received it?—For by grace you have been saved
through faith; and that not of yourselves, it is the gift of God; not
as a result of works, that no one should boast. For we are His
workmanship, created in Christ Jesus for good works, which God
prepared beforehand, that we should walk in them.

By the grace of God I am what I am, and His grace toward me
did not prove vain; but I labored even more than all of them, yet
not I, but the grace of God with me.—For from Him and through
Him and to Him are all things.—For all things come from Thee,
and from Thy hand we have given Thee.

Do not enter into judgment with Thy servant, for in Thy sight
no man living is righteous.

LK 17:10. Ro 3:27.—1 Co 4:7.—Eph 2:8–10. 1 Co 15:10.—
Ro 11:36.—1 Ch 29:14. Ps 143:2.

**He Himself knows our frame; He is mindful that we are but
dust.**

The Lord God formed man of dust from the ground, and
breathed into his nostrils the breath of life; and man became a
living being.

I will give thanks to Thee, for I am fearfully and wonderfully
made; wonderful are Thy works, and my soul knows it very well.
My frame was not hidden from Thee, when I was made in secret,
and skillfully wrought in the depths of the earth. Thine eyes have
seen my unformed substance; and in Thy book they were all
written, the days that were ordained for me, when as yet there
was not one of them.

Do we not all have one father? Has not one God created us?
—In Him we live and move and exist.—Just as a father has compassion on his children, so the Lord has compassion on those
who fear Him.

He, being compassionate, forgave their iniquity, and did not
destroy them; and often He restrained His anger, and did not
arouse all His wrath. Thus He remembered that they were but
flesh, a wind that passes and does not return.

PS 103:14. Gen 2:7. Ps 139:14–16. Mal 2:10.—Ac 17:28.—Ps 103:13.
Ps 78:38,39.

He will be quiet in His love.

The Lord did not set His love on you nor choose you because you were more in number than any of the peoples, for you were the fewest of all peoples, but because the Lord loved you.—We love, because He first loved us.—He has now reconciled you in His fleshly body through death, in order to present you before Him holy and blameless and beyond reproach.

In this is love, not that we loved God, but that He loved us and sent His Son to be the propitiation for our sins.—God demonstrates His own love toward us, in that while we were yet sinners, Christ died for us.

Behold, a voice out of the heavens, saying, This is My beloved Son, in whom I am well pleased.—For this reason the Father loves Me, because I lay down My life that I may take it again.—His Son . . . He is the radiance of His glory and the exact representation of His nature, and upholds all things by the word of His power. When He had made purification of sins, He sat down at the right hand of the Majesty on high.

ZEP 3:17. Deu 7:7,8.—1 Jn 4:19.—Col 1:22. 1 Jn 4:10.—Ro 5:8.
Mt 3:17.—Jn 10:17.—Heb 1:2,3.

A new and living way.

Cain went out from the presence of the Lord.—Your iniquities have made a separation between you and your God, and your sins have hidden His face from you.—Sanctification without which no one will see the Lord.

I am the way, and the truth, and the life; no one comes to the Father, but through Me.—Our Savior Christ Jesus, who abolished death, and brought life and immortality to light through the gospel.

The way into the holy place has not yet been disclosed; while the outer tabernacle is still standing.—He Himself is our peace, who made both groups into one, and broke down the barrier of the dividing wall.—The veil of the temple was torn in two from top to bottom.

The gate is small, and the way is narrow that leads to life, and few are those who find it.—Thou wilt make known to me the path of life; in Thy presence is fulness of joy; in Thy right hand there are pleasures forever.

HEB 10:20. Gen 4:16.—Is 59:2.—Heb 12:14. Jn 14:6.—2 Ti 1:10.
Heb 9:8.—Eph 2:14.—Mt 27:51. Mt 7:14.—Ps 16:11.

(You) ought to pray and not to lose heart.

Suppose one of you shall have a friend, and shall go to him at midnight, and say to him, Friend, lend me three loaves; for a friend of mine has come to me from a journey, and I have nothing to set before him; and from inside he shall answer and say, Do not bother me; the door has already been shut and my children and I are in bed; I cannot get up and give you anything. I tell you, even though he will not get up and give him anything because he is his friend, yet because of his persistence he will get up and give him as much as he needs.—With all prayer and petition pray at all times in the Spirit, and with this in view, be on the alert with all perseverance and petition for all the saints.

I will not let you go unless you bless me. . . . You have striven with God and with me and have prevailed.—Devote yourselves to prayer, keeping alert in it with an attitude of thanksgiving.

(Jesus) went off to the mountain to pray, and He spent the whole night in prayer to God.

LK 18:1. Lk 11:5–8.—Eph 6:18. Gen 32:26,28.—Col 4:2. Lk 6:12.

Forgive all my sins.

Come now, and let us reason together, says the LORD, though your sins are as scarlet, they will be as white as snow; though they are red like crimson, they will be like wool.

Take courage, My son, your sins are forgiven.—I, even I, am the one who wipes out your transgressions for My own sake; and I will not remember your sins.

The Son of Man has authority on earth to forgive sins.—In Him we have redemption through His blood, the forgiveness of our trespasses, according to the riches of His grace.—He saved us, not on the basis of deeds which we have done in righteousness, but according to His mercy, by the washing of regeneration and renewing by the Holy Spirit, whom He poured out upon us richly through Jesus Christ our Savior.—Having forgiven us all our transgressions, having cancelled out the certificate of debt consisting of decrees against us and which was hostile to us; and He has taken it out of the way, having nailed it to the cross.

Bless the LORD, O my soul . . . who pardons all your iniquities.

PS 25:18. Is 1:18. Mt 9:2.—Is 43:25. Mt 9:6.—Eph 1:7.—
Titus 3:5,6.—Col 2:13,14. Ps 103:2,3.

The LORD caused all that he did to prosper in his hand.

How blessed is everyone who fears the LORD, who walks in His ways. When you shall eat of the fruit of your hands, you will be happy and it will be well with you.—Trust in the LORD, and do good; dwell in the land and cultivate faithfulness. Delight yourself in the LORD; and He will give you the desires of your heart. —Do not tremble or be dismayed, for the LORD your God is with you wherever you go.

Seek first His kingdom and His righteousness; and all these things shall be added to you.

As long as he sought the LORD, God prospered him.—Beware lest you forget the LORD your God by not keeping His commandments and His ordinances and His statutes which I am commanding you today. Otherwise, you may say in your heart, My power and the strength of my hand made me this wealth.

Is not the LORD your God with you? And has He not given you rest on every side?

GEN 39:3. Ps 128:1,2.—Ps 37:3,4.—Jos 1:9. Mt 6:33. 2 Ch 26:5.—
Deu 8:11,17. 1 Ch 22:18.

Why are you reasoning about these things in your hearts?

Without becoming weak in faith (Abraham) contemplated his own body, now as good as dead since he was about a hundred years old, and the deadness of Sarah's womb; yet, with respect to the promise of God, he did not waver in unbelief, but grew strong in faith, giving glory to God.

Which is easier, to say to the paralytic, Your sins are forgiven; or to say, Arise, and take up your pallet and walk?—If You can! All things are possible to him who believes.

All authority has been given to Me in heaven and on earth.— Why are you so timid? How is it that you have no faith?—Look at the birds of the air . . . your heavenly Father feeds them. Are you not worth much more than they?—Why do you discuss among yourselves because you have no bread? Do you not . . . remember the five loaves of the five thousand?

My God shall supply all your needs according to His riches in glory in Christ Jesus.

MK 2:8. Ro 4:19,20. Mk 2:9.—Mk 9:23. Mt 28:18.—Mk 4:40.—
Mt 6:26.—Mt 16:8,9. Phil 4:19.

Never did a man speak the way this man speaks.

Thou art fairer than the sons of men; grace is poured upon Thy lips; therefore God has blessed Thee forever.—The Lord GOD has given Me the tongue of disciples, that I may know how to sustain the weary one with a word.—His mouth is full of sweetness. And he is wholly desirable. This is my beloved and this is my friend.

All were speaking well of Him, and wondering at the gracious words which were falling from His lips.—He was teaching them as one having authority, and not as their scribes.

Let the word of Christ richly dwell within you; with all wisdom.—The sword of the Spirit, which is the word of God.—The word of God is living and active and sharper than any two-edged sword.—The weapons of our warfare are not of the flesh, but divinely powerful for the destruction of fortresses . . . destroying speculations and every lofty thing raised up against the knowledge of God, and we are taking every thought captive to the obedience of Christ.

JN 7:46. Ps 45:2.—Is 50:4.—Song 5:16. Lk 4:22.—Mt 7:29.
Col 3:16.—Eph 6:17.—Heb 4:12.—2 Co 10:4,5.

The triumphing of the wicked is short.

You shall bruise him on the heel.—This hour and the power of darkness are yours.—Since then the children share in flesh and blood, He Himself likewise also partook of the same, that through death He might render powerless him who had the power of death, that is, the devil.—When He had disarmed the rulers and authorities, He made a public display of them, having triumphed over them through Him.

Be of sober spirit, be on the alert. Your adversary, the devil, prowls about like a roaring lion, seeking someone to devour. But resist him, firm in your faith.—Resist the devil and he will flee from you.

The wicked plots against the righteous, and gnashes at him with his teeth. The LORD laughs at him; for He sees his day is coming.—The God of peace will soon crush Satan under your feet.—The devil . . . was thrown into the lake of fire and brimstone . . . and will be tormented day and night forever and ever.

JOB 20:5. Gen 3:15.—Lk 22:53.—Heb 2:14.—Col 2:15. 1 Pe 5:8,9.—
Ja 4:7. Ps 37:12,13.—Ro 16:20.—Rev 20:10.

The younger son gathered everything together and went on a journey into a distant country, and there he squandered his estate with loose living.

And such were some of you; but you were washed, but you were sanctified, but you were justified in the name of the Lord Jesus Christ, and in the Spirit of our God.—We too all formerly lived in the lusts of our flesh, indulging the desires of the flesh and of the mind, and were by nature children of wrath, even as the rest. But God, being rich in mercy, because of His great love with which He loved us, even when we were dead in our transgressions, made us alive together with Christ (by grace you have been saved), and raised us up with Him, and seated us with Him in the heavenly places, in Christ Jesus.

In this is love, not that we loved God, but that He loved us and sent His Son to be the propitiation for our sins.

God demonstrates His own love toward us, in that while we were yet sinners, Christ died for us. For if while we were enemies, we were reconciled to God through the death of His Son, much more, having been reconciled, we shall be saved by His life.

LK 15:13. 1 Co 6:11.—Eph 2:3–6. 1 Jn 4:10. Ro 5:8,10.

As the Lord forgave you, so also should you.

A certain money-lender had two debtors: one owed five hundred denarii, and the other fifty. When they were unable to repay, he graciously forgave them both.—I forgave you all that debt. . . . Should you not also have had mercy on your fellow-slave, even as I had mercy on you?

Whenever you stand praying, forgive, if you have anything against anyone; so that your Father also who is in heaven may forgive you your transgressions.—Chosen of God, holy and beloved, put on a heart of compassion, kindness, humility, gentleness and patience; bearing with one another, and forgiving each other, whoever has a complaint against any one.

How often shall my brother sin against me and I forgive him? Up to seven times? Jesus said to him, I do not say to you, up to seven times, but up to seventy times seven.

Love . . . is the perfect bond of unity.

COL 3:13. Lk 7:41,42.—Mt 18:32,33. Mk 11:25.—Col 3:12,13.
Mt 18:21,22. Col 3:14.

He got up and came to his father. But while he was still a long way off, his father saw him ... and ran and embraced him, and kissed him.

The LORD is compassionate and gracious, slow to anger and abounding in lovingkindness. He will not always strive with us; nor will He keep His anger forever. He has not dealt with us according to our sins, nor rewarded us according to our iniquities. For as high as the heavens are above the earth, so great is His lovingkindness toward those who fear Him. As far as the east is from the west, so far has He removed our transgressions from us. Just as a father has compassion on his children, so the LORD has compassion on those who fear Him.

You have not received a spirit of slavery leading to fear again, but you have received a spirit of adoption as sons by which we cry out, Abba! Father! The Spirit Himself bears witness with our spirit that we are children of God.—Now in Christ Jesus you who formerly were far off have been brought near by the blood of Christ. So then you are no longer strangers and aliens, but you are fellow-citizens with the saints, and are of God's household.

LK 15:20. Ps 103:8–13. Ro 8:15,16.—Eph 2:13,19.

Behold, I am making all things new.

Unless one is born again, he cannot see the kingdom of God. —If any man is in Christ, he is a new creature; the old things passed away; behold, new things have come.

I will give you a new heart and put a new spirit within you; and I will remove the heart of stone from your flesh and give you a heart of flesh.—Clean out the old leaven, that you may be a new lump.—The new self, which in the likeness of God has been created in righteousness and holiness of the truth.

You will be called by a new name, which the mouth of the LORD will designate.

Behold, I create new heavens and a new earth; and the former things shall not be remembered or come to mind.—Since all these things are to be destroyed in this way, what sort of people ought you to be in holy conduct and godliness.

REV 21:5. Jn 3:3.—2 Co 5:17. Eze 36:26.—1 Co 5:7.—Eph 4:24. Is 62:2. Is 65:17.—2 Pe 3:11.

Everything that can stand the fire, you shall pass through the fire, and it shall be clean.

The LORD your God is testing you to find out if you love the LORD your God with all your heart and with all your soul.—He will sit as a smelter and purifier of silver, and He will purify the sons of Levi and refine them like gold and silver, so that they may present to the LORD offerings in righteousness.—Each man's work will become evident; for the day will show it, because it is to be revealed with fire; and the fire itself will test the quality of each man's work.

I will also turn My hand against you, and will smelt away your dross . . . and remove all your alloy.—I will refine them and assay them.

Thou hast tried us, O God; Thou hast refined us as silver is refined. . . . We went through fire and through water; yet Thou didst bring us out into a place of abundance.

When you walk through the fire, you will not be scorched, nor will the flame burn you.

NUM 31:23. Deu 13:3.—Mal 3:3.—1 Co 3:13. Is 1:25.—Jer 9:7.
Ps 66:10,12. Is 43:2.

We might die to sin and live to righteousness.

In reference to your former manner of life, you lay aside the old self, which is being corrupted in accordance with the lusts of deceit, and . . . be renewed in the spirit of your mind, and put on the new self, which in the likeness of God has been created in righteousness and holiness of the truth.

You have died and your life is hidden with Christ in God.—As Christ was raised from the dead through the glory of the Father, so we too might walk in newness of life. Knowing this, that our old self was crucified with Him, that our body of sin might be done away with, that we should no longer be slaves to sin; for he who has died is freed from sin. Consider yourselves to be dead to sin, but alive to God in Christ Jesus. Therefore do not let sin reign in your mortal body that you should obey its lusts . . . but present . . . your members as instruments of righteousness to God.

1 PE 2:24. Eph 4:22–24. Col 3:3.—Ro 6:4,6,7,11–13.

Abide in Me, and I in you.

I have been crucified with Christ; and it is no longer I who live, but Christ lives in me; and the life which I now live in the flesh I live by faith in the Son of God, who loved me, and delivered Himself up for me.

I know that nothing good dwells in me, that is, in my flesh; for the wishing is present in me, but the doing of the good is not. Wretched man that I am! Who will set me free from the body of this death? Thanks be to God through Jesus Christ our Lord!— If Christ is in you, though the body is dead because of sin, yet the spirit is alive because of righteousness.—If you continue in the faith firmly established and steadfast, and not moved away from the hope of the gospel that you have heard.

Little children, abide in Him, so that when He appears, we may have confidence and not shrink away from Him in shame at His coming.—The one who says he abides in Him ought himself to walk in the same manner as He walked.

JN 15:4. Gal 2:20. Ro 7:18,24,25.—Ro 8:10.—Col 1:23. 1 Jn 2:28.—
1 Jn 2:6.

Do you believe in the Son of Man?

Who is He, Lord, that I may believe in Him?

He is the radiance of His glory and the exact representation of His nature.—He who is the blessed and only Sovereign, the King of kings and the Lord of lords; who alone possesses immortality and dwells in unapproachable light; whom no man has seen or can see. To Him be honor and eternal dominion! Amen.—I am the Alpha and the Omega, says the Lord God, who is and who was and who is to come, the Almighty.

Lord, I believe.—I know whom I have believed and I am convinced that He is able to guard what I have entrusted to Him until that day.

Behold I lay in Zion a choice stone, a precious corner stone, and he who believes in Him shall not be disappointed. This precious value, then, is for you who believe.

JN 9:35. Jn 9:36. Heb 1:3.—1 Ti 6:15,16.—Rev 1:8. Jn 9:38.—
2 Ti 1:12. 1 Pe 2:6,7.

Just as the sufferings of Christ are ours in abundance, so also our comfort is abundant through Christ.

The fellowship of His sufferings.—To the degree that you share the sufferings of Christ, keep on rejoicing; so that also at the revelation of His glory, you may rejoice with exultation.—If we died with Him, we shall also live with Him.—If children, heirs also, heirs of God and fellow-heirs with Christ, if indeed we suffer with Him in order that we may also be glorified with Him.

God, desiring even more to show to the heirs of the promise the unchangeableness of His purpose, interposed with an oath, in order that by two unchangeable things, in which it is impossible for God to lie, we may have strong encouragement, we who have fled for refuge in laying hold of the hope set before us.— Our Lord Jesus Christ Himself and God our Father, who has loved us and given us eternal comfort and good hope by grace, comfort and strengthen your hearts in every good work and word.

2 CO 1:5. Phil 3:10.—1 Pe 4:13.—2 Ti 2:11.—Ro 8:17. Heb 6:17,18.—2 Th 2:16,17.

Martha, Martha, you are worried and bothered about so many things.

Consider the ravens, for they neither sow nor reap. . . . Consider the lilies, how they grow; they neither toil nor spin. . . . Do not seek what you shall eat, and what you shall drink, and do not keep worrying. . . . Your Father knows that you need these things.

If we have food and covering, with these we shall be content. But those who want to get rich fall into temptation and a snare and many foolish and harmful desires which plunge men into ruin and destruction. For the love of money is a root of all sorts of evil, and some by longing for it have wandered away from the faith, and pierced themselves with many a pang.

The worries of the world, and the deceitfulness of riches, and the desires for other things enter in and choke the word, and it becomes unfruitful.

Let us also lay aside every encumbrance, and the sin which so easily entangles us, and let us run with endurance the race that is set before us.

LK 10:41. Lk 12:24,27,29,30. 1 Ti 6:8–10. Mk 4:19. Heb 12:1.

The secret things belong to the LORD our God, but the things revealed belong to us.

O LORD, my heart is not proud, nor my eyes haughty; nor do I involve myself in great matters, or in things too difficult for me. Surely I have composed and quieted my soul; like a weaned child rests against his mother, my soul is like a weaned child within me.

The secret of the LORD is for those who fear Him, and He will make them know His covenant.—There is a God in heaven who reveals mysteries.—Behold, these are the fringes of His ways; and how faint a word we hear of Him!

No longer do I call you slaves; for the slave does not know what his master is doing; but I have called you friends, for all things that I have heard from My Father I have made known to you. —If you love Me, you will keep My commandments. And I will ask the Father, and He will give you another Helper, that He may be with you forever; that is the Spirit of truth.

DEU 29:29. Ps 131:1,2. Ps 25:14.—Dan 2:28.—Job 26:14.
Jn 15:15.—Jn 14:15–17.

The Spirit . . . intercedes for the saints according to the will of God.

If you shall ask the Father for anything, He will give it to you in My name. Until now you have asked for nothing in My name; ask, and you will receive, that your joy may be made full.—With all prayer and petition pray at all times in the Spirit.

This is the confidence which we have before Him, that, if we ask anything according to His will, He hears us. And if we know that He hears us in whatever we ask, we know that we have the requests which we have asked from Him.—This is the will of God, your sanctification.

God has . . . called us for the purpose of . . . sanctification . . . the God who gives His Holy Spirit to you.

Rejoice always; pray without ceasing; in everything give thanks; for this is God's will for you in Christ Jesus. Do not quench the Spirit.

RO 8:27. Jn 16:23,24.—Eph 6:18. 1 Jn 5:14,15.—1 Th 4:3.
1 Th 4:7,8. 1 Th 5:16–19.

Be careful how you walk, not as unwise men, but as wise, making the most of your time, because the days are evil.

Be very careful to observe the commandment and the law . . . to love the LORD your God and walk in all His ways and keep His commandments and hold fast to Him and serve Him with all your heart and with all your soul.—Conduct yourselves with wisdom toward outsiders, making the most of the opportunity. Let your speech always be with grace, seasoned, as it were, with salt, so that you may know how you should respond to each person.—Abstain from every form of evil.

Now while the bridegroom was delaying, they all got drowsy and began to sleep. But at midnight there was a shout, Behold, the bridegroom! Come out to meet him. Be on the alert then, for you do not know the day nor the hour.

Brethren, be all the more diligent to make certain about His calling and choosing you; for as long as you practice these things, you will never stumble.—Blessed are those slaves whom the master shall find on the alert when he comes.

EPH 5:15,16. Jos 22:5.—Col 4:5,6.—1 Th 5:22. Mt 25:5,6,13.
2 Pe 1:10.—Lk 12:37.

Hold fast what you have, in order that no one take your crown.

If I only touch His garment, I shall get well.—Lord, if You are willing, You can make me clean. . . . I am willing; be cleansed.— Faith as a mustard seed.

Do not throw away your confidence, which has a great reward. —Work out your salvation with fear and trembling; for it is God who is at work in you, both to will and to work for His good pleasure.

First the blade, then the head, then the mature grain in the head.—So let us know, let us press on to know the LORD.—The kingdom of heaven suffers violence, and violent men take it by force.—Run in such a way that you may win.

I have fought the good fight, I have finished the course, I have kept the faith; in the future there is laid up for me the crown of righteousness, which the Lord, the righteous Judge, will award to me on that day.

REV 3:11. Mt 9:21.—Mt 8:2,3.—Mt 17:20. Heb 10:35.—Phil 2:12,13.
Mk 4:28.—Ho 6:3.—Mt 11:12.—1 Co 9:24. 2 Ti 4:7,8.

In everything by prayer and supplication with thanksgiving let your requests be made known to God.

I love the LORD, because He hears my voice and my supplications. Because He has inclined His ear to me, therefore I shall call upon Him as long as I live.

When you are praying, do not use meaningless repetition, as the Gentiles do, for they suppose that they will be heard for their many words.—The Spirit also helps our weakness; for we do not know how to pray as we should, but the Spirit Himself intercedes for us with groanings too deep for words.

I want the men in every place to pray, lifting up holy hands, without wrath and dissension.—With prayer and petition pray at all times in the Spirit, . . . be on the alert with all perseverance and petition for all the saints.

If two of you agree on earth about anything that they may ask, it shall be done for them by My Father who is in heaven.

PHIL 4:6. Ps 116:1,2. Mt 6:7.—Ro 8:26. 1 Ti 2:8.—Eph 6:18.
Mt 18:19.

All Thy works shall give thanks to Thee, O LORD, and Thy godly ones shall bless Thee.

Bless the LORD, O my soul; and all that is within me, bless His holy name. Bless the LORD, O my soul, and forget none of His benefits.—I will bless the LORD at all times; His praise shall continually be in my mouth.—Every day I will bless Thee, and I will praise Thy name forever and ever.

Because Thy lovingkindness is better than life, my lips will praise Thee. So I will bless Thee as long as I live; I will lift up my hands in Thy name. My soul is satisfied as with marrow and fatness. And my mouth offers praises with joyful lips.

My soul exalts the Lord, and my spirit has rejoiced in God my Savior.

Worthy art Thou, our Lord and our God, to receive glory and honor and power; for Thou didst create all things, and because of Thy will they existed, and were created.

PS 145:10. Ps 103:1,2.—Ps 34:1.—Ps 145:2. Ps 63:3–5. Lk 1:46,47.
Rev 4:11.

You shall put the mercy seat on top of the ark. . . . and there I will meet with you.

The way into the holy place has not yet been disclosed.—Jesus cried out again with a loud voice, and yielded up His spirit. And behold, the veil of the temple was torn in two from top to bottom.

Therefore, brethren, we have confidence to enter the holy place by the blood of Jesus, by a new and living way which He inaugurated for us through the veil, that is, His flesh. Let us draw near with a sincere heart in full assurance of faith, having our hearts sprinkled clean from an evil conscience and our body washed with pure water.—Let us therefore draw near with confidence to the throne of grace, that we may receive mercy and may find grace to help in time of need.

Christ Jesus; whom God displayed publicly as a propitiation (mercy seat) in His blood through faith. This was to demonstrate His righeousness, because in the forbearance of God He passed over the sins previously committed.—Through Him we . . . have our access in one Spirit to the Father.

EX 25:21,22. Heb 9:8.—Mt 27:50,51. Heb 10:19,20,22.—Heb 4:16.
Ro 3:24,25.—Eph 2:18.

Faith as a mustard seed.

Barak said to her (Deborah), If you will go with me, then I will go; but if you will not go with me, I will not go. God subdued on that day Jabin the king of Canaan.—Gideon . . . was too afraid of his father's household and the men of the city to do it by day, that he did it by night. Gideon said to God, If Thou wilt deliver Israel through me, as Thou hast spoken . . . please let me make a test. . . . And God did so.

Because you have a little power, and have kept My word, and have not denied My name.—Who has despised the day of small things?

We ought always to give thanks to God for you, brethren, as is only fitting, because your faith is greatly enlarged.—Lord, increase our faith!—I will be like the dew to Israel; he will blossom like the lily and he will take root like the cedars of Lebanon. His shoots will sprout, and his beauty will be like the olive tree, and his fragrance like the cedars of Lebanon.

MT 17:20. Judg 4:8,23.—Judg 6:27,36,39,40. Rev 3:8.—Zec 4:10.
2 Th 1:3.—Lk 17:5.—Ho 14:5,6.

Peace with all men, and . . . the sanctification without which no one will see the Lord.

Unless one is born again, he cannot see the kingdom of God. —No one who practices abomination . . . shall ever come into it. —There is no blemish in you.

You shall be holy, for I the LORD your God am holy.—As obedient children, do not be conformed to the former lusts which were yours in your ignorance, but like the Holy One who called you, be holy yourselves also in all your behavior; because it is written, You shall be holy, for I am holy. And if you address as Father the One who impartially judges according to each man's work, conduct yourselves in fear during the time of your stay upon earth.—Lay aside the old self, which is being corrupted in accordance with the lusts of deceit, and . . . be renewed in the spirit of your mind, and put on the new self, which in the likeness of God has been created in righteousness and holiness of the truth.—He chose us in Him before the foundation of the world, that we should be holy and blameless before Him.

HEB 12:14. Jn 3:3.—Rev 21:27.—Song 4:7. Lev 19:2.—
1 Pe 1:14–17.—Eph 4:22–24.—Eph 1:4.

Gold refined by fire.

There is no one who has left house or brothers or sisters or mother or father or children or farms, for My sake and for the gospel's sake, but that he shall receive a hundred times as much now in the present age, houses and brothers and sisters and mothers and children and farms, along with persecutions; and in the world to come, eternal life.

Beloved, do not be surprised at the fiery ordeal among you, which comes upon you for your testing, as though some strange thing were happening to you.—Now for a little while, if necessary, you have been distressed by various trials, that the proof of your faith, being more precious than gold which is perishable, even though tested by fire, may be found to result in praise and glory and honor at the revelation of Jesus Christ.

After you have suffered for a little while, the God of all grace, who called you to His eternal glory in Christ, will Himself perfect, confirm, strengthen and establish you.—In the world you have tribulation, but take courage; I have overcome the world.

REV 3:18. Mk 10:29,30. 1 Pe 4:12.—1 Pe 1:6,7. 1 Pe 5:10.—
Jn 16:33.

Take this child away and nurse him for me and I shall give you your wages.

You too go into the vineyard, and whatever is right I will give you.—Whoever gives you a cup of water to drink because of your name as followers of Christ, truly I say to you, he shall not lose his reward.—The generous man will be prosperous, and he who waters will himself be watered.—God is not unjust so as to forget your work and the love ... in having ministered and in still ministering to the saints.

Each will receive his own reward according to his own labor.

Lord, when did we see You hungry, and feed You, or thirsty, and give You drink? And when did we see You a stranger, and invite You in, or naked, and clothe You? And the King will answer and say to them. ... To the extent that you did it to one of these brothers of Mine, even the least of them, you did it to me. ... Come, you who are blessed of My Father, inherit the kingdom prepared for you from the foundation of the world.

EX 2:9. Mt 20:4.—Mk 9:41.—Pr 11:25.—Heb 6:10. 1 Co 3:8.
Mt 25:37,38,40,34.

Thou dost scrutinize my path and my lying down.

Jacob awoke from his sleep and said, Surely the LORD is in this place, and I did not know it. And he was afraid and said, How awesome is this place! This is none other than the house of God, and this is the gate of heaven.

The eyes of the LORD move to and fro throughout the earth that He may strongly support those whose heart is completely His.

In peace I will both lie down and sleep, for Thou alone, O LORD, dost make me to dwell in safety.

For you have made the LORD, my refuge, even the Most High, your dwelling place. No evil will befall you, nor will any plague come near your tent. For He will give His angels charge concerning you, to guard you in all your ways.—When you lie down, you will not be afraid; when you lie down, your sleep will be sweet. —For He gives to His beloved even in his sleep.

PS 139:3. Gen 28:16,17. 2 Ch 16:9. Ps 4:8. Ps 91:9–11.—Pr 3:24.—
Ps 127:2.

Christ also suffered for you, leaving you an example for you to follow in His steps.

Even the Son of Man did not come to be served, but to serve. —Whoever wishes to be first among you shall be slave of all.

Jesus of Nazareth . . . went about doing good.—Bear one another's burdens, and thus fulfill the law of Christ.

The meekness and gentleness of Christ.—With humility of mind let each of you regard one another as more important than himself.

Father forgive them; for they do not know what they are doing.—Be kind to one another, tender-hearted, forgiving each other, just as God in Christ also has forgiven you.

The one who says he abides in Him ought himself to walk in the same manner as He walked.—Fixing our eyes on Jesus, the author and perfecter of faith, who for the joy set before Him endured the cross, despising the shame, and has sat down at the right hand of the throne of God.

1 PE 2:21. Mk 10:45.—Mk 10:44. Ac 10:38.—Gal 6:2. 2 Co 10:1.— Phil 2:3. Lk 23:34.—Eph 4:32. 1 Jn 2:6.—Heb 12:2.

I searched for him, but I did not find him; I called him, but he did not answer me.

O Lord, what can I say since Israel has turned their back before their enemies? So the LORD said to Joshua, Rise up! Why is it that you have fallen on your face? Israel has sinned . . . they have even taken some of the things under the ban . . . they have also put them among their own things.

Behold, the LORD's hand is not so short that it cannot save; neither is His ear so dull that it cannot hear. But your iniquities have made a separation between you and your God, and your sins have hidden His face from you, so that He does not hear.

If I regard wickedness in my heart, the Lord will not hear.

Beloved, if our heart does not condemn us, we have confidence before God; and whatever we ask we receive from Him, because we keep His commandments and do the things that are pleasing in His sight.

SONG 5:6. Jos 7:8,10,11. Is 59:1,2. Ps 66:18 1 Jn 3:21,22.

You have died and your life is hidden with Christ in God.

How shall we who died to sin still live in it?—I have been crucified with Christ; and it is no longer I who live, but Christ lives in me; and the life which I now live in the flesh I live by faith in the Son of God, who loved me, and delivered Himself up for me.—He died for all, that they who live should no longer live for themselves, but for Him who died and rose again on their behalf. —If any man is in Christ, he is a new creature; the old things passed away; behold, new things have come.

We are in Him who is true, in His Son Jesus Christ.—As Thou, Father, art in Me, and I in Thee, that they also may be in Us.— Now you are Christ's body, and individually members of it.— Because I live, you shall live also.

To him who overcomes, to him I will give some of the hidden manna, and I will give him a white stone, and a new name written on the stone which no one knows but he who receives it.

COL 3:3. Ro 6:2.—Gal 2:20.—2 Co 5:15.—2 Co 5:17. 1 Jn 5:20.— Jn 17:21.—1 Co 12:27.—Jn 14:19. Rev 2:17.

Behold how He loved.

He died for all.—Greater love has no one than this, that one lay down his life for his friends.

He always lives to make intercession for them.—I go to prepare a place for you.

I will come again, and receive you to Myself; that where I am, there you may be also.—Father, I desire that they also, whom Thou hast given Me, be with Me where I am.—Having loved His own who were in the world, He loved them to the end.

We love, because He first loved us.—The love of Christ controls us, having concluded this, that one died for all, therefore all died; and He died for all, that they who live should no longer live for themselves, but for Him who died and rose again on their behalf.

If you keep My commandments, you will abide in My love; just as I have kept My Father's commandments, and abide in His love.

JN 11:36. 2 Co 5:15.—Jn 15:13. Heb 7:25.—Jn 14:2. Jn 14:3.— Jn 17:24.—Jn 13:1. 1 Jn 4:19.—2 Co 5:14,15. Jn 15:10.

I will ask the Father, and He will give you another Helper, that He may be with you forever; that is the Spirit of truth.

It is to your advantage that I go away; for if I do not go away, the Helper shall not come to you; but if I go, I will send Him to you.

The Spirit Himself bears witness with our spirit that we are children of God.—You have not received a spirit of slavery leading to fear again, but you have received a spirit of adoption as sons by which we cry out, Abba! Father!—The Spirit also helps our weakness; for we do not know how to pray as we should, but the Spirit Himself intercedes for us with groanings too deep for words.

The God of hope fill you with all joy and peace in believing, that you may abound in hope by the power of the Holy Spirit. —Hope does not disappoint; because the love of God has been poured out within our hearts through the Holy Spirit who was given to us.

By this we know that we abide in Him and He in us, because He has given us of His Spirit.

JN 14:16,17. Jn 16:7. Ro 8:16.—Ro 8:15.—Ro 8:26. Ro 15:13.—
Ro 5:5. 1 Jn 4:13.

Shall I not seek security for you, that it may be well with you?

There remains . . . a rest for the people of God.—Then my people will live in a peaceful habitation, and in secure dwellings and in undisturbed resting places.—There the wicked cease from raging, and there the weary are at rest.—They . . . rest from their labors.

Jesus has entered as a forerunner for us, having become a high priest forever according to the order of Melchizedek.

Come to Me, all who are weary and heavy laden, and I will give you rest. Take My yoke upon you, and learn from Me, for I am gentle and humble in heart; and you shall find rest for your souls. For My yoke is easy, and My load is light.—In repentance and rest you shall be saved, in quietness and trust is your strength.

The LORD is my shepherd, I shall not want. He makes me lie down in green pastures; He leads me beside quiet waters.

RUTH 3:1. Heb 4:9.—Is 32:18.—Job 3:17.—Rev 14:13. Heb 6:20.
Mt 11:28–30.—Is 30:15. Ps 23:1,2.

The ark of the covenant of the LORD journeying in front of them ... to seek out a resting place for them.

My times are in Thy hand.—He chooses our inheritance for us.
—O LORD, lead me in Thy righteousness ... make Thy way straight before me.

Commit your way to the LORD, trust also in Him, and He will do it.—In all your ways acknowledge Him, and He will make your paths straight.—Your ears will hear a word behind you, This is the way, walk in it, whenever you turn to the right or to the left.

The LORD is my shepherd, I shall not want. He makes me lie down in green pastures; He leads me beside quiet waters.—Just as a father has compassion on his children, so the LORD has compassion on those who fear Him. For He Himself knows our frame; He is mindful that we are but dust.—Your heavenly Father knows that you need all these things.—Casting all your anxiety upon Him, because He cares for you.

NUM 10:33. Ps 31:15.—Ps 47:4.—Ps 5:8. Ps 37:5.—Pr 3:6.—Is 30:21.
Ps 23:1,2.—Ps 103:13,14.—Mt 6:32.—1 Pe 5:7.

Rabbi (... Teacher), where are You staying? He said to them, Come, and you will see.

In My Father's house are many dwelling places; if it were not so, I would have told you; for I go to prepare a place for you. And if I go and prepare a place for you, I will come again, and receive you to Myself; that where I am, there you may be also.—He who overcomes, I will grant to him to sit down with Me on my throne.

Thus says the high and exalted One who lives forever, whose name is Holy, I dwell on a high and holy place, and also with the contrite and lowly of spirit in order to revive the spirit of the lowly and to revive the heart of the contrite.

Behold, I stand at the door and knock; if any one hears My voice and opens the door, I will come in to him, and will dine with him, and he with Me.

Lo, I am with you always, even to the end of the age.—How precious is Thy lovingkindness, O God! And the children of men take refuge in the shadow of Thy wings.

JN 1:38,39. Jn 14:2,3.—Rev 3:21. Is 57:15. Rev 3:20. Mt 28:20.—
Ps 36:7.

We know that, when He appears, we shall be like Him, because we shall see Him just as He is.

As many as received Him, to them He gave the right to become children of God, even to those who believe in His name. —He has granted to us His precious and magnificent promises, in order that by them you might become partakers of the divine nature, having escaped the corruption that is in the world by lust.

For from of old they have not heard nor perceived by ear, neither has the eye seen a God besides Thee, who acts in behalf of the one who waits for Him.

Now we see in a mirror dimly, but then face to face; now I know in part, but then I shall know fully just as I also have been fully known.—Christ ... will transform the body of our humble state into conformity with the body of His glory, by the exertion of the power that He has even to subject all things to Himself. —As for me, I shall behold Thy face in righteousness; I will be satisfied with Thy likeness when I awake.

1 JN 3:2. Jn 1:12.—2 Pe 1:4. Is 64:4. 1 Co 13:12.—Phil 3:20,21.— Ps 17:15.

The man, My Associate, declares the LORD of hosts.

In Him all the fulness of Deity dwells in bodily form.—I have given help to one who is mighty; I have exalted one chosen from the people.—I have trodden the wine trough alone, and from the peoples there was no man with Me.

Great is the mystery of godliness: He who was revealed in the flesh.—A child will be born to us, a son will be given to us; and the government will rest on His shoulders; and His name will be called Wonderful Counselor, Mighty God, Eternal Father, Prince of Peace.

He is the radiance of His glory and the exact representation of His nature, and upholds all things by the word of His power. When He had made purification of sins, He sat down at the right hand of the Majesty on high. ... but of the Son He says, Thy Throne, O God, is forever and ever.

Let all the angels of God worship Him.

KING OF KINGS, AND LORD OF LORDS.

ZEC 13:7. Col 2:9.—Ps 89:19.—Is 63:3. 1 Ti 3:16.—Is 9:6. Heb 1:3,8. Heb 1:6. Rev 19:16.

Oh that Thou wouldst bless me indeed ... and that Thou wouldst keep me from harm, ... and God granted him what he requested.

It is the blessing of the LORD that makes rich, and He adds no sorrow to it.—When He keeps quiet, who then can condemn? And when He hides His face, who then can behold Him?

Salvation belongs to the LORD; Thy blessing be upon Thy people!—How great is Thy goodness, which Thou hast stored up for those who fear Thee, which Thou hast wrought for those who take refuge in Thee, before the sons of men!—I do not ask Thee to take them out of the world, but to keep them from the evil one.

Ask, and it shall be given to you; seek, and you shall find; knock, and it shall be opened to you. For every one who asks receives, and he who seeks finds, and to him who knocks it shall be opened. —The LORD redeems the soul of His servants; and none of those who take refuge in Him will be condemned.

1 CH 4:10. Pr 10:22.—Job 34:29. Ps 3:8.—Ps 31:19.—Jn 17:15. Mt 7:7,8.—Ps 34:22.

It is a night to be observed for the LORD for having brought them out from the land of Egypt.

The Lord Jesus in the night in which He was betrayed took bread; and when He had given thanks, He broke it, and said, This is My body, which is for you; do this in remembrance of Me. In the same way the cup also, after supper, saying, This cup is the new covenant in my blood; do this, as often as you drink it, in remembrance of Me.

He knelt down and began to pray. And being in agony He was praying very fervently; and His sweat became like drops of blood, falling down upon the ground.

It was the day of preparation for the Passover ... about the sixth hour. . . . They took Jesus ... to the place called ... Golgotha. There they crucified Him.

Christ our Passover also has been sacrificed. Let us therefore celebrate the feast.

EX 12:42. 1 Co 11:23–25. Lk 22:41,44. Jn 19:14,16–18. 1 Co 5:7,8.

Who is able to stand?

Who can endure the day of His coming? And who can stand when He appears? For He is like a refiner's fire and like fullers' soap.

I looked, and behold, a great multitude, which no one could count, from every nation and all tribes and peoples and tongues, standing before the throne and before the Lamb, clothed in white robes, and palm branches were in their hands. These are the ones who come out of the great tribulation, and they have washed their robes and made them white in the blood of the Lamb. They shall hunger no more, neither thirst any more; neither shall the sun beat down on them, nor any heat; for the Lamb in the center of the throne . . . shall guide them to springs of the water of life; and God shall wipe every tear from their eyes.

There is therefore now no condemnation for those who are in Christ Jesus.—Christ set us free; therefore keep standing firm.

REV 6:17. Mal 3:2. Rev 7:9,14,16,17. Ro 8:1.—Gal 5:1.

Do not enter into judgment with Thy servant, for in Thy sight no man living is righteous.

Come now, and let us reason together, says the LORD, though your sins are as scarlet, they will be as white as snow; though they are red like crimson, they will be like wool.

Let him rely on My protection, let him make peace with Me, let him make peace with Me.—Yield now and be at peace with Him.

Having been justified by faith, we have peace with God through our Lord Jesus Christ.—Man is not justified by the works of the law but through faith in Christ Jesus.—By the works of the law no flesh will be justified in His sight.

Through Him everyone who believes is freed from all things, from which you could not be freed through the Law of Moses.

Thanks be to God, who gives us the victory through our Lord Jesus Christ.

PS 143:2. Is 1:18. Is 27:5.—Job 22:21. Ro 5:1.—Gal 2:16.—Ro 3:20.
Ac 13:39. 1 Co 15:57.

I know that my Redeemer lives.

If while we were enemies, we were reconciled to God through the death of His Son, much more, having been reconciled, we shall be saved by His life.—Because He abides forever, holds His priesthood permanently . . . He is able to save forever those who draw near to God through Him, since He always lives to make intercession for them.

Because I live, you shall live also.—If we have only hoped in Christ in this life, we are of all men most to be pitied. But now Christ has been raised from the dead, the first fruits of those who are asleep.

A Redeemer will come to Zion, and to those who turn from transgression in Jacob, declares the LORD.—We have redemption through His blood, the forgiveness of our trespasses, according to the riches of His grace.—You were not redeemed with perishable things like silver or gold from your futile way of life inherited from your forefathers, but with precious blood, as of a lamb unblemished and spotless, the blood of Christ.

JOB 19:25. Ro 5:10.—Heb 7:24,25. Jn 14:19.—1 Co 15:19,20.
Is 59:20.—Eph 1:7.—1 Pe 1:18,19.

The Spirit explicitly says that in later times some will fall away from the faith, paying attention to deceitful spirits.

Therefore take care how you listen.—Let the word of Christ richly dwell within you; with all wisdom.—In addition to all, taking up the shield of faith with which you will be able to extinguish all the flaming missiles of the evil one.

Those who love Thy law have great peace, and nothing causes them to stumble. How sweet are Thy words to my taste! Yes, sweeter than honey to my mouth! From Thy precepts I get understanding; therefore I hate every false way.

Thy word is a lamp to my feet, and a light to my path. I have more insight than all my teachers, for Thy testimonies are my meditation.

Even Satan disguises himself as an angel of light.—But even though we, or an angel from heaven, should preach to you a gospel contrary to that which we have preached to you, let him be accursed.

1 TI 4:1. Lk 8:18.—Col 3:16.—Eph 6:16. Ps 119:165,103,104.
Ps 119:105,99. 2 Co 11:14.—Gal 1:8.

His commandments are not burdensome.

For this is the will of My Father, that every one who beholds the Son, and believes in Him, may have eternal life.—Whatever we ask we receive from Him, because we keep His commandments and do the things that are pleasing in His sight.

My yoke is easy, and My load is light.—If you love Me, you will keep My commandments. He who has My commandments, and keeps them, he it is who loves Me; and he who loves Me shall be loved by My Father, and I will love him, and will disclose Myself to him.

How blessed is the man who finds wisdom, and the man who gains understanding. Her ways are pleasant ways, and all her paths are peace.—Those who love Thy law have great peace, and nothing causes them to stumble.—I joyfully concur with the law of God in the inner man.

This is His commandment, that we believe in the name of His Son Jesus Christ, and love one another.—Love does no wrong to a neighbor; love therefore is the fulfillment of the law.

1 JN 5:3. Jn 6:40.—1 Jn 3:22. Mt 11:30.—Jn 14:15,21. Pr 3:13,17. Ps 119:165.—Ro 7:22. 1 Jn 3:23.—Ro 13:10.

Do not remember the sins of my youth or my transgressions.

I have wiped out your transgressions like a thick cloud, and your sins like a heavy mist.—I, even I, am the one who wipes out your transgressions for My own sake; and I will not remember your sins.—Come now, and let us reason together, says the LORD, though your sins are as scarlet, they will be as white as snow; though they are red like crimson, they will be like wool. —I will forgive their iniquity, and their sin I will remember no more.—Thou wilt cast all their sins into the depths of the sea.

Thou who hast kept my soul from the pit of nothingness, for Thou hast cast all my sins behind Thy back.—Who is a God like Thee, who pardons iniquity ... He does not retain His anger forever, because He delights in unchanging love.—To Him who loves us, and released us from our sins by His blood ... to Him be the glory and the dominion forever and ever. Amen.

PS 25:7. Is 44:22.—Is 43:25.—Is 1:18.—Jer 31:34.—Mic 7:19. Is 38:17.—Mic 7:18.—Rev 1:5,6.

Those whom I love, I reprove and discipline.

My son, do not regard lightly the discipline of the Lord, nor faint when you are reproved by Him; for those whom the Lord loves He disciplines, and He scourges every son whom He receives.—Even as a father the son in whom he delights.—He inflicts pain, and gives relief; He wounds, and His hands also heal. —Humble yourselves, therefore, under the mighty hand of God, that He may exalt you at the proper time.—I have tested you in the furnace of affliction.

He does not afflict willingly, or grieve the sons of men.—He has not dealt with us according to our sins, nor rewarded us according to our iniquities. For as high as the heavens are above the earth, so great is His lovingkindness toward those who fear Him. As far as the east is from the west, so far has He removed our transgressions from us. Just as a father has compassion on his children, so the Lord has compassion on those who fear Him. For He Himself knows our frame; He is mindful that we are but dust.

REV 3:19. Heb 12:5,6.—Pr 3:12.—Job 5:18.—1 Pe 5:6.—Is 48:10. Lam 3:33.—Ps 103:10–14.

God is in heaven and you are on the earth; therefore let your words be few.

When you are praying, do not use meaningless repetition, as the Gentiles do, for they suppose that they will be heard for their many words. Therefore do not be like them; for your Father knows what you need, before you ask Him.

They . . . called on the name of Baal from morning until noon saying, O Baal, answer us.

Two men went up into the temple to pray, one a Pharisee, and the other a tax-gatherer. The Pharisee stood and was praying thus to himself, God, I thank Thee that I am not like other people, swindlers, unjust, adulterers, or even like this tax-gatherer. But the tax-gatherer, standing some distance away, was even unwilling to lift up his eyes to heaven, but was beating his breast, saying, God, be merciful to me, the sinner! I tell you, this man went down to his house justified rather than the other.

Lord, teach us to pray.

EC 5:2. Mt 6:7,8. 1 Ki 18:26. Lk 18:10,11,13,14. Lk 11:1.

The fruit of the Spirit is ... goodness.

Be imitators of God, as beloved children.—Love your enemies, and pray for those who persecute you; in order that you may be sons of your Father who is in heaven; for He causes His sun to rise on the evil and the good, and sends rain on the righteous and the unrighteous.—Be merciful, just as your Father is merciful.

The fruit of the light consists in all goodness and righteousness and truth.

When the kindness of God our Savior and His love for mankind appeared, He saved us, not on the basis of deeds which we have done in righteousness, but according to His mercy, by the washing of regeneration and renewing by the Holy Spirit, whom He poured out upon us richly through Jesus Christ our Savior.—The LORD is good to all, and His mercies are over all His works.—He who did not spare His own Son, but delivered Him up for us all, how will He not also with Him freely give us all things?

GAL 5:22. Eph 5:1.—Mt 5:44,45.—Lk 6:36. Eph 5:9. Titus 3:4–6.—
Ps 145:9.—Ro 8:32.

Ebenezer ... Thus far the LORD has helped us.

I was brought low, and He saved me.—Blessed be the LORD, because He has heard the voice of my supplication. The LORD is my strength and my shield; my heart trusts in Him, and I am helped; therefore my heart exults, and with my song I shall thank Him.

It is better to take refuge in the LORD than to trust in man. It is better to take refuge in the LORD than to trust in princes.— How blessed is he whose help is the God of Jacob, whose hope is in the LORD his God.—He led them also by a straight way, to go to an inhabited city.—Not one of the good promises which the LORD had made to the house of Israel failed; all came to pass.

When I sent you out without purse and bag and sandals, you did not lack anything, did you? And they said, No, nothing.— Thou hast been my help, and in the shadow of Thy wings I sing for joy.

1 SA 7:12. Ps 116:6.—Ps 28:6,7. Ps 118:8,9.—Ps 146:5.—Ps 107:7.—
Jos 21:45. Lk 22:35.—Ps 63:7.

This is the ordinance of the Passover: no foreigner is to eat of it.

We have an altar, from which those who serve the tabernacle have no right to eat.—Unless one is born again, he cannot see the kingdom of God.—Remember that you were at that time separate from Christ, excluded from the commonwealth of Israel, and strangers to the covenants of promise, having no hope and without God in the world. But now in Christ Jesus you who formerly were far off have been brought near by the blood of Christ.

He Himself is our peace, who made both groups into one . . . by abolishing in His flesh the enmity, which is the Law of commandments contained in ordinances, that in Himself He might make the two into one new man, thus establishing peace.

So then you are no longer strangers and aliens, but you are fellow-citizens with the saints, and are of God's household.

If any one hears My voice and opens the door, I will come in to him, and will dine with him, and he with Me.

EX 12:43. Heb 13:10.—Jn 3:3.—Eph 2:12,13. Eph 2:14,15.
Eph 2:19. Rev 3:20.

(Jesus) went away and prayed a third time, saying the same thing once more.

In the days of His flesh, He offered up both prayers and supplications with loud crying and tears to the One able to save Him from death.

So let us know, let us press on to know the LORD.—Devoted to prayer.—With all prayer and petition pray at all times in the Spirit, and with this in view, be on the alert with all perseverance and petition.—By prayer and supplication with thanksgiving let your requests be made known to God. And the peace of God, which surpasses all comprehension, shall guard your hearts and your minds in Christ Jesus.

Yet not as I will, but as Thou wilt.—This is the confidence which we have before Him, that, if we ask anything according to His will, He hears us.

Delight yourself in the LORD; and He will give you the desires of your heart. Commit your way to the LORD, trust also in Him, and He will do it.

MT 26:44. Heb 5:7. Hos 6:3.—Ro 12:12.—Eph 6:18.—Phil 4:6,7.
Mt 26:39.—1 Jn 5:14. Ps 37:4,5.

If children, heirs also, heirs of God and fellow-heirs with Christ.

If you belong to Christ, then you are Abraham's offspring, heirs according to promise.

See how great a love the Father has bestowed upon us, that we should be called children of God.—You are no longer a slave, but a son; and if a son, then an heir through God.—He predestined us to adoption as sons through Jesus Christ to Himself, according to the kind intention of His will.

Father, I desire that they also whom Thou hast given Me be with Me where I am, in order that they may behold My glory, which Thou hast given Me.

He who overcomes, and he who keeps My deeds until the end, to him I will give authority over the nations.—He who overcomes, I will grant to him to sit down with Me on My throne, as I also overcame and sat down with My Father on His throne.

RO 8:17. Gal 3:29. 1 Jn 3:1.—Gal 4:7.—Eph 1:5. Jn 17:24.
Rev 2:26.—Rev 3:21.

Things . . . despised, God has chosen.

Why, are not all these who are speaking Galileans?

(Jesus) saw two brothers . . . casting a net into the sea; for they were fishermen. And He said to them, Follow Me.—Now as they observed the confidence of Peter and John, and understood that they were uneducated and untrained men, they were marveling, and began to recognize them as having been with Jesus.

My message and my preaching were not in persuasive words of wisdom, but in demonstration of the Spirit and of power, that your faith should not rest on the wisdom of men, but on the power of God.

You did not choose Me, but I chose you, and appointed you, that you should go and bear fruit. . . . He who abides in Me, and I in him, he bears much fruit; for apart from Me you can do nothing.—We have this treasure in earthen vessels, that the surpassing greatness of the power may be of God.

1 CO 1:28. Ac 2:7. Mt 4:18,19.—Ac 4:13. 1 Co 2:4,5. Jn 15:16,5.—
2 Co 4:7.

Reclining on Jesus' breast.

As one whom his mother comforts, so I will comfort you.—And they began bringing children to Him, so that He might touch them. And He took them in His arms and began blessing them, laying His hands upon them.—Jesus summoned to Himself His disciples, and said, I feel compassion for the multitude, because they have remained with Me now for three days and have nothing to eat; and I do not wish to send them away hungry, lest they faint on the way.—A high priest who can . . . sympathize with our weaknesses.—In His love and in His mercy He redeemed them.

I will not leave you as orphans; I will come to you.—Can a woman forget her nursing child, and have no compassion on the son of her womb? Even these may forget, but I will not forget you.

The Lamb in the center of the throne shall be their shepherd, and shall guide them to springs of the water of life; and God shall wipe every tear from their eyes.

JN 13:23. Is 66:13.—Mk 10:13,16.—Mt 15:32.—Heb 4:15.—Is 63:9.
Jn 14:18.—Is 49:15. Rev 7:17.

Jesus Christ the righteous . . . the propitiation for our sins.

The faces of the cherubim are to be turned toward the mercy seat. And you shall put the mercy seat on top of the ark, and in the ark you shall put the testimony which I shall give you. And there I will meet with you, . . . from above the mercy seat.

Surely His salvation is near to those who fear Him . . . lovingkindness and truth have met together; righteousness and peace have kissed each other.

If Thou, LORD, shouldst mark iniquities, O Lord, who could stand? But there is forgiveness with Thee, that Thou mayest be feared. O Israel, hope in the LORD; for with the LORD there is lovingkindness, and with Him is abundant redemption. And He will redeem Israel from all his iniquities.—For all have sinned and fall short of the glory of God, being justified as a gift by His grace through the redemption which is in Christ Jesus; whom God displayed publicly as a propitiation in His blood through faith. This was to demonstrate His righteousness . . . over the sins previously committed.

1 JN 2:1,2. Ex 25:20–22. Ps 85:9,10. Ps 130:3,4,7,8.—Ro 3:23–25.

**We have come to know and have believed the love which God
has for us.**

God, being rich in mercy, because of His great love with which
He loved us, even when we were dead in our transgressions,
made us alive together with Christ (by grace you have been
saved), and raised us up with Him, and seated us with Him in the
heavenly places, in Christ Jesus, in order that in the ages to come
He might show the surpassing riches of His grace in kindness
toward us in Christ Jesus.

God so loved the world, that He gave His only begotten Son,
that whoever believes in Him should not perish, but have eternal
life.—He who did not spare His own Son, but delivered Him up
for us all, how will He not also with Him freely give us all things?
—The LORD is good to all, and His mercies are over all His works.

We love, because He first loved us.

Blessed is she who believed that there would be a fulfillment
of what had been spoken to her by the Lord.

1 JN 4:16. Eph 2:4–7. Jn 3:16—Ro 8:32.—Ps 145:9. 1 Jn 4:19.
Lk 1:45.

Do not be haughty in mind, but associate with the lowly.

My brethren, do not hold your faith in our glorious Lord Jesus
Christ with an attitude of personal favoritism. Did not God
choose the poor of this world to be rich in faith and heirs of the
kingdom which He promised to those who love Him?

Let no one seek his own good, but that of his neighbor.—If we
have food and covering, with these we shall be content. But
those who want to get rich fall into temptation and a snare and
many foolish and harmful desires which plunge men into ruin
and destruction.

But God has chosen the foolish things of the world to shame
the wise, and God has chosen the weak things of the world to
shame the things which are strong, and the base things of the
world and the despised, God has chosen, the things that are not,
that He might nullify the things that are, that no man should
boast before God.

O LORD, my heart is not proud, nor my eyes haughty.

RO 12:16. Ja 2:1,5. 1 Co 10:24.—1 Ti 6:8,9. 1 Co 1:27–29. Ps 131:1.

Let your speech always be with grace.

Like apples of gold in settings of silver is a word spoken in right circumstances. Like an earring of gold and an ornament of fine gold is a wise reprover to a listening ear.—Let no unwholesome word proceed from your mouth, but only such a word as is good for edification according to the need of the moment, that it may give grace to those who hear.—The good man out of his good treasure brings forth what is good; and the evil man out of his evil treasure brings forth what is evil. By your words you shall be justified.—The tongue of the wise brings healing.

Those who feared the LORD spoke to one another, and the LORD gave attention and heard it, and a book of remembrance was written before Him for those who fear the LORD and esteem His name.

If you extract the precious from the worthless, you will become My spokesman.—Just as you abound in everything, in faith and utterance and knowledge and in all earnestness . . . see that you abound in this gracious work also.

COL 4:6. Pr 25:11,12.—Eph 4:29.—Mt 12:35,37.—Pr 12:18.
Mal 3:16. Jer 15:19.—2 Co 8:7.

Thy lovingkindness is before my eyes.

The LORD is gracious and merciful; slow to anger and great in lovingkindness.—Your Father who is in heaven . . . He causes His sun to rise on the evil and the good, and sends rain on the righteous and the unrighteous.

Be imitators of God, as beloved children; and walk in love, just as Christ also loved you, and gave Himself up for us, an offering and a sacrifice to God as a fragrant aroma.—Be kind to one another, tender-hearted, forgiving each other, just as God in Christ also has forgiven you.—Since you have in obedience to the truth purified your souls for a sincere love of the brethren, fervently love one another from the heart.—The love of Christ controls us.

Love your enemies, and do good, and lend, expecting nothing in return; and your reward will be great, and you will be sons of the Most High; for He Himself is kind to ungrateful and evil men. Be merciful, just as your Father is merciful.

PS 26:3. Ps 145:8.—Mt 5:45. Eph 5:1,2.—Eph 4:32.—1 Pe 1:22.—
2 Co 5:14. Lk 6:35,36.

Then Jesus was led up by the Spirit into the wilderness to be tempted by the devil.

In the days of His flesh, He offered up both prayers and supplications with loud crying and tears to the One able to save Him from death, and He was heard because of His piety. Although He was a Son, He learned obedience from the things which He suffered. And having been made perfect, He became to all those who obey Him the source of eternal salvation.—We do not have a high priest who cannot sympathize with our weaknesses, but one who has been tempted in all things as we are, yet without sin.

No temptation has overtaken you but such as is common to man; and God is faithful, who will not allow you to be tempted beyond what you are able; but with the temptation will provide the way of escape also, that you may be able to endure it.—My grace is sufficient for you, for power is perfected in weakness.

MT 4:1. Heb 5:7–9.—Heb 4:15. 1 Co 10:13.—2 Co 12:9.

The Son of Man did . . . come . . . to give His life a ransom for many.

If the blood of goats and bulls and the ashes of a heifer sprinkling those who have been defiled, sanctify for the cleansing of the flesh, how much more will the blood of Christ, who through the eternal Spirit offered Himself without blemish to God, cleanse your conscience from dead works to serve the living God?

He . . . like a lamb that is led to slaughter.—I lay down My life for the sheep. No one has taken it away from Me, but I lay it down on My own initiative. I have authority to lay it down, and I have authority to take it up again.

For the life of the flesh is in the blood, and I have given it to you on the altar to make atonement for your souls; for it is the blood by reason of the life that makes atonement.—Without shedding of blood there is no forgiveness.

While we were yet sinners, Christ died for us. Much more then, having now been justified by His blood, we shall be saved from the wrath of God through Him.

MT 20:28. Heb 9:13,14. Is 53:7.—Jn 10:15,18. Lev 17:11.— Heb 9:22. Ro 5:8,9.

If we confess our sins, He is faithful and righteous to forgive us our sins and to cleanse us from all unrighteousness.

I know my transgressions, and my sin is ever before me. Against Thee, Thee only, I have sinned, and done what is evil in Thy sight.

And he got up and came to his father. But while he was still a long way off, his father saw him, and felt compassion for him, and ran and embraced him, and kissed him.—I have wiped out your transgressions like a thick cloud, and your sins like a heavy mist. Return to Me, for I have redeemed you.—Your sins are forgiven you for His name's sake.—God in Christ also has forgiven you.—That He might be just and the justifier of the one who has faith in Jesus.

I will sprinkle clean water on you, and you will be clean.—They will walk with Me in white; for they are worthy.

This is the one who came by water and blood, Jesus Christ; not with the water only, but with the water and with the blood.

1 JN 1:9. Ps 51:3,4. Lk 15:20.—Is 44:22.—1 Jn 2:12.—Eph 4:32.—
Ro 3:26. Eze 36:25.—Rev 3:4. 1 Jn 5:6.

Can a throne of destruction be allied with Thee?

Indeed our fellowship is with the Father, and with His Son Jesus Christ.—Beloved, now we are children of God, and it has not appeared as yet what we shall be. We know that, when He appears, we shall be like Him, because we shall see Him just as He is. And every one who has this hope fixed on Him purifies himself, just as He is pure.

The ruler of the world is coming, and he has nothing in Me.—A high priest, holy, innocent, undefiled.

Our struggle is not against flesh and blood, but against the rulers, against the powers, against the world-forces of this darkness, against the spiritual forces of wickedness in the heavenly places.—The prince of the power of the air, of the spirit that is now working in the sons of disobedience.

We know that no one who is born of God sins; but He who was born of God keeps him and the evil one does not touch him. We know that we are of God, and the whole world lies in the power of the evil one.

PS 94:20. 1 Jn 1:3.—1 Jn 3:2,3. Jn 14:30.—Heb 7:26. Eph 6:12.—
Eph 2:2. 1 Jn 5:18,19.

**I have taken your iniquity away from you and will clothe you
with festal robes.**

Blessed is he whose transgression is forgiven, whose sin is covered!—All of us have become like one who is unclean.—I know
that nothing good dwells in me, that is, in my flesh; for the
wishing is present in me, but the doing of the good is not.

All of you who were baptized into Christ have clothed yourselves with Christ.—You laid aside the old self with its evil practices, and have put on the new self who is being renewed to a
true knowledge according to the image of the One who created
him.—Not having a righteousness of my own derived from the
Law, but . . . through faith in Christ, the righteousness which
comes from God on the basis of faith.

Bring out the best robe and put it on him.—Fine linen is the
righteous acts of the saints.—I will rejoice greatly in the LORD,
my soul will exult in my God; for He has clothed me with garments of salvation, He has wrapped me with a robe of righteousness.

ZEC 3:4. Ps 32:1.—Is 64:6.—Ro 7:18. Gal 3:27.—Col 3:9,10.—
Phil 3:9. Lk 15:22.—Rev 19:8.—Is 61:10.

The day will show it.

Do not go on passing judgment before the time, but wait until
the Lord comes who will both bring to light the things hidden
in the darkness and disclose the motives of men's hearts; and
then each man's praise will come to him from God.

Why do you judge your brother? Or you again, why do you
regard your brother with contempt? For we shall all stand before
the judgment-seat of God. So then each one of us shall give
account of himself to God. Therefore let us not judge one another any more.

God will judge the secrets of men through Christ Jesus.—Not
even the Father judges any one, but He has given all judgment
to the Son. He gave Him authority to execute judgment, because
he is the Son of Man.

O great and mighty God, The LORD of hosts is His name; great
in counsel and mighty in deed, whose eyes are open to all the
ways of the sons of men, giving to every one according to his
ways and according to the fruit of his deeds.

1 CO 3:13. 1 Co 4:5. Ro 14:10,12,13. Ro 2:16.—Jn 5:22,27.
Jer 32:18,19.

A disciple is not above his teacher.

You call Me Teacher, and Lord; and you are right; for so I am.
It is enough for the disciple that he become as his teacher, and
the slave as his master.—If they persecuted Me, they will also
persecute you; if they kept My word, they will keep yours also.
—I have given them Thy word; and the world has hated them,
because they are not of the world, even as I am not of the world.

Consider Him who has endured such hostility by sinners
against Himself, so that you may not grow weary and lose heart.
You have not yet resisted to the point of shedding blood in your
striving against sin.

Let us run with endurance the race that is set before us, fixing
our eyes on Jesus, the author and perfecter of faith, who for the
joy set before Him endured the cross, despising the shame, and
has sat down at the right hand of the throne of God.—Therefore,
since Christ has suffered in the flesh, arm yourselves also with the
same purpose.

MT 10:24. Jn 13:13. Mt 10:25.—Jn 15:20.—Jn 17:14. Heb 12:3,4.
Heb 12:1,2.—1 Pe 4:1.

Give me your heart, my son.

Oh that they had such a heart in them, that they would fear
Me, and keep all My commandments always, that it may be well
with them and with their sons forever!

Your heart is not right before God.—Because the mind set on
the flesh is hostile toward God; for it does not subject itself to the
Law of God, for it is not even able to do so; and those who are
in the flesh cannot please God.

They first gave themselves to the Lord.—Every work which he
(Hezekiah) began ... seeking his God, he did with all his heart
and prospered.

Watch over your heart with all diligence, for from it flow the
springs of life.

Whatever you do, do your work heartily, as for the Lord.—As
slaves of Christ, doing the will of God from the heart. With good
will render service, as to the Lord, and not to men.

I shall run the way of Thy commandments, for Thou wilt enlarge my heart.

PR 23:26. Deu 5:29. Ac 8:21.—Ro 8:7,8. 2 Co 8:5.—2 Ch 31:21.
Pr 4:23. Col 3:23.—Eph 6:6,7. Ps 119:32.

I am with you to save you.

Can the prey be taken from the mighty man, or the captives of a tyrant be rescued? Surely thus says the LORD, Even the captives of the mighty man will be taken away, and the prey of the tyrant will be rescued; for I will contend with the one who contends with you. . . . And all flesh will know that I, the LORD, am your Saviour, and your Redeemer, the Mighty One of Jacob.—Do not fear, for I am with you; do not anxiously look about you, for I am your God. I will strengthen you, surely I will help you, surely, I will uphold you with My righteous right hand.

We do not have a high priest who cannot sympathize with our weaknesses, but one who has been tempted in all things as we are, yet without sin.—Since He Himself was tempted in that which He has suffered, He is able to come to the aid of those who are tempted.—The steps of a man are established by the LORD; and He delights in his way. When he falls, he shall not be hurled headlong; because the LORD is the One who holds his hand.

JER 15:20. Is 49:24–26.—Is 41:10. Heb 4:15.—Heb 2:18.—
Ps 37:23,24.

He has satisfied the thirsty soul, and the hungry soul He has filled with what is good.

You have tasted the kindness of the Lord.

O GOD, Thou art my God; I shall seek Thee earnestly; my soul thirsts for Thee, my flesh yearns for Thee, in a dry and weary land where there is no water. . . . To see Thy power and Thy glory.—My soul longed and even yearned for the courts of the LORD; my heart and my flesh sing for joy to the living God.— Having the desire to depart and be with Christ, for that is very much better.

I will be satisfied with Thy likeness when I awake.—They shall hunger no more, neither thirst any more; neither shall the sun beat down on them, nor any heat; for the Lamb in the center of the throne shall be their shepherd, and shall guide them to springs of the water of life; and God shall wipe every tear from their eyes.—They drink their fill of the abundance of Thy house; and Thou dost give them to drink of the river of Thy delights. —My people shall be satisfied with My goodness, declares the LORD.

PS 107:9. 1 Pe 2:3. Ps 63:1,2.—Ps 84:2.—Phil 1:23. Ps 17:15.—
Rev 7:16,17.—Ps 36:8.—Jer 31:14.

JULY 12   MORNING

My presence shall go with you, and I will give you rest.

Be strong and courageous, do not be afraid or tremble at them, for the LORD your God is the one who goes with you. He will not fail you or forsake you. The LORD is the one who goes ahead of you; He will be with you. He will not fail you or forsake you. Do not fear, or be dismayed.—Have I not commanded you? Be strong and courageous! Do not tremble or be dismayed, for the LORD your God is with you wherever you go.—In all your ways acknowledge Him, and He will make your paths straight.

I will never desert you, nor will I ever forsake you, so that we confidently say, The Lord is my helper, I will not be afraid. What shall man do to me?—Our adequacy is from God.

Do not lead us into temptation.—I know, O LORD, that a man's way is not in himself; nor is it in a man who walks to direct his steps.—My times are in Thy hand.

EX 33:14. Deu 31:6,8.—Jos 1:9.—Pr 3:6. Heb 13:5,6.—2 Cor 3:5.
Mt 6:13.—Jer 10:23.—Ps 31:15.

JULY 12   EVENING

Let us consider how to stimulate one another to love and good deeds.

Honest words are not painful.—I am stirring up your sincere mind by way of reminder.

Those who feared the LORD spoke to one another, and the LORD gave attention and heard it, and a book of remembrance was written before Him for those who fear the LORD and who esteem His name.—If two of you agree on earth about anything that they may ask, it shall be done for them by My Father who is in heaven.

The LORD God said, It is not good for the man to be alone.— Two are better than one because they have a good return for their labor. For if either of them falls, the one will lift up his companion. But woe to the one who falls when there is not another to lift him up.

Determine this—not to put an obstacle or a stumbling block in a brother's way.—Bear one another's burdens and thus fulfill the law of Christ. Each one looking to yourself, lest you too be tempted.

HEB 10:24. Job 6:25.—2 Pe 3:1. Mal 3:16.—Mt 18:19. Gen 2:18.—
Ec 4:9,10. Ro 14:13.—Gal 6:2,1.

I am my beloved's, and his desire is for me.

I know whom I have believed and I convinced that He is able to guard what I have entrusted to Him until that day.—I am convinced that neither death, nor life, nor angels, nor principalities, nor things present, nor things to come, nor powers, nor height, nor depth, nor any other created thing, shall be able to separate us from the love of God, which is in Christ Jesus our Lord.—Them . . . which Thou hast given me; . . . I guarded them, and not one of them perished.

The LORD takes pleasure in His people.—Having my delight in the sons of men.—His great love with which He loved us.—Greater love has no one than this, that one lay down his life for his friends.

You have been bought with a price: therefore glorify God in your body.—If we live, we live for the Lord, or if we die, we die for the Lord; therefore whether we live or die, we are the Lord's.

SONG 7:10. 2 Ti 1:12.—Ro 8:38,39.—Jn 17:12. Ps 149:4.—Pr 8:31.—
Eph 2:4.—Jn 15:13. 1 Co 6:20.—Ro 14:8.

Seek from the book of the LORD.

You shall therefore impress these words of mine on your heart and on your soul; and you shall bind them as a sign on your hand, and they shall be as frontals on your forehead.—This book of the law shall not depart from your mouth, but you shall meditate on it day and night, so that you may be careful to do according to all that is written in it; for then you will make your way prosperous, and then you will have success.

The Law of his God is in his heart; his steps do not slip.—By the word of Thy lips I have kept from the paths of the violent. —Thy word I have treasured in my heart, that I may not sin against Thee.

We have the prophetic word made more sure, to which you do well to pay attention as to a lamp shining in a dark place, until the day dawns and the morning star arises in your hearts.—That through perseverance and the encouragement of the Scriptures we might have hope.

IS 34:16. Deu 11:18.—Jos 1:8. Ps 37:31.—Ps 17:4.—Ps 119:11.
2 Pe 1:19.—Ro 15:4.

The mouth speaks out of that which fills the heart.

Let the word of Christ richly dwell within you; with all wisdom.

Watch over your heart with all diligence, for from it flow the springs of life.—Death and life are in the power of the tongue.—The mouth of the righteous utters wisdom, and his tongue speaks justice. The Law of his God is in his heart; his steps do not slip.—Let no unwholesome word proceed from your mouth, but only such a word as is good for edification according to the need of the moment, that it may give grace to those who hear.

We cannot stop speaking what we have seen and heard.—I believed . . . I said.

Every one . . . who shall confess Me before men, I will also confess him before My Father who is in heaven.—With the heart man believes, resulting in righteousness, and with the mouth he confesses, resulting in salvation.

MT 12:34. Col 3:16. Pr 4:23.—Pr 18:21.—Ps 37:30,31.—Eph 4:29.
Ac 4:20.—Ps 116:10. Mt 10:32.—Ro 10:10.

I hope to see you shortly, and we shall speak face to face.

O that Thou wouldst rend the heavens and come down.—As the deer pants for the water brooks, so my soul pants for Thee, O God. My soul thirsts for God, for the living God; when shall I come and appear before God?—Hurry, my beloved, and be like a gazelle or a young stag on the mountains of spices.

Our citizenship is in heaven, from which also we eagerly wait for a Savior, the Lord Jesus Christ.—The blessed hope . . . our great God and Savior, Christ Jesus.—God our Savior . . . Christ Jesus, who is our hope.—You love Him . . . though you do not see Him now.

He who testifies to these things says, Yes, I am coming quickly. Amen. Come, Lord Jesus.—It will be said in that day, Behold, this is our God for whom we have waited that He might save us. This is the LORD for whom we have waited; let us rejoice and be glad in His salvation.

3 JN 14. Is 64:1.—Ps 42:1,2.—Song 8:14. Phil 3:20.—Titus 2:13.—
1 Ti 1:1.—1 Pe 1:8. Rev 22:20.—Is 25:9.

Thy will be done, on earth as it is in heaven.

Bless the LORD, you His angels, mighty in strength, who perform His word, obeying the voice of His word! Bless the LORD, all you His hosts, you who serve Him, doing His will.

I have come down from heaven, not to do My own will, but the will of Him who sent Me.—I delight to do Thy will, O my God; Thy Law is within my heart.—My Father, if this cannot pass away unless I drink it, Thy will be done.

Not every one who says to Me, Lord, Lord, will enter the kingdom of heaven; but he who does the will of My Father, who is in heaven.—Not the hearers of the Law are just before God, but the doers of the Law will be justified.—If you know these things, you are blessed if you do them.—To one who knows the right thing to do, and does not do it, to him it is sin.

Do not be conformed to this world, but be transformed by the renewing of your mind.

MT 6:10. Ps 103:20,21. Jn 6:38.—Ps 40:8.—Mt 26:42. Mt 7:21.—
Ro 2:13.—Jn 13:17.—Ja 4:17. Ro 12:2.

The ear tests words, as the palate tastes food.

Beloved, do not believe every spirit, but test the spirits to see whether they are from God; because many false prophets have gone out into the world.—Do not judge according to appearance, but judge with righteous judgment.—I speak as to wise men; you judge what I say.—Let the word of Christ richly dwell within you; with all wisdom.

He who has an ear, let him hear what the Spirit says.—He who is spiritual appraises all things.

Take care what you listen to.—I know your deeds . . . and you put to the test those who call themselves apostles, and they are not, and you found them to be false.—Examine everything carefully; hold fast to that which is good.

He calls his own sheep by name, and leads them out. When he puts forth all his own, he goes before them, and the sheep follow him because they know his voice. And a stranger they simply will not follow, but will flee from him, because they do not know the voice of strangers.

JOB 34:3. 1 Jn 4:1.—Jn 7:24.—1 Co 10:15.—Col 3:16. Rev 2:29.—
1 Co 2:15. Mk 4:24.—Rev 2:2.—1 Th 5:21. Jn 10:3-5.

You shall be to Me a kingdom of priests and a holy nation.

Thou wast slain, and didst purchase for God with Thy blood men from every tribe and tongue and people and nation. And Thou hast made them to be a kingdom and priests to our God. —You are a chosen race, a royal priesthood, a holy nation, a people for God's own possession, that you may proclaim the excellencies of Him who has called you out of darkness into His marvelous light.

You will be called the priests of the LORD; you will be spoken of as ministers of our God.—Priests of God and of Christ.

Therefore, holy brethren, partakers of a heavenly calling, consider Jesus, the Apostle and High Priest of our confession.— Through Him then let us continually offer up a sacrifice of praise to God, that is, the fruit of lips that give thanks to His name.

We are His workmanship, created in Christ Jesus for good works, which God prepared beforehand, that we should walk in them.—The temple of God is holy, and that is what you are.

EX 19:6. Rev 5:9,10.—1 Pe 2:9. Is 61:6.—Rev 20:6. Heb 3:1.—
Heb 13:15. Eph 2:10.—1 Co 3:17.

We prayed to our God, and . . . set up a guard against them.

Keep watching and praying, that you may not enter into temptation.—Devote yourselves to prayer, keeping alert in it with an attitude of thanksgiving.—Casting all your anxiety upon Him, because He cares for you. Be of sober spirit, be on the alert. Your adversary, the devil, prowls about like a roaring lion, seeking someone to devour. But resist him, firm in your faith.

Why do you call Me, Lord, Lord, and do not do what I say?— Prove yourselves doers of the word, and not merely hearers who delude themselves.

Why are you crying out to Me? Tell the sons of Israel to go forward.

Be anxious for nothing, but in everything by prayer and supplication with thanksgiving let your requests be made known to God. And the peace of God, which surpasses all comprehension, shall guard your hearts and your minds in Christ Jesus.

NEH 4:9. Mt 26:41.—Col 4:2.—1 Pe 5:7–9. Lk 6:46.—Ja 1:22.
Ex 14:15. Phil 4:6,7.

Thou art a gracious and compassionate God, slow to anger and
abundant in lovingkindness, and One who relents concerning
calamity.

Now, I pray, let the power of the Lord be great, just as Thou
hast declared, the LORD is slow to anger and abundant in lovingkindness, forgiving iniquity and transgression; but He will by no
means clear the guilty; visiting the iniquity of the fathers on the
children to the third and fourth generations.

Do not remember the iniquities of our forefathers against us;
let Thy compassion come quickly to meet us. . . . Help us, O God
of our salvation, for the glory of Thy name; and deliver us, and
forgive our sins, for Thy name's sake.—Although our iniquities
testify against us, O LORD, act for Thy name's sake!—Truly our
apostasies have been many, we have sinned against Thee.—We
know our wickedness, O LORD, the iniquity of our fathers, for we
have sinned against Thee.

If Thou, LORD, shouldst mark iniquities, O Lord, who could
stand? But there is forgiveness with Thee, that Thou mayest be
feared.

JON 4:2. Num 14:17,18. Ps 79:8,9.—Jer 14:7.—Jer 14:20. Ps 130:3,4.

Sanctification by the Spirit.

Awake, O north wind, and come, wind of the south; make my
garden breathe out fragrance.

Behold what earnestness this very thing, this godly sorrow, has
produced in you, what vindication of yourselves, what indignation, what fear, what longing, what zeal, what avenging of
wrong!—(for the fruit of the light consists in all goodness and
righteousness and truth), trying to learn what is pleasing to the
Lord.

The Helper, the Holy Spirit.—The love of God has been
poured out within our hearts through the Holy Spirit who was
given to us.

The fruit of the Spirit is love, joy, peace.

In a great ordeal of affliction their abundance of joy and their
deep poverty overflowed in the wealth of their liberality.

The same Spirit works all these things, distributing to each one
individually just as He wills.

2 TH 2:13. Song 4:16. 2 Co 7:11.—Eph 5:9,10. Jn 14:26.—Ro 5:5.
Gal 5:22. 2 Co 8:2. 1 Co 12:11.

He calls his own sheep by name, and leads them out.

The firm foundation of God stands, having this seal, The Lord knows those who are His, and, Let every one who names the name of the Lord abstain from wickedness.—Many will say to Me on that day, Lord, Lord, did we not prophesy in Your name, and in Your name cast out demons, and in Your name perform many miracles? And then I will declare to them, I never knew you; depart from Me, you who practice lawlessness.—The LORD knows the way of the righteous, but the way of the wicked will perish.

Behold, I have inscribed you on the palms of My hands; your walls are continually before Me.—Put me like a seal over your heart, like a seal on your arm.—The LORD is good, a stronghold in the day of trouble, and He knows those who take refuge in Him.

I go to prepare a place for you. And if I go and prepare a place for you, I will come again, and receive you to Myself; that where I am, there you may be also.

JN 10:3. 2 Ti 2:19.—Mt 7:22,23.—Ps 1:6. Is 49:16.—Song 8:6.—
Nah 1:7. Jn 14:2,3.

She has done what she could.

This poor widow put in more than all of them.—Whoever gives you a cup of water to drink because of your name as followers of Christ, truly I say to you, he shall not lose his reward.—If the readiness is present, it is acceptable according to what a man has, not according to what he does not have.

Let us not love with word or with tongue, but in deed and truth.—If a brother or sister is without clothing and in need of daily food, and one of you says to them, Go in peace, be warmed and be filled; and yet you do not give them what is necessary for their body; what use is that?—He who sows sparingly shall also reap sparingly; and he who sows bountifully shall also reap bountifully. Let each one do just as he has purposed in his heart; not grudgingly or under compulsion; for God loves a cheerful giver.

When you do all the things which are commanded you, say, We are unworthy slaves; we have done only that which we ought to have done.

MK 14:8. Lk 21:3.—Mk 9:41.—2 Co 8:12. 1 Jn 3:18.—Ja 2:15,16.—
2 Co 9:6,7. Lk 17:10.

The Mighty One has done great things for me; and holy is His name.

Who is like Thee among the gods, O Lord? Who is like Thee, majestic in holiness, awesome in praises, working wonders?— There is no one like Thee among the gods, O Lord; nor are there any works like Thine.—Who will not fear, O Lord, and glorify Thy name? For Thou alone art holy.—Hallowed be Thy name.
Blessed be the Lord God of Israel, for He has visited us and accomplished redemption for His people.
Who is this who comes from Edom, with garments of glowing colors from Bozrah, this one who is majestic in His apparel, marching in the greatness of His strength? It is I who speak in righteousness, mighty to save.—I have given help to one who is mighty; I have exalted one chosen from the people.
Now to Him who is able to do exceeding abundantly beyond all that we ask or think, according to the power that works within us ... be the glory.

LK 1:49. Ex 15:11.—Ps 86:8.—Rev 15:4.—Mt 6:9. Lk 1:68.
Is 63:1.—Ps 89:19. Eph 3:20,21.

The dew of Hermon.

Mount Sion (that is, Hermon).—For there the Lord commanded the blessing—life forever.—I will be like the dew to Israel; he will blossom like the lily and he will take root like the cedars of Lebanon.
Let my teaching drop as the rain, my speech distill as the dew, as the droplets on the fresh grass and as the showers on the herb. —For as the rain and the snow come down from heaven, and do not return there without watering the earth, and making it bear and sprout, and furnishing seed to the sower and bread to the eater; so shall My word be which goes forth from My mouth; it shall not return to Me empty, without accomplishing what I desire, and without succeeding in the matter for which I sent it.
God ... gives the Spirit without measure.—Of His fulness we have all received, and grace upon grace.—It is like the precious oil upon the head ... even Aaron's ... coming down upon the edge of his robes.

PS 133:3. Deu 4:48.—Ps 133:3.—Ho 14:5. Deu 32:2.—Is 55:10,11.
Jn 3:34.—Jn 1:16.—Ps 133:2.

They are not of the world, even as I am not of the world.

He was despised and forsaken of men, a man of sorrows, and acquainted with grief.—In the world you have tribulation, but take courage; I have overcome the world.

It was fitting that we should have such a high priest, holy, innocent, undefiled, separated from sinners.—That you may prove yourselves to be blameless and innocent, children of God above reproach in the midst of a crooked and perverse generation.

Jesus of Nazareth . . . He went about doing good, and healing all who were oppressed by the devil; for God was with Him.—While we have opportunity, let us do good to all men, and especially to those who are of the household of faith.

There was the true light which, coming into the world, enlightens every man.—You are the light of the world. A city set on a hill cannot be hidden. Let your light shine before men in such a way that they may see your good works, and glorify your Father who is in heaven.

JN 17:16. Is 53:3.—Jn 16:33. Heb 7:26.—Phil 2:15. Ac 10:38.—
Gal 6:10. Jn 1:9.—Mt 5:14,16.

A cheerful heart has a continual feast.

The joy of the LORD is your strength.—The kingdom of God is not eating and drinking, but righteousness and peace and joy in the Holy Spirit.—Be filled with the Spirit, speaking to one another in psalms and hymns and spiritual songs, singing and making melody with your heart to the Lord; always giving thanks for all things in the name of our Lord Jesus Christ.

Through Him then let us continually offer up a sacrifice of praise to God, that is, the fruit of lips that give thanks to His name.

Though the fig tree should not blossom, and there be no fruit on the vines, though the yield of the olive should fail, and the fields produce no food, though the flock should be cut off from the fold, and there be no cattle in the stalls, yet I will exult in the LORD, I will rejoice in the God of my salvation.—As sorrowful yet always rejoicing.—We also exult in our tribulations.

PR 15:15. Neh 8:10.—Ro 14:17.—Eph 5:18–20. Heb 13:15.
Hab 3:17,18.—2 Co 6:10.—Ro 5:3.

What is the benefit of circumcision?

Great in every respect.—Circumcise yourselves to the Lord and remove the foreskins of your heart.—If their uncircumcised heart becomes humbled so that they then make amends for their iniquity, then I will remember My covenant with Jacob, and I will remember also My covenant with Isaac, and My covenant with Abraham as well.

Christ has become a servant to the circumcision on behalf of the truth of God to confirm the promises given to the fathers.— In Him you were also circumcised with a circumcision made without hands, in the removal of the body of the flesh by the circumcision of Christ.—When you were dead in your transgressions and the uncircumcision of your flesh, He made you alive together with Him, having forgiven us all our transgressions.

Lay aside the old self, which is being corrupted in accordance with the lusts of deceit, and that you be renewed in the spirit of your mind, and put on the new self, which in the likeness of God has been created in righteousness.

RO 3:1. Ro 3:2.—Jer 4:4.—Lev 26:41,42. Ro 15:8.—Col 2:11.—
Col 2:13. Eph 4:22–24.

The veil of the temple was torn in two from top to bottom.

The Lord Jesus in the night in which He was betrayed took bread; and when He had given thanks, He broke it, and said, This is My body, which is for you; do this in remembrance of Me.— The bread . . . which I shall give for the life of the world is My flesh.

Unless you eat the flesh of the Son of Man and drink His blood, you have no life in yourselves. He who eats My flesh and drinks My blood has eternal life. . . . He who eats My flesh and drinks My blood abides in Me, and I in him. As the living Father sent Me, and I live because of the Father; so he who eats Me, he also shall live because of Me. Does this cause you to stumble? What then if you should behold the Son of Man ascending where He was before? It is the Spirit who gives life; the flesh profits nothing.

A new and living way which He inaugurated for us through the veil, that is, His flesh. Let us draw near.

MT 27:51. 1 Co 11:23,24.—Jn 6:51. Jn 6:53,54,56,57,61–63.
Heb 10:20,22.

For the death that He died, He died to sin, once for all; but the life that He lives, He lives to God.

He . . . was numbered with the transgressors.—Christ . . . having been offered once to bear the sins of many.—He Himself bore our sins in His body on the cross, that we might die to sin and live to righteousness; for by His wounds you were healed.—By one offering He has perfected for all time those who are sanctified.

He abides forever, holds His priesthood permanently. Hence also He is able to save forever those who draw near to God through Him, since He always lives to make intercession for them.—God demonstrates His own love toward us, in that while we were yet sinners, Christ died for us. Much more then, having now been justified by His blood, we shall be saved from the wrath of God through Him.

Therefore, since Christ has suffered in the flesh, arm yourselves also with the same purpose, because he who has suffered in the flesh has ceased from sin, so as to live the rest of the time in the flesh no longer for the lusts of men, but for the will of God.

RO 6:10. Is 53:12.—Heb 9:28.—1 Pe 2:24.—Heb 10:14.
Heb 7:24,25.—Ro 5:8,9. 1 Pe 4:1,2.

Keep yourselves in the love of God.

Abide in Me, and I in you. As the branch cannot bear fruit of itself, unless it abides in the vine, so neither can you, unless you abide in Me. I am the vine, you are the branches; he who abides in Me, and I in him, he bears much fruit; for apart from Me you can do nothing.

The fruit of the Spirit is love.

By this is My Father glorified, that you bear much fruit, and so prove to be My disciples. Just as the Father has loved Me, I have also loved you; abide in My love. If you keep My commandments, you will abide in My love; just as I have kept My Father's commandments and abide in His love.—Whoever keeps His word, in him the love of God has truly been perfected.

This is My commandment, that you love one another, just as I have loved you.—God demonstrates His own love toward us, in that while we were yet sinners, Christ died for us.—God is love, and the one who abides in love abides in God, and God abides in him.

JUDE 21. Jn 15:4,5. Gal 5:22. Jn 15:8–10.—1 Jn 2:5. Jn 15:12.—
Ro 5:8.—1 Jn 4:16.

Then comes the end.

But of that day or hour no one knows, not even the angels in heaven, nor the Son, but the Father alone. Take heed, keep on the alert; for you do not know when the appointed time is. What I say to you I say to all, Be on the alert!—The Lord is not slow about His promise, as some count slowness, but is patient toward you, not wishing for any to perish but for all to come to repentance.—The coming of the Lord is at hand. ... The Judge is standing right at the door.—Yes, I am coming quickly.

Since all these things are to be destroyed in this way, what sort of people ought you to be in holy conduct and godliness.

The end of all things is at hand; therefore, be of sound judgment and sober spirit for the purpose of prayer.—Be dressed in readiness, and keep your lamps alight. And be like men who are waiting for their master when he returns from the wedding feast, so that they may immediately open the door to him when he comes and knocks.

1 CO 15:24. Mk 13:32,33,37.—2 Pe 3:9.—Ja 5:8,9.—Rev 22:20.
2 Pe 3:11. 1 Pe 4:7.—Lk 12:35,36.

Brethren, pray for us.

Is anyone among you sick? Let him call for the elders of the church, and let them pray over him ... and the prayer offered in faith will restore the one who is sick, and the Lord will raise him up. ... Pray for one another, so that you may be healed. The effective prayer of a righeous man can accomplish much. Elijah was a man with a nature like ours, and he prayed earnestly that it might not rain; and it did not rain on the earth for three years and six months. And he prayed again, and the sky poured rain, and the earth produced its fruit.

With all prayer and petition pray at all times in the Spirit ... be on the alert with all perseverance and petition for all the saints.

How unceasingly I make mention of you.—Always laboring earnestly for you in ... prayers, that you may stand perfect and fully assured in all the will of God.

1 TH 5:25. Ja 5:14–18. Eph 6:18. Ro 1:9.—Col 4:12.

Persevering in tribulation.

It is the LORD; let Him do what seems good to Him.—For though I were right, I could not answer; I would have to implore the mercy of my Judge.—The LORD gave and the LORD has taken away. Blessed be the name of the LORD.—Shall we indeed accept good from God and not accept adversity?

Jesus wept.—A man of sorrows, and acquainted with grief. . . . Surely our griefs He Himself bore, and our sorrows He carried.

For those whom the Lord loves He disciplines, and He scourges every son whom He receives. All discipline for the moment seems not to be joyful, but sorrowful; yet to those who have been trained by it, afterwards it yields the peaceful fruit of righteousness.—Strengthened with all power, according to His glorious might, for the attaining of all steadfastness and patience, joyously.—In the world you have tribulation, but take courage; I have overcome the world.

RO 12:12. 1 Sa 3:18.—Job 9:15.—Job 1:21.—Job 2:10. Jn 11:35.—
Is 53:3,4. Heb 12:6,11.—Col 1:11.—Jn 16:33.

With respect to the promise of God, he did not waver in unbelief.

Have faith in God. . . . Whoever says to this mountain, Be taken up and cast into the sea, and does not doubt in his heart, but believes that what he says is going to happen; it shall be granted him. Therefore I say to you, all things for which you pray and ask, believe that you have received them, and they shall be granted you.—Without faith it is impossible to please Him, for he who comes to God must believe that He is, and that He is a rewarder of those who seek Him.

By faith Abraham . . . he who had received the promises was offering up his only begotten son; it was he to whom it was said, In Isaac your descendants shall be called. He considered that God is able to raise men even from the dead.—Being fully assured that what He had promised, He was able also to perform.

Is anything too difficult for the LORD?—With God all things are possible.—Lord, increase our faith!

RO 4:20. Mk 11:22–24.—Heb 11:6. Heb 11:17–19.—Ro 4:21.
Gen 18:14.—Mt 19:26.—Lk 17:5.

We know that we have passed out of death into life.

He who hears My word, and believes Him who sent Me, has eternal life, and does not come into judgment, but has passed out of death into life.—He who has the Son has the life; he who does not have the Son of God does not have the life.

He who establishes us with you in Christ and anointed us is God, who also sealed us and gave us the Spirit in our hearts as a pledge.—We shall know by this that we are of the truth, and shall assure our heart before Him. Beloved, if our heart does not condemn us, we have confidence before God.—We know that we are of God, and the whole world lies in the power of the evil one.

You were dead in your trespasses and sins. . . . Alive together with Christ.—He delivered us from the domain of darkness, and transferred us to the kingdom of His beloved Son.

1 JN 3:14. Jn 5:24.—1 Jn 5:12. 2 Co 1:21,22.—1 Jn 3:19,21.—
1 Jn 5:19. Eph 2:1,5.—Col 1:13.

Thou wilt make known to me the path of life.

Thus says the LORD, Behold, I set before you the way of life and the way of death.—I will instruct you in the good and right way. —I am the way, and the truth, and the life; no one comes to the Father, but through Me.—Follow Me.

There is a way which seems right to a man, but its end is the way of death.—The gate is wide, and the way is broad that leads to destruction, and many are those who enter by it. For the gate is small, and the way is narrow that leads to life, and few are those who find it.

And a highway will be there, a roadway, and it will be called the highway of holiness. The unclean will not travel on it, but it will be for him who walks that way, and fools will not wander on it.—So let us know, let us press on to know the LORD.

In My Father's house are many dwelling places; if it were not so, I would have told you; for I go to prepare a place for you.

PS 16:11. Jer 21:8.—1 Sa 12:23.—Jn 14:6.—Mt 4:19. Pr 14:12.—
Mt 7:13,14. Is 35:8.—Ho 6:3. Jn 14:2.

By faith Abraham, when he was called, obeyed by going out to a place which he was to receive for an inheritance.

He chooses our inheritance for us.—He encircled him, He cared for him, He guarded him as the pupil of His eye. Like an eagle that stirs up its nest, that hovers over its young, He spread His wings and caught them, He carried them on His pinions. The LORD alone guided him, and there was no foreign god with him.

I am the LORD your God, who teaches you to profit, who leads you in the way you should go.—Who is a teacher like Him?

We walk by faith, not by sight.—Here we do not have a lasting city, but we are seeking the city which is to come.—Beloved, I urge you as aliens and strangers to abstain from fleshly lusts, which wage war against the soul.—Arise and go, for this is no place of rest because of the uncleanness that brings on destruction, a painful destruction.

HEB 11:8. Ps 47:4.—Deu 32:10–12. Is 48:17.—Job 36:22.
2 Co 5:7.—Heb 13:14.—1 Pe 2:11.—Mic 2:10.

Give thanks to His holy name.

The heavens are not pure in His sight; how much less one who is detestable and corrupt, man, who drinks iniquity like water!—The stars are not pure in His sight, how much less man . . . that worm!

Who is like Thee among the gods, O LORD? Who is like Thee, majestic in holiness.—Holy, Holy, Holy, is the LORD of hosts.

Like the Holy One who called you, be holy yourselves also in all your behavior; because it is written, You shall be holy, for I am holy.—We . . . share His holiness.

The temple of God is holy, and that is what you are.—What sort of people ought you to be in holy conduct and godliness. . . . spotless and blameless.

Let no unwholesome word proceed from your mouth, but only such a word as is good for edification. . . . And do not grieve the Holy Spirit of God, by whom you were sealed for the day of redemption.

PS 97:12. Job 15:15,16.—Job 25:5,6. Ex 15:11.—Is 6:3.
1 Pe 1:15,16.—Heb 12:10. 1 Co 3:17.—2 Pe 3:11,14. Eph 4:29,30.

Christ, who is the image of God.

The glory of the LORD will be revealed, and all flesh will see it together.—No man has seen God at any time; the only begotten God, who is in the bosom of the Father, He has explained Him. And the Word became flesh, and dwelt among us, and we beheld His glory, glory as of the only begotten from the Father, full of grace and truth.—He who has seen Me has seen the Father.—He is the radiance of His glory and the exact representation of His nature.—He . . . was revealed in the flesh.

In whom we have redemption, the forgiveness of sins. And He is the image of the invisible God, the first-born of all creation.— Whom He foreknew, He also predestined to become conformed to the image of His Son, that He might be the first-born among many brethren.

Just as we have borne the image of the earthy, we shall also bear the image of the heavenly.

2 CO 4:4. Is 40:5.—Jn 1:18,14.—Jn 14:9.—Heb 1:3.—1 Ti 3:16.
Col 1:14,15.—Ro 8:29. 1 Co 15:49.

Thou hast girded me with strength for battle.

When I am weak, then I am strong.

Then Asa called to the LORD his God, and said, Lord, there is no one besides Thee to help in the battle between the powerful and those who have no strength; so help us, O LORD our God, for we trust in Thee, and in Thy name have come against this multitude. O LORD, Thou art our God; let not man prevail against Thee.—Jehoshaphat cried out, and the LORD helped him.

It is better to take refuge in the LORD than to trust in man. It is better to take refuge in the LORD than to trust in princes.— The king is not saved by a mighty army; a warrior is not delivered by great strength. A horse is a false hope for victory; nor does it deliver anyone by its great strength.

For our struggle is not against flesh and blood, but against the rulers, against the powers, against the world-forces of this darkness, against the spiritual forces of wickedness in the heavenly places. Therefore take up the full armor of God.

PS 18:39. 2 Co 12:10. 2 Ch 14:11.—2 Ch 18:31. Ps 118:8,9.—
Ps 33:16,17. Eph 6:12,13.

Walk in love.

A new commandment I give to you, that you love one another, even as I have loved you, that you also love one another.—Above all, keep fervent in your love for one another, because love covers a multitude of sins.—Love covers all transgressions.

Whenever you stand praying, forgive, if you have anything against anyone; so that your Father also who is in heaven may forgive you your transgressions.—Love your enemies, and do good, and lend, expecting nothing in return.—Do not rejoice when your enemy falls, and do not let your heart be glad when he stumbles.—Not returning evil for evil, or insult for insult, but giving a blessing instead; for you were called for the very purpose that you might inherit a blessing.—If possible, so far as it depends on you, be at peace with all men.—Be kind to one another, tender-hearted, forgiving each other, just as God in Christ also has forgiven you.

Little children, let us not love with word or with tongue, but in deed and truth.

EPH 5:2. Jn 13:34.—1 Pe 4:8.—Pr 10:12. Mk 11:25.—Lk 6:35.— Pr 24:17.—1 Pe 3:9.—Ro 12:18.—Eph 4:32. 1 Jn 3:18.

Let your requests be made known to God.

Abba (Father), all things are possible for Thee; remove this cup from Me; yet not what I will, but what Thou wilt.—There was given me a thorn in the flesh. . . . Concerning this I entreated the Lord three times that it might depart from me. And He has said to me, My grace is sufficient for you, for power is perfected in weakness. Most gladly, therefore, I will rather boast about my weaknesses.

I pour out my complaint before Him; I declare my trouble before Him.—Hannah . . . greatly distressed, prayed to the LORD and wept bitterly. And she made a vow and said, O LORD of hosts, if Thou wilt indeed look on the affliction of Thy maidservant and . . . wilt give Thy maidservant a son, then I will give him to the LORD all the days of his life. . . . the LORD remembered her.

We do not know how to pray as we should.—He chooses our inheritance for us.

PHIL 4:6. Mk 14:36.—2 Co 12:7-9. Ps 142:2.—1 Sa 1:9-11,19. Ro 8:26.—Ps 47:4.

O that Thou wouldst rend the heavens and come down.

Hurry, my beloved, and be like a gazelle or a young stag on the mountains of spices.—We ourselves groan within ourselves, waiting eagerly for our adoption as sons, the redemption of our body. —Bow Thy heavens, O LORD, and come down; touch the mountains, that they may smoke.

This Jesus, who has been taken up from you into heaven, will come in just the same way as you have watched Him go into heaven.—Christ . . . shall appear a second time for salvation without reference to sin, to those who eagerly await Him.—It will be said in that day, Behold, this is our God for whom we have waited that He might save us. This is the LORD for whom we have waited; let us rejoice and be glad in His salvation.

He who testifies to these things says, Yes, I am coming quickly. Amen. Come, Lord Jesus.—The blessed hope and the appearing of the glory of our great God and Savior, Christ Jesus.—Our citizenship is in heaven.

IS 64:1. Song 8:14.—Ro 8:23.—Ps 144:5. Ac 1:11.—Heb 9:28.— Is 25:9. Rev 22:20.—Titus 2:13.—Phil 3:20.

Thou hast given me the inheritance of those who fear Thy name.

No weapon that is formed against you shall prosper; and every tongue that accuses you in judgment you will condemn. This is the heritage of the servants of the LORD, and their vindication is from Me, declares the LORD.—The angel of the LORD encamps around those who fear Him, and rescues them. O taste and see that the LORD is good; how blessed is the man who takes refuge in Him! O fear the LORD, you His saints; for to those who fear Him, there is no want. The young lions do lack and suffer hunger; but they who seek the LORD shall not be in want of any good thing.—The lines have fallen to me in pleasant places; indeed, my heritage is beautiful to me.

But for you who fear My name the sun of righteousness will rise with healing in its wings; and you will go forth and skip about like calves from the stall.—He who did not spare His own Son, but delivered Him up for us all, how will He not also with Him freely give us all things?

PS 61:5. Is 54:17.—Ps 34:7–10.—Ps 16:6. Mal 4:2.—Ro 8:32.

Keep seeking the things above, where Christ is, seated at the right hand of God.

Acquire wisdom! Acquire understanding!—The wisdom from above.—The deep says, It is not in me; and the sea says, It is not with me.—We have been buried with Him through baptism into death, in order that as Christ was raised from the dead through the glory of the Father, so we too might walk in newness of life. For if we have become united with Him in the likeness of His death, certainly we shall be also in the likeness of His resurrection.

Let us also lay aside every encumbrance, and the sin which so easily entangles us, and let us run with endurance the race that is set before us.—God . . . made us alive together with Christ . . . and raised us up with Him, and seated us with Him in the heavenly places, in Christ Jesus.

Those who say such things make it clear that they are seeking a country of their own.—Seek the LORD, all you humble of the earth who have carried out His ordinances; seek righteousness, seek humility.

COL 3:1. Pr 4:5.—Ja 3:17.—Job 28:14.—Ro 6:4,5. Heb 12:1.—
Eph 2:4–6. Heb 11:14.—Zep 2:3.

Nicodemus . . . (he who came to Him before).

Peter also followed Him at a distance.—Many even of the rulers believed in Him, but because of the Pharisees they were not confessing Him, lest they should be put out of the synagogue; for they loved the approval of men rather than the approval of God.—The fear of man brings a snare, but he who trusts in the LORD will be exalted.

The one who comes to Me I will certainly not cast out.—A bruised reed He will not break, and a dimly burning wick He will not extinguish.—Faith as a mustard seed.

God has not given us a spirit of timidity, but of power and love and discipline. Therefore do not be ashamed of the testimony of our Lord.—Little children, abide in Him, so that when He appears, we may have confidence and not shrink away from Him in shame at His coming.—Every one therefore who shall confess Me before men, I will also confess him before My Father who is in heaven.

JN 7:50. Mt 26:58.—Jn 12:42,43.—Pr 29:25. Jn 6:37.—Is 42:3.—
Mt 17:20. 2 Ti 1:7,8.—1 Jn 2:28.—Mt 10:32.

Suffer hardship with me, as a good soldier of Christ Jesus.

I have made him a witness to the peoples, a leader and commander for the peoples.—It was fitting for Him, for whom are all things, and through whom are all things, in bringing many sons to glory, to perfect the author of their salvation through sufferings.—Through many tribulations we must enter the kingdom of God.

For our struggle is not against flesh and blood, but against the rulers, against the powers, against the world-forces of this darkness, against the spiritual forces of wickedness in the heavenly places. Therefore take up the full armor of God.—We do not war according to the flesh, for the weapons of our warfare are not of the flesh, but divinely powerful for the destruction of fortresses.

After you have suffered for a little while, the God of all grace, who called you to His eternal glory in Christ, will Himself perfect, confirm, strengthen and establish you.

2 TI 2:3. Is 55:4.—Heb 2:10.—Ac 14:22. Eph 6:12,13.—2 Co 10:3,4.
1 Pe 5:10.

The unity of the Spirit.

There is one body and one Spirit.—Through Him we both have our access in one Spirit to the Father. So then you are no longer strangers and aliens, but you are fellow-citizens with the saints, and are of God's household, having been built upon the foundation of the apostles and prophets, Christ Jesus Himself being the cornerstone, in whom the whole building, being fitted together is growing into a holy temple in the Lord; in whom you also are being built together into a dwelling of God in the Spirit.

Behold, how good and how pleasant it is for brothers to dwell together in unity! It is like the precious oil upon the head, coming down upon the beard, even Aaron's beard, coming down upon the edge of his robes.

Since you have in obedience to the truth purified your souls for a sincere love of the brethren, fervently love one another from the heart.

EPH 4:3. Eph 4:4.—Eph 2:18–22. Ps 133:1,2. 1 Pe 1:22.

The fruit of the Spirit is ... faithfulness.

By grace you have been saved through faith; and that not of yourselves, it is the gift of God.—Without faith it is impossible to please Him.—He who believes in Him is not judged; he who does not believe has been judged already, because he has not believed in the name of the only begotten Son of God.—I do believe; help my unbelief.

Whoever keeps His word, in him the love of God has truly been perfected. By this we know that we are in Him.—Faith working through love.—Faith without works is useless.

We walk by faith, not by sight.—I have been crucified with Christ; and it is no longer I who live, but Christ lives in me; and the life which I now live in the flesh I live by faith in the Son of God, who loved me, and delivered Himself up for me.—Though you have not seen Him, you love Him, and though you do not see Him now, but believe in Him, you greatly rejoice with joy inexpressible and full of glory, obtaining as the outcome of your faith the salvation of your souls.

GAL 5:22. Eph 2:8.—Heb 11:6.—Jn 3:18.—Mk 9:24. 1 Jn 2:5.—
Gal 5:6.—Ja 2:20. 2 Co 5:7.—Gal 2:20.—1 Pe 1:8,9.

The Lord is full of compassion and is merciful.

Just as a father has compassion on his children, so the LORD has compassion on those who fear Him.—The LORD is gracious and compassionate. He will remember His covenant forever.

He who keeps you will not slumber. Behold, He who keeps Israel will neither slumber nor sleep.—Like an eagle that stirs up its nest, that hovers over its young, He spread His wings and caught them, He carried them on His pinions. The LORD alone guided him, and there was no foreign god with him.

His compassions never fail. They are new every morning; great is Thy faithfulness.

When He came out, He saw a great multitude, and felt compassion for them, and healed their sick.—The same yesterday and today, yes and forever.

The very hairs of your head are all numbered. Are not two sparrows sold for a cent? And yet not one of them will fall to the ground apart from your Father. Therefore do not fear.

JA 5:11. Ps 103:13.—Ps 111:4,5. Ps 121:3,4.—Deu 32:11,12.
Lam 3:22,23. Mt 14:14.—Heb 13:8. Mt 10:30,29,31.

From the foundation of the world . . . the Lamb who has been slain.

Your lamb shall be . . . unblemished . . . the whole assembly of the congregation of Israel is to kill it at twilight. . . . they shall take some of the blood and put it on the two doorposts and on the lintel of the houses in which they eat it. . . . and when I see the blood I will pass over you.—The sprinkled blood.—Christ our Passover also has been sacrificed.—This Man, delivered up by the predetermined plan and foreknowledge of God.—According to His own purpose and grace which was granted us in Christ Jesus from all eternity.

In Him we have redemption through His blood, the forgiveness of our trespasses.

Therefore, since Christ has suffered in the flesh, arm yourselves also with the same purpose, because he who has suffered in the flesh has ceased from sin, so as to live the rest of the time in the flesh no longer for the lusts of men, but for the will of God.

REV 13:8. Ex 12:5–7,13.—Heb 12:24.—1 Co 5:7.—Ac 2:23.—
2 Ti 1:9. Eph 1:7. 1 Pe 4:1,2.

I have trodden the wine trough alone.

Who is like Thee among the gods, O LORD? Who is like Thee, majestic in holiness, awesome in praises, working wonders?—He saw that there was no man, and was astonished that there was no one to intercede; then His own arm brought salvation to Him; and His righteousness upheld Him.—He Himself bore our sins in His body on the cross.—Become a curse for us.

O sing to the LORD a new song, for He has done wonderful things, His right hand and His holy arm have gained the victory for Him.—When he had disarmed the rulers and authorities, He made a public display of them, having triumphed over them through Him.—As a result of the anguish of His soul, He will see it and be satisfied; by His knowledge the Righteous One, My Servant, will justify the many, as He will bear their iniquities.

O my soul, march on with strength.—We overwhelmingly conquer through Him who loved us.—They overcame . . . because of the blood of the Lamb and because of the word of their testimony.

IS 63:3. Ex 15:11.—Is 59:16.—1 Pe 2:24.—Gal 3:13. Ps 98:1.—
Col 2:15.—Is 53:11. Judg 5:21.—Ro 8:37.—Rev 12:11.

His mercy is upon ... those who fear Him.

How great is Thy goodness, which Thou hast stored up for those who fear Thee, which Thou hast wrought for those who take refuge in Thee, before the sons of men! Thou dost hide them in the secret place of Thy presence from the conspiracies of man; Thou dost keep them secretly in a shelter from the strife of tongues.

If you address as Father the One who impartially judges according to each man's work, conduct yourselves in fear during the time of your stay upon earth.—The LORD is near to all who call upon Him ... in truth. He will fulfill the desire of those who fear Him; He will also hear their cry and will save them.

Because your heart was tender and you humbled yourself before the LORD ... and you have torn your clothes and wept before Me, I truly have heard you, declares the LORD.—To this one I will look, to him who is humble and contrite of spirit, and who trembles at My word.—The LORD is near to the broken-hearted, and saves those who are crushed in spirit.

LK 1:50. Ps 31:19,20. 1 Pe 1:17.—Ps 145:18,19. 2 Ki 22:19.—
Is 66:2.—Ps 34:18.

Those who honor Me I will honor.

Every one therefore who shall confess Me before men, I will also confess him before My Father who is in heaven.—He who loves father or mother more than Me is not worthy of Me; and he who loves son or daughter more than Me is not worthy of Me. And he who does not take his cross and follow after Me is not worthy of Me. He who has found his life shall lose it, and he who has lost his life for My sake shall find it.

Blessed is a man who perseveres under trial; for once he has been approved, he will receive the crown of life, which the Lord has promised to those who love him.

Do not fear what you are about to suffer. ... Be faithful until death, and I will give you the crown of life.

For momentary, light affliction is producing for us an eternal weight of glory far beyond all comparison.—Praise and glory and honor at the revelation of Jesus Christ.

1 SA 2:30. Mt 10:32.—Mt 10:37–39. Ja 1:12. Rev 2:10. 2 Co 4:17.—
1 Pe 1:7.

It is finished! And he bowed His head, and gave up His spirit.

Jesus, the author and perfecter of faith.—I glorified Thee on the earth, having accomplished the work which Thou hast given Me to do.—We have been sanctified through the offering of the body of Jesus Christ once for all. And every priest stands daily ministering and offering time after time the same sacrifices, which can never take away sins; but He, having offered one sacrifice for sins for all time, sat down at the right hand of God, waiting from that time onward until His enemies be made a footstool for His feet. For by one offering He has perfected for all time those who are sanctified.—Having cancelled out the certificate of debt consisting of decrees against us and which was hostile to us; and He has taken it out of the way, having nailed it to the cross.

I lay down My life that I may take it again. No one has taken it away from Me, but I lay it down on My own initiative. I have authority to lay it down, and I have authority to take it up again. —Greater love has no one than this, that one lay down his life for his friends.

JN 19:30. Heb 12:2.—Jn 17:4.—Heb 10:10–14.—Col 2:14.
Jn 10:17,18.—Jn 15:13.

He sent from on high, He took me; He drew me out of many waters.

He brought me up out of the pit of destruction, out of the miry clay; and He set my feet upon a rock making my footsteps firm. —You were dead in your trespasses and sins, in which you formerly walked according to the course of this world. . . . We . . . all formerly lived in the lusts of our flesh.

Hear my cry, O God; give heed to my prayer. From the end of the earth I call to Thee, when my heart is faint.—I cried for help from the depth of Sheol; Thou didst hear my voice. For Thou hadst cast me into the deep, into the heart of the seas, and the current engulfed me. All Thy breakers and billows passed over me.—We went through fire and through water; yet Thou didst bring us out into a place of abundance.

When you pass through the waters, I will be with you; and through the rivers, they will not overflow you.

PS 18:16. Ps 40:2.—Eph 2:1–3. Ps 61:1,2.—Jon 2:2,3.—Ps 66:12.
Is 43:2.

Walk in newness of life.

Just as you presented your members as slaves to impurity and to lawlessness ... so now present your members as slaves to righteousness, resulting in sanctification.—I urge you ... brethren, by the mercies of God, to present your bodies a living and holy sacrifice, acceptable to God, which is your spiritual service of worship. Do not be conformed to this world, but be transformed by the renewing of your mind.

If any man is in Christ, he is a new creature; the old things passed away; behold, new things have come.—For neither is circumcision anything, nor uncircumcision, but a new creation. And those who will walk by this rule, peace and mercy be upon them.—This I say therefore, and affirm together with the Lord, that you walk no longer just as the Gentiles also walk, in the futility of their mind. You did not learn Christ in this way, if indeed you have heard Him and have been taught in Him, just as truth is in Jesus. Put on the new self, which in the likeness of God has been created in righteousness and holiness of the truth.

RO 6:4. Ro 6:19.—Ro 12:1,2. 2 Co 5:17.—Gal 6:15,16.— Eph 4:17,20,21,24.

Thy will be done.

I know, O LORD, that a man's way is not in himself; nor is it in a man who walks to direct his steps.—Not as I will, but as Thou wilt.—Surely I have composed and quieted my soul; like a weaned child rests against his mother, my soul is like a weaned child within me.

We do not know how to pray as we should, but the Spirit Himself intercedes for us with groanings too deep for words; and He who searches the hearts knows what the mind of the Spirit is, because He intercedes for the saints according to the will of God.

You do not know what you are asking.—So He gave them their request, but sent a wasting disease among them.—Now these things happened as examples for us, that we should not crave evil things, as they also craved.

I want you to be free from concern.—The steadfast of mind Thou wilt keep in perfect peace, because he trusts in Thee.

MT 26:42. Jer 10:23.—Mt 26:39.—Ps 131:2. Ro 8:26,27. Mt 20:22.— Ps 106:15.—1 Co 10:6. 1 Co 7:32.—Is 26:3.

Whom the LORD loves He reproves.

See now that I, I am He, and there is no god besides Me; it is I who put to death and give life. I have wounded, and it is I who heal; and there is no one who can deliver from My hand.—I know the plans that I have for you, declares the LORD, plans for welfare and not for calamity to give you a future and a hope.—My thoughts are not your thoughts, neither are your ways My ways, declares the LORD.

I will allure her, bring her into the wilderness, and speak kindly to her.—The LORD your God was disciplining you just as a man disciplines his son.—All discipline for the moment seems not to be joyful, but sorrowful; yet to those who have been trained by it, afterwards it yields the peaceful fruit of righteousness.—Humble yourselves, therefore, under the mighty hand of God, that He may exalt you at the proper time.

I know, O LORD, that Thy judgments are righteous, and that in faithfulness Thou hast afflicted me.

PR 3:12. Deu 32:39.—Jer 29:11.—Is 55:8. Ho 2:14.—Deu 8:5.—
Heb 12:11.—1 Pe 5:6. Ps 119:75.

The earth is the LORD'S, and all it contains.

She does not know that it was I who gave her the grain, the new wine, and the oil, and lavished on her silver and gold. Therefore, I will take back My grain at harvest time and My new wine in its season. I will also take away My wool and My flax.

All things come from Thee, and from Thy hand we have given Thee. For we are sojourners before Thee . . . as all our fathers were; our days on the earth are like a shadow, and there is no hope. O LORD our God, all this abundance, . . . it is from Thy hand, and all is Thine.—From Him and through Him and to Him are all things. To Him be the glory forever. Amen.

God who richly supplies us with all things to enjoy.—Everything created by God is good, and nothing is to be rejected, if it is received with gratitude; for it is sanctified by means of the word of God and prayer.

My God shall supply all your needs according to His riches in glory in Christ Jesus.

PS 24:1. Ho 2:8,9. 1 Ch 29:14–16.—Ro 11:36. 1 Ti 6:17.—1 Ti 4:4,5.
Phil 4:19.

The Helper, the Holy Spirit, whom the Father will send in My name.

If you knew the gift of God, and who it is who says to you, Give Me a drink, you would have asked Him, and He would have given you living water.—If you then, being evil, know how to give good gifts to your children, how much more shall your Heavenly Father give the Holy Spirit to those who ask Him?—Truly, truly, I say to you, if you shall ask the Father for anything, He will give it to you in My name. Until now you have asked for nothing in My name; ask, and you will receive, that your joy may be made full.—You do not have because you do not ask.

When He, the Spirit of truth, comes, He will guide you into all the truth; for He will not speak on His own initiative, but whatever He hears, He will speak; and He will disclose to you what is to come. He shall glorify Me; for He shall take of Mine, and shall disclose it to you.

They rebelled and grieved His Holy Spirit; therefore, He turned Himself to become their enemy, He fought against them.

JN 14:26. Jn 4:10.—Lk 11:13.—Jn 16:23,24.—Ja 4:2. Jn 16:13,14.
Is 63:10.

What do you think about the Christ?

Lift up your heads, O gates, and lift them up, O ancient doors, that the King of glory may come in! Who is this King of glory? The Lord of hosts, He is the King of glory.—On His robe and on His thigh He has a name written, KING OF KINGS, AND LORD OF LORDS.

Precious value ... for you who believe, but for those who disbelieve, The stone which the builders rejected, this became the very corner stone.—Christ crucified, to Jews a stumbling block, and to Gentiles foolishness, but to those who are the called, both Jews and Greeks, Christ the power of God and the wisdom of God.

I count all things to be loss in view of the surpassing value of knowing Christ Jesus my Lord, for whom I have suffered the loss of all things, and count them but rubbish in order that I may gain Christ.—Lord, You know all things; You know that I love You.

MT 22:42. Ps 24:9,10.—Rev 19:16. 1 Pe 2:7.—1 Co 1:23,24.
Phil 3:8.—Jn 21:17.

The path of the righteous is like the light of dawn, that shines brighter and brighter until the full day.

Not that I have already obtained it, or have already become perfect, but I press on in order that I may lay hold of that for which also I was laid hold of by Christ Jesus.—So . . . let us press on to know the LORD.

Then the righteous will shine forth as the sun in the kingdom of their Father.—We all, with unveiled face beholding as in a mirror the glory of the Lord, are being transformed into the same image from glory to glory, just as from the Lord, the Spirit. —When the perfect comes, the partial will be done away. For now we see in a mirror dimly, but then face to face; now I know in part, but then I shall know fully just as I also have been fully known.—Beloved, now we are children of God, and it has not appeared as yet what we shall be. We know that, when He appears, we shall be like Him, because we shall see Him just as He is. And every one who has this hope fixed on Him purifies himself, just as He is pure.

PR 4:18. Phil 3:12.—Ho 6:3. Mt 13:43.—2 Co 3:18.—
1 Co 13:10,12.—1 Jn 3:2,3.

Whoever will call upon the name of the Lord will be saved.

The one who comes to Me I will certainly not cast out.—Jesus, remember me when You come in Your kingdom! And He said to him, Truly I say to you, today you shall be with Me in Paradise. —What do you wish Me to do for you? They said to Him, Lord, we want our eyes to be opened. And moved with compassion, Jesus touched their eyes; and immediately they received their sight, and followed Him.

If you then, being evil, know how to give good gifts to your children, how much more shall your Heavenly Father give the Holy Spirit to those who ask Him?—I will put My Spirit within you. . . . Thus says the Lord God, . . . ask Me to do.

This is the confidence which we have before Him, that, if we ask anything according to His will, He hears us. And if we know that He hears us in whatever we ask, we know that we have the requests which we have asked from Him.

RO 10:13. Jn 6:37.—Lk 23:42,43.—Mt 20:32-34. Lk 11:13.—
Eze 36:27,37. 1 Jn 5:14,15.

You are altogether beautiful, my darling, and there is no blemish in you.

The whole head is sick, and the whole heart is faint. From the sole of the foot even to the head there is nothing sound in it. Only bruises, welts, and raw wounds, not pressed out or bandaged, nor softened with oil.—All of us have become like one who is unclean, and all our righteous deeds are like a filthy garment.—I know that nothing good dwells in me, that is, in my flesh.

You were washed . . . you were sanctified . . . you were justified in the name of the Lord Jesus Christ, and in the Spirit of our God. —The King's daughter is all glorious within.—Perfect because of My splendor which I bestowed on you, declares the Lord God.

Let the favor of the Lord our God be upon us.

These are the ones who . . . have washed their robes and made them white in the blood of the Lamb.—The church in all her glory, having no spot or wrinkle or any such thing; but . . . holy and blameless.—In Him you have been made complete.

SONG 4:7. Is 1:5,6.—Is 64:6.—Ro 7:18. 1 Co 6:11.—Ps 45:13.—
Eze 16:14. Ps 90:17. Rev 7:14.—Eph 5:27.—Col 2:10.

Broken cisterns, that can hold no water.

Eve . . . gave birth to Cain, and she said, I have gotten a manchild with the help of the Lord.

Come, let us build for ourselves a city, and a tower whose top will reach into heaven. . . . The Lord scattered them.—Lot chose for himself all the valley of the Jordan. It was well watered everywhere . . . like the garden of the Lord. Now the men of Sodom were wicked exceedingly and sinners against the Lord.

I set my mind to know wisdom and to know madness and folly; I realized that this also is striving after wind. Because in much wisdom there is much grief, and increasing knowledge results in increasing pain.—I enlarged my works; I built houses for myself, I planted vineyards for myself. Also, I collected for myself silver and gold. Thus I considered . . . and behold all was vanity and striving after wind.

If any man is thirsty, let him come to Me and drink.—He has satisfied the thirsty soul, and the hungry soul He has filled with what is good.

Set your mind on the things above, not on the things that are on earth.

JER 2:13. Gen 4:1. Gen 11:4,8.—Gen 13:11,10,13. Ec 1:17,18.—
Ec 2:4,8,11. Jn 7:37.—Ps 107:9. Col 3:2.

I do not ask Thee to take them out of the world, but to keep them from the evil one.

Blameless and innocent, children of God, above reproach in the midst of a crooked and perverse generation, among whom you appear as lights in the world.—You are the salt of the earth . . . the light of the world. Let your light shine before men in such a way that they may see your good works, and glorify your Father who is in heaven.

I also kept you from sinning against Me.

The Lord is faithful, and He will strengthen and protect you from the evil one.—I did not do so because of the fear of God. —Who gave Himself for our sins, that He might deliver us out of this present evil age, according to the will of our God and Father.—Now to Him who is able to keep you from stumbling, and to make you stand in the presence of His glory blameless with great joy, to the only God our Savior, through Jesus Christ our Lord, be glory, majesty, dominion and authority, before all time and now and forever. Amen.

JN 17:15. Phil 2:15.—Mt 5:13,14,16. Gen 20:6. 2 Th 3:3.— Neh 5:15.—Gal 1:4.—Jude 24,25.

He who trusts in the Lord will be exalted.

The Lord is exalted, for He dwells on high.—The Lord is high above all nations; His glory is above the heavens. He raises the poor from the dust, and lifts the needy from the ash heap, to make them sit with princes.

God, being rich in mercy, because of His great love with which He loved us, even when we were dead in our transgressions, made us alive together with Christ (by grace you have been saved), and raised us up with Him, and seated us with Him in the heavenly places, in Christ Jesus.

He who did not spare His own Son, but delivered Him up for us all, how will He not also with Him freely give us all things? For I am convinced that neither death, nor life, nor angels, nor principalities, nor things present, nor things to come, nor powers, nor height, nor depth, nor any other created thing, shall be able to separate us from the love of God, which is in Christ Jesus our Lord.

PR 29:25. Is 33:5.—Ps 113:4,7,8. Eph 2:4–6. Ro 8:32,38,39.

That through death He might render powerless him who had the power of death.

Our Savior Christ Jesus, who abolished death, and brought life and immortality to light through the gospel.—He will swallow up death for all time, and the Lord GOD will wipe tears away from all faces, and He will remove the reproach of His people from all the earth; for the LORD has spoken.—When this perishable will have put on the imperishable, and this mortal will have put on immortality, then will come about the saying that is written, Death is swallowed up in victory. ... O death, where is your sting? The sting of death is sin, and the power of sin is the law; but thanks be to God, who gives us the victory through our Lord Jesus Christ.

God has not given us a spirit of timidity, but of power and love and discipline.—Even though I walk through the valley of the shadow of death, I fear no evil; for Thou art with me; Thy rod and Thy staff, they comfort me.

HEB 2:14. 2 Ti 1:10.—Is 25:8.—1 Co 15:54–57. 2 Ti 1:7.—Ps 23:4.

Where is the way to the dwelling of light?

God is light, and in Him there is no darkness at all.—While I am in the world, I am the light of the world.

If we say that we have fellowship with Him and yet walk in the darkness, we lie and do not practice the truth; but if we walk in the light as He Himself is in the light, we have fellowship with one another, and the blood of Jesus His Son cleanses us from all sin.—The Father, who has qualified us to share in the inheritance of the saints in light. For He delivered us from the domain of darkness, and transferred us to the kingdom of His beloved Son, in whom we have redemption, the forgiveness of sins.

You are all sons of light and sons of day. We are not of night nor of darkness.—You are the light of the world. A city set on a hill cannot be hidden. Let your light shine before men in such a way that they may see your good works, and glorify your Father who is in heaven.

JOB 38:19. 1 Jn 1:5.—Jn 9:5. 1 Jn 1:6,7.—Col 1:12–14. 1 Th 5:5.—
Mt 5:14,16.

For the Lord will not reject forever, for if He causes grief, then He will have compassion.

Do not fear, declares the LORD, for I am with you . . . I shall not make a full end of you; but I shall correct you properly.—For a brief moment I forsook you, but with great compassion I will gather you. In an outburst of anger I hid My face from you for a moment; but with everlasting lovingkindness I will have compassion on you, says the LORD your Redeemer. For the mountains may be removed and the hills may shake, but My lovingkindness will not be removed from you, and My covenant of peace will not be shaken, says the LORD who has compassion on you. O afflicted one, storm-tossed, and not comforted, behold, I will set your stones in antimony, and your foundations I will lay in sapphires.

I will bear the indignation of the LORD because I have sinned against Him, until He pleads my case and executes justice for me. He will bring me out to the light, and I will see His righteousness.

LAM 3:31,32. Jer 46:28.—Is 54:7,8,10,11. Mic 7:9.

God has chosen the foolish things of the world to shame the wise.

When the sons of Israel cried to the LORD, the LORD raised up a deliverer for them, Ehud . . . a left-handed man. And after him came Shamgar . . . who struck down six hundred Philistines with an oxgoad; and he also saved Israel.

The LORD looked at him (Gideon) and said, Go in this your strength . . . Have I not sent you? And he said to Him, O Lord, how shall I deliver Israel? Behold, my family is the least in Manasseh, and I am the youngest in my father's house.

The LORD said to Gideon, The people who are with you are too many for Me . . . lest Israel become boastful, saying, My own power has delivered me.

Not by might nor by power, but by My Spirit, says the LORD of hosts.—Be strong in the Lord, and in the strength of His might.

1 CO 1:27. Judg 3:15,31. Judg 6:14,15. Judg 7:2. Zec 4:6.—
Eph 6:10.

He has prepared a city for them.

If I go and prepare a place for you, I will come again, and receive you to Myself; that where I am, there you may be also. —An inheritance which is imperishable and undefiled and will not fade away, reserved in heaven for you.—Here we do not have a lasting city, but we are seeking the city which is to come.

This Jesus, who has been taken up from you into heaven, will come in just the same way as you have watched Him go into heaven.—Be patient, therefore, brethren, until the coming of the Lord. Behold, the farmer waits for the precious produce of the soil, being patient about it, until it gets the early and late rains. You too be patient; strengthen your hearts, for the coming of the Lord is at hand.—For yet in a very little while, He who is coming will come, and will not delay.

Then we who are alive and remain shall be caught up together with them in the clouds to meet the Lord in the air, and thus we shall always be with the Lord.

HEB 11:16. Jn 14:3.—1 Pe 1:4.—Heb 13:14. Ac 1:11.—Ja 5:7,8.—
Heb 10:37. 1 Th 4:17,18.

Base things of the world . . . God has chosen.

Do not be deceived; neither fornicators, nor idolaters, nor adulterers, nor effeminate, nor homosexuals, nor thieves, nor covetous, nor drunkards, nor revilers, nor swindlers, shall inherit the kingdom of God. And such were some of you; but you were washed, but you were sanctified, but you were justified in the name of the Lord Jesus Christ, and in the Spirit of our God.

You were dead in your trespasses and sins, in which you formerly walked according to the course of this world. . . . Among them we too all formerly lived . . . indulging the desires of the flesh and of the mind.

He saved us, . . . by the washing of regeneration and renewing by the Holy Spirit, whom He poured out upon us richly through Jesus Christ our Savior.

My thoughts are not your thoughts, neither are your ways My ways, declares the LORD.

1 CO 1:28. 1 Co 6:9–11. Eph 2:1–3. Titus 3:5,6. Is 55:8.

The joy of the LORD is your strength.

Shout for joy, O heavens! And rejoice, O earth! Break forth into joyful shouting, O mountains! For the LORD has comforted His people, and will have compassion on His afflicted.—Behold, God is my salvation, I will trust and not be afraid; for the LORD GOD is my strength and song, and He has become my salvation. —The LORD is my strength and my shield; my heart trusts in Him, and I am helped; therefore my heart exults, and with my song I shall thank Him.—I will rejoice greatly in the LORD, my soul will exult in my God; for He has clothed me with garments of salvation, He has wrapped me with a robe of righteousness, as a bridegroom decks himself with a garland, and as a bride adorns herself with her jewels.

Therefore in Christ Jesus I have found reason for boasting in things pertaining to God.—We also exult in God through our Lord Jesus Christ, through whom we have now received the reconciliation.—I will rejoice in the God of my salvation.

NEH 8:10. Is 49:13.—Is 12:2.—Ps 28:7.—Is 61:10. Ro 15:17.—
Ro 5:11.—Hab 3:18.

He has made an everlasting covenant with me, ordered in all things, and secured.

I am convinced that He is able to guard what I have entrusted to Him until that day.

Blessed be the God and Father of our Lord Jesus Christ, who has blessed us with every spiritual blessing in the heavenly places in Christ, just as He chose us in Him before the foundation of the world, that we should be holy and blameless before Him. In love He predestined us to adoption as sons through Jesus Christ to Himself, according to the kind intention of His will.

We know that God causes all things to work together for good to those who love God, to those who are called according to His purpose. For whom He foreknew, He also predestined to become conformed to the image of His Son, that He might be the first-born among many brethren; and whom He predestined, these He also called; and whom He called, these He also justified; and whom He justified, these He also glorified.

2 SA 23:5. 2 Ti 1:12. Eph 1:3–5. Ro 8:28–30.

The God of peace . . . equip you in every good thing to do His will.

Rejoice, be made complete, be comforted, be like-minded, live in peace; and the God of love and peace shall be with you.

By grace you have been saved through faith; and that not of yourselves, it is the gift of God; not as a result of works, that no one should boast.—Every good thing bestowed and every perfect gift is from above, coming down from the Father of lights, with whom there is no variation, or shifting shadow.

Work out your salvation with fear and trembling; for it is God who is at work in you, both to will and to work for His good pleasure.—Be transformed by the renewing of your mind, that you may prove what the will of God is, that which is good and acceptable and perfect.—Filled with the fruit of righteousness which comes through Jesus Christ, to the glory and praise of God.

Not that we are adequate in ourselves to consider anything as coming from ourselves, but our adequacy is from God.

HEB 13:20,21. 2 Co 13:11. Eph 2:8,9.—Ja 1:17. Phil 2:12,13.—
Ro 12:2.—Phil 1:11. 2 Co 3:5.

I will allure her, bring her into the wilderness, and speak kindly to her.

Come out from their midst and be separate, says the Lord. And do not touch what is unclean; and I will welcome you. And I will be a father to you, and you shall be sons and daughters to Me, says the Lord Almighty.—Having these promises, beloved, let us cleanse ourselves from all defilement of flesh and spirit, perfecting holiness in the fear of God.

Jesus . . . that He might sanctify the people through His own blood, suffered outside the gate. Hence, let us go out to Him outside the camp, bearing His reproach.

He said . . . Come away by yourselves to a lonely place and rest a while.—The LORD is my shepherd, I shall not want. He makes me lie down in green pastures; He leads me beside quiet waters. He restores my soul; He guides me in the paths of righteousness for His name's sake.

HO 2:14. 2 Co 6:17,18.—2 Co 7:1. Heb 13:12,13. Mk 6:31.—
Ps 23:1–3.

The house that is to be built for the LORD shall be exceedingly magnificent.

You . . . as living stones, are being built up as a spiritual house. —Do you not know that you are a temple of God, and that the Spirit of God dwells in you? If any man destroys the temple of God, God will destroy him, for the temple of God is holy, and that is what you are.—Do you not know that your body is a temple of the Holy Spirit who is in you, . . . and that you are not your own? For you have been bought with a price: therefore glorify God in your body.—Or what agreement has the temple of God with idols? For we are the temple of the living God; just as God said, I will dwell in them and walk among them; and I will be their God, and they shall be My people.—You . . . having been built upon the foundation of the apostles and prophets, Christ Jesus Himself being the cornerstone, in whom the whole building, being fitted together is growing into a holy temple in the Lord; in whom you also are being built together into a dwelling of God in the Spirit.

1 CH 22:5. 1 Pe 2:5.—1 Co 3:16,17.—1 Co 6:19,20.—2 Co 6:16.—
Eph 2:19–22.

He is before all things.

The Amen . . . the Beginning of the creation of God.—He is the beginning, the firstborn from the dead; so that He Himself might come to have first place in everything.

The LORD possessed me at the beginning of His way, before His works of old. From everlasting I was established from the beginning, from the earliest times of the earth. When He established the heavens, I was there, when He inscribed a circle on the face of the deep, when He made firm the skies above, when the springs of the deep became fixed, when He set for the sea its boundary, so that the water should not transgress His command, when He marked out the foundations of the earth . . . I was daily His delight, rejoicing always before Him.—Even from eternity I am He.

From the foundation of the world . . . the Lamb who has been slain.—The author and perfecter of faith, who for the joy set before Him endured the cross, despising the shame, and has sat down at the right hand of the throne of God.

COL 1:17. Rev 3:14.—Col 1:18. Pr 8:22,23,27–30.—Is 43:13.
Rev 13:8.—Heb 12:2.

Pray for one another, so that you may be healed.

Abraham answered and said, Now behold, I have ventured to speak to the Lord, although I am but dust and ashes. Suppose the fifty righteous are lacking five, wilt Thou destroy the whole city because of five? And He said, I will not destroy it if I find forty-five there.

Father forgive them; for they do not know what they are doing.—Pray for those who persecute you.

I ask on their behalf; I do not ask on behalf of the world, but of those whom Thou hast given Me; for they are Thine. I do not ask in behalf of these alone, but for those also who believe in Me through their word.—Bear one another's burdens, and thus fulfill the law of Christ.

The effective prayer of a righteous man can accomplish much. Elijah was a man with a nature like ours, and he prayed earnestly that it might not rain; and it did not rain on the earth for three years and six months.

JA 5:16. Gen 18:27,28. Lk 23:34.—Mt 5:44. Jn 17:9,20.—Gal 6:2. Ja 5:16,17.

As for man, his days are like grass; as a flower of the field, so he flourishes. When the wind has passed over it, it is no more; and its place acknowledges it no longer.

So teach us to number our days, that we may present to Thee a heart of wisdom.—What does it profit a man to gain the whole world, and forfeit his soul?

Surely the people are grass. The grass withers, the flower fades, but the word of our God stands forever.—The world is passing away, and also its lusts; but the one who does the will of God abides forever.

Behold, now is the acceptable time, behold, now is the day of salvation.—The time has been shortened, so that ... those who use the world (shall be) as though they did not make full use of it; for the form of this world is passing away.—Let us consider how to stimulate one another to love and good deeds, not forsaking our own assembling together, as is the habit of some, but encouraging one another; and all the more, as you see the day drawing near.

PS 103:15,16. Ps 90:12.—Mk 8:36. Is 40:7,8.—1 Jn 2:17. 2 Co 6:2.— 1 Co 7:29,31.—Heb 10:24,25.

What god is there in heaven or on earth who can do such works and mighty acts as Thine?

Who in the skies is comparable to the LORD? Who among the sons of the mighty is like the LORD? O Lord GOD of hosts, who is like Thee, O mighty LORD? Thy faithfulness also surrounds Thee.—There is no one like Thee among the gods, O Lord; nor are there any works like Thine.—For the sake of Thy word, and according to Thine own heart, Thou hast done all this greatness to let Thy servant know. For this reason Thou art great, O Lord GOD; for there is none like Thee, and there is no God besides Thee, according to all that we have heard with our ears.

Things which eye has not seen and ear has not heard, and which have not entered the heart of man, all that God has prepared for those who love Him. For to us God revealed them through the Spirit.—The secret things belong to the LORD our God, but the things revealed belong to us and to our sons forever.

DEU 3:24. Ps 89:6,8.—Ps 86:8.—2 Sa 7:21,22. 1 Co 2:9,10.—
Deu 29:29.

Let him who boasts, boast in the Lord.

Let not a wise man boast of his wisdom, and let not the mighty man boast of his might, let not a rich man boast of his riches; but let him who boasts boast of this, that he understands and knows Me, that I am the LORD.

I count all things to be loss in view of the surpassing value of knowing Christ Jesus my Lord, for whom I have suffered the loss of all things, and count them but rubbish in order that I may gain Christ.—I am not ashamed of the gospel, for it is the power of God for salvation to every one who believes.—Therefore in Christ Jesus I have found reason for boasting in things pertaining to God.

Whom have I in heaven but Thee? And besides Thee, I desire nothing on earth.—My heart exults in the LORD . . . I rejoice in Thy salvation.

Not to us, O LORD, not to us, but to Thy name give glory because of Thy lovingkindness, because of Thy truth.

1 CO 1:31. Jer 9:23,24. Phil 3:8.—Ro 1:16.—Ro 15:17. Ps 73:25.—
1 Sa 2:1. Ps 115:1.

Like the Holy One who called you, be holy yourselves also in all your behavior.

You know how we were exhorting and encouraging and imploring each one of you ... so that you may walk in a manner worthy of the God who calls you into His own kingdom and glory. —You may proclaim the excellencies of Him who has called you out of darkness into His marvelous light.

For you were formerly darkness, but now you are light in the Lord; walk as children of light (for the fruit of the light consists in all goodness and righteousness and truth), trying to learn what is pleasing to the Lord. And do not participate in the unfruitful deeds of darkness, but instead even expose them.—Having been filled with the fruit of righteousness which comes through Jesus Christ, to the glory and praise of God.

Let your light shine before men in such a way that they may see your good works, and glorify your Father who is in heaven. —Whether, then, you eat or drink or whatever you do, do all to the glory of God.

1 PE 1:15. 1 Th 2:11,12.—1 Pe 2:9. Eph 5:8–11.—Phil 1:11. Mt 5:16.—1 Co 10:31.

Ask Me about the things to come concerning my sons, and you shall commit to Me the work of My hands.

I will give you a new heart and put a new spirit within you; and I will remove the heart of stone from your flesh and give you a heart of flesh. And I will put My Spirit within you and cause you to walk in My statutes. Thus says the Lord God, This also I will let the house of Israel ask Me to do for them.

If two of you agree on earth about anything that they may ask, it shall be done for them by My Father who is in heaven. For where two or three have gathered together in My name, there I am in their midst.

Have faith in God. Truly I say to you, whoever says to this mountain, Be taken up and cast into the sea, and does not doubt in his heart, but believes that what he says is going to happen, it shall be granted him.

IS 45:11. Eze 36:26,27,37. Mt 18:19,20. Mk 11:22,23.

God is not a man, that He should lie, nor a son of man, that He should repent.

The Father of lights, with whom there is no variation, or shifting shadow.—Jesus Christ is the same yesterday and today, yes and forever.

His faithfulness is a shield and bulwark.

God, desiring even more to show to the heirs of the promise the unchangeableness of His purpose, interposed with an oath, in order that by two unchangeable things, in which it is impossible for God to lie, we may have strong encouragement, we who have fled for refuge in laying hold of the hope set before us.

The faithful God, who keeps His covenant and His lovingkindness to a thousandth generation with those who love Him and keep His commandments.—All the paths of the LORD are lovingkindness and truth to those who keep His covenant and His testimonies.—How blessed is he whose help is the God of Jacob, whose hope is in the LORD his God . . . who keeps faith forever.

NUM 23:19. Ja 1:17.—Heb 13:8. Ps 91:4. Heb 6:17,18. Deu 7:9.—
Ps 25:10.—Ps 146:5,6.

If you are slack in the day of distress, your strength is limited.

He gives strength to the weary, and to him who lacks might He increases power.—My grace is sufficient for you, for power is perfected in weakness.—He will call upon Me, and I will answer him; I will be with him in trouble; I will rescue him, and honor him.—The eternal God is a dwelling place, and underneath are the everlasting arms; and He drove out the enemy from before you.

I looked for sympathy, but there was none; and for comforters, but I found none.

Every high priest taken from among men is appointed on behalf of men in things pertaining to God . . . he can deal gently with the ignorant and misguided. . . . So also Christ . . . although He was a Son, He learned obedience from the things which He suffered. And having been made perfect, He became to all those who obey Him the source of eternal salvation.—Surely our griefs He Himself bore, and our sorrows He carried.

PR 24:10. Is 40:29.—2 Co 12:9.—Ps 91:15.—Deu 33:27. Ps 69:20.
Heb 5:1,2,5,8,9.—Is 53:4.

The LORD is my portion.

All things belong to you, and you belong to Christ; and Christ belongs to God.—Our . . . Savior, Christ Jesus; who gave Himself for us.—Gave Him as head over all things to the church.—Christ also loved the church and gave Himself up for her; that He might present to Himself the church in all her glory, having no spot or wrinkle or any such thing; but that she should be holy and blameless.

My soul shall make its boast in the LORD.—I will rejoice greatly in the LORD, my soul will exult in my God; for He has clothed me with garments of salvation, He has wrapped me with a robe of righteousness.

Whom have I in heaven but Thee? And besides Thee, I desire nothing on earth. My flesh and my heart may fail; but God is the strength of my heart and my portion forever.—I said to the LORD, Thou art my LORD. The LORD is the portion of my inheritance and my cup; Thou dost support my lot. The lines have fallen to me in pleasant places; indeed, my heritage is beautiful to me.

PS 119:57. 1 Co 3:21,23.—Titus 2:13,14.—Eph 1:22.—Eph 5:25,27. Ps 34:2.—Is 61:10. Ps 73:25,26.—Ps 16:2,5,6.

There is a way which seems right to a man, but its end is the way of death.

He who trusts in his own heart is a fool.

Thy word is a lamp to my feet, and a light to my path.—As for the deeds of men, by the word of Thy lips I have kept from the paths of the violent.

If a prophet or a dreamer of dreams arises among you . . . saying, Let us go after other gods (whom you have not known) and let us serve them, you shall not listen to the words of that prophet or that dreamer of dreams; for the LORD your God is testing you to find out if you love the LORD your God with all your heart and with all your soul. You shall follow the LORD your God and fear Him; and you shall keep His commandments, listen to His voice, serve Him, and cling to Him.

I will instruct you and teach you in the way which you should go; I will counsel you with My eye upon you.

PR 14:12. Pr 28:26. Ps 119:105.—Ps 17:4. Deu 13:1–4. Ps 32:8.

Not one of us lives for himself, and not one dies for himself.

For if we live, we live for the Lord, or if we die, we die for the Lord; therefore whether we live or die, we are the Lord's.—Let no one seek his own good, but that of his neighbor.—You have been bought with a price: therefore glorify God in your body.

Christ shall even now, as always, be exalted in my body, whether by life or by death. For to me, to live is Christ, and to die is gain. But if I am to live on in the flesh, this will mean fruitful labor for me; and I do not know which to choose. But I am hard pressed from both directions, having the desire to depart and be with Christ, for that is very much better.

For through the Law I died to the Law, that I might live to God. Christ lives in me; and the life which I now live in the flesh I live by faith in the Son of God, who loved me, and delivered Himself up for me.

RO 14:7. Ro 14:8.—1 Co 10:24.—1 Co 6:20. Phil 1:20–23.
Gal 2:19,20.

God gave Solomon . . . breadth of mind, like the sand that is on the seashore.

Behold, something greater than Solomon is here.—Prince of Peace.

For one will hardly die for a righteous man; though perhaps for the good man someone would dare even to die. But God demonstrates His own love toward us, in that while we were yet sinners, Christ died for us.—Who, although He existed in the form of God, did not regard equality with God a thing to be grasped, but emptied Himself, taking the form of a bond-servant, and being made in the likeness of men. And being found in appearance as a man, He humbled Himself by becoming obedient to the point of death, even death on a cross.—The love of Christ which surpasses knowledge.

Christ the power of God and the wisdom of God.—In whom are hidden all the treasures of wisdom and knowledge.—The unfathomable riches of Christ.—By His doing you are in Christ Jesus, who became to us wisdom from God, and righteousness and sanctification, and redemption.

1 KI 4:29. Mt 12:42.—Is 9:6. Ro 5:7,8.—Phil 2:6–8.—Eph 3:19.
1 Co 1:24.—Col 2:3.—Eph 3:8.—1 Co 1:30.

I have loved you with an everlasting love; therefore I have drawn you with lovingkindness.

We should always give thanks to God for you, brethren beloved by the Lord, because God has chosen you from the beginning for salvation through sanctification by the Spirit and faith in the truth. And it was for this He called you through our gospel, that you may gain the glory of our Lord Jesus Christ.— God; who has saved us, and called us with a holy calling, not according to our works, but according to His own purpose and grace which was granted us in Christ Jesus from all eternity.— Thine eyes have seen my unformed substance; and in Thy book they were all written, the days that were ordained for me, when as yet there was not one of them.

God so loved the world, that He gave His only begotten Son, that whoever believes in Him should not perish, but have eternal life.

In this is love, not that we loved God, but that He loved us and sent His Son to be the propitiation for our sins.

JER 31:3. 2 Th 2:13,14.—2 Ti 1:8,9.—Ps 139:16. Jn 3:16. 1 Jn 4:10.

I have done it, and I shall carry you.

Thus says the LORD, your creator, O Jacob, and He who formed you, O Israel: Do not fear, for I have redeemed you; I have called you by name; you are Mine! When you pass through the waters, I will be with you; and through the rivers, they will not overflow you.—Even to your old age, I shall be the same: and even to your graying years I shall bear you!

Like an eagle that stirs up its nest, that hovers over its young, He spread His wings and caught them, He carried them on His pinions. The LORD alone guided him.—He lifted them and carried them all the days of old.

Jesus Christ is the same yesterday and today, yes and forever. —For I am convinced that neither . . . height, nor depth, nor any other created thing, shall be able to separate us from the love of God, which is in Christ Jesus our Lord.

Can a woman forget her nursing child, and have no compassion on the son of her womb? Even these may forget, but I will not forget you.

IS 46:4. Is 43:1,2.—Is 46:4. Deu 32:11,12.—Is 63:9. Heb 13:8.— Ro 8:38,39. Is 49:15.

I am aware of their sufferings.

A man of sorrows, and acquainted with grief.—Tempted in all things as we are, yet without sin.

He Himself took our infirmities, and carried away our diseases. —Jesus . . . being wearied from His journey, was sitting thus by the well.

Jesus . . . saw her weeping, and the Jews who came with her, also weeping, He was deeply moved in spirit, and was troubled. Jesus wept.—Since He Himself was tempted in that which He has suffered, He is able to come to the aid of those who are tempted.

He looked down from His holy height; from heaven the LORD gazed upon the earth, to hear the groaning of the prisoner; to set free those who were doomed to death.—He knows the way I take; when He has tried me, I shall come forth as gold.—When my spirit was overwhelmed within me; Thou didst know my path.

He who touches you, touches the apple of His eye.—In all their affliction He was afflicted, and the angel of His presence saved them.

EX 3:7. Is 53:3.—Heb 4:15. Mt 8:17.—Jn 4:6. Jn 11:33,35.—
Heb 2:18. Ps 102:19,20.—Job 23:10.—Ps 142:3. Zec 2:8.—Is 63:9.

We must work the works of Him who sent Me, as long as it is day.

The soul of the sluggard craves and gets nothing, but the soul of the diligent is made fat.—He who waters will himself be watered.

My food is to do the will of Him who sent Me, and to accomplish His work. Do you not say, There are yet four months, and then comes the harvest? Behold, I say to you, lift up your eyes, and look on the fields, that they are white for harvest. Already he who reaps is receiving wages, and is gathering fruit for life eternal; that he who sows and he who reaps may rejoice together. —For the kingdom of heaven is like a landowner who went out early in the morning to hire laborers for his vineyard. And when he had agreed with the laborers for a denarius for the day, he sent them into his vineyard.

Preach the word; be ready in season and out of season.—Do business . . . until I come.

I labored even more than all of them, yet not I, but the grace of God with me.

JN 9:4. Pr 13:4.—Pr 11:25. Jn 4:34–36.—Mt 20:1,2. 2 Ti 4:2.—
Lk 19:13. 1 Co 15:10.

Look to the rock from which you were hewn, and to the quarry from which you were dug.

Behold, I was brought forth in iniquity, and in sin my mother conceived me.—No eye looked with pity on you. . . . Rather you were thrown out into the open field, for you were abhorred on the day you were born. When I passed by and saw you squirming in your blood, I said to you . . . Live!

He brought me up out of the pit of destruction, out of the miry clay; and He set my feet upon a rock making my footsteps firm. And He put a new song in my mouth, a song of praise to our God.

For while we were still helpless, at the right time Christ died for the ungodly. For one will hardly die for a righteous man; though perhaps for the good man someone would dare even to die. But God demonstrates His own love toward us, in that while we were yet sinners, Christ died for us.—God, being rich in mercy, because of His great love with which He loved us, even when we were dead in our transgressions, made us alive together with Christ.

IS 51:1. Ps 51:5.—Eze 16:5,6. Ps 40:2,3. Ro 5:6–8.—Eph 2:4,5.

I will rejoice greatly in the LORD, my soul will exult in my God.

I will bless the LORD at all times; His praise shall continually be in my mouth. My soul shall make its boast in the LORD; the humble shall hear it and rejoice. O magnify the LORD with me, and let us exalt His name together.—The LORD gives grace and glory; no good thing does He withhold from those who walk uprightly. O LORD of hosts, how blessed is the man who trusts in Thee!—Bless the LORD, O my soul; and all that is within me, bless His holy name.

Is anyone cheerful? Let him sing praises.—Be filled with the Spirit, speaking to one another in psalms and hymns and spiritual songs, singing and making melody with your heart to the Lord; always giving thanks for all things.—Singing with thankfulness in your hearts to God.

About midnight Paul and Silas were praying and singing hymns of praise to God, and the prisoners were listening to them. —Rejoice in the Lord always; again I will say, rejoice!

IS 61:10. Ps 34:1–3.—Ps 84:11,12.—Ps 103:1. Ja 5:13.—
Eph 5:18–20.—Col 3:16. Ac 16:25.—Phil 4:4.

You shall also make a plate of pure gold and shall engrave on it, like the engravings of a seal, Holy to the LORD.

Sanctification without which no one will see the Lord.—God is spirit; and those who worship Him must worship in spirit and truth.—For all of us have become like one who is unclean, and all our righteous deeds are like a filthy garment.—By those who come near Me I will be treated as holy, and before all the people I will be honored.

This is the law of the house: its entire area on the top of the mountain all around shall be most holy.—Holiness befits Thy house, O LORD, for evermore.

For their sakes I sanctify Myself, that they themselves also may be sanctified in truth.—Since then we have a great high priest who has passed through the heavens, Jesus the Son of God, let us... therefore draw near with confidence to the throne of grace, that we may receive mercy and may find grace to help in time of need.

EX 28:36. Heb 12:14.—Jn 4:24.—Is 64:6.—Lev 10:3. Eze 43:12.—
Ps 93:5. Jn 17:19.—Heb 4:14,16.

My cup overflows.

O taste and see that the LORD is good; how blessed is the man who takes refuge in Him! O fear the LORD, you His saints; for to those who fear Him, there is no want. The young lions do lack and suffer hunger; but they who seek the LORD shall not be in want of any good thing.—His compassions never fail. They are new every morning; great is Thy faithfulness.

The LORD is the portion of my inheritance and my cup; Thou dost support my lot. The lines have fallen to me in pleasant places; indeed, my heritage is beautiful to me.—Whether... the world or life or death or things present or things to come; all things belong to you.—Blessed be the God and Father of our Lord Jesus Christ, who has blessed us with every spiritual blessing in the heavenly places in Christ.

I have learned to be content in whatever circumstances I am. —Godliness actually is a means of great gain, when accompanied by contentment.—My God shall supply all your needs according to His riches in glory in Christ Jesus.

PS 23:5. Ps 34:8–10.—Lam 3:22,23. Ps 16:5,6.—1 Co 3:22.—
Eph 1:3. Phil 4:11.—1 Ti 6:6.—Phil 4:19.

Thy word is a lamp to my feet, and a light to my path.

By the word of Thy lips I have kept from the paths of the violent. My steps have held fast to Thy paths. My feet have not slipped.—When you walk about, they will guide you; when you sleep, they will watch over you; and when you awake, they will talk to you. For the commandment is a lamp, and the teaching is light.—Your ears will hear a word behind you, This is the way, walk in it, whenever you turn to the right or to the left.

I am the light of the world; he who follows Me shall not walk in the darkness, but shall have the light of life.—We have the prophetic word made more sure, to which you do well to pay attention as to a lamp shining in a dark place.—Now we see in a mirror dimly, but then face to face; now I know in part, but then I shall know fully just as I also have been fully known.— They shall not have need of the light of a lamp nor the light of the sun, because the Lord God shall illumine them; and they shall reign forever and ever.

PS 119:105. Ps 17:4,5.—Pr 6:22,23.—Is 30:21. Jn 8:12.—2 Pe 1:19.—
1 Co 13:12.—Rev 22:5.

How is it that you are sleeping? Get up.

This is no place of rest because of the uncleanness that brings on destruction, a painful destruction.—Set your minds on the things above, not on the things that are on earth.—If riches increase, do not set your heart upon them.—Set your heart and your soul to seek the LORD your God; arise, therefore.

Why are you sleeping? Rise and pray that you may not enter into temptation.—Be on guard, that your hearts may not be weighted down with dissipation and drunkenness and the worries of life, and that day come on you suddenly like a trap.

Now while the bridegroom was delaying, they all got drowsy and began to sleep.—Yet in a very little while, He who is coming will come, and will not delay.—It is already the hour for you to awaken from sleep; for now salvation is nearer to us than when we believed.—Therefore, be on the alert—for you do not know when the master of the house is coming, whether in the evening, at midnight, at cockcrowing, or in the morning—lest he come suddenly and find you asleep.

JON 1:6. Mic 2:10.—Col 3:2.—Ps 62:10.—1 Ch 22:19. Lk 22:46.—
Lk 21:34. Mt 25:5.—Heb 10:37.—Ro 13:11.—Mk 13:35,36.

The accuser of our brethren has been thrown down, who accuses them before our God day and night.

They overcame him because of the blood of the Lamb and because of the word of their testimony.—Who will bring a charge against God's elect? God is the one who justifies; who is the one who condemns? Christ Jesus is He who died, yes, rather who was raised, who is at the right hand of God, who also intercedes for us.

When He had disarmed the rulers and authorities, He made a public display of them.—That through death He might render powerless him who had the power of death, that is, the devil; and might deliver those who through fear of death were subject to slavery all their lives.—In all these things we overwhelmingly conquer through Him who loved us.—Put on the full armor of God, that you may be able to stand firm against the schemes of the devil. And take . . . the sword of the Spirit, which is the word of God.—Thanks be to God, who gives us the victory through our Lord Jesus Christ.

REV 12:10. Rev 12:11.—Ro 8:33,34. Col 2:15.—Heb 2:14,15.—
Ro 8:37.—Eph 6:11,17.—1 Co 15:57.

The tree of life.

God has given us eternal life, and this life is in His Son.—He gave His only begotten Son, that whoever believes in Him should not perish, but have eternal life.—Just as the Father raises the dead and gives them life, even so the Son also gives life to whom He wishes. As the Father has life in Himself, even so He gave to the Son also to have life in Himself.

To him who overcomes, I will grant to eat of the tree of life, which is in the Paradise of God.—In the middle of its street. And on either side of the river was the tree of life, bearing twelve kinds of fruit, yielding its fruit every month; and the leaves of the trees were for the healing of the nations.

How blessed is the man who finds wisdom. . . . Long life is in her right hand. . . . She is a tree of life to those who take hold of her, and happy are all who hold her fast.—Christ Jesus, who became to us wisdom.

GEN 2:9. 1 Jn 5:11.—Jn 3:16.—Jn 5:21,26. Rev 2:7.—Rev 22:2.
Pr 3:13,16,18.—1 Co 1:30.

Blessed is he who trusts in the LORD.

(Abraham) with respect to the promise of God, did not waver in unbelief, but grew strong in faith, giving glory to God, and being fully assured that what He had promised, He was able also to perform.—The sons of Judah conquered because they trusted in the LORD, the God of their fathers.

God is our refuge and strength, a very present help in trouble. Therefore we will not fear, though the earth should change, and though the mountains slip into the heart of the sea.—It is better to take refuge in the LORD than to trust in man. It is better to take refuge in the LORD than to trust in princes.—The steps of a man are established by the LORD; and He delights in his way. When he falls, he shall not be hurled headlong; because the LORD is the One who holds his hand.

O taste and see that the LORD is good; how blessed is the man who takes refuge in Him! O fear the LORD, you His saints; for to those who fear Him, there is no want.

PR 16:20. Ro 4:20,21.—2 Ch 13:18. Ps 46:1,2.—Ps 118:8,9.—
Ps 37:23,24. Ps 34:8,9.

In peace I will both lie down and sleep, for Thou alone, O LORD, dost make me to dwell in safety.

You will not be afraid of the terror by night. He will cover you with His pinions, and under His wings you may seek refuge.— The way a hen gathers her chicks under her wings.—He will not allow your foot to slip; He who keeps you will not slumber. Behold, He who keeps Israel will neither slumber nor sleep. The LORD is your keeper; the LORD is your shade on your right hand.

Let me dwell in Thy tent forever; let me take refuge in the shelter of Thy wings.—Even the darkness is not dark to Thee, and the night is as bright as the day. Darkness and light are alike to Thee.

He who did not spare His own Son, but delivered Him up for us all, how will He not also with Him freely give us all things?— You belong to Christ; and Christ belongs to God.—I will trust and not be afraid.

PS 4:8. Ps 91:5,4.—Mt 23:37.—Ps 121:3–5. Ps 61:4.—Ps 139:12.
Ro 8:32.—1 Co 3:23.—Is 12:2.

The king extended to Esther the golden scepter . . . So Esther came near and touched the top of the scepter.

It shall come about that when he cries out to Me, I will hear him, for I am gracious.

We have come to know and have believed the love which God has for us. God is love, and the one who abides in love abides in God, and God abides in him. By this, love is perfected with us, that we may have confidence in the day of judgment; because as He is, so also are we in this world. There is no fear in love; but perfect love casts out fear, because fear involves punishment, and the one who fears is not perfected in love. We love, because He first loved us.

Let us draw near with a sincere heart in full assurance of faith, having our hearts sprinkled clean from an evil conscience and our body washed with pure water.—Through Him we . . . have our access in one Spirit to the Father.—We have boldness and confident access through faith in Him.—Let us therefore draw near with confidence to the throne of grace, that we may receive mercy and may find grace to help in time of need.

EST 5:2. Ex 22:27. 1 Jn 4:16–19. Heb 10:22.—Eph 2:18.—
Eph 3:12.—Heb 4:16.

What is it? . . . Moses said to them, It is the bread which the LORD has given you to eat.

By common confession great is the mystery of godliness: He who was revealed in the flesh.—The bread of God is that which comes down out of heaven, and gives life to the world.

Your fathers ate the manna in the wilderness, and they died. If any one eats of this bread, he shall live forever; and the bread also which I shall give for the life of the world is My flesh. My flesh is true food, and My blood is true drink.

The sons of Israel . . . some gathered much and some little. . . . He who had gathered much had no excess, and he who had gathered little had no lack; every man gathered as much as he should eat.

Do not be anxious then, saying, What shall we eat? or, What shall we drink? . . . Your heavenly Father knows that you need all these things. But seek first His kingdom, and His righteousness; and all these things shall be added to you.

EX 16:15. 1 Ti 3:16.—Jn 6:33. Jn 6:49,51,55. Ex 16:17,18.
Mt 6:31–33.

The free gift arose from many transgressions resulting in justification.

Though your sins are as scarlet, they will be as white as snow; though they are red like crimson, they will be like wool.—I, even I, am the one who wipes out your transgressions for My own sake; and I will not remember your sins. Put me in remembrance; let us argue our case together, state your cause, that you may be proved right.—I have wiped out your transgressions like a thick cloud, and your sins like a heavy mist. Return to Me, for I have redeemed you.

God so loved the world, that He gave His only begotten Son, that whoever believes in Him should not perish, but have eternal life.—The free gift is not like the transgression. For if by the transgression of the one the many died, much more did the grace of God and the gift by the grace of the one Man, Jesus Christ, abound to the many.—Such were some of you; but you were washed, but you were sanctified, but you were justified in the name of the Lord Jesus Christ, and in the Spirit of our God.

RO 5:16. Is 1:18.—Is 43:25,26.—Is 44:22. Jn 3:16.—Ro 5:15.—
1 Co 6:11.

Do business ... until I come.

Like a man, away on a journey, who upon leaving his house and putting his slaves in charge, assigning to each one his task, also commanded the doorkeeper to stay on the alert.—To one he gave five talents, to another, two, and to another, one, each according to his own ability; and he went on his journey.

We must work the works of Him who sent Me, as long as it is day; night is coming, when no man can work.—Did you not know that I had to be in My Father's house?—Leaving you an example for you to follow in His steps.

Preach the word; be ready in season and out of season; reprove, rebuke, exhort, with great patience and instruction.— Each man's work will become evident; for the day will show it. —Therefore, my beloved brethren, be steadfast, immovable, always abounding in the work of the Lord, knowing that your toil is not in vain in the Lord.

LK 19:13. Mk 13:34.—Mt 25:15. Jn 9:4.—Lk 2:49.—1 Pe 2:21.
2 Ti 4:2.—1 Co 3:13.—1 Co 15:58.

The fruit of the Spirit is ... gentleness.

The afflicted also shall increase their gladness in the LORD, and the needy of mankind shall rejoice in the Holy One of Israel.— Truly I say to you, unless you are converted and become like children, you shall not enter the kingdom of heaven. Whoever then humbles himself as this child, he is the greatest in the kingdom of heaven.—The imperishable quality of a gentle and quiet spirit, which is precious in the sight of God.—Love does not brag and is not arrogant.

Pursue ... gentleness.—Take My yoke upon you, and learn from Me, for I am gentle and humble in heart.—He was oppressed and He was afflicted, yet He did not open His mouth; like a lamb that is led to slaughter, and like a sheep that is silent before its shearers, so He did not open His mouth.—Christ also suffered for you, leaving you an example for you to follow in His steps, who committed no sin, nor was any deceit found in His mouth; and while being reviled, He did not revile in return ... but kept entrusting Himself to Him who judges righteously.

GAL 5:22,23. Is 29:19.—Mt 18:3,4.—1 Pe 3:4.—1 Co 13:4.
1 Ti 6:11.—Mt 11:29.—Is 53:7.—1 Pe 2:21-23.

If anyone wishes to come after Me, let him deny himself, and take up his cross daily, and follow Me.

By glory and dishonor, by evil report and good report.—All who desire to live godly in Christ Jesus will be persecuted.—The stumbling block of the cross.

If I were still trying to please men, I would not be a bond-servant of Christ.

If you are reviled for the name of Christ, you are blessed. ... By no means let any of you suffer as a murderer, or thief, or evildoer, or a troublesome meddler; but if anyone suffers as a Christian, let him not feel ashamed, but in that name let him glorify God.

To you it has been granted for Christ's sake, not only to believe in Him, but also to suffer for His sake.—One died for all, therefore all died; and He died for all, that they who live should no longer live for themselves, but for Him who died and rose again on their behalf.—If we endure, we shall also reign with Him.

LK 9:23. 2 Co 6:8.—2 Ti 3:12.—Gal 5:11. Gal 1:10. 1 Pe 4:14-16.
Phil 1:29.—2 Co 5:14,15.—2 Ti 2:12.

Wait for the LORD; be strong, and let your heart take courage.

Do you not know? Have you not heard? The everlasting God, the LORD, the creator of the ends of the earth does not become weary or tired. He gives strength to the weary, and to him who lacks might He increases power.—Do not fear, for I am with you; do not anxiously look about you, for I am your God. I will strengthen you, surely I will help you, surely, I will uphold you with My righteous right hand.—For Thou hast been a defense for the helpless, a defense for the needy in his distress, a refuge from the storm, a shade from the heat; for the breath of the ruthless is like a rain storm against a wall.

The testing of your faith produces endurance. And let endurance have its perfect result, that you may be perfect and complete, lacking in nothing.—Therefore, do not throw away your confidence, which has a great reward. For you have need of endurance, so that when you have done the will of God, you may receive what was promised.

PS 27:14. Is 40:28,29.—Is 41:10.—Is 25:4. Ja 1:3,4.—Heb 10:35,36.

He makes me lie down in green pastures.

But the wicked are like the tossing sea, for it cannot be quiet. . . . There is no peace, says my God, for the wicked.

Come to Me, all who are weary and heavy laden, and I will give you rest.—Rest in the LORD.—For the one who has entered His rest has himself also rested from his works.

Do not be carried away by varied and strange teachings; for it is good for the heart to be strengthened by grace.—We are no longer to be children, tossed here and there by . . . every wind of doctrine, by the trickery of men, by craftiness in deceitful scheming; but speaking the truth in love, we are to grow up in all aspects into Him, who is the head, even Christ.

In his shade I took great delight and sat down, and his fruit was sweet to my taste. He has brought me to his banquet hall, and his banner over me is love.

PS 23:2. Is 57:20,21. Mt 11:28.—Ps 37:7.—Heb 4:10. Heb 13:9.— Eph 4:14,15. Song 2:3,4.

Nothing leavened shall be seen among you, nor . . . in all your borders.

The fear of the Lord is to hate evil.—Abhor what is evil.—Abstain from every form of evil.—See to it that no one comes short of the grace of God; that no root of bitterness springing up cause trouble, and by it many be defiled.

If I regard wickedness in my heart, the Lord will not hear.

Do you not know that a little leaven leavens the whole lump of dough? Clean out the old leaven, that you may be a new lump, just as you are in fact unleavened. For Christ our Passover also has been sacrificed. Let us therefore celebrate the feast, not with old leaven, nor with the leaven of malice and wickedness, but with the unleavened bread of sincerity and truth.—Let a man examine himself, and so let him eat of the bread and drink of the cup.

Let every one who names the name of the Lord abstain from wickedness.—It was fitting that we should have such a high priest, holy, innocent, undefiled, separated from sinners.—In Him there is no sin.

EX 13:7. Pr 8:13.—Ro 12:9.—1 Th 5:22.—Heb 12:15. Ps 66:18.
1 Co 5:6–8.—1 Co 11:28. 2 Ti 2:19.—Heb 7:26.—1 Jn 3:5.

The serpent said to the woman, You surely shall not die! . . . your eyes will be opened, and you will be like God, knowing good and evil.

I am afraid, lest as the serpent deceived Eve by his craftiness, your minds should be led astray from the simplicity and purity of devotion to Christ.

Be strong in the Lord, and in the strength of His might. Put on the full armor of God, that you may be able to stand firm against the schemes of the devil. Therefore take up the full armor of God, that you may be able to resist in the evil day, and having done everything, to stand firm. Stand firm therefore, having girded your loins with truth, and having put on the breastplate of righteousness, and having shod your feet with the preparation of the gospel of peace; in addition to all, taking up the shield of faith with which you will be able to extinguish all the flaming missiles of the evil one. And take the helmet of salvation, and the sword of the Spirit, which is the word of God.—In order that no advantage be taken of us by Satan; for we are not ignorant of his schemes.

GEN 3:4,5. 2 Co 11:3. Eph 6:10,11,13–17.—2 Co 2:11.

Wait, my daughter.

Take care, and be calm, have no fear and do not be faint-hearted.—Cease striving and know that I am God.—Did I not say to you, if you believe, you will see the glory of God?—The pride of man will be humbled, and the loftiness of men will be abased, and the LORD alone will be exalted in that day.

Mary, . . . was listening to the Lord's word, seated at His feet. Mary has chosen the good part, which shall not be taken away from her.—In repentance and rest you shall be saved, in quietness and trust is your strength.—Meditate in your heart upon your bed, and be still.

Rest in the LORD and wait patiently for Him; fret not yourself because of him who prospers in his way, because of the man who carries our wicked schemes.

He will not fear evil tidings; his heart is steadfast, trusting in the LORD. His heart is upheld.

He who believes . . . will not be disturbed.

RU 3:18. Is 7:4.—Ps 46:10.—Jn 11:40.—Is 2:17. Lk 10:39,42.—
Is 30:15.—Ps 4:4. Ps 37:7.Ps 112:7,8. Is 28:16.

What I do you do not realize now; but you shall understand hereafter.

You shall remember all the way which the LORD your God has led you in the wilderness these forty years, that He might humble you, testing you, to know what was in your heart, whether you would keep His commandments or not.

Then I passed by you and saw you, and behold, you were at the time for love. . . . I also swore to you and entered into a covenant with you so that you became Mine, declares the Lord GOD.— Those whom the Lord loves He disciplines.

Beloved, do not be surprised at the fiery ordeal among you, which comes upon you for your testing, as though some strange thing were happening to you; but to the degree that you share the sufferings of Christ, keep on rejoicing; so that also at the revelation of His glory, you may rejoice with exultation.—For momentary, light affliction is producing for us an eternal weight of glory far beyond all comparison, while we look not at the things which are seen, but at the things which are not seen.

JN 13:7. Deu 8:22. Eze 16:8.—Heb 12:6. 1 Pe 4:12,13.—
2 Co 4:17,18.

As the body is one and yet has many members, . . . so also is Christ.

He is also head of the body, the church.—He . . . gave Him as head over all things to the church, which is His body, the fulness of Him who fills all in all.—We are members of His body.

A body Thou has prepared for Me.—Thine eyes have seen my unformed substance; and in Thy book they were all written, the days that were ordained for me, when as yet there was not one of them.

Thine they were, and Thou gavest them to Me.—He chose us in Him before the foundation of the world.—Whom He foreknew, He also predestined to become conformed to the image of His Son.

We are to grow up in all aspects into Him, who is the head, even Christ, from whom the whole body, being fitted and held together by that which every joint supplies . . . causes the growth of the body for the building up of itself in love.

1 CO 12:12. Col 1:18.—Eph 1:22,23.—Eph 5:30. Heb 10:5.—
Ps 139:16. Jn 17:6.—Eph 1:4.—Ro 8:29. Eph 4:15,16.

The fountain of living waters.

How precious is Thy lovingkindness, O God! And the children of men take refuge in the shadow of Thy wings. They drink their fill of the abundance of Thy house; and Thou dost give them to drink of the river of Thy delights. For with Thee is the fountain of life.

Thus says the Lord GOD, Behold, My servants shall eat, but you shall be hungry. Behold, My servants shall drink, but you shall be thirsty.—Whoever drinks of the water that I shall give him shall never thirst; but the water that I shall give him shall become in him a well of water springing up to eternal life.—He spoke of the Spirit, whom those who believed in Him were to receive.

Ho! Every one who thirsts, come to the waters.—The Spirit and the bride say, Come. And let the one who hears say, Come. And let the one who is thirsty come; let the one who wishes take the water of life without cost.

JER 2:13. Ps 36:7–9. Is 65:13.—Jn 4:14.—Jn 7:39. Is 55:1.—
Rev 22:17.

We lift up our heart and hands toward God in heaven.

Who is like the LORD our God, who is enthroned on high, who humbles Himself to behold the things that are in heaven and in the earth?—To Thee, O LORD, I lift up my soul.—I stretch out my hands to Thee; my soul longs for Thee, as a parched land. . . . Do not hide Thy face from me, lest I become like those who go down to the pit. Let me hear Thy lovingkindness in the morning; for I trust in Thee; teach me the way in which I should walk; for to Thee I lift up my soul.

Because Thy lovingkindness is better than life, my lips will praise Thee. So I will bless Thee as long as I live; I will lift up my hands in Thy name.—Make glad the soul of Thy servant, for to Thee, O Lord, I lift up my soul. For Thou, Lord, art good, and ready to forgive, and abundant in lovingkindness to all who call upon Thee.

Whatever you ask in My name, that will I do.

LAM 3:41. Ps 113:5,6.—Ps 25:1.—Ps 143:6–8. Ps 63:3,4.—Ps 86:4,5.
Jn 14:13.

Watchman, how far gone is the night?

It is already the hour for you to awaken from sleep; for now salvation is nearer to us than when we believed. The night is almost gone, and the day is at hand. Let us therefore lay aside the deeds of darkness and put on the armor of light.

Now learn the parable from the fig tree: when its branch has already become tender, and puts forth its leaves, you know that summer is near; even so you too, when you see all these things, recognize that He is near, right at the door. Heaven and earth will pass away, but My words shall not pass away.

I wait for the LORD, my soul does wait, and in His word do I hope. My soul waits for the Lord more than the watchmen for the morning; indeed, more than the watchmen for the morning.

He who testifies to these things says, Yes, I am coming quickly. Amen. Come, Lord Jesus.

Be on the alert then, for you do not know the day nor the hour.

IS 21:11. Ro 13:11,12. Mt 24:32,33,35. Ps 130:5,6. Rev 22:20.
Mt 25:13.

Rejoicing in hope.

The hope laid up for you in heaven.—If we have only hoped in Christ in this life, we are of all men most to be pitied.— Through many tribulations we must enter the kingdom of God. —Whoever does not carry his own cross and come after Me cannot be My disciple.—No man may be disturbed by these afflictions; for you yourselves know that we have been destined for this.

Rejoice in the Lord always; again I will say, rejoice!—May the God of hope fill you with all joy and peace in believing, that you may abound in hope by the power of the Holy Spirit.—Blessed be the God and Father of our Lord Jesus Christ, who according to His great mercy has caused us to be born again to a living hope through the resurrection of Jesus Christ from the dead.—Though you have not seen Him, you love Him, and though you do not see Him now, but believe in Him, you greatly rejoice with joy inexpressible and full of glory.—Through whom also we have obtained our introduction by faith into this grace in which we stand; and we exult in hope of the glory of God.

RO 12:12. Col 1:5.—1 Co 15:19.—Ac 14:22.—Lk 14:27.—1 Th 3:3.
Phil 4:4.—Ro 15:13.—1 Pe 1:3.—1 Pe 1:8.—Ro 5:2.

Since I am afflicted and needy, let the Lord be mindful of me.

For I know the plans that I have for you, declares the LORD, plans for welfare and not for calamity.—My thoughts are not your thoughts, neither are your ways My ways, declares the LORD. For as the heavens are higher than the earth, so are My ways higher than your ways, and My thoughts than your thoughts.

How precious also are Thy thoughts to me, O God! How vast is the sum of them! If I should count them, they would outnumber the sand. When I awake, I am still with Thee.—How great are Thy works, O LORD! Thy thoughts are very deep.—Many, O LORD my God, are the wonders which Thou hast done, and Thy thoughts toward us.

Consider your call, brethren, that there were not many wise . . . not many mighty, not many noble.—Did not God choose the poor of this world to be rich in faith and heirs of the kingdom? —Having nothing yet possessing all things.—The unfathomable riches of Christ.

PS 40:17. Jer 29:11.—Is 55:8,9. Ps 139:17,18.—Ps 92:5.—Ps 40:5.
1 Co 1:26.—Ja 2:5.—2 Co 6:10.—Eph 3:8.

You have been weighed on the scales and found deficient.

For the LORD is a God of knowledge, and with Him actions are weighed.—That which is highly esteemed among men is detestable in the sight of God.—Man looks at the outward appearance, but the LORD looks at the heart.—Do not be deceived, God is not mocked; for whatever a man sows, this he will also reap. For the one who sows to his own flesh shall from the flesh reap corruption, but the one who sows to the Spirit shall from the Spirit reap eternal life.

What will a man be profited, if he gains the whole world, and forfeits his soul? Or what will a man give in exchange for his soul? —Whatever things were gain to me, those things I have counted as loss for the sake of Christ.

Behold, Thou dost desire truth in the innermost being.—Thou hast tried my heart; Thou hast visited me by night; Thou hast tested me and dost find nothing.

DAN 5:27. 1 Sa 2:3.—Lk 16:15.—1 Sa 16:7.—Gal 6:7,8. Mt 16:26.—
Phil 3:7. Ps 51:6.—Ps 17:3.

Christ the first fruits.

Unless a grain of wheat falls into the earth and dies, it remains by itself alone; but if it dies, it bears much fruit.—If the first piece of dough be holy, the lump is also; and if the root be holy, the branches are too.—Now Christ has been raised from the dead, the first fruits of those who are asleep.—If we have become united with Him in the likeness of His death, certainly we shall be also in the likeness of His resurrection.—The Lord Jesus Christ; who will transform the body of our humble state into conformity with the body of His glory, by the exertion of the power that He has even to subject all things to Himself.

The first-born from the dead.—If the Spirit of Him who raised Jesus from the dead dwells in you, He who raised Christ Jesus from the dead will also give life to your mortal bodies through His Spirit who indwells you.

I am the resurrection, and the life; he who believes in Me shall live even if he dies.

1 CO 15:23. Jn 12:24.—Ro 11:16.—1 Co 15:20.—Ro 6:5.—
Phil 3:20,21. Col 1:18.—Ro 8:11. Jn 11:25.

He has filled the hungry with good things; and sent away the rich empty-handed.

You say, I am rich, and have become wealthy, and have need of nothing, and you do not know that you are wretched and miserable and poor and blind and naked. I advise you to buy from Me gold refined by fire, that you may become rich. . . . Those whom I love, I reprove and discipline; be zealous therefore, and repent.

Blessed are those who hunger and thirst for righteousness, for they shall be satisfied.—The afflicted and needy are seeking water, but there is none, and their tongue is parched with thirst; I the LORD will answer them Myself, as the God of Israel I will not forsake them.—I, the LORD, am your God, . . . open your mouth wide and I will fill it.

Why do you spend money for what is not bread, and your wages for what does not satisfy? Listen carefully to Me, and eat what is good, and delight yourself in abundance.—I am the bread of life; he who comes to Me shall not hunger, and he who believes in Me shall never thirst.

LK 1:53. Rev 3:17–19. Mt 5:6.—Is 41:17.—Ps 81:10. Is 55:2.—
Jn 6:35.

My feet came close to stumbling; my steps had almost slipped.

If I should say, My foot has slipped, Thy lovingkindness, O LORD, will hold me up.

Simon, Simon, behold, Satan has demanded permission to sift you like wheat; but I have prayed for you, that your faith may not fail.

A righteous man falls seven times, and rises again.—When he falls, he shall not be hurled headlong; because the LORD is the One who holds his hand.

Do not rejoice over me, O my enemy. Though I fall I will rise; though I dwell in darkness, the LORD is a light for me.—From six troubles He will deliver you, even in seven evil will not touch you.

If anyone sins, we have an Advocate with the Father, Jesus Christ the righteous.—He is able to save forever those who draw near to God through Him, since He always lives to make intercession for them.

PS 73:2. Ps 94:18. Lk 22:31,32. Pr 24:16.—Ps 37:24. Mic 7:8.—
Job 5:19. 1 Jn 2:1.—Heb 7:25.

I will give them one heart and one way, that they may fear Me always, for their own good, and for the good of their children after them.

I will give you a new heart and put a new spirit within you.— Good and upright is the LORD; therefore He instructs sinners in the way. He leads the humble in justice, and He teaches the humble His way. All the paths of the LORD are lovingkindness and truth to those who keep His covenant and His testimonies.

That they may all be one; even as Thou, Father, art in Me, and I in Thee, that they also may be in Us; that the world may believe that Thou didst send Me.

I . . . entreat you to walk in a manner worthy of the calling with which you have been called, with all humility and gentleness, . . . being diligent to preserve the unity of the Spirit in the bond of peace. There is one body and one Spirit, just as also you were called in one hope of your calling; one Lord, one faith, one baptism, one God and Father of all who is over all and through all and in all.

JER 32:39. Eze 36:26.—Ps 25:8–10. Jn 17:21. Eph 4:1–6.

Those who wait for the LORD will gain new strength.

When I am weak, then I am strong.—My God is My strength. —He has said to me, My grace is sufficient for you, for power is perfected in weakness. Most gladly, therefore, I will rather boast about my weaknesses, that the power of Christ may dwell in me. —Let him rely on My protection.

Cast your burden upon the LORD, and He will sustain you.— His arms are agile, from the hands of the Mighty One of Jacob.

I will not let you go unless you bless me.

You come to me with a sword, a spear, and a javelin, but I come to you in the name of the LORD of hosts, the God of the armies of Israel, whom you have taunted.—Contend, O LORD, with those who contend with me; fight against those who fight against me. Take hold of buckler and shield, and rise up for my help.

IS 40:31. 2 Co 12:10.— Is 49:5.—2 Co 12:9.—Is 27:5. Ps 55:22.— Gen 49:24. Gen 32:26. 1 Sa 17:45.—Ps 35:1,2.

Do not be conformed to this world, but be transformed by the renewing of your mind.

You shall not follow a multitude in doing evil.—Do you not know that friendship with the world is hostility toward God? Therefore whoever wishes to be a friend of the world makes himself an enemy of God.

What partnership have righteousness and lawlessness, or what fellowship has light with darkness? Or what harmony has Christ with Belial, or what has a believer in common with an unbeliever? Or what agreement has the temple of God with idols?—Do not love the world, nor the things in the world. If any one loves the world, the love of the Father is not in him. For all that is in the world . . . is passing away, and also its lusts; but the one who does the will of God abides forever.

In which you formerly walked according to the course of this world, according to the prince of the power of the air, of the spirit that is now working in the sons of disobedience.—But you did not learn Christ in this way, if indeed you have heard Him . . . just as truth is in Jesus.

RO 12:2. Ex 23:2. Ja 4:4. 2 Co 6:14–16.—1 Jn 2:15–17. Eph 2:2.—Eph 4:20,21.

Man goes forth to his work and to his labor until evening.

By the sweat of your face you shall eat bread, till you return to the ground.—This order: If anyone will not work, neither let him eat.—Make it your ambition to lead a quiet life and attend to your own business and work with your hands.

Whatever your hand finds to do, verily, do it with all your might; for there is no activity or planning or wisdom in Sheol where you are going.—Night is coming, when no man can work.

Let us not lose heart in doing good, for in due time we shall reap if we do not grow weary.—Always abounding in the work of the Lord, knowing that your toil is not in vain in the Lord.

There remains . . . a rest for the people of God.—To us who have borne the burden and the scorching heat of the day.—Here is rest, give rest to the weary, and, Here is repose.

PS 104:23. Gen 3:19.—2 Th 3:10.—1 Th 4:11. Ec 9:10.—Jn 9:4. Gal 6:9.—1 Co 15:58. Heb 4:9.—Mt 20:12.—Is 28:12.

I have seen his ways, but I will heal him.

I, the LORD, am your healer.
O LORD, Thou hast searched me and known me. Thou dost know when I sit down and when I rise up; Thou dost understand my thought from afar. Thou dost scrutinize my path and my lying down, and art intimately acquainted with all my ways.—Thou hast placed our iniquities before Thee, our secret sins in the light of Thy presence.—All things are open and laid bare to the eyes of Him with whom we have to do.

Come now, and let us reason together, says the LORD, though your sins are as scarlet, they will be as white as snow; though they are red like crimson, they will be like wool.—Let him be gracious to him, and say, deliver him from going down to the pit, I have found a ransom.—He was pierced through for our transgressions, He was crushed for our iniquities; the chastening for our well-being fell upon Him, and by His scourging we are healed.—He has sent me to bind up the brokenhearted.—Your faith has made you well; go in peace, and be healed of your affliction.

IS 57:18. Ex 15:26. Ps 139:1–3.—Ps 90:8.—Heb 4:13. Is 1:18.—
Job 33:24.—Is 53:5.—Is 61:1.—Mk 5:34.

The LORD is for me.

May the LORD answer you in the day of trouble! May the name of the God of Jacob set you securely on high! May He send you help from the sanctuary, and support you from Zion! We will sing for joy over your victory, and in the name of our God we will set up our banners. Some boast in chariots, and some in horses; but we will boast in the name of the LORD, our God. They have bowed down and fallen; but we have risen and stood upright.

For He will come like a rushing stream, which the wind of the LORD drives.—No temptation has overtaken you but such as is common to man; and God is faithful, who will not allow you to be tempted beyond what you are able; but with the temptation will provide the way of escape also, that you may be able to endure it.

If God is for us, who is against us?—The LORD is for me; I will not fear.

Our God whom we serve is able to deliver us . . . and He will deliver us.

PS 118:7. Ps 20:1,2,5,7,8. Is 59:19.—1 Co 10:13. Ro 8:31.—Ps 118:6.
Dan 3:17.

If any man is thirsty, let him come to Me and drink.

My soul longed and even yearned for the courts of the LORD; my heart and my flesh sing for joy to the living God.—O God, Thou art my God; I shall seek Thee earnestly; my soul thirsts for Thee, my flesh yearns for Thee, in a dry and weary land where there is no water. Thus I have beheld Thee in the sanctuary, to see Thy power and Thy glory.

Ho! Every one who thirsts, come to the waters; and you who have no money come, buy and eat. Come, buy wine and milk without money and without cost.—The Spirit and the bride say, Come. And let the one who hears say, Come. And let the one who is thirsty come; let the one who wishes take the water of life without cost.—Whoever drinks of the water that I shall give him shall never thirst; but the water that I shall give him shall become in him a well of water springing up to eternal life.—My blood is true drink.

Eat, friends; drink and imbibe deeply, O lovers.

JN 7:37. Ps 84:2.—Ps 63:1,2. Is 55:1.—Rev 22:17.—Jn 4:14.—Jn 6:55.
Song 5:1.

You are the salt of the earth.

Imperishable quality.—you have been born again not of seed which is perishable but imperishable, that is, through the living and abiding word of God.—He who believes in Me shall live even if he dies.—Sons of God, being sons of the resurrection.—The incorruptible God.

If anyone does not have the Spirit of Christ, he does not belong to Him. And if Christ is in you, though the body is dead because of sin, yet the spirit is alive because of righteousness. But if the Spirit of Him who raised Jesus from the dead dwells in you, He who raised Christ Jesus from the dead will also give life to your mortal bodies through His Spirit who indwells you.—It is sown a perishable body, it is raised an imperishable body.

Have salt in yourselves, and be at peace with one another.— Let no unwholesome word proceed from your mouth, but only such a word as is good for edification according to the need of the moment, that it may give grace to those who hear.

MT 5:13. 1 Pe 3:4.—1 Pe 1:23.—Jn 11:25.—Lk 20:36.—Ro 1:23.
Ro 8:9–11.—1 Co 15:42. Mk 9:50.—Eph 4:29.

I, even I, am He who comforts you.

Blessed be the God and Father of our Lord Jesus Christ, the Father of mercies and God of all comfort; who comforts us in all our affliction so that we may be able to comfort those who are in any affliction with the comfort with which we ourselves are comforted by God.—Just as a father has compassion on his children, so the LORD has compassion on those who fear Him. For He Himself knows our frame; He is mindful that we are but dust.—As one whom his mother comforts, so I will comfort you.—Casting all your anxiety upon Him, because He cares for you.

Thou, O Lord, art a God merciful and gracious, slow to anger and abundant in lovingkindness and truth.

Another Helper . . . that is the Spirit of truth.—The Spirit also helps our weakness.

He shall wipe away every tear from your eyes; and there shall no longer be any death; there shall no longer be any mourning, or crying, or pain; the first things have passed away.

IS 51:12. 2 Co 1:3,4.—Ps 103:13,14.—Is 66:13.—1 Pe 5:7. Ps 86:14.
Jn 14:16,17.—Ro 8:26. Rev 21:4.

You were called into fellowship with His Son.

When He received . . . glory from God the Father, such an utterance as this was made to Him by the Majestic Glory, This is My beloved Son with whom I am well pleased.—See how great a love the Father has bestowed upon us, that we should be called children of God.

Be imitators of God, as beloved children.—If children, heirs also, heirs of God and fellow-heirs with Christ.

He is the radiance of His glory and the exact representation of His nature.—Let your light shine before men in such a way that they may see your good works, and glorify your Father who is in heaven.

Jesus, the author and perfecter of faith, who for the joy set before Him endured the cross, despising the shame.

These things I speak in the world, that they may have My joy made full in themselves.—Just as the sufferings of Christ are ours in abundance, so also our comfort is abundant through Christ.

1 CO 1:9. 2 Pe 1:17.—1 Jn 3:1. Eph 5:1.—Ro 8:17. Heb 1:3.—
Mt 5:16. Heb 12:2.—Jn 17:13.—2 Co 1:5.

Sin shall not be master over you, for you are not under law, but under grace.

What then? Shall we sin because we are not under law but under grace? May it never be!—My brethren, you also were made to die to the Law through the body of Christ, that you might be joined to another, to Him who was raised from the dead, that we might bear fruit for God.—Though not being without the law of God but under the law of Christ.—The sting of death is sin, and the power of sin is the law; but thanks be to God, who gives us the victory through our Lord Jesus Christ.

The law of the Spirit of life in Christ Jesus has set you free from the law of sin and of death.—Every one who commits sin is the slave of sin. If therefore the Son shall make you free, you shall be free indeed.

Christ set us free; therefore keep standing firm and do not be subject again to a yoke of slavery.

RO 6:14. Ro 6:15.—Ro 7:4.—1 Co 9:21.—1 Co 15:56,57. Ro 8:2.—
Jn 8:34,36. Gal 5:1.

A double-minded man, unstable in all his ways.

No one, after putting his hand to the plow and looking back, is fit for the kingdom of God.

He who comes to God must believe that He is, and that He is a rewarder of those who seek Him.—Let him ask in faith without any doubting, for the one who doubts is like the surf of the sea driven and tossed by the wind. For let not that man expect that he will receive anything from the Lord.—All things for which you pray and ask, believe that you have received them, and they shall be granted you.

We are no longer to be children, tossed here and there by waves, and carried about by every wind of doctrine, by the trickery of men, by craftiness in deceitful scheming; but speaking the truth in love, we are to grow up in all aspects into Him, who is the head, even Christ.

Abide in Me.—Be steadfast, immovable, always abounding in the work of the Lord, knowing that your toil is not in vain in the Lord.

JA 1:8. Lk 9:62. Heb 11:6.—Ja 1:6,7.—Mk 11:24. Eph 4:14,15.
Jn 15:4.—1 Co 15:58.

The LORD weighs the hearts.

The LORD knows the way of the righteous, but the way of the wicked will perish.—The LORD will show who is His, and who is holy.—Your Father who sees in secret will repay you.

Search me, O God, and know my heart; try me and know my anxious thoughts; and see if there be any hurtful way in me, and lead me in the everlasting way.—There is no fear in love; but perfect love casts out fear.

Lord, all my desire is before Thee; and my sighing is not hidden from Thee.—When my spirit was overwhelmed within me; Thou didst know my path.—He who searches the hearts knows what the mind of the Spirit is, because He intercedes for the saints according to the will of God.

The firm foundation of God stands, having this seal, The Lord knows those who are His, and, Let every one who names the name of the Lord abstain from wickedness.

PR 21:2. Ps 1:6.—Num 16:5.—Mt 6:4. Ps 139:23,24.—1 Jn 4:18.
Ps 38:9.—Ps 142:3.—Ro 8:27. 2 Ti 2:19.

Weeping may last for the night, but a shout of joy comes in the morning.

So that no man may be disturbed by these afflictions; for you yourselves know that we have been destined for this. For indeed when we were with you, we kept telling you in advance that we were going to suffer affliction.—In Me ... have peace. In the world you have tribulation, but take courage; I have overcome the world.

I will be satisfied with Thy likeness when I awake.—The night is almost gone, and the day is at hand.—As the light of the morning when the sun rises, a morning without clouds, when the tender grass springs out of the earth, through sunshine after rain.

He will swallow up death for all time, and the Lord GOD will wipe tears away from all faces.—There shall no longer be any death; there shall no longer be any mourning, or crying, or pain; the first things have passed away.—Then we who are alive and remain shall be caught up together with them in the clouds to meet the Lord in the air.... Therefore comfort one another with these words.

PS 30:5. 1 Th 3:3,4.—Jn 16:33. Ps 17:15.—Ro 13:12.—2 Sa 23:4.
Is 25:8.—Rev 21:4.—1 Th 4:17,18.

A battered reed He will not break off.

The sacrifices of God are a broken spirit; a broken and a contrite heart, O God, Thou wilt not despise.—He heals the brokenhearted, and binds up their wounds.—For thus says the high and exalted One who lives forever, whose name is Holy, I dwell on a high and holy place, and also with the contrite and lowly of spirit in order to revive the spirit of the lowly and to revive the heart of the contrite. For I will not contend forever, neither will I always be angry; for the spirit would grow faint before Me, and the breath of those whom I have made.

I will seek the lost, bring back the scattered, bind up the broken, and strengthen the sick.—Therefore, strengthen the hands that are weak and the knees that are feeble, and make straight paths for your feet, so that the limb which is lame may not be put out of joint, but rather be healed.—Behold, your God . . . He will save you.

MT 12:20. Ps 51:17.—Ps 147:3.—Is 57:15,16. Eze 34:16.—
Heb 12:12,13.—Is 35:4.

O taste and see that the LORD is good; how blessed is the man who takes refuge in Him!

When the headwaiter tasted the water which had become wine, and did not know where it came from . . . (he) said . . . Every man serves the good wine first, and when men have drunk freely, then that which is poorer; you have kept the good wine until now.

For the ear tests words, as the palate tastes food.—I believed. —I know whom I have believed.—In his shade I took great delight and sat down, and his fruit was sweet to my taste.

The kindness of God.—He who did not spare His own Son, but delivered Him up for us all, how will He not also with Him freely give us all things?

Like newborn babes, long for the pure milk of the word, that by it you may grow in respect to salvation, if you have tasted the kindness of the Lord.

Let all who take refuge in Thee be glad, let them ever sing for joy.

PS 34:8. Jn 2:9,10. Job 34:3.—2 Co 4:13.—2 Ti 1:12.—Song 2:3.
Ro 2:4.—Ro 8:32. 1 Pe 2:2,3. Ps 5:11.

Open my eyes, that I may behold wonderful things from Thy law.

He opened their minds to understand the Scriptures.—To you it has been granted to know the mysteries of the kingdom of heaven, but to them it has not been granted.—I praise Thee, O Father, Lord of heaven and earth, that Thou didst hide these things from the wise and intelligent and didst reveal them to babes.—Now we have received, not the spirit of the world, but the Spirit who is from God, that we might know the things freely given to us by God.—How precious also are Thy thoughts to me, O God! How vast is the sum of them! If I should count them, they would outnumber the sand.—Oh the depth of the riches both of the wisdom and knowledge of God! How unsearchable are His judgments and unfathomable His ways! For who has known the mind of the Lord, or who became His counselor? For from Him and through Him and to Him are all things. To Him be the glory forever. Amen.

PS 119:18. Lk 24:45.—Mt 13:11.—Mt 11:25,26.—1 Co 2:12.—
Ps 139:17,18.—Ro 11:33,34,36.

En-hakkore (The well of him that cried).

If you knew the gift of God, and who it is who says to you, Give Me a drink, you would have asked Him, and He would have given you living water.—If any man is thirsty, let him come to Me and drink. This He spoke of the Spirit, whom those who believed in Him were to receive.

Test Me now . . . says the Lord of hosts, if I will not open for you the windows of heaven, and pour out for you a blessing until there is no more need.—If you then, being evil, know how to give good gifts to your children, how much more shall your Heavenly Father give the Holy Spirit to those who ask Him?—Ask, and it shall be given to you; seek, and you shall find.

Because you are sons, God has sent forth the Spirit of His Son into our hearts, crying, Abba! Father!—You have not received a spirit of slavery leading to fear again, but you have received a spirit of adoption as sons by which we cry out, Abba! Father!

JUDG 15:19. Jn 4:10.—Jn 7:37,39. Mal 3:10.—Lk 11:13.—Lk 11:9.
Gal 4:6.—Ro 8:15.

The God of all grace.

I Myself . . . will proclaim the name of the LORD before you; and I will be gracious to whom I will be gracious.—Be gracious to him, and say, Deliver him from going down to the pit, I have found a ransom.—Being justified as a gift by His grace through the redemption which is in Christ Jesus; whom God displayed publicly as a propitiation in His blood through faith. This was to demonstrate His righteousness, because in the forbearance of God He passed over the sins previously committed.—Grace and truth were realized through Jesus Christ.

By grace you have been saved through faith; and that not of yourselves, it is the gift of God.—Grace, mercy and peace from God the Father and Christ Jesus our Lord.—To each one of us grace was given according to the measure of Christ's gift.—As each one has received a special gift, employ it in serving one another, as good stewards of the manifold grace of God.—He gives a greater grace.

Grow in the grace and knowledge of our Lord and Savior Jesus Christ. To Him be the glory, both now and to the day of eternity. Amen.

1 PE 5:10. Ex 33:19.—Job 33:24.—Ro 3:24,25.—Jn 1:17. Eph 2:8.—
1 Ti 1:2.—Eph 4:7.—1 Pe 4:10.—Ja 4:6. 2 Pe 3:18.

I will lift up my eyes to the mountains; from whence shall my help come? My help comes from the LORD, who made heaven and earth.

As the mountains surround Jerusalem, so the LORD surrounds His people from this time forth and forever.

To Thee I lift up my eyes, O Thou who art enthroned in the heavens! Behold, as the eyes of servants look to the hand of their master, as the eyes of a maid to the hand of her mistress; so our eyes look to the LORD our God, until He shall be gracious to us. —For Thou hast been my help, and in the shadow of Thy wings I sing for joy.

O our God, wilt Thou not judge them? For we are powerless before this great multitude who are coming against us; nor do we know what to do, but our eyes are on Thee.—My eyes are continually toward the LORD, for He will pluck my feet out of the net. —Our help is in the name of the LORD, who made heaven and earth.

PS 121:1,2. Ps 125:2. Ps 123:1,2.—Ps 63:7. 2 Ch 20:12.—Ps 25:15.—
Ps 124:8.

How blessed is the man who finds wisdom, and the man who gains understanding.

For he who finds me finds life, and obtains favor from the LORD.

Thus says the LORD, Let not a wise man boast of his wisdom, and let not the mighty man boast of his might . . . but let him who boasts boast of this, that he understands and knows Me, that I am the LORD.—The fear of the LORD is the beginning of wisdom.

But whatever things were gain to me, those things I have counted as loss for the sake of Christ. More than that, I count all things to be loss in view of the surpassing value of knowing Christ Jesus my Lord, for whom I have suffered the loss of all things, and count them but rubbish in order that I may gain Christ.—In whom are hidden all the treasures of wisdom and knowledge.—Counsel is mine and sound wisdom; I am understanding, power is mine.

Christ Jesus, who became to us wisdom from God, and righteousness and sanctification, and redemption.

He who is wise wins souls.

PR 3:13. Pr 8:35. Jer 9:23,24.—Pr 9:10. Phil 3:7,8.—Col 2:3.—
Pr 8:14. 1 Co 1:30. Pr 11:30.

Poor yet making many rich.

For you know the grace of our Lord Jesus Christ, that though He was rich, yet for your sake He became poor, that you through His poverty might become rich.—Of His fulness we have all received, and grace upon grace.—My God shall supply all your needs according to His riches in glory in Christ Jesus.—God is able to make all grace abound to you, that always having all sufficiency in everything, you may have an abundance for every good deed.

Did not God choose the poor of this world to be rich in faith and heirs of the kingdom which He promised to those who love Him?—Not many wise according to the flesh, not many mighty, not many noble; but God has chosen the foolish things of the world to shame the wise, and God has chosen the weak things of the world to shame the things which are strong.

We have this treasure in earthen vessels, that the surpassing greatness of the power may be of God and not from ourselves.

2 CO 6:10. 2 Co 8:9.—Jn 1:16.—Phil 4:19.—2 Co 9:8. Ja 2:5.—
1 Co 1:26,27. 2 Co 4:7.

**We know that God causes all things to work together for good
to those who love God.**

For the wrath of man shall praise Thee; with a remnant of
wrath Thou shalt gird Thyself.—You meant evil against me, but
God meant it for good.

All things belong to you . . . the world or life or death or things
present or things to come; all things belong to you, and you
belong to Christ; and Christ belongs to God.—All things are for
your sakes, that the grace which is spreading to more and more
people may cause the giving of thanks to abound to the glory of
God. Therefore we do not lose heart, but though our outer man
is decaying, yet our inner man is being renewed day by day. For
momentary, light affliction is producing for us an eternal weight
of glory far beyond all comparison.

Consider it all joy, my brethren, when you encounter various
trials; knowing that the testing of your faith produces endurance.
And let endurance have its perfect result, that you may be perfect and complete, lacking in nothing.

RO 8:28. Ps 76:10.—Gen 50:20. 1 Co 3:21–23.—2 Co 4:15–17.
Ja 1:2–4.

The fellowship of the Holy Spirit, be with you all.

And I will ask the Father, and He will give you another Helper,
that He may be with you forever; that is the Spirit of truth, whom
the world cannot receive, because it does not behold Him or
know Him, but you know Him because He abides with you, and
will be in you.—He will not speak on His own initiative . . . He
shall glorify Me; for He shall take of Mine, and shall disclose it to
you.

The love of God has been poured out within our hearts
through the Holy Spirit who was given to us.

The one who joins himself to the Lord is one spirit with Him.
Do you not know that your body is a temple of the Holy Spirit
who is in you, whom you have from God, and that you are not
your own?

Do not grieve the Holy Spirit of God, by whom you were
sealed for the day of redemption.—The Spirit also helps our
weakness; for we do not know how to pray as we should, but the
Spirit Himself intercedes for us with groanings too deep for
words.

2 CO 13:14. Jn 14:16,17.—Jn 16:13,14. Ro 5:5. 1 Co 6:17,19.
Eph 4:30.—Ro 8:26.

Let my meditation be pleasing to Him; as for me, I shall be glad in the LORD.

Like an apple tree among the trees of the forest, so is my beloved among the young men. In his shade I took great delight and sat down, and his fruit was sweet to my taste.—Who in the skies is comparable to the LORD? Who among the sons of the mighty is like the LORD?

My beloved is dazzling and ruddy, outstanding among ten thousand.—One pearl of great value.—Ruler of the kings of the earth.

His head is like gold, pure gold; his locks are like clusters of dates, and black as a raven.—Head over all things.—He is also head of the body, the church.

His cheeks are like a bed of balsam, banks of sweet-scented herbs.—He could not escape notice.

His lips are lilies, dripping with liquid myrrh.—Never did a man speak the way this man speaks.

His appearance is like Lebanon, choice as the cedars.—Make Thy face to shine upon thy servant.—Lift up the light of Thy countenance upon us, O LORD!

PS 104:34. Song 2:3.—Ps 89:6. Song 5:10.—Mt 13:46.—Rev 1:5. Song 5:11.—Eph 1:22.—Col 1:18. Song 5:13.—Mk 7:24. Song 5:13.— Jn 7:46. Song 5:15.—Ps 31:16.—Ps 4:6.

My Father, if it is possible, let this cup pass from Me; yet not as I will, but as Thou wilt.

Now My soul has become troubled; and what shall I say, Father, save Me from this hour? But for this purpose I came to this hour.

I have come down from heaven, not to do My own will, but the will of Him who sent Me.—He ... becoming obedient to the point of death, even death on a cross.—In the days of His flesh, He offered up both prayers and supplications with loud crying and tears to the One able to save Him from death, and He was heard because of His piety. Although He was a Son, He learned obedience from the things which He suffered.

Do you think that I cannot appeal to My Father, and He will at once put at My disposal more than twelve legions of angels? —Thus it is written, that the Christ should suffer and rise again from the dead the third day; and that repentance for forgiveness of sins should be proclaimed in His name to all the nations— beginning from Jerusalem.

MT 26:39. Jn 12:27. Jn 6:38.—Phil 2:8.—Heb 5:7,8. Mt 26:53.— Lk 24:46,47.

Our God has not forsaken us.

Beloved, do not be surprised at the fiery ordeal among you, which comes upon you for your testing, as though some strange thing were happening to you.—It is for discipline that you endure; God deals with you as with sons; for what son is there whom his father does not discipline? But if you are without discipline, of which all have become partakers, then you are illegitimate children and not sons.

The LORD your God is testing you to find out if you love the LORD your God with all your heart and with all your soul.

The LORD will not abandon His people on account of His great name, because the LORD has been pleased to make you a people for Himself.—Can a woman forget her nursing child, and have no compassion on the son of her womb? Even these may forget, but I will not forget you.—How blessed is he whose help is the God of Jacob, whose hope is in the LORD his God.

Shall not God bring about justice for His elect, who cry to Him day and night, and will He delay long over them? I tell you that He will bring about justice for them speedily.

EZRA 9:9. 1 Pe 4:12.—Heb 12:7,8. Deu 13:3. 1 Sa 12:22.—
Is 49:15.—Ps 146:5. Lk 18:7,8.

He who overcomes shall inherit these things.

If we have only hoped in Christ in this life, we are of all men most to be pitied.—They desire a better country, that is a heavenly one. Therefore God is not ashamed to be called their God; for He has prepared a city for them.—To obtain an inheritance which is imperishable and undefiled and will not fade away, reserved in heaven for you.

All things belong to you . . . the world or life or death or things present or things to come; all things belong to you.—Things which eye has not seen and ear has not heard, and which have not entered the heart of man, all that God has prepared for those who love Him. For to us God revealed them through the Spirit.

Watch yourselves, that you might not lose what we have accomplished, but that you may receive a full reward.—Let us . . . lay aside every encumbrance, and the sin which so easily entangles us, and let us run with endurance the race that is set before us.

REV 21:7. 1 Co 15:19.—Heb 11:16.—1 Pe 1:4. 1 Co 3:21,22.—
1 Co 2:9,10. 2 Jn 8.—Heb 12:1.

The nearness of God is my good.

O LORD, I love the habitation of Thy house, and the place where Thy glory dwells.—A day in Thy courts is better than a thousand outside. I would rather stand at the threshold of the house of my God, than dwell in the tents of wickedness.—How blessed is the one whom Thou dost choose, and bring near to Thee, to dwell in Thy courts. We will be satisfied with the goodness of Thy house, Thy holy temple.

The LORD is good to those who wait for Him, to the person who seeks Him.—Therefore the LORD longs to be gracious to you, and therefore He waits on high to have compassion on you. For the LORD is a God of justice; how blessed are all those who long for Him.

Therefore, brethren, we have confidence to enter the holy place by the blood of Jesus, by a new and living way which He inaugurated for us . . . let us draw near with a sincere heart in full assurance of faith, having our hearts sprinkled clean from an evil conscience.

PS 73:28. Ps 26:8.—Ps 84:10.—Ps 65:4. Lam 3:25.—Is 30:18.
Heb 10:19,20,22.

The grace of our Lord Jesus Christ.

The Word became flesh, and dwelt among us, and we beheld His glory, glory as of the only begotten from the Father, full of grace and truth.—Thou art fairer than the sons of men; grace is poured upon Thy lips.—All were speaking well of Him, and wondering at the gracious words which were falling from His lips.

You have tasted the kindness of the Lord.—The one who believes in the Son of God has the witness in himself.—We speak that which we know, and bear witness of that which we have seen.

O taste and see that the LORD is good; how blessed is the man who takes refuge in Him!—In his shade I took great delight and sat down, and his fruit was sweet to my taste.

He said to me, My grace is sufficient for you, for power is perfected in weakness.—To each one of us grace was given according to the measure of Christ's gift.—As each one has received a special gift, employ it in serving one another, as good stewards of the manifold grace of God.

2 CO 8:9. Jn 1:14.—Ps 45:2.—Lk 4:22. 1 Pe 2:3.—1 Jn 5:10.—
Jn 3:11. Ps 34:8.—Song 2:3. 2 Co 12:9.—Eph 4:7.—1 Pe 4:10.

Let endurance have its perfect result, that you may be perfect and complete, lacking in nothing.

Now for a little while, if necessary, you have been distressed by various trials, that the proof of your faith, being more precious than gold which is perishable, even though tested by fire, may be found to result in praise and glory and honor at the revelation of Jesus Christ.—We . . . exult in our tribulations; knowing that tribulation brings about perseverance; and perseverance, proven character; and proven character, hope.

It is good that he waits silently for the salvation of the LORD.—You have for yourselves a better possession and an abiding one. Therefore, do not throw away your confidence, which has a great reward. For you have need of endurance, so that when you have done the will of God, you may receive what was promised.—Now may our Lord Jesus Christ Himself and God our Father, who has loved us and given us eternal comfort and good hope by grace, comfort and strengthen your hearts in every good work and word.

JA 1:4. 1 Pe 1:6,7.—Ro 5:3,4. Lam 3:26.—Heb 10:34–36.—
2 Th 2:16,17.

God will judge the secrets of men through Christ Jesus.

Therefore do not go on passing judgment before the time, but wait until the Lord comes who will both bring to light the things hidden in the darkness and disclose the motives of men's hearts; and then each man's praise will come to him from God.—Not even the Father judges any one, but He has given all judgment to the Son . . . because He is the Son of Man.—The Son of God, who has eyes like a flame of fire.

They say, How does God know? And is there knowledge with the Most High?—These things you have done, and I kept silence; you thought that I was just like you; I will reprove you, and state the case in order before your eyes.—There is nothing covered up that will not be revealed, and hidden that will not be known.

Lord, all my desire is before Thee; and my sighing is not hidden from Thee.—Examine me, O LORD, and try me; test my mind and my heart.

RO 2:16. 1 Co 4:5.—Jn 5:22,27.—Rev 2:18. Ps 73:11.—Ps 50:21.—
Lk 12:2. Ps 38:9.—Ps 26:2.

A God of faithfulness and without injustice.

Him who judges righteously.—We must all appear before the judgment-seat of Christ, that each one may be recompensed for his deeds in the body, according to what he has done, whether good or bad.—Each one of us shall give account of himself to God.—The soul who sins will die.

Awake, O sword, against My Shepherd, and against the man, My Associate, declares the LORD of hosts. Strike the Shepherd. —The LORD has caused the iniquity of us all to fall on Him.— Lovingkindness and truth have met together; righteousness and peace have kissed each other.—Mercy triumphs over judgment. —The wages of sin is death, but the free gift of God is eternal life in Christ Jesus our Lord.

A righteous God and a Savior; there is none except Me.—Just and the justifier of the one who has faith in Jesus.—Justified as a gift by His grace through the redemption which is in Christ Jesus.

DEU 32:4. 1 Pe 2:23.—2 Co 5:10.—Ro 14:12.—Eze 18:4.
Zec 13:7.—Is 53:6.—Ps 85:10.—Ja 2:13.—Ro 6:23. Is 45:21.—
Ro 3:26.—Ro 3:24.

Death is swallowed up in victory.

Thanks be to God, who gives us the victory through our Lord Jesus Christ.

Since then the children share in flesh and blood, He Himself likewise also partook of the same, that through death He might render powerless him who had the power of death, that is, the devil; and might deliver those who through fear of death were subject to slavery all their lives.

If we have died with Christ, we believe that we shall also live with Him, knowing that Christ, having been raised from the dead, is never to die again; death no longer is master over Him. For the death that He died, He died to sin, once for all; but the life that He lives, He lives to God.

Even so consider yourselves to be dead to sin, but alive to God in Christ Jesus.

In all these things we overwhelmingly conquer through Him who loved us.

1 CO 15:54. 1 Co 15:57. Heb 2:14,15. Ro 6:8–10. Ro 6:11. Ro 8:37.

Humble yourselves . . . under the mighty hand of God, that He may exalt you at the proper time.

Everyone who is proud in heart is an abomination to the LORD; assuredly, he will not be unpunished.

O LORD, Thou art our Father, we are the clay, and Thou our potter; and all of us are the work of Thy hand. Do not be angry beyond measure, O LORD, neither remember iniquity forever; behold, look now, all of us are Thy people.—Thou hast chastised me, and I was chastised, like an untrained calf; bring me back that I may be restored, for Thou art the LORD my God. For after I turned back, I repented; and after I was instructed, I smote on my thigh; I was ashamed, and also humiliated, because I bore the reproach of my youth.—It is good for a man that he should bear the yoke in his youth.

For affliction does not come from the dust, neither does trouble sprout from the ground, for man is born for trouble, as sparks fly upward.

1 PE 5:6. Pr 16:5. Is 64:8,9.—Jer 31:18,19.—Lam 3:27. Job 5:6,7.

Indeed, has God said?

The tempter came and said to Him (Jesus), If you are the Son of God . . . But He answered and said, It is written . . . it is written . . . it is written . . . Then the devil left Him.

I cannot return with you. . . . For a command came to me by the word of the LORD, You shall eat no bread, nor drink water there . . . He said to him, I also am a prophet like you, and an angel spoke to me by the word of the LORD, saying, Bring him back with you to your house, that he may eat bread and drink water. But he lied to him. So he went back with him. . . . The man of God, who disobeyed the command of the LORD . . . the LORD has given . . . to the lion, which has torn him and killed him, according to the word of the LORD.—Though we, or an angel from heaven, should preach to you a gospel contrary to that which we have preached to you, let him be accursed.—Thy word I have treasured in my heart, that I may not sin against Thee.

GEN 3:1. Mt 4:3,4,7,10,11. 1 Ki 13:16–19,26.—Gal 1:8.—Ps 119:11.

They shall invoke My name on the sons of Israel, and I then will bless them.

O LORD our God, other masters besides Thee have ruled us; but through Thee alone we confess Thy name.—We have become like those over whom Thou hast never ruled, like those who were not called by Thy name.

All the peoples of the earth shall see that you are called by the name of the LORD; and they shall be afraid of you.—The LORD will not abandon His people on account of His great name, because the LORD has been pleased to make you a people for Himself.

O Lord, Hear! O Lord, forgive! O Lord, listen and take action! For Thine own sake, O my God, do not delay, because Thy city and Thy people are called by Thy name.—Help us, O God of our salvation, for the glory of Thy name; and deliver us, and forgive our sins, for Thy name's sake. Why should the nations say, Where is their God?—The name of the LORD is a strong tower; the righteous runs into it and is safe.

NUM 6:27. Is 26:13.—Is 63:19. Deu 28:10.—1 Sa 12:22. Dan 9:19.—
Ps 79:9,10.—Pr 18:10.

The heavens are telling of the glory of God; and the firmament is declaring the work of His hands.

Since the creation of the world His invisible attributes, His eternal power and divine nature, have been clearly seen, being understood through what has been made.—He did not leave Himself without witness.—Day to day pours forth speech, and night to night reveals knowledge. There is no speech, nor are there words; their voice is not heard.

When I consider Thy heavens, the work of Thy fingers, the moon and the stars, which Thou hast ordained; what is man, that Thou dost take thought of him? And the son of man, that Thou dost care for him?

There is one glory of the sun, and another glory of the moon, and another glory of the stars; for star differs from star in glory. So also is the resurrection of the dead.—Those who have insight will shine brightly like the brightness of the expanse of heaven, and those who lead the many to righteousness, like the stars forever and ever.

PS 19:1. Ro 1:20.—Ac 14:17.—Ps 19:2,3. Ps 8:3,4. 1 Co 15:41,42.—
Dan 12:3.

We know love by this, that He laid down His life for us.

The love of Christ which surpasses knowledge.—Greater love has no one than this, that one lay down his life for his friends.—You know the grace of our Lord Jesus Christ, that though He was rich, yet for your sake He became poor, that you through His poverty might become rich.—Beloved, if God so loved us, we also ought to love one another.—Be kind to one another, tenderhearted, forgiving each other, just as God in Christ also has forgiven you.—Bearing with one another, and forgiving each other, whoever has a complaint against any one; just as the Lord forgave you, so also should you.—For even the Son of Man did not come to be served, but to serve, and to give His life a ransom for many.—Christ . . . suffered for you, leaving you an example for you to follow in His steps.

If I then, the Lord and the Teacher, washed your feet, you also ought to wash one another's feet.—We ought to lay down our lives for the brethren.

1 JN 3:16. Eph 3:19.—Jn 15:13.—2 Co 8:9.—1 Jn 4:11.—Eph 4:32.—Col 3:13.—Mk 10:45.—1 Pe 2:21. Jn 13:14.—1 Jn 3:16.

Whatever the Father does, these things the Son also does in like manner.

The LORD gives wisdom; from His mouth come knowledge and understanding.—I will give you utterance and wisdom which none of your opponents will be able to resist or refute.

Wait for the LORD; be strong, and let your heart take courage.—My grace is sufficient for you, for power is perfected in weakness.

Those who are the called, beloved in God the Father.—Both He who sanctifies and those who are sanctified are all from one Father; for which reason He is not ashamed to call them brethren.

Do I not fill the heavens and the earth? declares the LORD.—The fulness of Him who fills all in all.

I, even I, am the LORD; and there is no savior besides Me.—This One is indeed the Savior of the world.

Grace and peace from God the Father and Christ Jesus our Savior.

JN 5:19. Pr 2:6.—Lk 21:15. Ps 27:14.—2 Co 12:9. Jude 1.—Heb 2:11. Jer 23:24.—Eph 1:23. Is 43:11.—Jn 4:42. Titus 1:4.

He knows the way I take; when He has tried me, I shall come forth as gold.

He Himself knows our frame.—He does not afflict willingly, or grieve the sons of men.

The firm foundation of God stands, having this seal, The Lord knows those who are His, and, Let every one who names the name of the Lord abstain from wickedness. Now in a large house there are not only gold and silver vessels, but also vessels of wood and of earthenware, and some to honor and some to dishonor. Therefore, if a man cleanses himself from these things, he will be a vessel for honor, sanctified, useful to the Master, prepared for every good work.

He will sit as a smelter and purifier of silver, and He will purify the sons of Levi and refine them like gold and silver, so that they may present to the LORD offerings in righteousness.—I will . . . refine them as silver is refined. . . . They will call on My name, and I will answer them; I will say, They are My people, and they will say, The LORD is my God.

JOB 23:10. Ps 103:14.—Lam 3:33. 2 Ti 2:19–21. Mal 3:3.—Zec 13:9.

Make me know Thy ways, O LORD; teach me Thy paths.

Moses said to the LORD . . . I pray Thee, if I have found favor in Thy sight, let me know Thy ways, that I may know Thee. . . . And He said, My presence shall go with you, and I will give you rest.—He made known His ways to Moses, His acts to the sons of Israel.

He leads the humble in justice, and He teaches the humble His way. Who is the man who fears the LORD? He will instruct him in the way he should choose.—Trust in the LORD with all your heart, and do not lean on your own understanding. In all your ways acknowledge Him, and He will make your paths straight.

Thou wilt make known to me the path of life; in Thy presence is fulness of joy; in Thy right hand there are pleasures forever. —I will instruct you and teach you in the way which you should go; I will counsel you with My eye upon you.—The path of the righteous is like the light of dawn, that shines brighter and brighter until the full day.

PS 25:4. Ex 33:12–14.—Ps 103:7. Ps 25:9,12.—Pr 3:5,6. Ps 16:11.— Ps 32:8.—Pr 4:18.

The fruit of the Spirit is . . . self-control.

Everyone who competes in the games exercises self-control in all things. They then do it to receive a perishable wreath, but we an imperishable. Therefore I run in such a way, as not without aim; I box in such a way, as not beating the air; but I buffet my body and make it my slave, lest possibly, after I have preached to others, I myself should be disqualified.

Do not get drunk with wine, for that is dissipation, but be filled with the Spirit.

If any one wishes to come after Me, let him deny himself, and take up his cross, and follow Me.

Let us not sleep as others do, but let us be alert and sober. For those who sleep do their sleeping at night, and those who get drunk get drunk at night. But since we are of the day, let us be sober.—Deny ungodliness and worldly desires and . . . live sensibly, righteously and godly in the present age, looking for the blessed hope and the appearing of the glory of our great God and Savior, Christ Jesus.

GAL 5:22,23. 1 Co 9:25–27. Eph 5:18. Mt 16:24. 1 Th 5:6–8.—
Titus 2:12,13.

Grow up in all aspects into Him, who is the head, even Christ.

First the blade, then the head, then the mature grain in the head.—Until we all attain to the unity of the faith, and of the knowledge of the Son of God, to a mature man, to the measure of the stature which belongs to the fulness of Christ.

They measure themselves by themselves, and compare themselves with themselves, they are without understanding. But he who boasts, let him boast in the Lord. For not he who commends himself is approved, but whom the Lord commends.

The substance belongs to Christ. Let no one keep defrauding you of your prize by delighting in self-abasement and the worship of the angels, taking his stand on visions he has seen, inflated without cause by his fleshly mind, and not holding fast to the Head, from whom the entire body, being supplied and held together by the joints and ligaments, grows with a growth which is from God.

Grow in the grace and knowledge of our Lord and Savior Jesus Christ.

EPH 4:15. Mk 4:28.—Eph 4:13. 2 Co 10:12,17,18. Col 2:17–19.
2 Pe 3:18.

The goat shall bear on itself all their iniquities to a solitary land; and he shall release the goat in the wilderness.

As far as the east is from the west, so far has He removed our transgressions from us.—In those days and at that time, declares the LORD, search will be made for the iniquity of Israel, but there will be none; and for the sins of Judah, but they will not be found; for I shall pardon those whom I leave as a remnant.—Yes, Thou wilt cast all their sins into the depths of the sea. Who is a God like Thee, who pardons iniquity?

All of us like sheep have gone astray, each of us has turned to his own way; but the LORD has caused the iniquity of us all to fall on Him.—He will bear their iniquities. Therefore, I will allot Him a portion with the great, and He will divide the booty with the strong; because He poured out Himself to death, and was numbered with the transgressors; yet He Himself bore the sin of many, and interceded for the transgressors.—The Lamb of God who takes away the sin of the world!

LEV 16:22. Ps 103:12.—Jer 50:20.—Mic 7:19,18. Is 53:6.—
Is 53:11,12.—Jn 1:29.

Who regards you as superior? And what do you have that you did not receive?

By the grace of God I am what I am.—In the exercise of His will He brought us forth by the word of truth.—So then it does not depend on the man who wills or the man who runs, but on God who has mercy.—Where then is boasting? It is excluded.—Christ Jesus who became to us wisdom . . . and righteousness and sanctification, and redemption . . . Let him who boasts, boast in the Lord.

You were dead in your trespasses and sins, in which you formerly walked according to the course of this world, according to the prince of the power of the air, of the spirit that is now working in the sons of disobedience. Among them we too all formerly lived in the lusts of our flesh, indulging the desires of the flesh and of the mind, and were by nature children of wrath, even as the rest.—You were washed . . . you were sanctified . . . you were justified in the name of the Lord Jesus Christ, and in the Spirit of our God.

1 CO 4:7. 1 Co 15:10.—Ja 1:18.—Ro 9:16.—Ro 3:27.—1 Co 1:30,31.
Eph 2:1–3.—1 Co 6:11.

To Him who loves us, and released us from our sins by His blood.

Many waters cannot quench love, nor will rivers overflow it. Love is as strong as death.—Greater love has no one than this, that one lay down his life for his friends.

He Himself bore our sins in His body on the cross, that we might die to sin and live to righteousness; for by His wounds you were healed.—In Him we have redemption through His blood, the forgiveness of our trespasses, according to the riches of His grace.

You were washed . . . you were sanctified . . . you were justified in the name of the Lord Jesus Christ, and in the Spirit of our God. —You are a chosen race, a royal priesthood, a holy nation, a people for God's own possession, that you may proclaim the excellencies of Him who has called you out of darkness into His marvelous light.—I urge you . . . brethren, by the mercies of God, to present your bodies a living and holy sacrifice, acceptable to God, which is your spiritual service of worship.

REV 1:5. Song 8:7,6.—Jn 15:13. 1 Pe 2:24.—Eph 1:7. 1 Co 6:11.—
1 Pe 2:9.—Ro 12:1.

There are varieties of ministries, and the same Lord.

Azmaveth the son of Adiel had charge of the king's storehouses. Jonathan . . . had charge of the storehouses in the country . . . the cities . . . the villages, and in the towers. Ezri . . . had charge of the agricultural workers who tilled the soil. Shimei . . . had charge of the vineyards. . . . These were overseers of the property which belonged to King David.

God has appointed in the church, first apostles, second prophets, third teachers, then miracles, then gifts of healings, helps, administrations, various kinds of tongues. But one and the same Spirit works all these things, distributing to each one individually just as He wills.

As each one has received a special gift, employ it in serving one another, as good stewards of the manifold grace of God. Whoever speaks, let him speak, as it were, the utterances of God; whoever serves, let him do so as by the strength which God supplies; so that in all things God may be glorified through Jesus Christ, to whom belongs the glory and dominion forever and ever. Amen.

1 CO 12:5. 1 Ch 27:25–27,31. 1 Co 12:28,11. 1 Pe 4:10,11.

**Moses did not know that the skin of his face shone because of
his speaking with Him.**

Not to us, O LORD, not to us, but to Thy name give glory.—
Lord, when did we see You hungry, and feed You, or thirsty, and
give You drink?—With humility of mind let each of you regard
one another as more important than himself.—Clothe yourselves
with humility.

He (Jesus) was transfigured before them; and His face shone
like the sun, and His garments became as white as light.—Fixing
their gaze on him (Stephen), all who were sitting in the Council
saw his face like the face of an angel.—The glory which Thou hast
given Me I have given to them.—We all, with unveiled face
beholding as in a mirror the glory of the Lord, are being transformed into the same image from glory to glory, just as from the
Lord, the Spirit.

You are the light of the world. A city set on a hill cannot be
hidden. Nor do men light a lamp, and put it under the peck-
measure, but on the lampstand; and it gives light to all who are
in the house.

EX 34:29. Ps 115:1.—Mt 25:37.—Phil 2:3.—1 Pe 5:5. Mt 17:2.—
Ac 6:15.—Jn 17:22.—2 Co 3:18. Mt 5:14,15.

**There are varieties of effects, but the same God who works all
things in all persons.**

From Manasseh also some defected to David.... And they
helped David against the band of raiders, for they were all
mighty men of valor.—To each one is given the manifestation of
the Spirit for the common good.

Of the sons of Issachar, men who understood the times, with
knowledge of what Israel should do.—For to one is given the
word of wisdom through the Spirit, and to another the word of
knowledge according to the same Spirit.

Of Zebulun, there were 50,000 who went out in the army, who
could draw up in battle formation with all kinds of weapons of
war and helped David with an undivided heart.—A double-
minded man, unstable in all his ways.

There should be no division in the body, but that the members
should have the same care for one another. If one member
suffers, all the members suffer with it; if one member is honored,
all the members rejoice with it.

One Lord, one faith, one baptism.

1 CO 12:6. 1 Ch 12:19,21.—1 Co 12:7. 1 Ch 12:32.—1 Co 12:8.
1 Ch 12:33.—Ja 1:8. 1 Co 12:25,26. Eph 4:5.

Call upon Me in the day of trouble; I shall rescue you, and you will honor me.

Why are you in despair, O my soul? And why have you become disturbed within me? Hope in God, for I shall yet praise Him, the help of my countenance, and my God.—O LORD, Thou hast heard the desire of the humble; Thou wilt strengthen their heart, Thou wilt incline Thine ear.—For Thou, Lord, art good, and ready to forgive, and abundant in lovingkindness to all who call upon Thee.

Jacob said to his household . . . and let us arise and go up to Bethel; and I will make an altar there to God, who answered me in the day of my distress, and has been with me wherever I have gone.—Bless the LORD, O my soul, and forget none of His benefits.

I love the LORD, because He hears my voice and my supplications. Because He has inclined His ear to me, therefore I shall call upon Him as long as I live. The cords of death encompassed me, and the terrors of Sheol came upon me; I found distress and sorrow. Then I called upon the name of the LORD.

PS 50:15. Ps 42:11.—Ps 10:17.—Ps 86:5. Gen 35:2,3.—Ps 103:2. Ps 116:1–4.

For yet in a very little while, He who is coming will come, and will not delay.

Record the vision and inscribe it on tablets, that the one who reads it may run. For the vision is yet for the appointed time; it hastens toward the goal, and it will not fail. Though it tarries, wait for it; for it will certainly come, it will not delay.

Do not let this one fact escape your notice, beloved, that with the Lord one day is as a thousand years, and a thousand years as one day. The Lord is not slow about His promise, as some count slowness, but is patient toward you, not wishing for any to perish but for all to come to repentance.—Thou, O LORD, art a God merciful and gracious, slow to anger and abundant in lovingkindness and truth.—O that Thou wouldst rend the heavens and come down, that the mountains might quake at Thy presence. For from of old they have not heard nor perceived by ear, neither has the eye seen a God besides Thee, who acts in behalf of the one who waits for Him.

HEB 10:37. Hab 2:2,3. 2 Pe 3:8,9.—Ps 86:15.—Is 64:1,4.

The Lord our God, the Almighty, reigns.

I know that Thou canst do all things.—The things impossible with men are possible with God.—He does according to His will in the host of heaven and among the inhabitants of earth; and no one can ward off His hand or say to Him, What hast Thou done? —There is none who can deliver out of My hand; I act and who can reverse it?—Abba (Father), all things are possible for Thee.

Do you believe that I am able to do this? They said to Him, Yes, Lord. Then He touched their eyes, saying, Be it done to you according to your faith.—Lord, if You are willing, You can make me clean. And stretching out His hand, He touched him, saying, I am willing; be cleansed.—Mighty God.—All authority has been given to Me in heaven and on earth.

Some boast in chariots, and some in horses; but we will boast in the name of the LORD, our God.—Be strong and courageous, do not fear or be dismayed . . . for the one with us is greater than the one with him.

REV 19:6. Job 42:2.—Lk 18:27.—Dan 4:35.—Is 43:13.—Mk 14:36. Mt 9:28,29.—Mt 8:2,3.—Is 9:6.—Mt 28:18. Ps 20:7.—2 Ch 32:7.

What is the word that He spoke to you?

He has told you, O man, what is good; and what does the LORD require of you but to do justice, to love kindness, and to walk humbly with your God?—To keep the LORD's commandments and His statutes which I am commanding you today for your good?

For as many as are of the works of the Law are under a curse; for it is written, Cursed is every one who does not abide by all things written in the book of the Law, to perform them. Now that no one is justified by the Law before God is evident; for, The righteous man shall live by faith. Why the Law then? It was added because of transgressions . . . until the seed should come to whom the promise had been made.

God, after He spoke long ago to the fathers in the prophets in many portions and in many ways, in these last days has spoken to us in His Son.

Speak, LORD, for Thy servant is listening.

1 SA 3:17. Mic 6:8.—Deu 10:13. Gal 3:10,11,19. Heb 1:1,2.
1 Sa. 3:9.

He teaches the humble His way.

Blessed are the gentle (humble), for they shall inherit the earth.

I again saw under the sun that the race is not to the swift, and the battle is not to the warriors, and neither is bread to the wise, nor wealth to the discerning, nor favor to men of ability.—The mind of man plans his way, but the LORD directs his steps.

To Thee I lift up my eyes, O Thou who art enthroned in the heavens! Behold, as the eyes of servants look to the hand of their master . . . so our eyes look to the LORD our God.—Teach me the way in which I should walk; for to Thee I lift up my soul.

O our God, wilt Thou not judge them? For we are powerless before this great multitude who are coming against us; nor do we know what to do, but our eyes are on Thee.

If any of you lacks wisdom, let him ask of God, who gives to all men generously and without reproach, and it will be given to him.

When He, the Spirit of truth, comes, He will guide you into all the truth.

PS 25:9. Mt 5:5. Ec 9:11.—Pr 16:9. Ps 123:1,2.—Ps 143:8.
2 Ch 20:12. Ja 1:5. Jn 16:13.

O Lord GOD ... with Thy blessing may the house of Thy servant be blessed forever.

Thou, O LORD, hast blessed, and it is blessed forever.—The blessing of the LORD that makes rich, and He adds no sorrow to it.

Remember the words of the Lord Jesus, that He Himself said, It is more blessed to give than to receive.—When you give a reception, invite the poor, the crippled, the lame, the blind, and you will be blessed, since they do not have the means to repay you; for you will be repaid at the resurrection of the righteous. —Come, you who are blessed of My Father, inherit the kingdom prepared for you from the foundation of the world. For I was hungry, and you gave Me something to eat; I was thirsty, and you gave Me drink; I was a stranger, and you invited Me in; naked, and you clothed Me; I was sick, and you visited Me; I was in prison, and you came to Me.

How blessed is he who considers the helpless; the LORD will deliver him in a day of trouble.

The LORD God is a sun and shield.

2 SA 7:29. 1 Ch 17:27.—Pr 10:22. Ac 20:35.—Lk 14:13,14.—
Mt 25:34–36. Ps 41:1. Ps 84:11.

I will not be afraid. What shall man do to me?

Who shall separate us from the love of Christ? Shall tribulation, or distress, or persecution, or famine, or nakedness, or peril, or sword? In all these things we overwhelmingly conquer through Him who loved us.

Do not be afraid of those who kill the body, and after that have no more that they can do. But I will warn you whom to fear: Fear the One who after He has killed has authority to cast into hell; yes, I tell you, fear Him!

Blessed are those who have been persecuted for the sake of righteousness, for theirs is the kingdom of heaven. Blessed are you when men revile you, and persecute you, and say all kinds of evil against you falsely, on account of Me. Rejoice, and be glad, for your reward in heaven is great.—But I do not consider my life of any account as dear to myself, in order that I may finish my course.—I will also speak of Thy testimonies before kings, and shall not be ashamed.

HEB 13:6. Ro 8:35,37. Lk 12:4,5. Mt 5:10–12.—Ac 20:24.—
Ps 119:46.

He set my feet upon a rock.

The rock was Christ.—Simon Peter . . . said, Thou art the Christ, the Son of the living God. . . . Upon this rock I will build My church; and the gates of Hades shall not overpower it.—There is salvation in no one else; for there is no other name under heaven that has been given among men, by which we must be saved.

Full assurance of faith . . . our hope without wavering.—Faith without any doubting, for the one who doubts is like the surf of the sea driven and tossed by the wind.

Who shall separate us from the love of Christ? Shall tribulation, or distress, or persecution, or famine, or nakedness, or peril, or sword? In all these things we overwhelmingly conquer through Him who loved us. For I am convinced that neither death, nor life, nor angels, nor principalities, nor things present, nor things to come, nor powers, nor height, nor depth, nor any other created thing, shall be able to separate us from the love of God, which is in Christ Jesus our Lord.

PS 40:2. 1 Co 10:4.—Mt 16:16,18.—Ac 4:12. Heb 10:22,23.—Ja 1:6.
Ro 8:35,37–39.

Thou art a God of forgiveness, gracious and compassionate.

The Lord is not slow about His promise, as some count slowness, but is patient toward you, not wishing for any to perish but for all to come to repentance.—Regard the patience of our Lord to be salvation.

For this reason I found mercy, in order that in me ... Jesus Christ might demonstrate His perfect patience, as an example for those who would believe in Him for eternal life.—Whatever was written in earlier times was written for our instruction, that through perseverance and the encouragement of the Scriptures we might have hope.

Do you think lightly of the riches of His kindness and forbearance and patience, not knowing that the kindness of God leads you to repentance?—Rend your heart and not your garments. Now return to the LORD your God, for He is gracious and compassionate, slow to anger, abounding in lovingkindness, and relenting of evil.

NEH 9:17. 2 Pe 3:9.—2 Pe 3:15. 1 Ti 1:16.—Ro 15:4. Ro 2:4.—
Joel 2:13.

The words of the LORD are pure words.

Thy word is very pure, therefore Thy servant loves it.—The precepts of the LORD are right, rejoicing the heart; the commandment of the LORD is pure, enlightening the eyes.—Every word of God is tested; He is a shield to those who take refuge in Him. Do not add to His words lest He reprove you, and you be proved a liar.

Thy word I have treasured in my heart. .... I will meditate on Thy precepts, and regard Thy ways.—Brethren, whatever is true, whatever is honorable, whatever is right, whatever is pure, whatever is lovely, whatever is of good repute, if there is any excellence and if anything worthy of praise, let your mind dwell on these things.—Like newborn babes, long for the pure milk of the word, that by it you may grow.

We are not like many, peddling the word of God, but as from sincerity, but as from God, we speak in Christ.—Not ... adulterating the word of God.

PS 12:6. Ps 119:140.—Ps 19:8.—Pr 30:5,6. Ps 119:11,15.—Phil 4:8.—
1 Pe 2:2. 2 Co 2:17.—2 Co 4:2.

Every family in heaven and on earth.

One God and Father of all who is over all and through all and in all.—You are all sons of God through faith in Christ Jesus.—With a view . . . to the fulness of the times, that is, the summing up of all things in Christ, things in the heavens and things upon the earth.

He is not ashamed to call them brethren.—Behold, My mother and My brothers! For whoever shall do the will of My Father who is in heaven, he is My brother and sister and mother.—Go to My brethren, and say to them, I ascend to My Father and your Father.

I saw underneath the altar the souls of those who had been slain because of the word of God, and because of the testimony which they had maintained. And there was given to each of them a white robe; and they were told that they should rest for a little while longer, until the number of their fellow-servants and their brethren who were to be killed even as they had been, should be completed also.—So that apart from us they should not be made perfect.

> EPH 3:15. Eph 4:6.—Gal 3:26.—Eph 1:10. Heb 2:11.—
> Mt 12:49,50.—Jn 20:17. Rev 6:9,11.—Heb 11:40.

Pray, then, in this way: Our Father who art in heaven.

Jesus spoke; and lifting up His eyes to heaven, He said, Father. —My Father and your Father.

You are all sons of God through faith in Christ Jesus.—You have not received a spirit of slavery leading to fear again, but you have received a spirit of adoption as sons by which we cry out, Abba! Father! The Spirit Himself bears witness with our spirit that we are children of God.

Because you are sons, God has sent forth the Spirit of His Son into our hearts, crying, Abba! Father! Therefore you are no longer a slave, but a son.

Truly, truly, I say to you, if you shall ask the Father for anything, He will give it to you in My name. Until now you have asked for nothing in My name; ask, and you will receive, that your joy may be made full.

I will welcome you. And I will be a Father to you, and you shall be sons and daughters to Me, says the Lord Almighty.

> MT 6:9. Jn 17:1.—Jn 20:17. Gal 3:26.—Ro 8:15,16. Gal 4:6,7.
> Jn 16:23,24. 2 Co 6:17,18.

Be not far from me, for trouble is near.

How long, O LORD? Wilt Thou forget me forever? How long wilt Thou hide Thy face from me? How long shall I take counsel in my soul, having sorrow in my heart all the day?—Do not hide Thy face from me, do not turn Thy servant away in anger; Thou hast been my help; do not abandon me nor forsake me, O God of my salvation!

He will call upon Me, and I will answer him; I will be with him in trouble; I will rescue him, and honor him.—The LORD is near to all who call upon Him, to all who call upon Him in truth. He will fulfill the desire of those who fear Him; He will also hear their cry and will save them.

I will not leave you as orphans; I will come to you.—Lo, I am with you always, even to the end of the age.

God is our refuge and strength, a very present help in trouble. —My soul waits in silence for God only; from Him is my salvation. My soul, wait in silence for God only, for my hope is from Him.

PS 22:11. Ps 13:1,2.—Ps 27:9. Ps 91:15.—Ps 145:18,19. Jn 14:18.— Mt 28:20. Ps 46:1.—Ps 62:1,5.

Hallowed be Thy name.

You shall not worship any other god, for the LORD, whose name is Jealous, is a jealous God.

Who is like Thee among the gods, O LORD? Who is like Thee, majestic in holiness, awesome in praises, working wonders?— Holy, Holy, Holy, is the Lord God, the Almighty.

Worship the Lord in holy array.—I saw the Lord sitting on a throne, lofty and exalted, with the train of His robe filling the temple. Seraphim stood above Him. . . . One called out to another and said, Holy, Holy, Holy, is the LORD of hosts, the whole earth is full of His glory. Then I said, Woe is me, for I am ruined! —I have heard of Thee by the hearing of the ear; but now my eye sees Thee; therefore I retract.

The blood of Jesus His Son cleanses us from all sin.—That we may share His holiness.—We have confidence to enter the holy place by the blood of Jesus. Let us draw near with a sincere heart.

MT 6:9. Ex 34:14. Ex 15:11.—Rev 4:8. 1 Ch 16:29.—Is 6:1–3,5.— Job 42:5,6. 1 Jn 1:7.—Heb 12:10.—Heb 10:19,22.

God was in Christ reconciling the world to Himself, not counting their trespasses against them.

It was the Father's good pleasure for all the fulness to dwell in Him, and through Him to reconcile all things to Himself.—Lovingkindness and truth have met together; righteousness and peace have kissed each other.

I know the plans that I have for you, declares the Lord, plans for welfare and not for calamity.—Come now, and let us reason together, says the Lord, Though your sins are as scarlet, they will be as white as snow; though they are red like crimson, they will be like wool.

Who is a God like Thee, who pardons iniquity?

Yield now and be at peace with Him.—Work out your salvation with fear and trembling; for it is God who is at work in you, both to will and to work for His good pleasure.—Lord, Thou wilt establish peace for us, since Thou hast also performed for us all our works.

2 CO 5:19. Col 1:19,20.—Ps 85:10. Jer 29:11.—Is 1:18. Mic 7:18. Job 22:21.—Phil 2:12,13.—Is 26:12.

Thy kingdom come.

In the days of those kings the God of heaven will set up a kingdom which will never be destroyed, and that kingdom will not be left for another people; it will crush and put an end to all these kingdoms, but it will itself endure forever.—A stone was cut out without hands.—Not by might nor by power, but by My Spirit, says the Lord of hosts.—The kingdom of God is not coming with signs to be observed; nor will they say, Look, here it is! or, There it is! For behold, the kingdom of God is in your midst.

To you has been given the mystery of the kingdom of God. The kingdom of God is like a man who casts seed upon the ground; and goes to bed at night and gets up by day, and the seed sprouts up and grows—how, he himself does not know. But when the crop permits, he immediately puts in the sickle, because the harvest has come.

For this reason you be ready too; for the Son of Man is coming at an hour when you do not think He will.

The Spirit and the bride say, Come. And let the one who hears say, Come.

MT 6:10. Dan 2:44.—Dan 2:34.—Zec 4:6.—Lk 17:20,21.
Mk 4:11,26,27,29. Mt 24:44. Rev 22:17.

For from the first day that you set your heart on understanding this and on humbling yourself before your God, your words were heard.

Thus says the high and exalted One who lives forever, whose name is Holy, I dwell on a high and holy place, and also with the contrite and lowly of spirit in order to revive the spirit of the lowly and to revive the heart of the contrite.—The sacrifices of God are a broken spirit; a broken and a contrite heart, O God, Thou wilt not despise.—For though the LORD is exalted, yet He regards the lowly; but the haughty He knows from afar.—Humble yourselves, therefore, under the mighty hand of God, that He may exalt you at the proper time.—God is opposed to the proud, but gives grace to the humble. Submit therefore to God.

Thou, Lord, art good, and ready to forgive, and abundant in lovingkindness to all who call upon Thee. Give ear, O LORD, to my prayer; and give heed to the voice of my supplications! In the day of my trouble I shall call upon Thee, for Thou wilt answer me.

DAN 10:12. Is 57:15.—Ps 51:17.—Ps 138:6.—1 Pe 5:6.—Ja 4:6,7.
Ps 86:5–7.

Thy will be done, on earth as it is in heaven.

Understand what the will of the Lord is.

It is not the will of your Father who is in heaven that one of these little ones perish.

This is the will of God, your sanctification.—Live the rest of the time in the flesh no longer for the lusts of men, but for the will of God.—In the exercise of His will He brought us forth by the word of truth. Therefore putting aside all filthiness.

You shall be holy, for I am holy.—(Jesus) said . . . whoever does the will of God, he is My brother and sister and mother.—Every one who hears these words of Mine, and acts upon them, may be compared to a wise man, who built his house upon the rock; and the rain descended, and the floods came, and the winds blew, and burst against that house; and yet it did not fall; for it had been founded upon the rock.—The world is passing away, and also its lusts; but the one who does the will of God abides forever.

MT 6:10. Eph 5:17. Mt 18:14. 1 Th 4:3.—1 Pe 4:2.—Ja 1:18,21.
1 Pe 1:16.—Mk 3:34,35.—Mt 7;24,25.—1 Jn 2:17.

**To this end Christ died and lived again, that He might be Lord
both of the dead and of the living.**

The LORD was pleased to crush Him, putting Him to grief; if
He would render Himself as a guilt offering, He will see His
offspring, He will prolong His days, and the good pleasure of the
LORD will prosper in His hand. As a result of the anguish of His
soul, He will see it and be satisfied; by His knowledge the Righteous One, My Servant, will justify the many, as He will bear
their iniquities.—Was it not necessary for the Christ to suffer
these things and to enter into His glory?—Having concluded this,
that one died for all, therefore all died; and He died for all, that
they who live should no longer live for themselves, but for Him
who died and rose again on their behalf.

Therefore let all the house of Israel know for certain that God
has made Him both Lord and Christ—this Jesus whom you crucified.—He was foreknown before the foundation of the world,
but has appeared in these last times for the sake of you who
through Him are believers in God.

RO 14:9. Is 53:10,11.—Lk 24:26.—2 Co 5:14,15. Ac 2:36.—
1 Pe 1:20,21.

Give us this day our daily bread.

I have been young, and now I am old; yet I have not seen the
righteous forsaken, or his descendants begging bread.—His
bread will be given him; his water will be sure.—The ravens
brought him bread and meat in the morning and bread and meat
in the evening, and he would drink from the brook.

My God shall supply all your needs according to His riches in
glory in Christ Jesus.—Being content with what you have; for He
Himself has said, I will never desert you, nor will I ever forsake
you.

He humbled you and let you be hungry, and fed you with
manna . . . that He might make you understand that man does
not live by bread alone, but man lives by everything that proceeds out of the mouth of the LORD.—Jesus . . . said to them,
Truly, truly, I say to you, it is not Moses who has given you the
bread out of heaven, but it is My Father who gives you the true
bread out of heaven. For the bread of God is that which comes
down out of heaven, and gives life to the world. They said . . . to
Him, Lord, evermore give us this bread.

MT 6:11. Ps 37:25.—Is 33:16.—1 Ki 17:6. Phil 4:19.—Heb 13:5.
Deu 8:3.—Jn 6:32–34.

God is my stronghold.

The LORD is my rock and my fortress and my deliverer; my God, my rock, in whom I take refuge: my shield and the horn of my salvation, my stronghold and my refuge: My savior.—The LORD is my strength and my shield; my heart trusts in Him, and I am helped; therefore my heart exults, and with my song I shall thank Him.

For He will come like a rushing stream, which the wind of the LORD drives.—We confidently say, The Lord is my helper, I will not be afraid. What shall man do to me?

The LORD is my light and my salvation; whom shall I fear? The LORD is the defense of my life; whom shall I dread?

As the mountains surround Jerusalem, so the LORD surrounds His people from this time forth and forever.—For Thou hast been my help, and in the shadow of Thy wings I sing for joy.

For Thy name's sake Thou wilt lead me and guide me.

PS 59:9. 2 Sa 22:2,3.—Ps 28:7. Is 59:19.—Heb 13:6. Ps 27:1.
Ps 125:2.—Ps 63:7. Ps 31:3.

Forgive us our debts, as we also have forgiven our debtors.

Lord, how often shall my brother sin against me and I forgive him? Up to seven times? Jesus said to him, I do not say to you, up to seven times, but up to seventy times seven.—You wicked slave, I forgave you all that debt because you entreated me. Should you not also have had mercy on your fellow-slave, even as I had mercy on you? And his lord, moved with anger, handed him over to the torturers until he should repay all that was owed him. So shall My heavenly Father also do to you, if each of you does not forgive his brother from your heart.—Be kind to one another, tender-hearted, forgiving each other, just as God in Christ also has forgiven you.—He made you alive together with Him, having forgiven us all our transgressions, having cancelled out the certificate of debt consisting of decrees against us and which was hostile to us; and He has taken it out of the way, having nailed it to the cross.—Just as the Lord forgave you, so also should you.

MT 6:12. Mt 18:21,22.—Mt 18:32–35.—Eph 4:32.—Col 2:13,14.—
Col 3:13.

Not lagging behind in diligence, fervent in spirit, serving the Lord.

Whatever your hand finds to do, verily, do it with all your might; for there is no activity or planning or wisdom in Sheol where you are going.—Whatever you do, do your work heartily, as for the Lord rather than for men; knowing that from the Lord you will receive the reward of the inheritance. It is the Lord Christ whom you serve.—Whatever good thing each one does, this he will receive back from the Lord.

We must work the works of Him who sent Me, as long as it is day; night is coming, when no man can work.—Did you not know that I had to be in My Father's house?—Zeal for Thy house will consume me.

Brethren, be all the more diligent to make certain about His calling and choosing you; for as long as you practice these things, you will never stumble.—We desire that each one of you show the same diligence so as to realize the full assurance of hope until the end, that you may not be sluggish, but imitators of those who through faith and patience inherit the promises.—Run in such a way that you may win.

RO 12:11. Ec 9:10.—Col 3:23,24.—Eph 6:8. Jn 9:4.—Lk 2:49.—
Jn 2:17. 2 Pe 1:10.—Heb 6:11,12.—1 Co 9:24.

OCTOBER 16   EVENING

Do not lead us into temptation, but deliver us from evil.

He who trusts in his own heart is a fool, but he who walks wisely will be delivered.

Let no one say when he is tempted, I am being tempted by God; for God cannot be tempted by evil, and He Himself does not tempt any one. But each one is tempted when he is carried away and enticed by his own lust.—Therefore, come out from their midst and be separate, says the Lord. And do not touch what is unclean; and I will welcome you.

Lot lifted up his eyes and saw all the valley of the Jordan, that it was well watered everywhere ... like the garden of the LORD. . . . So Lot chose for himself all the valley of the Jordan. Now the men of Sodom were wicked exceedingly and sinners against the LORD.—He (the Lord) rescued righteous Lot, oppressed by the sensual conduct of unprincipled men. The Lord knows how to rescue the godly from temptation.—And stand he will, for the Lord is able to make him stand.

MT 6:13. Pr 28:26. Ja 1:13,14.—2 Co 6:17. Gen 13:10,11,13.—
2 Pe 2:7,9.—Ro 14:4.

In Thy name they rejoice all the day, and by Thy righteousness they are exalted.

Only in the LORD are righteousness and strength. Men will come to Him, and all who were angry at Him shall be put to shame. In the LORD all the offspring of Israel will be justified, and will glory.—Be glad in the LORD and rejoice you righteous ones, and shout for joy all you who are upright in heart.

Now apart from the Law the righteousness of God has been manifested, being witnessed by the Law and Prophets; even the righteousness of God through faith in Jesus Christ for all those who believe. . . . for the demonstration . . . of His righteousness at the present time, that He might be . . . the justifier of the one who has faith in Jesus.

Rejoice in the Lord always; again I will say, rejoice!—Though you have not seen Him, you love Him, and though you do not see Him now, but believe in Him, you greatly rejoice with joy inexpressible and full of glory.

PS 89:16. Is 45:24,25.—Ps 32:11. Ro 3:21,22,26. Phil 4:4.—1 Pe 1:8.

Thine is the kingdom, and the power, and the glory, forever.

The LORD reigns, He is clothed with majesty. Thy throne is established from of old; Thou art from everlasting.

The LORD is . . . great in power.—If God is for us, who is against us?—Our God whom we serve is able to deliver us . . . and He will deliver us.—My Father, who has given them to Me, is greater than all; and no one is able to snatch them out of the Father's hand.—Greater is He who is in you than he who is in the world.

Not to us, O LORD, not to us, but to Thy name give glory.— Thine, O LORD, is the greatness and the power and the glory and the victory and the majesty, indeed everything that is in the heavens and the earth; Thine is the dominion, O LORD, and Thou dost exalt Thyself as head over all. Now therefore, our God, we thank Thee, and praise Thy glorious name. But who am I and who are my people that we should be able to offer as generously as this? For all things come from Thee, and from Thy hand we have given Thee.

MT 6:13. Ps 93:1,2. Nah 1:3.—Ro 8:31.—Dan 3:17.—Jn 10:29.— 1 Jn 4:4. Ps 115:1.—1 Ch 29:11,13,14.

One of the soldiers pierced His side with a spear, and immediately there came out blood and water.

Behold, the blood of the covenant, which the LORD has made with you.—For the life of the flesh is in the blood, and I have given it to you on the altar to make atonement for your souls.—It is impossible for the blood of bulls and goats to take away sins.

He (Jesus) said to them, This is My blood of the covenant, which is to be shed on behalf of many.—Through His own blood, He entered the holy place once for all, having obtained eternal redemption.—Peace through the blood of His cross.

Knowing that you were not redeemed with perishable things like silver or gold . . . but with precious blood, as of a lamb unblemished and spotless, the blood of Christ. He . . . appeared in these last times for the sake of you.

I will sprinkle clean water on you, and you will be clean; I will cleanse you from all . . . your idols.—Let us draw near with a sincere heart in full assurance of faith, having our hearts sprinkled clean from an evil conscience.

JN 19:34. Ex 24:8.—Lev 17:11.—Heb 10:4. Mk 14:24.—Heb 9:12.—
Col 1:20. 1 Pe 1:18–20. Eze 36:25.—Heb 10:22.

Amen.

Amen! Thus may the LORD . . . say.—He who is blessed in the earth shall be blessed by the God of truth (Heb., The Amen); and he who swears in the earth shall swear by the God of truth (The Amen).

When God made the promise to Abraham, since He could swear by no one greater, He swore by Himself. For men swear by one greater than themselves, and with them an oath given as confirmation is an end of every dispute. In the same way God, desiring even more to show to the heirs of the promise the unchangeableness of His purpose, interposed with an oath, in order that by two unchangeable things, in which it is impossible for God to lie, we may have strong encouragement, we who have fled for refuge in laying hold of the hope set before us.

The Amen, the faithful and true Witness . . . says this.—For as many as may be the promises of God, in Him they are yes; wherefore also by Him is our Amen to the glory of God through us.

Blessed be the LORD God, the God of Israel, who alone works wonders. And blessed be His glorious name forever . . . Amen, and Amen.

MT 6:13. 1 Ki 1:36.—Is 65:16. Heb 6:13,16–18. Rev 3:14.—
2 Co 1:20. Ps 72:18,19.

The LORD will be your confidence, and will keep your foot from being caught.

The wrath of man shall praise Thee; with a remnant of wrath Thou shalt gird Thyself.—The king's heart is like channels of water in the hand of the LORD; He turns it wherever He wishes. —When a man's ways are pleasing to the LORD, He makes even his enemies to be at peace with him.

I wait for the LORD, my soul does wait, and in His word do I hope. My soul waits for the Lord more than the watchmen for the morning; indeed, more than the watchmen for the morning. —I sought the LORD, and He answered me, and delivered me from all my fears.

The eternal God is a dwelling place, and underneath are the everlasting arms; and He drove out the enemy from before you, and said, Destroy!—Blessed is the man who trusts in the LORD and whose trust is the LORD.

What then shall we say to these things? If God is for us, who is against us?

PR 3:26. Ps 76:10.—Pr 21:1.—Pr 16:7. Ps 130:5,6.—Ps 34:4.
Deu 33:27.—Jer 17:7. Ro 8:31.

Encouragement in Christ . . . consolation of love . . . fellowship of the Spirit.

Man, who is born of woman, is short-lived and full of turmoil. Like a flower he comes forth and withers. He also flees like a shadow and does not remain.—My flesh and my heart may fail; but God is the strength of my heart and my portion forever.

The Father . . . will give you another Helper, that He may be with you forever; . . . the Holy Spirit, whom the Father will send in My name.—Blessed be the God and Father of our Lord Jesus Christ, the Father of mercies and God of all comfort; who comforts us in all our affliction so that we may be able to comfort those who are in any affliction with the comfort with which we ourselves are comforted by God.

We believe that Jesus died and rose again, even so God will bring with Him those who have fallen asleep in Jesus. . . . Thus we shall always be with the Lord. Therefore comfort one another with these words.

PHIL 2:1. Job 14:1,2.—Ps 73:26. Jn 14:16,26.—2 Co 1:3,4.
1 Th 4:14,17,18.

I joyfully concur with the law of God in the inner man.

O how I love Thy law! It is my meditation all the day.—Thy words were found and I ate them, and Thy words became for me a joy and the delight of my heart.—In his shade I took great delight and sat down, and his fruit was sweet to my taste.—I have treasured the words of His mouth more than my necessary food.

I delight to do Thy will, O my God; Thy Law is within my heart.—My food is to do the will of Him who sent Me, and to accomplish His work.

The precepts of the LORD are right, rejoicing the heart; the commandment of the LORD is pure, enlightening the eyes. They are more desirable than gold, yes, than much fine gold; sweeter also than honey and the drippings of the honeycomb.—Prove yourselves doers of the word, and not merely hearers who delude themselves. For if any one is a hearer of the word and not a doer, he is like a man who looks at his natural face in a mirror.

RO 7:22. Ps 119:97.—Jer 15:16.—Song 2:3.—Job 23:12. Ps 40:8.—
Jn 4:34. Ps 19:8,10.—Ja 1:22,23.

May the LORD your God accept you.

With what shall I come to the LORD and bow myself before the God on high? Shall I come to Him with burnt offerings, with yearling calves? Does the LORD take delight in thousands of rams, in ten thousand rivers of oil? Shall I present my first-born for my rebellious acts, the fruit of my body for the sin of my soul? He has told you, O man, what is good; and what does the LORD require of you but to do justice, to love kindness, and to walk humbly with your God?

All of us have become like one who is unclean, and all our righteous deeds are like a filthy garment.—There is none righteous, not even one. For all have sinned and fall short of the glory of God, being justified as a gift by His grace through the redemption which is in Christ Jesus; whom God displayed publicly as a propitiation in His blood through faith . . . for the demonstration . . . of His righteousness at the present time, that He might be just and the justifier of the one who has faith in Jesus.

In the Beloved.—In Him you have been made complete.

2 SA 24:23. Mic 6:6–8. Is 64:6.—Ro 3:10,23–26. Eph 1:6.—Col 2:10.

Of His fulness we have all received, and grace upon grace.

This is My beloved Son, with whom I am well pleased.—See how great a love the Father has bestowed upon us, that we should be called children of God.

His Son, whom He appointed heir of all things.—If children, heirs also, heirs of God and fellow-heirs with Christ, if indeed we suffer with Him in order that we may also be glorified with Him.

I and the Father are one. The Father is in Me, and I in the Father.—My father and your Father, and My God and your God. —I in them, and Thou in Me, that they may be perfected in unity.

The Church, which is His body, the fulness of Him who fills all in all.

Having these promises, beloved, let us cleanse ourselves from all defilement of flesh and spirit, perfecting holiness in the fear of God.

JN 1:16. Mt 17:5.—1 Jn 3:1. Heb 1:2.—Ro 8:17. Jn 10:30,38.— Jn 20:17.—Jn 17:23. Eph 1:22,23. 2 Co 7:1.

A slave is not greater than his master; neither one who is sent greater than the one who sent him. If you know these things, you are blessed if you do them.

There arose also a dispute among them as to which one of them was regarded to be greatest. And He said to them, The kings of the Gentiles lord it over them; and those who have authority over them are called Benefactors. But not so with you, but let him who is the greatest among you become as the youngest, and the leader as the servant. For who is greater, the one who reclines at table, or the one who serves? Is it not the one who reclines at table? But I am among you as the one who serves.— The Son of Man did not come to be served, but to serve, and to give His life a ransom for many.

Jesus . . . rose from supper, and laid aside His garments; and taking a towel, girded Himself about. Then He poured water into the basin, and began to wash the disciples' feet, and to wipe them with the towel with which He was girded.

JN 13:16,17. Lk 22:24–27.—Mt 20:28. Jn 13:3–5.

My heart is steadfast, O God.

The LORD is my light and my salvation; whom shall I fear? The LORD is the defense of my life; whom shall I dread?

The steadfast of mind Thou wilt keep in perfect peace, because he trusts in Thee.—He will not fear evil tidings; his heart is steadfast, trusting in the LORD. His heart is upheld, he will not fear, until he looks with satisfaction on his adversaries.

When I am afraid, I will put my trust in Thee.—For in the day of trouble He will conceal me in His tabernacle; in the secret place of His tent He will hide me; He will lift me up on a rock. And now my head will be lifted up above my enemies around me; and I will offer in His tent sacrifices with shouts of joy; I will sing, yes, I will sing praises to the LORD.

After you have suffered for a little while, the God of all grace, who called you to His eternal glory in Christ, will Himself perfect, confirm, strengthen and establish you. To Him be dominion forever and ever.

PS 108:1. Ps 27:1. Is 26:3.—Ps 112:7,8. Ps 56:3.—Ps 27:5,6.
1 Pe 5:10,11.

The LORD has established His throne in the heavens; and His sovereignty rules over all.

The lot is cast into the lap, but its every decision is from the LORD.—If calamity occurs in a city has not the LORD done it?

I am the LORD, and there is no other; besides Me there is no God. I will gird you, though you have not known Me; that men may know from the rising to the setting of the sun that there is no one besides Me. I am the LORD, and there is no other, the One forming light and creating darkness, causing well-being and creating calamity; I am the LORD who does all these.

He does according to His will in the host of heaven and among the inhabitants of earth; and no one can ward off His hand or say to Him, What hast Thou done?—If God is for us, who is against us?

He must reign until He has put all His enemies under His feet. —Do not be afraid, little flock, for your Father has chosen gladly to give you the kingdom.

PS 103:19. Pr 16:33.—Amos 3:6. Is 45:5–7. Dan 4:35.—Ro 8:31.
1 Co 15:25.—Lk 12:32.

Not even when one has an abundance does his life consist of his possessions.

Better is the little of the righteous than the abundance of many wicked.—Better is a little with the fear of the LORD, than great treasure and turmoil with it.—Godliness actually is a means of great gain, when accompanied by contentment. If we have food and covering, with these we shall be content.

Give me neither poverty nor riches, feed me with the food that is my portion, lest I be full and deny Thee and say, Who is the LORD? Or lest I be in want and steal, and profane the name of my God.—Give us this day our daily bread.

Do not be anxious for your life, as to what you shall eat, or what you shall drink; nor for your body, as to what you shall put on. Is not life more than food, and the body than clothing?—When I sent you out without purse and bag and sandals, you did not lack anything, did you? And they said, No, nothing.—Let your character be free from the love of money, being content with what you have; for He Himself has said, I will never desert you, nor will I ever forsake you.

LK 12:15. Ps 37:16.—Pr 15:16.—1 Ti 6:6,8. Pr 30:8,9.—Mt 6:11. Mt 6:25.—Lk 22:35.—Heb 13:5.

It is the Spirit who gives life.

The first man, Adam, became a living soul. The last Adam became a life-giving spirit.—That which is born of the flesh is flesh; and that which is born of the Spirit is spirit.—He saved us, not on the basis of deeds which we have done in righteousness, but according to His mercy, by the washing of regeneration and renewing by the Holy Spirit.

If anyone does not have the Spirit of Christ, he does not belong to Him. And if Christ is in you, though the body is dead because of sin, yet the spirit is alive because of righteousness. But if the Spirit of Him who raised Jesus from the dead dwells in you, He who raised Christ Jesus from the dead will also give life to your mortal bodies through His Spirit who indwells you.

It is no longer I who live, but Christ lives in me; and the life which I now live in the flesh I live by faith in the Son of God.—Consider yourselves to be dead to sin, but alive to God in Christ Jesus.

JN 6:63. 1 Co 15:45.—Jn 3:6.—Titus 3:5. Ro 8:9–11. Gal 2:20.—Ro 6:11.

I have been expelled from Thy sight. Nevertheless I will look again toward Thy holy temple.

Zion said, The LORD has forsaken me, and the Lord has forgotten me. Can a woman forget her nursing child, and have no compassion on the son of her womb? Even these may forget, but I will not forget you.

I have forgotten happiness. So I say, My strength has perished, and so has my hope from the LORD.—Arouse Thyself, why dost Thou sleep, O Lord? Awake, do not reject us forever.—Why do you say, O Jacob, and assert, O Israel, My way is hidden from the LORD and the justice due me escapes the notice of my God?—In an outburst of anger I hid My face from you for a moment; but with everlasting lovingkindness I will have compassion on you, says the LORD your Redeemer.

Why are you in despair, O my soul? And why have you become disturbed within me? Hope in God, for I shall again praise Him for the help of His presence.—We are afflicted in every way, but not crushed; perplexed, but not despairing; persecuted, but not forsaken; struck down, but not destroyed.

JON 2:4. Is 49:14,15. Lam 3:17,18.—Ps 44:23.—Is 40:27.—Is 54:8.
Ps 42:5.—2 Co 4:8,9.

The afflicted and needy are seeking water, but there is none, and their tongue is parched with thirst; I the LORD will answer them Myself.

Many are saying, Who will show us any good?—What does a man get in all his labor and in his striving with which he labors under the sun? Because all his days his task is painful and grievous; even at night his mind does not rest . . . because everything is futility and striving after wind.—They have forsaken Me, the fountain of living waters, to hew for themselves cisterns, broken cisterns, that can hold no water.

The one who comes to Me I will certainly not cast out.—I will pour out water on the thirsty.—Blessed are those who hunger and thirst for righteousness, for they shall be satisfied.

O God, Thou art my God; I shall seek Thee earnestly; my soul thirsts for Thee, my flesh yearns for Thee, in a dry and weary land where there is no water.

IS 41:17. Ps 4:6.—Ec 2:22,23,17.—Jer 2:13. Jn 6:37.—Is 44:3.—
Mt 5:6. Ps 63:1.

Lo, I am with you always, even to the end of the age.

If two of you agree on earth about anything that they may ask, it shall be done for them by My Father who is in heaven. For where two or three have gathered together in My name, there I am in their midst.—He who has My commandments, and keeps them, he it is who loves Me; and he who loves Me shall be loved by My Father, and I will love him, and will disclose Myself to him.

Lord, what then has happened that You are going to disclose Yourself to us, and not to the world? . . . If anyone loves Me, he will keep My word; and My Father will love him, and We will come to him, and make Our abode with Him.

Now to Him who is able to keep you from stumbling, and to make you stand in the presence of His glory blameless with great joy, to the only God our Savior, through Jesus Christ our Lord, be glory, majesty, dominion and authority, before all time and now and forever. Amen.

MT 28:20. Mt 18:19,20.—Jn 14:21. Jn 14:22,23. Jude 24,25.

The end of all things is at hand.

I saw a great white throne and Him who sat upon it, from whose presence earth and heaven fled away.—The present heavens and earth . . . are being reserved for fire, kept for the day of judgment.

God is our refuge and strength, a very present help in trouble. Therefore we will not fear, though the earth should change, and though the mountains slip into the heart of the sea; though its waters roar and foam, though the mountains quake at its swelling pride.—You will be hearing of wars and rumors of wars; see that you are not frightened.

We have a building from God, a house not made with hands, eternal in the heavens.—We are looking for new heavens and a new earth, in which righteousness dwells. Therefore, beloved, since you look for these things, be diligent to be found by Him in peace, spotless and blameless.

1 PE 4:7. Rev 20:11.—2 Pe 3:7. Ps 46:1–3.—Mt 24:6. 2 Co 5:1.—
2 Pe 3:13,14.

The LORD reigns.

Do you not fear Me? declares the LORD. Do you not tremble in My presence? For I have placed the sand as a boundary for the sea, an eternal decree, so it cannot cross over it. Though the waves toss, yet they cannot prevail; though they roar, yet they cannot cross over it.—Not from the east, nor from the west, nor from the desert comes exaltation; but God is the Judge; He puts down one, and exalts another.

It is He who changes the times and the epochs; He removes kings and establishes kings; He gives wisdom to wise men, and knowledge to men of understanding.—You will be hearing of wars and rumors of wars; see that you are not frightened.

If God is for us, who is against us?—Are not two sparrows sold for a cent? And yet not one of them will fall to the ground apart from your Father. But the very hairs of your head are all numbered. Therefore do not fear; you are of more value than many sparrows.

PS 99:1. Jer 5:22.—Ps 75:6,7. Dan 2:21.—Mt 24:6. Ro 8:31.—
Mt 10:29–31.

Take heed then, to your spirit.

Master, we saw someone casting out demons in Your name; and we tried to hinder him because he does not follow along with us. But Jesus said to him, Do not hinder him; for he who is not against you is for you. . . . Lord, do You want us to command fire to come down from heaven and consume them? But He turned and rebuked them.

Eldad and Medad are prophesying in the camp. Then Joshua the son of Nun, . . . answered and said, Moses, my lord, restrain them. But Moses said to him, Are you jealous for my sake? Would that all the LORD'S people were prophets, that the LORD would put His Spirit upon them!

The fruit of the spirit is love, joy, peace, patience, kindness, goodness, faithfulness, gentleness, self-control. . . . Now those who belong to Christ Jesus have crucified the flesh with its passions and desires. If we live by the Spirit, let us also walk by the Spirit. Let us not become boastful, challenging one another, envying one another.

MAL 2:15. Lk 9:49,50,54,55. Num 11:27–29. Gal 5:22–26.

He Himself took our infirmities, and carried away our diseases.

Then the priest shall give orders to take two live clean birds and cedar wood and a scarlet string and hyssop for the one who is to be cleansed. The priest shall also give orders to slay the one bird in an earthenware vessel over running water. As for the live bird, he shall take it, together with the cedar wood and the scarlet string and the hyssop, and shall dip them and the live bird in the blood of the bird that was slain over the running water. He shall then sprinkle seven times the one who is to be cleansed from the leprosy, and shall pronounce him clean, and shall let the live bird go free over the open field.

A man full of leprosy . . . when he saw Jesus, he fell on his face and implored Him, saying, Lord, If You are willing, You can make me clean.—And moved with compassion, He stretched out His hand and touched him, and said to him, I am willing; be cleansed. And immediately the leprosy left him and he was cleansed.

MT 8:17. Lev 14:4–7. Lk 5:12.—Mk 1:41,42.

EVENING

He whom you bless is blessed.

Blessed are the poor in spirit, for theirs is the kingdom of heaven.

Blessed are those who mourn, for they shall be comforted. Blessed are the gentle, for they shall inherit the earth. Blessed are those who hunger and thirst for righteousness, for they shall be satisfied. Blessed are the merciful, for they shall receive mercy. Blessed are the pure in heart, for they shall see God. Blessed are the peace-makers, for they shall be called sons of God. Blessed are those who have been persecuted for the sake of righteousness, for theirs is the kingdom of heaven. Blessed are you when men revile you, and persecute you, and say all kinds of evil against you falsely, on account of Me. Rejoice, and be glad, for your reward in heaven is great.—Blessed are those who hear the word of God, and observe it.

Blessed are those who wash their robes, that they may have the right to the tree of life, and may enter by the gates into the city.

Num 22:6. Mt 5:3–12.—Lk 11:28. Rev 22:14.

He saw that there was no man, and was astonished that there was no one to intercede; then His own arm brought salvation to Him.

Sacrifice and meal offering Thou hast not desired; my ears Thou hast opened; burnt offering and sin offering Thou hast not required. Then I said, Behold, I come; in the scroll of the book it is written of me; I delight to do Thy will, O my God; Thy Law is within my heart.—I lay down My life that I may take it again. No one has taken it away from Me, but I lay it down on My own initiative. I have authority to lay it down, and I have authority to take it up again.

There is no other God besides Me, a righteous God and a Savior; there is none except Me. Turn to Me, and be saved, all the ends of the earth; for I am God, and there is no other.—There is salvation in no one else; for there is no other name under heaven that has been given among men, by which we must be saved.

IS 59:16. Ps 40:6–8.—Jn 10:17,18. Is 45:21,22.—Ac 4:12. 2 Co 8:9.

The enemy.

Be of sober spirit, be on the alert. Your adversary, the devil, prowls about like a roaring lion, seeking someone to devour.—Resist the devil and he will flee from you.

Put on the full armor of God, that you may be able to stand firm against the schemes of the devil. For our struggle is not against flesh and blood, but against the rulers, against the powers, against the world-forces of this darkness, against the spiritual forces of wickedness in the heavenly places. Therefore take up the full armor of God, that you may be able to resist in the evil day, and having done everything, to stand firm. Stand firm therefore, having girded your loins with truth, and having put on the breastplate of righteousness, and having shod your feet with the preparation of the gospel of peace; in addition to all, taking up the shield of faith with which you will be able to extinguish all the flaming missiles of the evil one.

Do not rejoice over me, O my enemy. Though I fall I will rise; though I dwell in darkness, the LORD is a light for me.

LK 10:19. 1 Pe 5:8.—Ja 4:7. Eph 6:11–16. Mic 7:8.

He is wholly desirable.

Let my meditation be pleasing to Him.—My beloved is ... outstanding among ten thousand.—A choice stone, a precious corner stone, and he who believes in Him shall not be disappointed.—Thou art fairer than the sons of men; grace is poured upon Thy lips.—God highly exalted Him, and bestowed on Him the name which is above every name.—It was the Father's good pleasure for all the fulness to dwell in Him.

Though you have not seen Him, you love Him, and though you do not see Him now, but believe in Him, you greatly rejoice with joy inexpressible and full of glory.

I count all things to be loss in view of the surpassing value of knowing Christ Jesus my Lord, for whom I have suffered the loss of all things, and count them but rubbish in order that I may gain Christ, and may be found in Him, not having a righteousness of my own derived from the Law, but that which is through faith in Christ, the righteousness which comes from God on the basis of faith.

SONG 5:16. Ps 104:34.—Song 5:10.—1 Pe 2:6.—Ps 45:2.—
Phil 2:9.—Col 1:19. 1 Pe 1:8. Phil 3:8,9.

David strengthened himself in the LORD his God.

Lord, to whom shall we go? You have words of eternal life.—I know whom I have believed and I am convinced that He is able to guard what I have entrusted to Him until that day.

In my distress I called upon the LORD, and cried to my God for help; He heard my voice out of His temple, and my cry for help before Him came into His ears. They confronted me in the day of my calamity, but the LORD was my stay. He brought me forth also into a broad place; He rescued me, because He delighted in me.

I will bless the LORD at all times; His praise shall continually be in my mouth. My soul shall make its boast in the LORD; the humble shall hear it and rejoice. O magnify the LORD with me, and let us exalt His name together. I sought the LORD, and He answered me, and delivered me from all my fears. O taste and see that the LORD is good; how blessed is the man who takes refuge in Him!

1 SA 30:6. Jn 6:68.—2 Ti 1:12. Ps 18:6,18,19. Ps 34:1-4,8.

**It is good that he waits silently for the salvation of the
LORD.**

Has God forgotten to be gracious? Or has He in anger withdrawn His compassion?—I said in my alarm, I am cut off from
before Thine eyes; nevertheless Thou didst hear the voice of my
supplications when I cried to Thee.

Shall not God bring about justice for His elect, who cry to Him
day and night, and will He delay long over them? I tell you that
He will bring about justice for them speedily.—Wait for the
LORD, and He will save you.—Rest in the LORD and wait patiently for Him; fret not yourself because of him who prospers in
his way, because of the man who carries out wicked schemes.

You need not fight in this battle; station yourselves, stand and
see the salvation of the LORD.

Let us not lose heart in doing good, for in due time we shall
reap if we do not grow weary.—Behold, the farmer waits for the
precious produce of the soil, being patient about it, until it gets
the early and late rains.

LAM 3:26. Ps 77:9.—Ps 31:22. Lk 18:7,8.—Pr 20:22.—Ps 37:7.
2 Ch 20:17. Gal 6:9.—Ja 5:7.

**Catch the foxes for us, the little foxes that are ruining the
vineyards, while our vineyards are in blossom.**

Who can discern his errors? Acquit me of hidden faults.—See
to it that no one comes short of the grace of God; that no root
of bitterness springing up cause trouble, and by it many be defiled.—You were running well; who hindered you from obeying
the truth?

He who began a good work in you will perfect it until the day
of Christ Jesus. Only conduct yourselves in a manner worthy of
the gospel of Christ.—The tongue is a small part of the body, and
yet it boasts of great things. Behold, how great a forest is set
aflame by such a small fire! And the tongue is a fire, the very
world of iniquity; the tongue is set among our members as that
which defiles the entire body, and sets on fire the course of our
life, and is set on fire by hell. No one can tame the tongue; it is
a restless evil and full of deadly poison.—Let your speech always
be with grace, seasoned, as it were, with salt.

SONG 2:15. Ps 19:12.—Heb 12:15.—Gal 5:7. Phil 1:6,27.—
Ja 3:5,6,8.—Col 4:6.

**Not by might nor by power, but by My Spirit, says the
LORD of hosts.**

Who has directed the Spirit of the LORD, or as His counselor
has informed Him?

God has chosen the foolish things of the world to shame the
wise, and God has chosen the weak things of the world to shame
the things which are strong, and the base things of the world and
the despised, God has chosen, the things that are not, that He
might nullify the things that are, that no man should boast before
God.

The wind blows where it wishes and you hear the sound of it,
but do not know where it comes from and where it is going; so
is every one who is born of the Spirit.—Born not of blood, nor of
the will of the flesh, nor of the will of man, but of God.

My Spirit is abiding in your midst; do not fear!—The battle is
not yours but God's.

The LORD does not deliver by sword or by spear; for the battle
is the LORD'S.

ZEC 4:6. Is 40:13. 1 Co 1:27–29. Jn 3:8.—Jn 1:13. Hag 2:5.—
2 Ch 20:15. 1 Sa 17:47.

Do as Thou hast spoken.

Establish Thy word to Thy servant, as that which produces
reverence for Thee. So I shall have an answer for him who reproaches me, for I trust in Thy word. Remember the word to Thy
servant, in which Thou hast made me hope. Thy statutes are my
songs in the house of my pilgrimage. The law of Thy mouth is
better to me than thousands of gold and silver pieces. Forever,
O LORD, Thy word is settled in heaven. Thy faithfulness contin-
ues throughout all generations.

God, desiring even more to show to the heirs of the promise
the unchangeableness of His purpose, interposed with an oath,
in order that by two unchangeable things, in which it is impossible for God to lie, we may have strong encouragement, we who
have fled for refuge in laying hold of the hope set before us. This
hope we have as an anchor of the soul, a hope both sure and
steadfast and one which enters within the veil, where Jesus has
entered as a forerunner for us.

His precious and magnificent promises.

2 SA 7:25. Ps 119:38,42,49,54,72,89,90. Heb 6:17–20. 2 Pe 1:4.

Blessed is the man who listens to me, watching daily at my gates, waiting at my doorposts.

Behold, as the eyes of servants look to the hand of their master, as the eyes of a maid to the hand of her mistress; so our eyes look to the LORD our God, until He shall be gracious to us.

A continual burnt offering throughout your generations at the doorway of the tent of meeting before the LORD, where I will meet with you, to speak to you there.—In every place where I cause My name to be remembered, I will come to you and bless you.

Where two or three have gathered together in My name, there I am in their midst.

But an hour is coming, and now is, when the true worshipers shall worship the Father in spirit and truth; for such people the Father seeks to be His worshipers. God is spirit; and those who worship Him must worship in spirit and truth.

With all prayer and petition pray at all times in the Spirit.—Pray without ceasing.

PR 8:34. Ps 123:2. Ex 29:42.—Ex 20:24. Mt 18:20. Jn 4:23,24.
Eph 6:18.—Th 5:17.

His name will be called ... Counselor.

The Spirit of the LORD will rest on Him, the spirit of wisdom and understanding, the spirit of counsel and strength, the spirit of knowledge and the fear of the LORD. And He will delight in the fear of the LORD.

Does not wisdom call, and understanding lift up her voice? To you, O men, I call, and my voice is to the sons of men. O naive ones, discern prudence; and, O fools, discern wisdom. Listen, for I shall speak noble things; and the opening of my lips will produce right things. Counsel is mine and sound wisdom; I am understanding, power is mine.

The LORD of hosts, who has made His counsel wonderful and His wisdom great.—If any of you lacks wisdom, let him ask of God, who gives to all men generously and without reproach, and it will be given to him.—Trust in the LORD with all your heart, and do not lean on your own understanding. In all your ways acknowledge Him, and He will make your paths straight.

IS 9:6. Is 11:2,3. Pr 8:1,4–6,14. Is 28:29.—Ja 1:5.—Pr 3:5,6.

Seek after that which is good.

You have been called for this purpose, since Christ also suffered for you, leaving you an example for you to follow in His steps, who committed no sin, nor was any deceit found in His mouth; and while being reviled, He did not revile in return . . . but kept entrusting Himself to Him who judges righteously.— Consider Him who has endured such hostility by sinners against Himself, so that you may not grow weary and lose heart.

Let us also lay aside every encumbrance, and the sin which so easily entangles us, and let us run with endurance the race that is set before us, fixing our eyes on Jesus, the author and perfecter of faith, who for the joy set before Him endured the cross, despising the shame, and has sat down at the right hand of the throne of God.

Finally, brethren, whatever is true, whatever is honorable, whatever is right, whatever is pure, whatever is lovely, whatever is of good repute, if there is any excellence and if anything worthy of praise, let your mind dwell on these things.

1 TH 5:15. 1 Pe 2:21–23.—Heb 12:3. Heb 12:1,2. Phil 4:8.

Mighty God.

Thou art fairer than the sons of men; grace is poured upon Thy lips; therefore God has blessed Thee forever. Gird Thy sword on Thy thigh, O Mighty One, in Thy splendor and Thy majesty! And in Thy majesty ride on victoriously. . . . Thy throne, O God, is forever and ever; a scepter of uprightness is the scepter of Thy kingdom.—Once Thou didst speak in vision to Thy godly ones, and didst say, I have given help to one who is mighty.—The man, My Associate, declares the LORD of hosts.

Behold, God is my salvation, I will trust and not be afraid; for the LORD GOD is my strength and song, and He has become my salvation.—Thanks be to God, who always leads us in His triumph in Christ.

Now to Him who is able to keep you from stumbling, and to make you stand in the presence of His glory blameless with great joy, to the only God our Savior, through Jesus Christ our Lord, be glory, majesty, dominion and authority, before all time and now and forever.

IS 9:6. Ps 45:2–4,6.—Ps 89:19.—Zec 13:7. Is 12:2.—2 Co 2:14.
Jude 24,25.

The ways of the LORD are right, and the righteous will walk in them, but transgressors will stumble in them.

This precious value, then, is for you who believe, but for those who disbelieve . . . a stone of stumbling and a rock of offense.— The way of the LORD is a stronghold to the upright, but ruin to the workers of iniquity.

He who has ears to hear, let him hear.—Who is wise? Let him give heed to these things; and consider the lovingkindnesses of the LORD.—The lamp of the body is the eye; if therefore your eye is clear, your whole body will be full of light.—If any man is willing to do His will, he shall know of the teaching, whether it is of God.—Whoever has, to him shall more be given, and he shall have an abundance.

He who is of God hears the words of God; for this reason you do not hear them, because you are not of God.—You are unwilling to come to Me, that you may have life.—My sheep hear My voice, and I know them, and they follow Me.

HO 14:9. 1 Pe 2:7,8.—Pr 10:29. Mt 11:15.—Ps 107:43.—Mt 6:22.—
Jn 7:17.—Mt 13:12. Jn 8:47.—Jn 5:40.—Jn 10:27.

Eternal Father.

Hear, O Israel! The LORD is our God, the LORD is one!

I and the Father are one. The Father is in Me, and I in the Father.—If you knew Me, you would know My Father also.— Philip said to Him, Lord, show us the Father, and it is enough for us. Jesus said to him, Have I been so long with you, and yet you have not come to know Me, Philip? He who has seen Me has seen the Father.—Behold, I and the children whom God has given me.—As a result of the anguish of His soul, He will see it and be satisfied.—I am the Alpha and the Omega, says the Lord God, who is and who was and who is to come, the Almighty.—Before Abraham was born, I AM.—God said to Moses, I AM WHO I AM; and He said, Thus you shall say to the sons of Israel, I AM has sent me to you.

Of the Son He says, Thy throne, O God, is forever and ever. —He is before all things, and in Him all things hold together.— In Him all the fulness of Deity dwells in bodily form.

IS 9:6. Deu 6:4. Jn 10:30,38.—Jn 8:19.—Jn 14:8,9.—Heb 2:13.—
Is 53:11.—Rev 1:8.—Jn 8:58.—Ex 3:14. Heb 1:8.—Col 1:17.—
Col 2:9.

Now for a little while, if necessary, you have been distressed by various trials.

Beloved, do not be surprised at the fiery ordeal among you, which comes upon you for your testing, as though some strange thing were happening to you; but to the degree that you share the sufferings of Christ, keep on rejoicing; so that also at the revelation of His glory, you may rejoice with exultation.—The exhortation which is addressed to you as sons, My son, do not regard lightly the discipline of the Lord, nor faint when you are reproved by Him.—All discipline for the moment seems not to be joyful, but sorrowful; yet to those who have been trained by it, afterwards it yields the peaceful fruit of righteousness.

We do not have a high priest who cannot sympathize with our weaknesses, but one who has been tempted in all things as we are, yet without sin.—Since He Himself was tempted in that which He has suffered, He is able to come to the aid of those who are tempted.—God is faithful, who will not allow you to be tempted beyond what you are able.

1 PE 1:6. 1 Pe 4:12,13.—Heb 12:5.—Heb 12:11. Heb 4:15.— Heb 2:18.—1 Co 10:13.

Prince of Peace.

May he judge Thy people with righteousness, and Thine afflicted with justice. Let the moutains bring peace to the people, and the hills in righteousness. May he come down like rain upon the mown grass, like showers that water the earth. In his days may the righteous flourish, and abundance of peace till the moon is no more.—Glory to God in the highest, and on earth peace among men.

Because of the tender mercy of our God . . . the Sunrise from on high shall visit us, to shine upon those who sit in darkness and the shadow of death, to guide our feet into the way of peace.— Peace through Jesus Christ (He is Lord of all).

These things I have spoken to you, that in Me you may have peace. In the world you have tribulation, but take courage; I have overcome the world.—Peace I leave with you; My peace I give to you; not as the world gives, do I give to you.—The peace of God, which surpasses all comprehension, shall guard your hearts and your minds in Christ Jesus.

IS 9:6. Ps 72:2,3,6,7.—Lk 2:14. Lk 1:78,79.—Ac 10:36. Jn 16:33.— Jn 14:27.—Phil 4:7.

Take also for yourself the finest of spices ... and you shall make of these a holy anointing oil.

It shall not be poured on anyone's body, nor shall you make any like it, in the same proportions; it is holy, and it shall be holy to you.—One Spirit.—Varieties of gifts, but the same Spirit.

Thy God, has anointed Thee with the oil of joy above Thy fellows.—Jesus of Nazareth ... God anointed Him with the Holy Spirit and with power.—He gives the Spirit without measure.

Of His fulness we have all received.—As His anointing teaches you about all things, and is true and is not a lie, and just as it has taught you, you abide in Him.—He who ... anointed us is God, who also sealed us and gave us the Spirit in our hearts.

The fruit of the Spirit is love, joy, peace, patience, kindness, goodness, faithfulness, gentleness, self-control; against such things there is no law.

EX 30:23,25. Ex 30:32.—Eph 4:4.—1 Co 12:4. Ps 45:7.—Ac 10:38.— Jn 3:34. Jn 1:16.—1 Jn 2:27.—2 Co 1:21,22. Gal 5:22,23.

The form of this world is passing away.

All the days of Methuselah were nine hundred and sixty-nine years, and he died.

Let the brother of humble circumstances glory in his high position; and let the rich man glory in his humiliation, because like flowering grass he will pass away. For the sun rises with a scorching wind, and withers the grass; and its flower falls off, and the beauty of its appearance is destroyed; so too the rich man in the midst of his pursuits will fade away.—You do not know what your life will be like tomorrow. You are just a vapor that appears for a little while and then vanishes away.—The world is passing away, and also its lusts; but the one who does the will of God abides forever.

LORD, make me to know my end, and what is the extent of my days, let me know how transient I am.—While they are saying, Peace and safety! then destruction will come upon them suddenly like birth pangs upon a woman with child; and they shall not escape. But you, brethren, are not in darkness, that the day should overtake you like a thief.

1 CO 7:31. Gen 5:27. Ja 1:9–11.—Ja 4:14.—1 Jn 2:17. Ps 39:4.— 1 Th 5:3,4.

When Christ, who is our life, is revealed, then you also will be revealed with Him in glory.

I am the resurrection, and the life; he who believes in Me shall live even if he dies.—God has given us eternal life, and this life is in His Son. He who has the Son has the life; he who does not have the Son of God does not have the life.

The Lord Himself will descend from heaven with a shout, with the voice of the archangel, and with the trumpet of God; and the dead in Christ shall rise first. Then we who are alive and remain shall be caught up together with them in the clouds to meet the Lord in the air, and thus we shall always be with the Lord. Therefore comfort one another with these words.—When He appears, we shall be like Him, because we shall see Him just as He is.—It is sown in dishonor, it is raised in glory; it is sown in weakness, it is raised in power.

If I go and prepare a place for you, I will come again, and receive you to Myself; that where I am, there you may be also.

COL 3:4. Jn 11:25.—1 Jn 5:11,12. 1 Th 4:16–18.—1 Jn 3:2.—
1 Co 15:43. Jn 14:3.

Lead me in Thy truth and teach me.

When He, the Spirit of truth, comes, He will guide you into all the truth.—You have an anointing from the Holy One, and you all know.

To the law and to the testimony! If they do not speak according to this word, it is because they have no dawn.—All Scripture is inspired by God and profitable for teaching, for reproof, for correction, for training in righteousness; that the man of God may be adequate, equipped for every good work.—The sacred writings which are able to give you the wisdom that leads to salvation through faith which is in Christ Jesus.

I will instruct you and teach you in the way which you should go; I will counsel you with My eye upon you.—The lamp of the body is the eye; if therefore your eye is clear, your whole body will be full of light.—If any man is willing to do His will, he shall know of the teaching, whether it is of God.—It will be for him who walks that way, and fools will not wander on it.

PS 25:5. Jn 16:13.—1 Jn 2:20. Is 8:20.—2 Ti 3:16,17.—2 Ti 3:15.
Ps 32:8.—Mt 6:22.—Jn 7:17.—Is 35:8.

**Let them give thanks to the LORD for His lovingkindness, and
for His wonders to the sons of men!**

O taste and see that the LORD is good; how blessed is the man
who takes refuge in Him.—How great is Thy goodness, which
Thou hast stored up for those who fear Thee.

The people whom I formed for Myself, will declare My praise.
—He predestined us to adoption as sons through Jesus Christ to
Himself, according to the kind intention of His will, to the praise
of the glory of His grace, which He freely bestowed on us in the
Beloved. . . . That we who were the first to hope in Christ should
be to the praise of His glory.

What comeliness and beauty will be theirs!—The LORD is good
to all, and His mercies are over all His works. All Thy works shall
give thanks to Thee, O LORD, and Thy godly ones shall bless
Thee. They shall speak of the glory of Thy kingdom, and talk of
Thy power; to make known to the sons of men Thy mighty acts,
and the glory of the majesty of Thy kingdom.

PS 107:8. Ps 34:8.—Ps 31:19. Is 43:21.—Eph 1:5,6,12. Zec 9:17.—
Ps 145:9–12.

Behold, we count those blessed who endured.

We also exult in our tribulations; knowing that tribulation
brings about perseverance; and perseverance, proven character;
and proven character, hope; and hope does not disappoint; because the love of God has been poured out within our hearts
through the Holy Spirit who was given to us.—All discipline for
the moment seems not to be joyful, but sorrowful; yet to those
who have been trained by it, afterwards it yields the peaceful
fruit of righteousness.—Consider it all joy, my brethren, when
you encounter various trials; knowing that the testing of your
faith produces endurance. And let endurance have its perfect
result, that you may be perfect and complete, lacking in nothing.
—Blessed is a man who perseveres under trial; for once he has
been approved, he will receive the crown of life, which the Lord
has promised to those who love Him.—I will rather boast about
my weaknesses, that the power of Christ may dwell in me. . . .
For when I am weak, then I am strong.

JA 5:11. Ro 5:3–5.—Heb 12:11.—Ja 1:2–4.—Ja 1:12.—2 Co 12:9,10.

Since we are of the day, let us be sober, having put on the breastplate of faith and love, and as a helmet, the hope of salvation.

Gird your minds for action, keep sober in spirit, fix your hope completely on the grace to be brought to you at the revelation of Jesus Christ.—Stand firm therefore, having girded your loins with truth, and having put on the breastplate of righteousness, . . . in addition to all, taking up the shield of faith with which you will be able to extinguish all the flaming missiles of the evil one. And take the helmet of salvation, and the sword of the Spirit, which is the word of God.

He will swallow up death for all time, and the Lord God will wipe tears away from all faces, and He will remove the reproach of His people from all the earth; for the Lord has spoken. And it will be said in that day, Behold, this is our God for whom we have waited that He might save us. This is the Lord . . . let us rejoice and be glad in His salvation.

Faith is the assurance of things hoped for, the conviction of things not seen.

1 TH 5:8. 1 Pe 1:13.—Eph 6:14,16,17. Is 25:8,9. Heb 11:1.

The sons of Israel camped before them like two little flocks of goats, but the Syrians filled the country.

Thus says the Lord, Because the Syrians have said, The Lord is a god of the mountains, but He is not a god of the valleys; therefore I will give all this great multitude into your hand, and you shall know that I am the Lord. So they camped one over against the other seven days. And it came about that on the seventh day, the battle was joined, and the sons of Israel killed of the Syrians 100,000 foot soldiers in one day.—You are from God, little children, and have overcome them; because greater is He who is in you than he who is in the world.

Do not fear, for I am with you; do not anxiously look about you, for I am your God. I will strengthen you, surely I will help you, surely, I will uphold you with My righteous right hand.

They will fight against you, but they will not overcome you, for I am with you to deliver you, declares the Lord.

1 KI 20:27. 1 Ki 20:28,29.—1 Jn 4:4. Is 41:10.—Jer 1:19.

I have given help to one who is mighty; I have exalted one chosen from the people.

I, even I, am the LORD; and there is no savior besides Me.— There is one God, and one mediator also between God and men, the man Christ Jesus.—There is no other name under heaven that has been given among men, by which we must be saved.

Mighty God.—Emptied Himself, taking the form of a bond-servant, and being made in the likeness of men. And being found in appearance as a man, He humbled Himself by becoming obedient to the point of death, even death on a cross. Therefore also God highly exalted Him, and bestowed on Him the name which is above every name.—We do see Him who has been made for a little while lower than the angels, namely, Jesus, because of the suffering of death crowned with glory and honor, that by the grace of God He might taste death for every one.—Since then the children share in flesh and blood, He Himself likewise also partook of the same.

PS 89:19. Is 43:11.—1 Ti 2:5.— Ac 4:12. Is 9:6.—Phil 2:7–9.—
Heb 2:9.—Heb 2:14.

Gather My godly ones to Me, those who have made a covenant with Me by sacrifice.

Christ also, having been offered once to bear the sins of many, shall appear a second time for salvation without reference to sin, to those who eagerly await Him.—He is the mediator of a new covenant, in order that since a death has taken place . . . those who have been called may receive the promise of the eternal inheritance.

Father, I desire that they also whom Thou hast given Me be with Me where I am.—Then He will send forth the angels, and will gather together His elect from the four winds, from the farthest end of the earth, to the farthest end of heaven.—If your outcasts are at the ends of the earth, from there the LORD your God will gather you, and from there He will bring you back.

The dead in Christ shall rise first. Then we who are alive and remain shall be caught up together with them in the clouds to meet the Lord in the air, and thus we shall always be with the Lord.

PS 50:5. Heb 9:28.—Heb 9:15. Jn 17:24.—Mk 13:27.—Deu 30:4.
1 Th 4:16,17.

**Bearing fruit in every good work and increasing in the knowl-
edge of God.**

I urge you therefore, brethren, by the mercies of God, to
present your bodies a living and holy sacrifice, acceptable to God,
which is your spiritual service of worship. And do not be conformed to this world, but be transformed by the renewing of
your mind, that you may prove what the will of God is, that
which is good and acceptable and perfect.—As you presented
your members as slaves to impurity and to lawlessness, resulting
in further lawlessness, so now present your members as slaves to
righteousness, resulting in sanctification.—For neither is circumcision anything, nor uncircumcision, but a new creation. And
those who will walk by this rule, peace and mercy be upon them.

By this is My Father glorified, that you bear much fruit, and
so prove to be My disciples.—I chose you, and appointed you,
that you should go and bear fruit, and that your fruit should
remain; that whatever you ask of the Father in My name, He may
give to you.

COL 1:10. Ro 12:1,2.—Ro 6:19.—Gal 6:15,16. Jn 15:8.—Jn 15:16.

I sought him but did not find him.

Return ... to the LORD your God, for you have stumbled because of your iniquity. Take words with you and return to the
LORD. Say to Him, Take away all iniquity, and receive us graciously.

Let no one say when he is tempted, I am being tempted by
God. ... But each one is tempted when he is carried away and
enticed by his own lust. Do not be deceived, my beloved brethren. Every good thing bestowed and every perfect gift is from
above, coming down from the Father of lights, with whom there
is no variation or shifting shadow.

Wait for the LORD; be strong, and let your heart take courage;
yes, wait for the LORD.—It is good that he waits silently for the
salvation of the LORD.—Shall not God bring about justice for His
elect, who cry to Him day and night, and will He delay long over
them?

My soul waits in silence for God only; from Him is my salvation.
My soul, wait in silence for God only, for my hope is from Him.

SONG 3:1. Ho 14:1,2. Ja 1:13,14,16,17. Ps 27:14.—Lam 3:26.—
Lk 18:7. Ps 62:1,5.

He led them safely.

I walk in the way of righeousness, in the midst of the paths of justice.

Behold, I am going to send an angel before you to guard you along the way, and to bring you into the place which I have prepared.—In all their affliction He was afflicted, and the angel of His presence saved them; in His love and in His mercy He redeemed them; and He lifted them and carried them all the days of old.

For by their own sword they did not possess the land; and their own arm did not save them; but Thy right hand, and Thine arm, and the light of Thy presence, for Thou didst favor them.—So didst Thou lead Thy people, to make for Thyself a glorious name.

O LORD, lead me in Thy righteousness because of my foes; make Thy way straight before me.—O send out Thy light and Thy truth, let them lead me; let them bring me to Thy holy hill, and to Thy dwelling places. Then I will go to the altar of God, to God my exceeding joy; and upon the lyre I shall praise Thee, O God, my God.

PS 78:53. Pr 8:20. Ex 23:20.—Is 63:9. Ps 44:3.—Is 63:14. Ps 5:8.—
Ps 43:3,4.

You were washed . . . you were sanctified . . . you were justified.

The blood of Jesus His Son cleanses us from all sin.—The chastening for our well-being fell upon Him, and by His scourging we are healed.

Christ . . . loved the church and gave Himself up for her; that He might sanctify her, having cleansed her by the washing of water with the word, that He might present to Himself the church in all her glory, having no spot or wrinkle or any such thing; but that she should be holy and blameless.—And it was given to her to clothe herself in fine linen, bright and clean; for the fine linen is the righteous acts of the saints.—Let us draw near with a sincere heart in full assurance of faith, having our hearts sprinkled clean from an evil conscience and our body washed with pure water.

Who will bring a charge against God's elect? God is the one who justifies.—How blessed is he whose transgression is forgiven. . . . How blessed is the man to whom the LORD does not impute iniquity, and in whose spirit there is no deceit!

1 CO 6:11. 1 Jn 1:7.—Is 53:5. Eph 5:25–27.—Rev 19:8.—Heb 10:22.
Ro 8:33.—Ps 32:1,2.

Sorrow that is according to the will of God produces a repentance without regret.

Peter remembered the word which Jesus had said, Before a
cock crows, you will deny Me three times. And he went out and
wept bitterly.—If we confess our sins, He is faithful and righteous
to forgive us our sins and to cleanse us from all unrighteousness.
—The blood of Jesus His Son cleanses us from all sin.

My iniquities have overtaken me, so that I am not able to see;
they are more numerous than the hairs of my head; and my heart
has failed me. Be pleased, O LORD, to deliver me; make haste,
O LORD, to help me.

Return to your God, observe kindness and justice, and wait for
your God continually.

The sacrifices of God are a broken spirit; a broken and a contrite heart, O God, Thou wilt not despise.—He heals the brokenhearted, and binds up their wounds.—He has told you, O man,
what is good; and what does the LORD require of you but to do
justice, to love kindness, and to walk humbly with your God?

2 CO 7:10. Mt 26:75.—1 Jn 1:9.—1 Jn 1:7. Ps 40:12,13. Ho 12:6.
Ps 51:17.—Ps 147:3.—Mi 6:8.

Is it well with you? . . . And she answered, It is well.

Having the same spirit of faith.

As punished yet not put to death, as sorrowful yet always
rejoicing, as poor yet making many rich, as having nothing yet
possessing all things.

We are afflicted in every way, but not crushed; perplexed, but
not despairing; persecuted, but not forsaken; struck down, but
not destroyed; always carrying about in the body the dying of
Jesus, that the life of Jesus also may be manifested in our body.
Therefore we do not lose heart, but though our outer man is
decaying, yet our inner man is being renewed day by day. For
momentary, light affliction is producing for us an eternal weight
of glory far beyond all comparison, while we look not at the
things which are seen, but at the things which are not seen.

Beloved, I pray that in all respects you may prosper and be in
good health, just as your soul prospers.

2 KI 4:26. 2 Co 4:13. 2 Co 6:9,10. 2 Co 4:8–10,16–18. 3 Jn 2.

Christt also loved the church and gave Himself up for her; that He might sanctify her, having cleansed her by the washing of water with the word.

Walk in love, just as Christ also loved you, and gave Himself up for us, an offering and a sacrifice to God as a fragrant aroma.

You have been born again not of seed which is perishable but imperishable, that is, through the living and abiding word of God.—Sanctify them in the truth; Thy word is truth.—Unless one is born of water and the Spirit, he cannot enter into the kingdom of God.—Not on the basis of deeds which we have done in righteousness, but according to His mercy, by the washing of regeneration and renewing by the Holy Spirit.—Thy word has revived me.

The law of the LORD is perfect, restoring the soul; the testimony of the LORD is sure, making wise the simple. The precepts of the LORD are right, rejoicing the heart; the commandment of the LORD is pure, enlightening the eyes.

EPH 5:25,26. Eph 5:2. 1 Pe 1:23.—Jn 17:17.—Jn 3:5.—Titus 3:5.—
Ps 119:50.

Through Him we both have our access in one Spirit to the Father.

I in them, and Thou in Me, that they may be perfected in unity.

Whatever you ask in My name, that will I do, that the Father may be glorified in the Son. If you ask Me anything in My name, I will do it. I will ask the Father, and He will give you another Helper, that He may be with you forever; that is the Spirit of truth, whom the world cannot receive, because it does not behold Him or know Him, but you know Him because He abides with you, and will be in you.—There is one body and one Spirit, just as also you were called in one hope of your calling; one Lord, one faith, one baptism, one God and Father of all who is over all and through all and in all.—When you pray, say: Father, hallowed be Thy name.

Therefore, brethren, we have confidence to enter the holy place by the blood of Jesus, by a new and living way . . . let us draw near.

EPH 2:18. Jn 17:23. Jn 14:13,14,16,17.—Eph 4:4–6.—Lk 11:2.
Heb 10:19,20,22.

Thou art my help and my deliverer; do not delay, O my God.

The steps of a man are established by the LORD; and He delights in his way. When he falls, he shall not be hurled headlong; because the LORD is the One who holds his hand.—In the fear of the LORD there is strong confidence, and his children will have refuge.—Who are you that you are afraid of man who dies, and of the son of man who is made like grass; that you have forgotten the LORD your Maker?

I am with you to deliver you.—Be strong and courageous, do not be afraid or tremble at them, for the LORD your God is the one who goes with you. He will not fail you or forsake you.

I shall sing of Thy strength; yes, I shall joyfully sing of Thy lovingkindness in the morning, for Thou hast been my stronghold, and a refuge in the day of my distress.—Thou art my hiding place; Thou dost preserve me from trouble; Thou dost surround me with songs of deliverance.

PS 40:17. Ps 37:23,24.—Pr 14:26.—Is 51:12,13. Jer 1:8.—Deu 31:6.
Ps 59:16.—Ps 32:7.

How will you do in the thicket of the Jordan?

Jordan overflows all its banks all the days of harvest.

The priests who carried the ark of the covenant of the LORD stood firm on dry ground in the middle of the Jordan while all Israel crossed on dry ground, until all the nation had finished crossing the Jordan.

We do see Him who has been made for a little while lower than the angels, namely, Jesus, because of the suffering of death crowned with glory and honor, that by the grace of God He might taste death for every one.

Though I walk through the valley of the shadow of death, I fear no evil; for Thou art with me; Thy rod and Thy staff, they comfort me.—When you pass through the waters, I will be with you; and through the rivers, they will not overflow you.

Do not be afraid; I am the first and the last, and the living One; and I was dead, and behold, I am alive forevermore, and I have the keys of death and of Hades.

JER 12:5. Jos 3:15. Jos 3:17. Heb 2:9. Ps 23:4.—Is 43:2. Rev 1:17,18.

**God is faithful, through whom you were called into fellowship
with His Son, Jesus Christ our Lord.**

Let us hold fast the confession of our hope without wavering,
for He who promised is faithful.—God said, I will dwell in them
and walk among them; and I will be their God, and they shall be
My people.—Indeed our fellowship is with the Father, and with
His Son Jesus Christ.—To the degree that you share the sufferings of Christ, keep on rejoicing; so that also at the revelation of
His glory, you may rejoice with exultation.

That you, being rooted and grounded in love, may be able to
comprehend with all the saints what is the breadth and length
and height and depth, and to know the love of Christ which
surpasses knowledge, that you may be filled up to all the fulness
of God.

Whoever confesses that Jesus is the Son of God, God abides in
him, and he in God.—The one who keeps His commandments
abides in Him, and He in him.

1 CO 1:9. Heb 10:23.—2 Co 6:16.—1 Jn 1:3.—1 Pe 4:13.
Eph 3:17–19. 1 Jn 4:15.—1 Jn 3:24.

We are His workmanship.

They quarried great stones, costly stones, to lay the foundation
of the house with cut stones.—The house, while it was being
built, was built of stone prepared at the quarry, and there was
neither hammer nor axe nor any iron tool heard in the house
while it was being built.

You also, as living stones, are being built up as a spiritual house.
—Having been built upon the foundation of the apostles and
prophets, Christ Jesus Himself being the cornerstone, in whom
the whole building . . . being built together into a dwelling of
God in the Spirit.—For you once were not a people, but now you
are the people of God.

We are . . . God's building.—Therefore if any man is in Christ,
he is a new creature; the old things passed away; behold, new
things have come.—Now He who prepared us for this very purpose is God, who gave to us the Spirit as a pledge.

EPH 2:10. 1 Ki 5:17.—1 Ki 6:7. 1 Pe 2:5.—Eph 2:20–22.—
1 Pe 2:10. 1 Co 3:9.—2 Co 5:17.—2 Co 5:5.

Sanctify them in the truth; Thy word is truth.

You are already clean because of the word which I have spoken to you.—Let the word of Christ richly dwell within you; with all wisdom.

How can a young man keep his way pure? By keeping it according to Thy word. With all my heart I have sought Thee; do not let me wander from Thy commandments.

For wisdom will enter your heart, and knowledge will be pleasant to your soul; discretion will guard you, understanding will watch over you.

My foot has held fast to His path; I have kept His way and not turned aside. I have not departed from the command of His lips; I have treasured the words of His mouth more than my necessary food.—I have more insight than all my teachers, for Thy testimonies are my meditation.—If you abide in My word, then you are truly disciples of Mine; and you shall know the truth, and the truth shall make you free.

JN 17:17. Jn 15:3.—Col 3:16. Ps 119:9,10. Pr 2:10,11.
Job 23:11,12.—Ps 119:99.—Jn 8:31,32.

Fellow-citizens with the saints.

You have come to Mount Zion and to the city of the living God, the heavenly Jerusalem, and to myriads of angels, to the general assembly and church of the first-born who are enrolled in heaven, and to God the Judge of all, and to the spirits of righteous men made perfect.

All these died in faith, without receiving the promises, but having seen them and having welcomed them from a distance, and having confessed that they were strangers and exiles on the earth.—For our citizenship is in heaven, from which also we eagerly wait for a Savior, the Lord Jesus Christ; who will transform the body of our humble state into conformity with the body of His glory, by the exertion of the power that He has even to subject all things to Himself.—The Father . . . delivered us from the domain of darkness, and transferred us to the kingdom of His beloved Son.

As aliens and strangers to abstain from fleshly lusts, which wage war against the soul.

EPH 2:19. Heb 12:22,23. Heb 11:13.—Phil 3:20,21.—Col 1:12,13.
1 Pe 2:11.

Thy thoughts are very deep.

We have not ceased to pray for you and to ask that you may be filled with the knowledge of His will in all spiritual wisdom and understanding.—That you, being rooted and grounded in love, may be able to comprehend with all the saints what is the breadth and length and height and depth, and to know the love of Christ which surpasses knowledge, that you may be filled up to all the fulness of God.

Oh the depth of the riches both of the wisdom and knowledge of God! How unsearchable are His judgments and unfathomable His ways!—For My thoughts are not your thoughts, neither are your ways My ways, declares the LORD. For as the heavens are higher than the earth, so are My ways higher than your ways, and My thoughts than your thoughts.—Many, O LORD my God, are the wonders which Thou hast done, and Thy thoughts toward us; there is none to compare with Thee; if I would declare and speak of them, they would be too numerous to count.

PS 92:5. Col 1:9.—Eph 3:17–19. Ro 11:33.—Is 55:8,9.—Ps 40:5.

Whatever a man sows, this he will also reap.

Those who plow iniquity and those who sow trouble harvest it. —They sow the wind, and they reap the whirlwind.—The one who sows to his own flesh shall from the flesh reap corruption.

He who sows righteousness gets a true reward.—The one who sows to the Spirit shall from the Spirit reap eternal life. And let us not lose heart in doing good, for in due time we shall reap if we do not grow weary. So then, while we have opportunity, let us do good to all men, and especially to those who are of the household of the faith.

There is one who scatters, yet increases all the more, and there is one who withholds what is justly due, but it results only in want. The generous man will be prosperous, and he who waters will himself be watered.—He who sows sparingly shall also reap sparingly; and he who sows bountifully shall also reap bountifully.

GAL 6:7. Job 4:8.—Ho 8:7.—Gal 6:8. Pr 11:18.—Gal 6:8–10.
Pr 11:24,25.—2 Co 9:6.

With His fierce wind He has expelled them on the day of the east wind.

Let us now fall into the hand of the LORD for His mercies are great.—I am with you, declares the LORD, to save you . . . I will chasten you justly, and will by no means leave you unpunished. —He will not always strive with us; nor will He keep His anger forever. He has not dealt with us according to our sins, nor rewarded us according to our iniquities. For He Himself knows our frame; He is mindful that we are but dust.—I will spare them as a man spares his own son who serves him.

God is faithful, who will not allow you to be tempted beyond what you are able; but with the temptation will provide the way of escape also, that you may be able to endure it.—Satan has demanded permission to sift you like wheat; but I have prayed for you, that your faith may not fail.

Thou hast been a defense for the helpless. A defense for the needy in his distress, a refuge from the storm, a shade from the heat, for the breath of the ruthless is like a rain storm against a wall.

IS 27:8. 2 Sa 24:14.—Jer 30:11.—Ps 103:9,10,14.—Mal 3:17.
1 Co 10:13.—Lk 22:31,32.

I did not believe the reports, until I came and my eyes had seen it. And behold, the half was not told me.

The Queen of the South shall rise up with this generation at the judgment and shall condemn it; because she came from the ends of the earth to hear the wisdom of Solomon; and behold, something greater than Solomon is here.—We beheld His glory, glory as of the only begotten from the Father, full of grace and truth.

My message and my preaching were . . . in demonstration of the Spirit and of power, that your faith should not rest on the wisdom of men, but on the power of God. . . . As it is written, Things which eye has not seen and ear has not heard, and which have not entered the heart of man, all that God has prepared for those who love Him. For to us God revealed them through the Spirit; for the Spirit searches all things, even the depths of God.

Your eyes will see the king in his beauty.—We shall see Him just as He is.—From my flesh I shall see God.—I will be satisfied.

1 KI 10:7. Mt 12:42.—Jn 1:14. 1 Co 2:4,5,9,10. Is 33:17.—1 Jn 3:2.—
Job 19:26.—Ps 17:15.

You will know them by their fruits.

Little children, let no one deceive you; the one who practices righteousness is righteous, just as He is righteous.—Does a fountain send out from the same opening both fresh and bitter water? Can a fig tree, my brethren, produce olives, or a vine produce figs? Neither can salt water produce fresh. Who among you is wise and understanding? Let him show by his good behavior his deeds in the gentleness of wisdom.—Keep your behavior excellent among the Gentiles, so that in the thing in which they slander you as evildoers, they may on account of your good deeds, as they observe them, glorify God in the day of visitation.

Either make the tree good, and its fruit good; or make the tree rotten, and its fruit rotten; for the tree is known by its fruit.—The good man out of his good treasure brings forth what is good; and the evil man out of his evil treasure brings forth what is evil.

What more was there to do for My vineyard that I have not done in it?

MT 7:20. 1 Jn 3:7.—Ja 3:11–13.—1 Pe 2:12. Mt 12:33.—Mt 12:35.
Is 5:4.

I shall make the place of My feet glorious.

Thus says the LORD, Heaven is My throne, and the earth is My footstool.

Will God indeed dwell with mankind on the earth? Behold, heaven and the highest heaven cannot contain Thee; how much less this house which I have built.

Thus says the LORD of hosts, Once more in a little while, I am going to shake the heavens and the earth, the sea also and the dry land. And I will shake all the nations; and they will come with the wealth of all nations; and I will fill this house with glory, says the LORD of hosts. The latter glory of this house will be greater than the former, says the LORD of hosts.

I saw a new heaven and a new earth; for the first heaven and the first earth passed away, and there is no longer any sea. And I heard a loud voice from the throne, saying, Behold, the tabernacle of God is among men, and He shall dwell among them, and they shall be His peoples, and God Himself shall be among them.

IS 60:13. Is 66:1. 2 Ch 6:18. Hag 2:6,7,9. Rev 21:1,3.

Though I dwell in darkness, the LORD is a light for me.

When you pass through the waters, I will be with you; and through the rivers, they will not overflow you. When you walk through the fire, you will not be scorched, nor will the flame burn you. For I am the LORD your God, the Holy One of Israel, your Savior.—I will lead the blind by a way they do not know, in paths they do not know I will guide them. I will make darkness into light before them and rugged places into plains. These are the things I will do, and I will not leave them undone.

Even though I walk through the valley of the shadow of death, I fear no evil; for Thou art with me; Thy rod and Thy staff, they comfort me.—When I am afraid, I will put my trust in Thee. In God, whose word I praise, in God I have put my trust; I shall not be afraid. What can mere man do to me?—The LORD is my light and my salvation; whom shall I fear? The LORD is the defense of my life; whom shall I dread?

MIC 7:8. Is 43:2,3.—Is 42:16. Ps 23:4.—Ps 56:3,4.—Ps 27:1.

There is one God, and one mediator also between God and men, the man Christ Jesus.

Hear, O Israel! The LORD is our God, the LORD is one!—Now a mediator is not for one party only; whereas God is only one.

We have sinned like our fathers, we have committed iniquity, we have behaved wickedly. Our fathers in Egypt did not understand Thy wonders; they did not remember Thine abundant kindnesses. . . . Therefore He said that He would destroy them, had not Moses His chosen one stood in the breach before Him, to turn away His wrath from destroying them.

Therefore, holy brethren, partakers of a heavenly calling, consider Jesus, the Apostle and High Priest of our confession. He was faithful to Him who appointed Him, as Moses also was in all His house.

He is also the mediator of a better covenant, which has been enacted on better promises. For I will be merciful to their iniquities, and I will remember their sins no more.

1 TI 2:5. Deu 6:4.—Gal 3:20. Ps 106:6,7,23. Heb 3:1,2. Heb 8:6,12.

The one who comes to Me I will certainly not cast out.

It shall come about that when he cries out to Me, I will hear him, for I am gracious.—I will not reject them, nor will I so abhor them as to destroy them, breaking My covenant with them; for I am the LORD their God.—I will remember My covenant with you in the days of your youth, and I will establish an everlasting covenant with you.

Come now, and let us reason together, says the LORD, though your sins are as scarlet, they will be as white as snow; though they are red like crimson, they will be like wool.—Let the wicked forsake his way, and the unrighteous man his thoughts; and let him return to the LORD, and He will have compassion on him; and to our God, for He will abundantly pardon.—Jesus, remember me when You come in Your kingdom! And He said to him, Truly I say to you, today you shall be with Me in Paradise.

A bruised reed He will not break, and a dimly burning wick He will not extinguish.

JN 6:37. Ex 22:27.—Lev 26:44.—Eze 16:60. Is 1:18.—Is 55:7.—
Lk 23:42,43. Is 42:3.

His beloved Son.

Behold, a voice out of the heavens, saying, This is My Beloved Son, in whom I am well pleased.—My Servant, whom I uphold; My chosen one in whom My soul delights.—The only begotten God, who is in the bosom of the Father.

By this the love of God was manifested in us, that God has sent His only begotten Son into the world so that we might live through Him. In this is love, not that we loved God, but that He loved us and sent His Son to be the propitiation for our sins. And we have come to know and have believed the love which God has for us. God is love.

The glory which Thou hast given Me I have given to them; that they may be one, just as We are one; I in them, and Thou in Me, that they may be perfected in unity, that the world may know that Thou didst send Me, and didst love them, even as Thou didst love Me.—See how great a love the Father has bestowed upon us, that we should be called children of God.

COL 1:13. Mt 3:17.—Is 42:1.—Jn 1:18. 1 Jn 4:9,10,16.
Jn 17:22–23.—1 Jn 3:1.

Praying in the Holy Spirit.

God is spirit; and those who worship Him must worship in spirit and truth.—We ... have our access in one Spirit to the Father.

My Father, if it is possible, let this cup pass from Me; yet not as I will, but as Thou wilt.

The Spirit also helps our weakness; for we do not know how to pray as we should, but the Spirit Himself intercedes for us with groanings too deep for words; and He who searches the hearts knows what the mind of the Spirit is, because He intercedes for the saints according to the will of God.—This is the confidence which we have before Him, that, if we ask anything according to His will, He hears us.—When He, the Spirit of truth, comes, He will guide you into all the truth.

With all prayer and petition pray at all times in the Spirit, and with this in view, be on the alert with all perseverance and petition.

JUDE 20. Jn 4:24.—Eph 2:18. Mt 26:39. Ro 8:26,27.—1 Jn 5:14.—
Jn 16:13. Eph 6:18.

There is hope for a tree, when it is cut down, that it will sprout again, and its shoots will not fail.

A bruised reed He will not break.—He restores my soul.

The sorrow that is according to the will of God produces a repentance without regret, leading to salvation; but the sorrow of the world produces death.—All discipline for the moment seems not to be joyful, but sorrowful; yet to those who have been trained by it, afterwards it yields the peaceful fruit of righteousness.

Before I was afflicted I went astray, but now I keep Thy word. —After all that has come upon us for our evil deeds and our great guilt, since Thou our God hast requited us less than our iniquities deserve, and hast given us an escaped remnant as this.

Do not rejoice over me, O my enemy. Though I fall I will rise; though I dwell in darkness, the LORD is a light for me ... He will bring me out to the light, and I will see His righteousness.

JOB 14:7. Is 42:3.—Ps 23:3. 2 Co 7:10.—Heb 12:11. Ps 119:67.—
Ezra 9:13. Mic 7:8,9.

He who listens to me shall live securely, and shall be at ease from the dread of evil.

LORD, Thou hast been our dwelling place in all generations.— He who dwells in the shelter of the Most High will abide in the shadow of the Almighty.—His faithfulness is a shield and bulwark.

Your life is hidden with Christ in God.—He who touches you, touches the apple of His eye.—Do not fear! Stand by and see the salvation of the LORD. . . . The LORD will fight for you while you keep silent.—God is our refuge and strength, a very present help in trouble. Therefore we will not fear.

Jesus spoke to them, saying, Take courage, it is I; do not be afraid.—Why are you troubled, and why do doubts arise in your heart? See My hands and My feet, that it is I Myself; touch Me and see, for a spirit does not have flesh and bones as you see that I have.—I know whom I have believed and I am convinced that He is able to guard what I have entrusted to Him until that day.

PR 1:33. Ps 90:1.—Ps 91:1.—Ps 91:4. Col 3:3.—Zec 2:8.—
Ex 14:13,14.—Ps 46:1,2. Mt 14:27.—Lk 24:38,39.—2 Ti 1:12.

My kingdom is not of this world.

He, having offered one sacrifice for sins for all time, sat down at the right hand of God, waiting from that time onward until His enemies be made a footstool for His feet.—Hereafter you shall see the Son of Man sitting at the right hand of Power, and coming on the clouds of heaven.

He must reign until He has put all His enemies under His feet.

Thanks be to God, who gives us the victory through our Lord Jesus Christ.—He raised Him from the dead, and seated Him at His right hand in the heavenly places, far above all rule and authority and power and dominion, and every name that is named, not only in this age, but also in the one to come. And He put all things in subjection under His feet, and gave Him as head over all things to the church, which is His body, the fulness of Him who fills all in all.—He will bring about at the proper time —He who is the blessed and only Sovereign, the King of kings and Lord of lords.

JN 18:36. Heb 10:12,13.—Mt 26:64. 1 Co 15:25. 1 Co 15:57.—
Eph 1:20–23.—1 Ti 6:15.

My mother and My brothers are these who hear the word of God and do it.

Both He who sanctifies and those who are sanctified are all from one Father; for which reason He is not ashamed to call them brethren, saying, I will proclaim Thy name to My brethren, in the midst of the congregation I will sing Thy praise.—In Christ Jesus neither circumcision nor uncircumcision means anything, but faith working through love.—You are My friends, if you do what I command you.—Blessed are those who hear the word of God, and observe it.

Not everyone who says to Me, Lord, Lord, will enter the kingdom of heaven; but he who does the will of My Father, who is in heaven.—My food is to do the will of Him who sent Me.

If we say that we have fellowship with Him and yet walk in the darkness, we lie and do not practice the truth.—Whoever keeps His word, in him the love of God has truly been perfected. By this we know that we are in Him.

LK 8:21. Heb 2:11,12.—Gal 5:6.—Jn 15:14.—Lk 11:28. Mt 7:21.—
Jn 4:34. 1 Jn 1:6.—Jn 2:5.

What are you doing here, Elijah?

He knows the way I take.—O LORD, Thou hast searched me and known me. Thou dost know when I sit down and when I rise up; Thou dost understand my thought from afar. Thou dost scrutinize my path and my lying down, and art intimately acquainted with all my ways. Where can I go from Thy Spirit? Or where can I flee from Thy presence? If I take the wings of the dawn, if I dwell in the remotest part of the sea, even there Thy hand will lead me, and Thy right hand will lay hold of me.

Elijah was a man with a nature like ours.—The fear of man brings a snare, but he who trusts in the LORD will be exalted.—When he falls, he shall not be hurled headlong; because the LORD is the One who holds his hand.—A righteous man falls seven times, and rises again.

Let us not lose heart in doing good, for in due time we shall reap if we do not grow weary.—The spirit is willing, but the flesh is weak.—Just as a father has compassion on his children, so the LORD has compassion on those who fear Him.

1 KI 19:9. Job 23:10.—Ps 139:1-3,7,9,10. Ja 5:17.—Pr 29:25.—
Ps 37:24.—Pr 24:16. Gal 6:9.—Mt 26:41.—Ps 103:13.

Having been freed from sin, you became slaves of righteousness.

You cannot serve God and Mammon.—When you were slaves of sin, you were free in regard to righteousness. Therefore what benefit were you then deriving from the things of which you are now ashamed? For the outcome of those things is death. But now having been freed from sin and enslaved to God, you derive your benefit, resulting in sanctification, and the outcome, eternal life.

Christ is the end of the law for righteousness to everyone who believes.

If any one serves Me, let him follow Me; and where I am, there shall My servant also be; if any one serves Me, the Father will honor him.—Take My yoke upon you, and learn from Me, for I am gentle and humble in heart; and you shall find rest for your souls. For My yoke is easy, and My load is light.

O LORD our God, other masters besides Thee have ruled us; but through Thee alone we confess Thy name.—I shall run the way of Thy commandments, for Thou wilt enlarge my heart.

RO 6:18. Mt 6:24.—Ro 6:20-22. Ro 10:4. Jn 12:26.—Mt. 11:29,30. Is 26:13.—Ps 119:32.

Every one who calls on the name of the Lord shall be saved.

Manasseh . . . did evil in the sight of the LORD, according to the abominations of the nations . . . he erected altars for Baal. He built altars for all the host of heaven in the two courts of the house of the LORD. He made his son pass through the fire, practiced witchcraft and used divination, and dealt with mediums and spiritists. He did much evil in the sight of the LORD provoking Him to anger.—When he was in distress, he entreated the LORD his God and humbled himself greatly before the God of his fathers. When he prayed to Him, He was moved by his entreaty and heard his supplication.

Come now, and let us reason together, says the LORD, though your sins are as scarlet, they will be as white as snow; though they are red like crimson, they will be like wool.—The Lord is not slow about His promise . . . not wishing for any to perish.

AC 2:21. 2 Ki 21:1,2,3,5,6.—2 Ch 33:12,13. Is 1:18.—2 Pe 3:9.

The LORD delights in you.

Thus says the LORD your creator ... Do not fear, for I have redeemed you; I have called you by name; you are Mine!—Can a woman forget her nursing child, and have no compassion on the son of her womb? Even these may forget, but I will not forget you. Behold, I have inscribed you on the palms of My hands; your walls are continually before Me.

The steps of a man are established by the LORD; and He delights in his way.—My delight in the sons of men.—The LORD favors those who fear Him, those who wait for His lovingkindness.—They will be Mine, says the LORD of hosts, on the day that I prepare My own possession, and I will spare them as a man spares his own son who serves him.

You were formerly alienated and hostile in mind, engaged in evil deeds, yet He has now reconciled you in His fleshly body through death, in order to present you before Him holy and blameless and beyond reproach.

IS 62:4. Is 43:1.—Is 49:15,16. Ps 37:23.—Pr 8:31.—Ps 147:11.—
Mal 3:17. Col 1:21,22.

The sorrow of the world produces death.

When Ahithophel saw that his counsel was not followed, he saddled his donkey and arose and went to his home, to his city, and set his house in order, and strangled himself; thus he died. —A broken spirit who can bear?

Is there no balm in Gilead? Is there no physician there? Why then has not the health of the daughter of my people been restored?—The LORD has anointed me to bring good news to the afflicted; He has sent me to bind up the brokenhearted ... to comfort all who mourn, to grant those who mourn in Zion, giving them a garland instead of ashes, the oil of gladness instead of mourning, the mantle of praise instead of a spirit of fainting.— Come to Me, all who are weary and heavy laden, and I will give you rest. Take My yoke upon you, and learn from Me, for I am gentle and humble in heart; and you shall find rest for your souls. For My yoke is easy, and My load is light.

Philip ... preached Jesus to him.—He heals the brokenhearted, and binds up their wounds.

2 CO 7:10. 2 Sa 17:23.—Pr 18:14. Jer 8:22.—Is 61:1–3.—
Mt 11:28–30. Ac 8:35.—Ps 147:3.

The glory which Thou hast given Me I have given to them.

I saw the Lord sitting on a throne, lofty and exalted, with the train of His robe filling the temple. Seraphim stood above Him. . . . One called out to another and said, Holy, Holy, Holy, is the LORD of hosts, the whole earth is full of His glory.—These things Isaiah said, because he saw His glory, and he spoke of Him.—On that which resembled a throne, high up, was a figure with the appearance of a man. As the appearance of the rainbow in the clouds on a rainy day, so was the appearance of the surrounding radiance. Such was the appearance of the likeness of the glory of the LORD.

I pray Thee, show me Thy glory! But He said, You cannot see My face, for no man can see Me and live!—No man has seen God at any time; the only begotten God, who is in the bosom of the Father, He has explained Him.—God, who said, Light shall shine out of darkness, is the One who has shone in our hearts to give the light of the knowledge of the glory of God in the face of Christ.

JN 17:22. Is 6:1–3.—Jn 12:41.—Eze 1:26,28. Ex 33:18,20.—
Jn 1:18.—2 Co 4:6.

My son, if sinners entice you, do not consent.

She took from its fruit and ate; and she gave also to her husband with her, and he ate.—Did not Achan the son of Zerah act unfaithfully in the things under the ban, and wrath fall on all the congregation of Israel? And that man did not perish alone in his iniquity.

You shall not follow a multitude in doing evil.

The way is broad that leads to destruction, and many are those who enter by it.

Not one of us lives for himself.—You were called to freedom, brethren; only do not turn your freedom into an opportunity for the flesh, but through love serve one another.—Take care lest this liberty of yours somehow become a stumbling block to the weak. And thus, by sinning against the brethren and wounding their conscience when it is weak, you sin against Christ.

All of us like sheep have gone astray, each of us has turned to his own way; but the LORD has caused the iniquity of us all to fall on Him.

PR 1:10. Gen 3:6.—Jos 22:20. Ex 23:2. Mt 7:13. Ro 14:7.—
Gal 5:13.—1 Co 8:9,12. Is 53:6.

Just as the body without the spirit is dead, so also faith without works is dead.

Not every one who says to Me, Lord, Lord, will enter the kingdom of heaven; but he who does the will of My Father who is in heaven.—Sanctification without which no one will see the Lord.—In your faith supply moral excellence, and in your moral excellence, knowledge; and in your knowledge, self-control, and in your self-control, perseverance, and in your perseverance, godliness; and in your godliness, brotherly kindness, and in your brotherly kindness, Christian love. For if these qualities are yours and are increasing, they render you neither useless nor unfruitful in the true knowledge of our Lord Jesus Christ. For he who lacks these qualities is blind or short-sighted, having forgotten his purification from his former sins. Therefore, brethren, be all the more diligent to make certain about His calling and choosing you; for as long as you practice these things, you will never stumble.

By grace you have been saved through faith; and that not of yourselves, it is the gift of God; not as a result of works, that no one should boast.

JA 2:26. Mt 7:21.—Heb 12:14.—2 Pe 1:5–10. Eph 2:8,9.

Since then the children share in flesh and blood, He Himself likewise also partook of the same . . . and might deliver those who through fear of death were subject to slavery all their lives.

O death, where is your victory? O death, where is your sting? Thanks be to God, who gives us the victory through our Lord Jesus Christ.—Therefore we do not lose heart, but though our outer man is decaying, yet our inner man is being renewed day by day.

We know that if the earthly tent which is our house is torn down, we have a building from God, a house not made with hands, eternal in the heavens. Therefore, being always of good courage, and knowing that while we are at home in the body we are absent from the Lord . . . and prefer rather to be absent from the body and to be at home with the Lord.

Let not your heart be troubled; believe in God, believe also in Me. In My Father's house are many dwelling places; if it were not so, I would have told you; for I go to prepare a place for you. And if I go and prepare a place for you, I will come again, and receive you to Myself; that where I am, there you may be also.

HEB 2:14,15. 1 Co 15:55,57.—2 Co 4:16. 2 Co 5:1,6,8. Jn 14:1,2.

We will be satisfied with the goodness of Thy house.

One thing I have asked from the LORD, that I shall seek; that I may dwell in the house of the LORD all the days of my life, to behold the beauty of the LORD, and to meditate in His temple.

Blessed are those who hunger and thirst for righteousness, for they shall be satisfied.—He has filled the hungry with good things; and sent away the rich empty-handed.

He has satisfied the thirsty soul, and the hungry soul He has filled with what is good.—I am the bread of life; he who comes to Me shall not hunger, and he who believes in Me shall never thirst.

How precious is Thy lovingkindness, O God! And the children of men take refuge in the shadow of Thy wings. They drink their fill of the abundance of Thy house; and Thou dost give them to drink of the river of Thy delights. For with Thee is the fountain of life; in Thy light we see light.

PS 65:4. Ps 27:4. Mt 5:6.—Lk 1:53. Ps 107:9.—Jn 6:35. Ps 36:7–9.

Do you now believe?

What use is it, my brethren, if a man says he has faith, but he has no works? Can that faith save him? Faith, if it has no works, is dead, being by itself.

By faith Abraham, when he was tested, offered up Isaac; and he who had received the promises was offering up his only begotten son. He considered that God is able to raise men even from the dead.—Was not Abraham our father justified by works, when he offered up Isaac his son on the altar? You see that a man is justified by works, and not by faith alone.

One who looks intently at the perfect law, the law of liberty, and abides by it, not having become a forgetful hearer but an effectual doer, this man shall be blessed in what he does.

So then, you will know them by their fruits. Not every one who says to Me, Lord, Lord, will enter the kingdom of heaven; but he who does the will of My Father, who is in heaven.—If you know these things, you are blessed if you do them.

JN 16:31. Ja 2:14,17. Heb 11:17,19.—Ja 2:21,24. Ja 1:25.
Mt 7:20,21.—Jn 13:17.

The Lord of peace Himself continually grant you peace in every circumstance. The Lord be with you all!

Peace, from Him who is and who was and who is to come.— The peace of God, which surpasses all comprehension, shall guard your hearts and your minds in Christ Jesus.

He Himself stood in their midst.—Peace I leave with you; My peace I give to you; not as the world gives, do I give to you. Let not your heart be troubled, nor let it be fearful.

The Helper . . . the Spirit of truth.—The fruit of the Spirit is love, joy, peace.—The Spirit Himself bears witness with our spirit that we are children of God.

My presence shall go with you, and I will give you rest. Then he said to Him, If Thy presence does not go with us, do not lead us up from here. For how then can it be known that I have found favor in Thy sight, I and Thy people? Is it not by Thy going with us?

2 TH 3:16. Rev 1:4.—Phil 4:7. Lk 24:36.—Jn 14:27. Jn 15:26.— Gal 5:22.—Ro 8:16. Ex 33:14–16.

We also exult in our tribulations.

If we have only hoped in Christ in this life, we are of all men most to be pitied.

Beloved, do not be surprised at the fiery ordeal among you, which comes upon you for your testing, as though some strange thing were happening to you; but to the degree that you share the sufferings of Christ, keep on rejoicing; so that also at the revelation of His glory, you may rejoice with exultation.—Sorrowful yet always rejoicing.

Rejoice in the Lord always; again I will say, rejoice!—They went on their way from the presence of the Council, rejoicing that they had been considered worthy to suffer shame for His name.

The God of hope fill you with all joy and peace in believing.

Though the fig tree should not blossom, and there be no fruit on the vines, though the yield of the olive should fail, and the fields produce no food, though the flock should be cut off from the fold, and there be no cattle in the stalls, yet I will exult in the LORD, I will rejoice in the God of my salvation.

RO 5:3. 1 Co 15:19. 1 Pe 4:12,13.—2 Co 6:10. Phil 4:4.—Ac 5:41. Ro 15:13. Hab 3:17,18.

And each will be like a refuge from the wind, and a shelter from the storm.

Since then the children share in flesh and blood, He Himself likewise also partook of the same.—Against the man, My Associate, declares the LORD of hosts.—I and the Father are one.

He who dwells in the shelter of the Most High will abide in the shadow of the Almighty.—And there will be a shelter to give shade from the heat by day, and refuge and protection from the storm and the rain.—The LORD is your shade on your right hand. The sun will not smite you by day, nor the moon by night.

When my heart is faint; lead me to the rock that is higher than I.—Thou art my hiding place; Thou dost preserve me from trouble.—Thou hast been a defense for the helpless. A defense for the needy in his distress, a refuge from the storm, a shade from the heat, for the breath of the ruthless is like a rain storm against a wall.

IS 32:2. Heb 2:14.—Zec 13:7.—Jn 10:30. Ps 91:1.—4:6.— Ps 121:5,6.—Ps 61:2. Ps 32:7.—Is 25:4.

Behold, I create new heavens and a new earth.

Just as the new heavens and the new earth which I make will endure before Me . . . so your offspring and your name will endure.

According to His promise we are looking for new heavens and a new earth, in which righteousness dwells.

And I saw a new heaven and a new earth; for the first heaven and the first earth passed away, and there is no longer any sea. And I saw the holy city, new Jerusalem, coming down out of heaven from God, made ready as a bride adorned for her husband. And I heard a loud voice from the throne, saying, Behold, the tabernacle of God is among men, and He shall dwell among them, and they shall be His peoples, and God Himself shall be among them, and He shall wipe away every tear from their eyes; and there shall no longer be any death; there shall no longer be any mourning, or crying, or pain: the first things have passed away. And He who sits on the throne said, Behold, I am making all things new.

IS 65:17. Is 66:22. 2 Pe 3:13. Rev 21:1–5.

You have an anointing from the Holy One, and you all know.

Jesus of Nazareth . . . God anointed Him with the Holy Spirit and with power.—It was the Father's good pleasure for all the fulness to dwell in Him.—Of his fulness we have all received, and grace upon grace.

Thou hast anointed my head with oil.—The anointing which you received from Him abides in you, and you have no need for any one to teach you; but as His anointing teaches you about all things, and is true and is not a lie, and just as it has taught you, you abide in Him.

The Helper, the Holy Spirit, whom the Father will send in My name, He will teach you all things, and bring to your remembrance all that I said to you.

The Spirit also helps our weakness; for we do not know how to pray as we should, but the Spirit Himself intercedes for us with groanings too deep for words.

1 JN 2:20. Ac 10:38.—Col 1:19. Jn 1:16. Ps 23:5.—1 Jn 2:27.
Jn 14:26. Ro 8:26.

Our hearts sprinkled clean from an evil conscience.

If the blood of goats and bulls and the ashes of a heifer sprinkling those who have been defiled, sanctify for the cleansing of the flesh, how much more will the blood of Christ, who through the eternal Spirit offered Himself without blemish to God, cleanse your conscience from dead works to serve the living God?—Jesus . . . the sprinkled blood, which speaks better than the blood of Abel.

We have redemption through His blood, the forgiveness of our trespasses, according to the riches of His grace.

When every commandment had been spoken by Moses to all the people according to the Law, he took the blood of the calves and the goats, with water and scarlet wool and hyssop, and sprinkled both the book itself and all the people. In the same way he sprinkled both the tabernacle and all the vessels of the ministry with the blood. And according to the Law, one may almost say, all things are cleansed with blood, and without shedding of blood there is no forgiveness.

HEB 10:22. Heb 9:13,14.—Heb 12:24. Eph 1:7. Heb 9:19,21,22.

I would seek God, and I would place my cause before God.

Is anything too difficult for the LORD?—Commit your way to the LORD, trust also in Him, and He will do it.—Be anxious for nothing, but in everything by prayer and supplication with thanksgiving let your requests be made known to God.—Casting all your anxiety upon Him, because He cares for you.

Hezekiah took the letter from the hand of the messengers and read it, and he went up to the house of the LORD and spread it out before the LORD. And Hezekiah prayed to the LORD.

It will also come to pass that before they call, I will answer; and while they are still speaking, I will hear.—The effective prayer of a righteous man can accomplish much.

I love the LORD, because He hears my voice and my supplications. Because He has inclined His ear to me, therefore I shall call upon Him as long as I live.

JOB 5:8. Gen 18:14.—Ps 37:5.—Phil 4:6.—1 Pe 5:7. Is 37:14,15.
Is 65:24.—Ja 5:16. Ps 116:1,2.

Our body washed with pure water.

You shall make a laver of bronze . . . and you shall put it between the tent of meeting and the altar, and you shall put water in it. And Aaron and his sons shall wash their hands and their feet from it; when they enter the tent of meeting, they shall wash with water, that they may not die . . . they shall wash their hands and their feet, that they may not die.—Your body is a temple of the Holy Spirit who is in you.—If any man destroys the temple of God, God will destroy him, for the temple of God is holy, and that is what you are.

From my flesh I shall see God; whom I myself shall behold, and whom my eyes shall see and not another.—Nothing unclean . . . shall ever come into it.—Thine eyes are too pure to approve evil, and Thou canst not look on wickedness with favor.—I urge you, therefore, brethren, by the mercies of God, to present your bodies a living and holy sacrifice, acceptable to God, which is your spiritual service of worship.

HEB 10:22. Ex 30:18–21.—1 Co 6:19.—1 Co 3:17. Job 19:26,27.—
Rev 21:27.—Hab 1:13. Ro 12:1.

Where can wisdom be found?

If any of you lacks wisdom, let him ask of God, who gives to all men generously and without reproach, and it will be given to him.—Trust in the LORD with all your heart, and do not lean on your own understanding. In all your ways acknowledge Him, and He will make your paths straight.—The only God.—Do not be wise in your own eyes.

Alas, Lord GOD! Behold, I do not know how to speak, because I am a youth. . . . Everywhere I send you, you shall go, and all that I command you, you shall speak. Do not be afraid of them, for I am with you to deliver you, declares the LORD.

If you shall ask the Father for anything, He will give it to you in My name. Until now you have asked for nothing in My name; ask, and you will receive, that your joy may be made full.— Everything you ask in prayer, believing, you shall receive.

JOB 28:12. Ja 1:5,6.—Pr 3:5,6.—1 Ti 1:17.—Pr 3:7. Jer 1:6–8. Jn 16:23,24.—Mt 21:22.

I will not live forever.

I said, O that I had wings like a dove! I would fly away and be at rest. I would hasten to my place of refuge from the stormy wind and tempest.

In this house we groan, longing to be clothed with our dwelling from heaven. For indeed while we are in this tent, we groan, being burdened, because we do not want to be unclothed, but to be clothed, in order that what is mortal may be swallowed up by life.—Having the desire to depart and be with Christ, for that is very much better.

Let us run with endurance the race that is set before us, fixing our eyes on Jesus, the author and perfecter of faith, who for the joy set before Him endured the cross, despising the shame, and has sat down at the right hand of the throne of God. For consider Him who has endured such hostility by sinners against Himself, so that you may not grow weary and lose heart.

Let not your heart be troubled, nor let it be fearful.

JOB 7:16. Ps 55:6,8. 2 Co 5:2,4.—Phil 1:23. Heb 12:1–3. Jn 14:27.

**It is good for me that I was afflicted, that I may learn Thy
statutes.**

Although He was a Son, He learned obedience from the things
which He suffered.—If indeed we suffer with Him in order that
we may also be glorified with Him. For I consider that the sufferings of this present time are not worthy to be compared with the
glory that is to be revealed to us.

He knows the way I take; when He has tried me, I shall come
forth as gold . . . I have kept His way and not turned aside.

You shall remember all the way which the LORD your God has
led you in the wilderness these forty years, that He might humble you, testing you, to know what was in your heart, whether
you would keep His commandments or not. Thus you are to
know in your heart that the LORD your God was disciplining you
just as a man disciplines his son. Therefore, you shall keep the
commandments of the LORD your God, to walk in His ways and
to fear Him.

PS 119:71. Heb 5:8.—Ro 8:17,18. Job 23:10,11. Deu 8:2,5,6.

Not by might shall a man prevail.

Then David said to the Philistine, You come to me with a
sword, a spear, and a javelin, but I come to you in the name of
the LORD of hosts, the God of the armies of Israel, whom you
have taunted. And David put his hand into his bag and took from
it a stone and slung it. . . . Thus David prevailed over the Philistine with a sling and a stone.

The king is not saved by a mighty army; a warrior is not delivered by great strength. Behold, the eye of the LORD is on those
who fear Him, on those who hope for His lovingkindness.—Both
riches and honor come from Thee, and Thou dost rule over all,
and in Thy hand is power and might; and it lies in Thy hand to
make great, and to strengthen everyone.

I will rather boast about my weaknesses, that the power of
Christ may dwell in me. Therefore I am well content with weaknesses, with insults, with distresses, with persecutions, with difficulties, for Christ's sake; for when I am weak, then I am strong.

1 SA 2:9. 1 Sa 17:45,49,50. Ps 33:16,18.—1 Ch 29:12. 2 Co 12:9,10.

It is God who is at work in you.

Not that we are adequate in ourselves to consider anything as coming from ourselves, but our adequacy is from God.—A man can receive nothing, unless it has been given him from heaven.—No one can come to Me, unless the Father who sent Me draws him; and I will raise him up on the last day.—I will give them one heart and one way, that they may fear Me always.

Do not be deceived, my beloved brethren. Every good thing bestowed and every perfect gift is from above, coming down from the Father of lights, with whom there is no variation, or shifting shadow. In the exercise of His will He brought us forth by the word of truth, so that we might be as it were the first fruits among His creatures.

We are His workmanship, created in Christ Jesus for good works, which God prepared beforehand, that we should walk in them.

LORD, Thou wilt establish peace for us, since Thou hast also performed for us all our works.

PHIL 2:13. 2 Co 3:5.—Jn 3:27.—Jn 6:44.—Jer 32:39. Ja 1:16–18.
Eph 2:10. Is 26:12.

The spirit is willing, but the flesh is weak.

While following the way of Thy judgments, O LORD, we have waited for Thee eagerly; Thy name, even Thy memory, is the desire of our souls. At night my soul longs for Thee, indeed, my spirit within me seeks Thee diligently.

I know that nothing good dwells in me, that is, in my flesh; for the wishing is present in me, but the doing of the good is not. For I joyfully concur with the law of God in the inner man, but I see a different law in the members of my body, waging war against the law of my mind, and making me a prisoner of the law of sin which is in my members.—For the flesh sets its desire against the Spirit, and the Spirit against the flesh; for these are in opposition to one another, so that you may not do the things that you please.

I can do all things through Him who strengthens me.—Our adequacy is from God.—My grace is sufficient for you.

MT 26:41. Is 26:8,9. Ro 7:18,22,23.—Gal 5:17. Phil 4:13.—
2 Co 3:5.—2 Co 12:9.

He made Him who knew no sin to be sin on our behalf, that we might become the righteousness of God in Him.

The Lord has caused the iniquity of us all to fall on Him.—He Himself bore our sins in His body on the cross, that we might die to sin and live to righteousness; for by His wounds you were healed.—Through the one man's disobedience the many were made sinners, even so through the obedience of the One the many will be made righteous.

When the kindness of God our Savior and His love for mankind appeared, He saved us, not on the basis of deeds which we have done in righteousness, but according to His mercy, by the washing of regeneration and renewing by the Holy Spirit, whom He poured out upon us richly through Jesus Christ our Savior, that being justified by His grace we might be made heirs according to the hope of eternal life.—There is therefore now no condemnation for those who are in Christ Jesus.

The Lord our righteousness.

2 CO 5:21. Is 53:6.—1 Pe 2:24.—Ro 5:19. Titus 3:4–7.—Ro 8:1.
Jer 23:6.

I will be like the dew to Israel.

The meekness and gentleness of Christ.

A bruised reed He will not break, and a dimly burning wick He will not extinguish.

The Spirit of the Lord is upon Me, because He anointed Me to preach the gospel to the poor. He has sent Me to proclaim release to the captives, and recovery of sight to the blind, to set free those who are downtrodden, to proclaim the favorable year of the Lord. And He began to say to them, Today this Scripture has been fulfilled in your hearing. And all were speaking well of Him, and wondering at the gracious words which were falling from His lips.

And the Lord turned and looked at Peter. And Peter remembered the word of the Lord, how He had told him, Before a cock crows today, you will deny Me three times. And he went outside and wept bitterly.

Like a shepherd He will tend His flock, in His arm He will gather the lambs, and carry them in His bosom; He will gently lead the nursing ewes.

HO 14:5. 2 Co 10:1. Is 42:3. Lk 4:18,19,21,22. Lk 22:61,62. Is 40:11.

Through love serve one another.

Brethren, even if a man is caught in any trespass, you who are spiritual, restore such a one in a spirit of gentleness; each one looking to yourself, lest you too be tempted. Bear one another's burdens, and thus fulfil the law of Christ.

My brethren, if any among you strays from the truth, and one turns him back, let him know that he who turns a sinner from the error of his way will save his soul from death, and will cover a multitude of sins.—Since you have in obedience to the truth purified your souls for a sincere love of the brethren, fervently love one another from the heart.—Owe nothing to anyone except to love one another; for he who loves his neighbor has fulfilled the law.—Be devoted to one another in brotherly love; give preference to one another in honor.—All of you, clothe yourselves with humility toward one another, for God is opposed to the proud, but gives grace to the humble.

We who are strong ought to bear the weaknesses of those without strength and not just please ourselves.

GAL 5:13. Gal 6:1,2. Ja 5:19,20.—1 Pe 1:22.—Ro 13:8.—Ro 12:10.—
1 Pe 5:5. Ro 15:1.

The dust will return to the earth as it was.

It is sown a perishable body . . . it is sown in dishonor . . . it is sown in weakness . . . it is sown a natural body.—The first man is from the earth, earthy.

You are dust, and to dust you shall return.—One dies in his full strength, being wholly at ease and satisfied . . . While another dies with a bitter soul, never even tasting anything good. Together they lie down in the dust, and worms cover them.

My flesh also will dwell securely.—Even after my skin is destroyed, yet from my flesh I shall see God.—The Lord Jesus Christ who will transform the body of our humble state into conformity with the body of His glory, by the exertion of the power that He has even to subject all things to Himself.

Lord, make me to know my end, and what is the extent of my days, let me know how transient I am.—So teach us to number our days, that we may present to Thee a heart of wisdom.

EC 12:7. 1 Co 15:42–44.—1 Co 15:47. Gen 3:19.—Job 21:23,25,26.
Ps 16:9.—Job 19:26.—Phil 3:20,21. Ps 39:4.—Ps 90:12.

To do righteousness and justice is desired by the LORD rather than sacrifice.

He has told you, O man, what is good; and what does the LORD require of you but to do justice, to love kindness, and to walk humbly with your God?—Has the LORD as much delight in burnt offerings and sacrifices as in obeying the voice of the LORD? Behold, to obey is better than sacrifice, and to heed than the fat of rams.—To love Him with all the heart and with all the understanding and with all the strength, and to love one's neighbor as himself, is much more than all burnt offerings and sacrifices.

Therefore, return to your God, observe kindness and justice, and wait for your God continually.—Mary . . . was listening to the Lord's word, seated at His feet. A few things are necessary, really only one: for Mary has chosen the good part, which shall not be taken away from her.

It is God who is at work in you, both to will and to work for His good pleasure.

PR 21:3. Mic 6:8.—1 Sa 15:22.—Mk 12:33. Ho 12:6.—Lk 10:39,42. Phil 2:13.

The spirit will return to God who gave it.

The LORD God formed man of dust from the ground, and breathed into his nostrils the breath of life; and man became a living being.—It is a spirit in man, and the breath of the Almighty gives them understanding.—The first man, Adam, became a living soul.—The breath of man ascends upward.

While we are at home in the body we are absent from the Lord. We are of good courage, I say, and prefer rather to be absent from the body and to be at home with the Lord.—With Christ, for that is very much better.—We do not want you to be uninformed, brethren, about those who are asleep, that you may not grieve, as do the rest who have no hope. For if we believe that Jesus died and rose again, even so God will bring with Him those who have fallen asleep in Jesus.

I go to prepare a place for you. And if I go and prepare a place for you, I will come again, and receive you to Myself; that where I am, there you may be also.

EC 12:7. Gen 2:7.—Job 32:8.—1 Co 15:45.—Ec 3:21. 2 Co 5:6,8.— Phil 1:23.—1 Th 4:13,14. Jn 14:2,3.

No one is able to snatch them out of the Father's hand.

I know whom I have believed and I am convinced that He is able to guard what I have entrusted to Him until that day.—The Lord will deliver me from every evil deed, and will bring me safely to His heavenly kingdom.—In all these things we overwhelmingly conquer through Him who loved us. For I am convinced that neither death, nor life, nor angels, nor principalities, nor things present, nor things to come, nor powers, nor height, nor depth, nor any other created thing, shall be able to separate us from the love of God, which is in Christ Jesus our Lord.—Your life is hidden with Christ in God.

Did not God choose the poor of this world to be rich in faith and heirs of the kingdom which He promised to those who love Him?

Our Lord Jesus Christ Himself and God our Father, who has loved us and given us eternal comfort and good hope by grace, comfort and strengthen your hearts in every good work and word.

JN 10:29. 2 Ti 1:12.—2 Ti 4:18.—Ro 8:37–39.—Col 3:3. Ja 2:5.
2 Th 2:16,17.

The perfect law, the law of liberty.

You shall know the truth, and the truth shall make you free. Truly, truly, I say to you, every one who commits sin is the slave of sin. If therefore the Son shall make you free, you shall be free indeed.

Christ set us free; therefore keep standing firm and do not be subject again to a yoke of slavery. You were called to freedom, brethren; only do not turn your freedom into an opportunity for the flesh, but through love serve one another. For the whole Law is fulfilled in one word, in the statement, You shall love your neighbor as yourself.—Having been freed from sin, you became slaves of righteousness.—The married woman is bound by law to her husband while he is living; but if her husband dies, she is released from the law concerning the husband.

The law of the Spirit of life in Christ Jesus has set you free from the law of sin and of death.—I will walk at liberty, for I seek Thy precepts.

JA 1:25. Jn 8:32,34,36. Gal 5:1,13,14.—Ro 6:18.—Ro 7:2. Ro 8:2.—
Ps 119:45.

Do not let what is for you a good thing be spoken of as evil.

Abstain from every form of evil.—Have regard for what is honorable, not only in the sight of the Lord, but also in the sight of men.—Such is the will of God that by doing right you may silence the ignorance of foolish men.

By no means let any of you suffer as a murderer, or thief, or evil-doer, or a troublesome meddler; but if anyone suffers as a Christian, let him not feel ashamed, but in that name let him glorify God.

You were called to freedom, brethren; only do not turn your freedom into an opportunity for the flesh, but through love serve one another.—Take care lest this liberty of yours somehow become a stumbling block to the weak.—Whoever causes one of these little ones who believe in Me to stumble, it is better for him that a heavy millstone be hung around his neck, and that he be drowned in the depth of the sea.—To the extent that you did it to one of these brothers of Mine, even the least of them, you did it to Me.

RO 14:16. 1 Th 5:22.—2 Co 8:21.—1 Pe 2:15. 1 Pe 4:15,16.
Gal 5:13.—1 Co 8:9.—Mt 18:6.—Mt 25:40.

Awake, sleeper, and arise from the dead, and Christ will shine on you.

It is already the hour for you to awaken from sleep; for now salvation is nearer to us than when we believed.—Then let us not sleep as others do, but let us be alert and sober. For those who sleep do their sleeping at night, and those who get drunk get drunk at night. But since we are of the day, let us be sober, having put on the breastplate of faith and love, and as a helmet, the hope of salvation.

Arise, shine; for your light has come, and the glory of the LORD has risen upon you. For behold, darkness will cover the earth, and deep darkness the peoples; but the LORD will rise upon you, and His glory will appear upon you.

Gird your minds for action, keep sober in spirit, fix your hope completely on the grace to be brought to you at the revelation of Jesus Christ.—Be dressed in readiness, and keep your lamps alight. And be like men who are waiting for their master.

EPH 5:14. Ro 13:11.—1 Th 5:6–8. Is 60:1,2. 1 Pe 1:13.—
Lk 12:35,36.

The LORD is in your midst.

Do not fear, for I am with you; do not anxiously look about you, for I am your God. I will strengthen you, surely I will help you, surely, I will uphold you with My righteous right hand.—Encourage the exhausted, and strengthen the feeble. Say to those with anxious heart, Take courage, fear not. Behold, your God will come with vengeance; the recompense of God will come, but He will save you.—The LORD your God is in your midst, a victorious warrior. He will exult over you with joy, He will be quiet in His love, He will rejoice over you with shouts of joy.—Wait for the LORD; be strong, and let your heart take courage.

I heard a loud voice from the throne, saying, Behold, the tabernacle of God is among men, and He shall dwell among them, and they shall be His peoples, and God Himself shall be among them, and He shall wipe away every tear from their eyes; and there shall no longer be any death; there shall no longer be any mourning, or crying, or pain.

ZEP 3:15. Is 41:10.—Is 35:3,4.—Zep 3:17.—Ps 27:14. Rev 21:3,4.

Why are you crying out to Me? Tell the sons of Israel to go forward.

Be strong, and let us show ourselves courageous for the sake of our people and for the cities of our God; and may the LORD do what is good in His sight.—We prayed to our God, and . . . set up a guard against them day and night.

Not every one who says to Me, Lord, Lord, will enter the kingdom of heaven; but he who does the will of My Father, who is in heaven.—If any man is willing to do His will, he shall know of the teaching, whether it is of God.—So let us know, let us press on to know the LORD.

Keep watching and praying, that you may not enter into temptation.—Be on the alert, stand firm in the faith, act like men, be strong.—Not lagging behind in diligence, fervent in spirit, serving the Lord.

Encourage the exhausted, and strengthen the feeble. Say to those with anxious heart, Take courage, fear not.

EX 14:15. 1 Ch 19:13. Neh 4:9. Mt 7:21.—Jn 7:17.—Ho 6:3.
Mt 26:41.—1 Co 16:13.—Ro 12:11. Is 35:3,4.

Be strong in the grace that is in Christ Jesus.

Strengthened with all power, according to His glorious might. —As you therefore have received Christ Jesus the Lord, so walk in Him, having been firmly rooted and now being built up in Him and established in your faith, just as you were instructed, and overflowing with gratitude.—Oaks of righteousness, the planting of the LORD, that He may be glorified.—Built upon the foundation of the apostles and prophets, Christ Jesus Himself being the cornerstone, in whom the whole building, being fitted together is growing into a holy temple of the Lord; in whom you also are being built together into a dwelling of God in the Spirit.

I commend you to God and to the word of His grace, which is able to build you up and to give you the inheritance among all those who are sanctified.—Having been filled with the fruit of righteousness which comes through Jesus Christ, to the glory and praise of God.

Fight the good fight of faith.—In no way alarmed by your opponents.

2 TI 2:1. Col 1:11.—Col 2:6,7.—Is 61:3.—Eph 2:20–22. Ac 20:32.— Phil 1:11. 1 Ti 6:12.—Phil 1:28.

Thou dost recompense a man according to his work.

No man can lay a foundation other than the one which is laid, which is Jesus Christ. If any man's work which he has built upon it remains, he shall receive a reward. If any man's work is burned up, he shall suffer loss; but he himself shall be saved, yet so as through fire.—For we must all appear before the judgment-seat of Christ, that each one may be recompensed for his deeds in the body, according to what he has done, whether good or bad.

When you give alms, do not let your left hand know what your right hand is doing; that your alms may be in secret; and your Father who sees in secret will repay you.—After a long time the master of those slaves came and settled accounts with them.

Not that we are adequate in ourselves to consider anything as coming from ourselves, but our adequacy is from God.—LORD, Thou wilt establish peace for us, since Thou hast also performed for us all our works.

PS 62:12. 1 Co 3:11,14,15.—2 Co 5:10. Mt 6:3,4.—Mt 25:19. 2 Co 3:5.—Is 26:12.

Make His praise glorious.

The people whom I formed for Myself, will declare My praise. —I will cleanse them from all their iniquity by which they have sinned against Me, and I will pardon all their iniquities by which they have sinned against Me, and by which they have transgressed against Me. And it shall be to Me a name of joy, praise, and glory before all the nations of the earth.—Through Him then, let us continually offer up a sacrifice of praise to God, that is, the fruit of lips that give thanks to His name.

I will give thanks to Thee, O Lord my God, with all my heart, and will glorify Thy name forever. For Thy lovingkindness toward me is great, and Thou hast delivered my soul from the depths of Sheol.—Who is like Thee among the gods, O LORD? . . . majestic in holiness, awesome in praises, working wonders? —I will praise the name of God with song, and shall magnify Him with thanksgiving.—They sang the song of Moses the bondservant of God and the song of the Lamb, saying, Great and marvelous are Thy works, O Lord God, the Almighty.

PS 66:2. Is 43:21.—Jer 33:8,9.—Heb 13:15. Ps 86:12,13.—
Ex 15:11.—Ps 69:30.—Rev 15:3.

By nature children of wrath, even as the rest.

We also once were foolish ourselves, disobedient, deceived, enslaved to various lusts and pleasures, spending our life in malice and envy, hateful, hating one another.—Do not marvel that I said to you, You must be born again.

Job answered the LORD and said, Behold, I am insignificant; what can I reply to Thee? I lay my hand on my mouth.—The LORD said to Satan, Have you considered My servant Job? For there is no one like him on the earth, a blameless and upright man, fearing God and turning away from evil.

Behold, I was brought forth in iniquity, and in sin my mother conceived me.—David . . . concerning whom He . . . said, I have found David the son of Jesse, a man after My heart, who will do all My will.

Even though I was formerly a blasphemer and a persecutor and a violent aggressor . . . yet I was shown mercy.

That which is born of the flesh is flesh; and that which is born of the Spirit is spirit.

EPH 2:3. Titus 3:3.—Jn 3:7. Job 40:3,4.—Job 1:8. Ps 51:5.—
Ac 13:22. 1 Ti 1:13. Jn 3:6.

Bear one another's burdens, and thus fulfil the law of Christ.

Do not merely look out for your own personal interests, but also for the interests of others. Have this attitude in yourselves which was also in Christ Jesus . . . taking the form of a bond-servant.—Even the Son of Man did not come to be served, but to serve, and to give His life a ransom for many.—He died for all, that they who live should no longer live for themselves, but for Him who died and rose again on their behalf.

When Jesus . . . saw her weeping, and the Jews who came with her, also weeping, He was deeply moved in spirit, and was troubled. Jesus wept.—Rejoice with those who rejoice, and weep with those who weep.

Let all be harmonious, sympathetic, brotherly, kind-hearted, and humble in spirit; not returning evil for evil, or insult for insult, but giving a blessing instead; for you were called for the very purpose that you might inherit a blessing.

GAL 6:2. Phil 2:4,5,7.—Mk 10:45.—2 Co 5:15. Jn 11:33,35.—
Ro 12:15. 1 Pe 3:8,9.

Son, go work today in the vineyard.

You are no longer a slave, but a son; and if a son, then an heir through God.

Consider yourselves to be dead to sin, but alive to God in Christ Jesus. Therefore do not let sin reign in your mortal body that you should obey its lusts, and do not go on presenting the members of your body to sin as instruments of unrighteousness; but present yourselves to God as those alive from the dead, and your members as instruments of righteousness to God.—As obedient children, do not be conformed to the former lusts which were yours in your ignorance, but like the Holy One who called you, be holy yourselves also in all your behavior; because it is written, You shall be holy, for I am holy.—Sanctified, useful to the Master, prepared for every good work.

Therefore, my beloved brethren, be steadfast, immovable, always abounding in the work of the Lord, knowing that your toil is not in vain in the Lord.

MT 21:28. Gal 4:7. Ro 6:11–13.—1 Pe 1:14–16.—2 Ti 2:21.
1 Co 15:58.

Having loved His own who were in the world, He loved them to the end.

I ask on their behalf; I do not ask on behalf of the world, but of those whom Thou hast given me; for they are Thine; and all things that are Mine are Thine, and Thine are Mine; and I have been glorified in them. I do not ask Thee to take them out of the world, but to keep them from the evil one. They are not of the world, even as I am not of the world.

Just as the Father has loved Me, I have also loved you; abide in My love.—Greater love has no one than this, that one lay down his life for his friends. You are My friends, if you do what I command you.—A new commandment I give to you, that you love one another, even as I have loved you, that you also love one another.

He who began a good work in you will perfect it until the day of Christ Jesus.—Christ . . . loved the church and gave Himself up for her; that He might sanctify her, having cleansed her by the washing of water with the word.

JN 13:1. Jn 17:9,10,15,16. Jn 15:9.—Jn 15:13,14.—Jn 13:34.
Phil 1:6.—Eph 5:25,26.

The depths of God.

No longer do I call you slaves; for the slave does not know what his master is doing; but I have called you friends, for all things that I have heard from My Father I have made known to you. —To you it has been granted to know the mysteries of the kingdom of heaven.

We have received, not the spirit of the world, but the Spirit who is from God, that we might know the things freely given to us by God.

For this reason, I bow my knees before the Father, from whom every family in heaven and on earth derives its name, that He would grant you, according to the riches of His glory, to be strengthened with power through His Spirit in the inner man . . . that you, being rooted and grounded in love, may be able to comprehend with all the saints what is the breadth and length and height and depth, and to know the love of Christ which surpasses knowledge, that you may be filled up to all the fulness of God.

1 CO 2:10. Jn 15:15.—Mt 13:11. 1 Co 2:12. Eph 3:14–19.

Revive us, and we will call upon Thy name.

It is the Spirit who gives life.—The Spirit also helps our weakness; for we do not know how to pray as we should, but the Spirit Himself intercedes for us with groanings too deep for words; and He who searches the hearts knows what the mind of the Spirit is, because He intercedes for the saints according to the will of God.—With all prayer and petition pray at all times in the Spirit . . . be on the alert with all perseverance and petition.

I will never forget Thy precepts, for by them Thou hast revived me.—The words that I have spoken to you are spirit and are life.—The letter kills, but the Spirit gives life.—If you abide in Me, and My words abide in you, ask whatever you wish, and it shall be done for you.—This is the confidence which we have before Him, that, if we ask anything according to His will, He hears us.

No one can say, Jesus is Lord, except by the Holy Spirit.

PS 80:18. Jn 6:63.—Ro 8:26,27.—Eph 6:18. Ps 119:93.—Jn 6:63.— 2 Co 3:6.—Jn 15:7.—1 Jn 5:14. 1 Co 12:3.

Do not participate in the unfruitful deeds of darkness, but instead even expose them.

Do not be deceived: Bad company corrupts good morals.—Do you not know that a little leaven leavens the whole lump of dough? Clean out the old leaven. . . . I wrote you in my letter not to associate with immoral people; I did not at all mean with the immoral people of this world, or with the covetous and swindlers, or with idolaters; for then you would have to go out of the world. But actually, I wrote to you not to associate with any so-called brother if he should be an immoral person, or covetous, or an idolater, or a reviler, or a drunkard, or a swindler—not even to eat with such a one.—That you may prove yourselves to be blameless and innocent, children of God above reproach in the midst of a crooked and perverse generation, among whom you appear as lights in the world.

In a large house there are not only gold and silver vessels, but also vessels of wood and of earthenware, and some to honor and some to dishonor.

EPH 5:11. 1 Co 15:33. 1 Co 5:6,7,9–11.—Phil 2:15. 2 Ti 2:20.

Let us therefore draw near with confidence to the throne of grace, that we may receive mercy and may find grace to help in time of need.

Be anxious for nothing, but in everything by prayer and supplication with thanksgiving let your requests be made known to God. And the peace of God, which surpasses all comprehension, shall guard your hearts and your minds in Christ Jesus.—You have not received a spirit of slavery leading to fear again, but you have received a spirit of adoption as sons by which we cry out, Abba! Father!

I did not say to the offspring of Jacob, Seek Me in a waste place. —Therefore, brethren, we have confidence to enter the holy place by the blood of Jesus, by a new and living way which He inaugurated for us through the veil, that is, His flesh, and since we have a great priest over the house of God, let us draw near with a sincere heart in full assurance of faith, having our hearts sprinkled clean from an evil conscience and our body washed with pure water.—We confidently say, The Lord is my helper, I will not be afraid. What shall man do to me?

HEB 4:16. Phil 4:6,7.—Ro 8:15. Is 45:19.—Heb 10:19–22.— Heb 13:6.

You shall know the truth, and the truth shall make you free.

Where the Spirit of the Lord is, there is liberty.—The law of the Spirit of life in Christ Jesus has set you free from the law of sin and of death.—If . . . the Son shall make you free, you shall be free indeed.

Brethren, we are not children of a bondwoman, but of the free woman.—A man is not justified by the works of the Law but through faith in Christ Jesus, even we have believed in Christ Jesus, that we may be justified by faith in Christ, and not by the works of the Law; since by the works of the Law shall no flesh be justified.

One who looks intently at the perfect law, the law of liberty and abides by it, not having become a forgetful hearer but an effectual doer, this man shall be blessed in what he does.—It was for freedom that Christ set us free; therefore keep standing firm and do not be subject again to a yoke of slavery.

JN 8:32. 2 Co 3:17.—Ro 8:2.—Jn 8:36. Gal 4:31.—Gal 2:16. Ja 1:25.—Gal 5:1.

Light arises in the darkness for the upright.

Who is among you that fears the LORD, that obeys the voice of his Servant, that walks in darkness and has no light? Let him trust in the name of the LORD and rely on his God.—When he falls, he shall not be hurled headlong; because the LORD is the One who holds his hand.—The commandment is a lamp, and the teaching is light.

Do not rejoice over me, O my enemy. Though I fall I will rise; though I dwell in darkness, the LORD is a light for me. I will bear the indignation of the LORD because I have sinned against Him, until He pleads my case and executes justice for me. He will bring me out to the light, and I will see His righteousness.

The lamp of the body is the eye; if therefore your eye is clear, your whole body will be full of light. But if your eye is bad, your whole body will be full of darkness. If therefore the light that is in you is darkness, how great is the darkness!

PS 112:4. Is 50:10.—Ps 37:24.—Pr 6:23. Mic 7:8,9. Mt 6:22,23.

Like a shepherd He will tend His flock, in His arm He will gather the lambs, and carry them in His bosom; He will gently lead the nursing ewes.

I feel compassion for the multitude, because they have remained with Me now for three days and have nothing to eat; and I do not wish to send them away hungry, lest they faint on the way.—We do not have a high priest who cannot sympathize with our weaknesses.

They began bringing children to Him . . . and He took them in His arms and began blessing them.

I have gone astray like a lost sheep; seek Thy servant.—The Son of Man has come to seek and to save that which was lost.— You were continually straying like sheep, but now you have returned to the Shepherd and Guardian of your souls.

Do not be afraid, little flock, for your Father has chosen gladly to give you the kingdom.—I will feed My flock and I will lead them to rest, declares the Lord GOD.

IS 40:11. Mt 15:32.—Heb 4:15. Mk 10:13,16. Ps 119:176.—
Lk 19:10.—1 Pe 2:25. Lk 12:32.—Eze 34:15.

He chose us in Him before the foundation of the world.

That we should be holy and blameless before Him.

God has chosen you from the beginning for salvation through sanctification by the Spirit and faith in the truth ... for this He called you ... that you may gain the glory of our Lord Jesus Christ.—Whom He foreknew, He also predestined to become conformed to the image of His Son, that He might be the first-born among many brethren; and whom He predestined, these He also called; and whom He called, these He also justified; and whom He justified, these He also glorified.—Chosen according to the foreknowledge of God the Father, by the sanctifying work of the Spirit, that you may obey Jesus Christ and be sprinkled with His blood.

I will give you a new heart and put a new spirit within you; and I will remove the heart of stone from your flesh and give you a heart of flesh.—God has not called us for the purpose of impurity, but in sanctification.

EPH 1:14. Eph 1:4. 2 Th 2:13,14.—Ro 8:29,30.—1 Pe 1:1,2.
Eze 36:26.—1 Th 4:7.

If the LORD should make windows in heaven, could this thing be?

Have faith in God.—Without faith it is impossible to please Him.—With God all things are possible.

Is My hand so short that it cannot ransom? Or have I no power to deliver?

My thoughts are not your thoughts, neither are your ways My ways, declares the LORD. For as the heavens are higher than the earth, so are My ways higher than your ways, and My thoughts than your thoughts.—Test Me now in this, says the LORD of hosts, if I will not open for you the windows of heaven, and pour out for you a blessing until there is no more need.

Behold, the LORD's hand is not so short that it cannot save; neither is His ear so dull that it cannot hear.—Lord, there is no one besides Thee to help in the battle between the powerful and those who have no strength.

We should not trust in ourselves, but in God who raises the dead.

2 KI 7:2. Mk 11:22.—Heb 11:6.—Mt 19:26. Is 50:2. Is 55:8,9.—
Mal 3:10. Is 59:1.—2 Ch 14:11. 2 Co 1:9.

The days of your mourning will be finished.

In the world you have tribulation.—We know that the whole creation groans and suffers the pains of childbirth together until now. And not only this, but also we ourselves, having the first fruits of the Spirit, even we ourselves groan within ourselves, waiting eagerly for our adoption as sons, the redemption of our body.—Indeed while we are in this tent, we groan, being burdened, because we do not want to be unclothed, but to be clothed, in order that what is mortal may be swallowed up by life.

These are the ones who come out of the great tribulation, and they have washed their robes and made them white in the blood of the Lamb. For this reason, they are before the throne of God; and they serve Him day and night in His temple; and He who sits on the throne shall spread His tabernacle over them. They shall hunger no more, neither thirst any more; neither shall the sun beat down on them, nor any heat; for the Lamb in the center of the throne shall be their shepherd, and shall guide them to springs of the water of life; and God shall wipe every tear from their eyes.

IS 60:20. Jn 16:33.—Ro 8:22,23.—2 Co 5:4. Rev 7:14–17.

Teacher, do You not care that we are perishing?

The Lord is good to all, and His mercies are over all His works. Every moving thing that is alive shall be food for you; I give all to you, as I gave the green plant.—While the earth remains, seedtime and harvest, and cold and heat, and summer and winter, and day and night shall not cease.

The Lord is good, a stronghold in the day of trouble, and He knows those who take refuge in Him.—God heard the lad crying; and the angel of God called to Hagar from heaven, and said to her, What is the matter with you, Hagar? Do not fear, for God has heard the voice of the lad where he is. Then God opened her eyes and she saw a well of water; and she went and filled the skin with water, and gave the lad a drink.

Do not be anxious then, saying, What shall we eat? or, What shall we drink? . . . for your heavenly Father knows that you need all these things.

MK 4:38. Ps 145:9. Gen 9:3.—Gen 8:22. Nah 1:7.—Gen 21:17,19.
Mt 6:31,32.

Your work of faith.

This is the work of God, that you believe in Him whom He has sent.

Faith, if it has no works, is dead, being by itself.—Faith working through love.—The one who sows to his own flesh shall from the flesh reap corruption, but the one who sows to the Spirit shall from the Spirit reap eternal life.—We are His workmanship, created in Christ Jesus for good works, which God prepared beforehand, that we should walk in them.—Who gave Himself for us, that He might redeem us from every lawless deed and purify for Himself a people for His own possession, zealous for good deeds.

We ought always to give thanks to God for you, brethren, as is only fitting, because your faith is greatly enlarged, and the love of each one of you all toward one another grows ever greater. To this end also we pray for you always that our God may count you worthy of your calling, and fulfill every desire for goodness and the work of faith with power.—It is God who is at work in you, both to will and to work for His good pleasure.

1 TH 1:3. Jn 6:29. Ja 2:17.—Gal 5:6.—Gal 6:8.—Eph 2:10.—
Titus 2:14. 2 Th 1:3,11.—Phil 2:13.

Where is the promise of His coming?

Enoch, in the seventh generation from Adam, prophesied, saying, Behold, the Lord came with many thousands of His holy ones, to execute judgment upon all.—Behold, He is coming with the clouds, and every eye will see Him, even those who pierced Him; and all the tribes of the earth will mourn over Him.

For the Lord Himself will descend from heaven with a shout, with the voice of the archangel, and with the trumpet of God; and the dead in Christ shall rise first. Then we who are alive and remain shall be caught up together with them in the clouds to meet the Lord in the air, and thus we shall always be with the Lord.

The grace of God has appeared, bringing salvation to all men, instructing us to deny ungodliness and worldly desires and to live sensibly, righteously and godly in the present age, looking for the blessed hope and the appearing of the glory of our great God and Savior, Christ Jesus.

2 PE 3:4. Jude 14,15.—Rev 1:7. 1 Th 4:16,17. Titus 2:11–13.

Let him rely on My protection, let him make peace with Me.

I know the plans that I have for you, declares the LORD, plans for welfare and not for calamity.—There is no peace for the wicked, says the LORD.

In Christ Jesus you who formerly were far off have been brought near by the blood of Christ. For He Himself is our peace.

For it was the Father's good pleasure for all the fulness to dwell in Him, and through Him to reconcile all things to Himself.—Christ Jesus; whom God displayed publicly as a propitiation in His blood through faith. This was to demonstrate His righteousness, because in the forebearance of God He passed over the sins previously committed . . . that He might be just and the justifier of the one who has faith in Jesus.—If we confess our sins, He is faithful and righteous to forgive us our sins and to cleanse us from all unrighteousness.

Trust in the LORD forever, for in God the LORD, we have an everlasting Rock.

IS 27:5. Jer 29:11.—Is 48:22. Eph 2:13,14. Col 1:19,20.—
Ro 3:24–26.—1 Jn 1:9. Is 26:4.

God has given us eternal life, and this life is in His Son.

Just as the Father has life in Himself, even so He gave to the Son also to have life in Himself. For just as the Father raises the dead and gives them life, even so the Son also gives life to whom He wishes.

I am the resurrection, and the life; he who believes in Me shall live even if he dies, and everyone who lives and believes in Me shall never die.—I am the good shepherd; the good shepherd lays down His life for the sheep. . . . I lay down My life that I may take it again. No one has taken it away from Me, but I lay it down on My own initiative. I have authority to lay it down, and I have authority to take it up again. This commandment I received from My Father.—No one comes to the Father, but through Me.—He who has the Son has the life; he who does not have the Son of God does not have the life.—You have died and your life is hidden with Christ in God. When Christ, who is our life, is revealed, then you also will be revealed with Him in glory.

1 JN 5:11. Jn 5:26,21. Jn 11:25,26.—Jn 10:11,17,18.—Jn 14:6.—
1 Jn 5:12.—Col 3:3,4.

If you are living according to the flesh, you must die; but if by the Spirit you are putting to death the deeds of the body, you will live.

Now the deeds of the flesh are evident, which are: immorality, impurity . . . and things like these, of which I forewarn you just as I have forewarned you that those who practice such things shall not inherit the kingdom of God. But the fruit of the Spirit is love, joy, peace, patience, kindness, goodness, faithfulness, gentleness, self-control; against such things there is no law. Now those who belong to Christ Jesus have crucified the flesh with its passions and desires. If we live by the Spirit, let us also walk by the Spirit.

The grace of God has appeared, bringing salvation to all men, instructing us to deny ungodliness and worldly desires and to live sensibly, righteously and godly in our present age, looking for the blessed hope and the appearing of the glory of our great God and Savior, Christ Jesus; who gave Himself for us, that He might redeem us from every lawless deed.

RO 8:13. Gal 5:19,21–25. Titus 2:11–14.

Then the commanders of the Philistines said, What are these Hebrews doing here?

If you are reviled for the name of Christ, you are blessed, because the Spirit of glory and of God rests upon you. By no means let any of you suffer as a murderer, or thief, or evildoer, or a troublesome meddler.

Do not let what is for you a good thing be spoken of as evil.—Keep your behavior excellent among the Gentiles.

Do not be bound together with unbelievers; for what partnership have righteousness and lawlessness, or what fellowship has light with darkness? . . . We are the temple of the living God. . . . Therefore, come out from their midst and be separate, says the Lord. And do not touch what is unclean.

You are a chosen race, a royal priesthood, a holy nation, a people for God's own possession, that you may proclaim the excellencies of Him who has called you out of darkness into His marvelous light.

1 SA 29:3. 1 Pe 4:14,15. Ro 14:16.—Pe 2:12. 2 Co 6:14,16,17.
1 Pe 2:9.

**The kindness of God our Savior and His love for mankind
appeared.**

I have loved you with an everlasting love.

By this the love of God was manifested in us, that God has sent
His only begotten Son into the world so that we might live
through Him. In this is love, not that we loved God, but that He
loved us and sent His Son to be the propitiation for our sins.

When the fulness of the time came, God sent forth His Son,
born of a woman, born under the Law, in order that He might
redeem those who were under the Law, that we might receive
the adoption as sons.—The Word became flesh, and dwelt among
us, and we beheld His glory, glory as of the only begotten from
the Father, full of grace and truth.—Great is the mystery of
godliness: He who was revealed in the flesh.

Since then the children share in flesh and blood, He Himself
likewise also partook of the same, that through death He might
render powerless him who had the power of death, that is, the
devil.

TITUS 3:4. Jer 31:3. 1 Jn 4:9,10. Gal 4:4,5.—Jn 1:14.—1 Ti 3:16.
Heb 2:14.

Thanks be to God for His indescribable gift!

Shout joyfully to the LORD, all the earth. Serve the LORD with
gladness; come before Him with joyful singing. Enter His gates
with thanksgiving, and His courts with praise. Give thanks to
Him; bless His name.—For a child will be born to us, a son will
be given to us; and the government will rest on His shoulders;
and His name will be called Wonderful Counselor, Mighty God,
Eternal Father, Prince of Peace.

He . . . did not spare His own Son, but delivered Him up for
us all.—He had one . . . a beloved son; he sent him.

Let them give thanks to the LORD for His lovingkindness, and
for His wonders to the sons of men! . . . Bless the LORD, O my soul;
and all that is within me, bless His holy name.

My soul exalts the Lord, and my spirit has rejoiced in God my
Savior.

2 CO 9:15. Ps 100:1,2,4.—Is 9:6. Ro 8:32.—Mk 12:6. Ps 107:21.—
Ps 103:1.

Be steadfast, immovable, always abounding in the work of the Lord.

Knowing that your toil is not in vain in the Lord.—As you therefore have received Christ Jesus the Lord, so walk in Him, having been firmly rooted and now being built up in Him and established in your faith, just as you were instructed, and overflowing with gratitude.—The one who endures to the end, it is he who shall be saved.—The seed in the good ground, these are the ones who have heard the word in an honest and good heart, and hold it fast, and bear fruit with perseverance.

In your faith you are standing firm.

We must work the works of Him who sent Me, as long as it is day; night is coming, when no man can work.

The one who sows to his own flesh shall from the flesh reap corruption, but the one who sows to the Spirit shall from the spirit reap eternal life. And let us not lose heart in doing good, for in due time we shall reap if we do not grow weary. So then, while we have opportunity, let us do good to all men, and especially to those who are of the household of faith.

1 CO 15:58. 1 Co 15:58.—Col 2:6,7.—Mt 24:13.—Lk 8:15.
2 Co 1:24. Jn 9:4. Gal 6:8–10.

He is able to save forever those who draw near to God through Him.

I am the way, and the truth, and the life; no one comes to the Father, but through Me.—There is salvation in no one else; for there is no other name under heaven that has been given among men, by which we must be saved.

My sheep hear My voice, and I know them, and they follow Me; and I give eternal life to them; and they shall never perish, and no one shall snatch them out of My hand.—He who began a good work in you will perfect it until the day of Christ Jesus. —Is anything too difficult for the LORD?

Now to Him who is able to keep you from stumbling, and to make you stand in the presence of His glory blameless with great joy, to the only God our Savior, through Jesus Christ our Lord, be glory, majesty, dominion and authority, before all time and now and forever. Amen.

HEB 7:25. Jn 14:6.—Ac 4:12. Jn 10:27,28.—Phil 1:6.—Gen 18:14.
Jude 24,25.

We look not at the things which are seen, but at the things which are not seen; for the things which are seen are temporal, but the things which are not seen are eternal.

Here we do not have a lasting city.—You have for yourselves a better possession and an abiding one.

Do not be afraid, little flock, for your Father has chosen gladly to give you the kingdom.

Now for a little while, if necessary, you have been distressed by various trials.—There the wicked cease from raging, and there the weary are at rest.

While we are in this tent, we groan, being burdened.—He shall wipe away every tear from their eyes; and there shall no longer be any death; there shall no longer be any mourning, or crying, or pain; the first things have passed away.

The sufferings of this present time are not worthy to be compared with the glory that is to be revealed to us.—For momentary, light affliction is producing for us an eternal weight of glory far beyond all comparison.

2 CO 4:18. Heb 13:14.—Heb 10:34. Lk 12:32. 1 Pe 1:6.—Job 3:17. 2 Co 5:4.—Rev 21:4. Ro 8:18.—2 Co 4:17.

He Himself is our peace.

God was in Christ reconciling the world to Himself, not counting their trespasses against them, and He has committed to us the word of reconciliation.—Through Him to reconcile all things to Himself, having made peace through the blood of His cross . . . and although you were formerly alienated and hostile in mind, engaged in evil deeds, yet He has now reconciled you in His fleshly body through death, in order to present you before Him holy and blameless and beyond reproach.—Having cancelled out the certificate of debt consisting of decrees against us and which was hostile to us; and He has taken it out of the way, having nailed it to the cross.—By abolishing in His flesh the enmity, which is the Law of commandments contained in ordinances, that in Himself He might make the two into one new man, thus establishing peace.

Peace I leave with you; My peace I give to you; not as the world gives, do I give to you. Let not your heart be troubled, nor let it be fearful.

EPH 2:14. 2 Co 5:19.—Col 1:20–22.—Col 2:14.—Eph 2:15. Jn 14:27.

Your sins are forgiven.

I will forgive their iniquity, and their sin I will remember no more.—Who can forgive sins but God alone?

I am the one who wipes out your transgressions for My own sake; and I will not remember your sins.—How blessed is he whose transgression is forgiven, whose sin is covered! How blessed is the man to whom the LORD does not impute iniquity. —Who is a God like Thee, who pardons iniquity?

God in Christ also has forgiven you.—The blood of Jesus His Son cleanses us from all sin. If we say that we have no sin, we are deceiving ourselves, and the truth is not in us. If we confess our sins, He is faithful and righteous to forgive us our sins and to cleanse us from all unrighteousness.

As far as the east is from the west, so far has He removed our transgressions from us.—Sin shall not be master over you, for you are not under law, but under grace. Having been freed from sin, you became slaves of righteousness.

MK 2:5. Jer 31:34.—Mk 2:7. Is 43:25.—Ps 32:1,3.—Mic 7:18.
Eph 4:32.—1 Jn 1:7–9. Ps 103:12.—Ro 6:14,18.

We wish to see Jesus.

O LORD, we have waited for Thee eagerly; Thy name, even Thy memory, is the desire of our souls.

The LORD is near to all who call upon Him, to all who call upon Him in truth.

Where two or three have gathered together in My name, there I am in their midst.—I will not leave you as orphans; I will come to you.—Lo, I am with you always, even to the end of the age.

Let us run with endurance the race that is set before us, fixing our eyes on Jesus, the author and perfecter of faith.

Now we see in a mirror dimly, but then face to face.—Having the desire to depart and be with Christ, for that is very much better.

Beloved, now we are children of God, and it has not appeared as yet what we shall be. We know that, when He appears, we shall be like Him, because we shall see Him just as He is. And every one who has this hope fixed on Him purifies himself, just as He is pure.

JN 12:21. Is 26:8. Ps 145:18. Mt 18:20.—Jn 14:18.—Mt 28:20.
Heb 12:1,2. 1 Co 13:12.—Phil 1:23. 1 Jn 3:2,3.

Understand what the will of the Lord is.

This is the will of God, your sanctification.—Yield now and be at peace with Him; thereby good will come to you.—This is eternal life, that they may know Thee the only true God, and Jesus Christ whom Thou hast sent.—We know that the Son of God has come, and has given us understanding, in order that we might know Him who is true, and we are in Him who is true, in His Son Jesus Christ. This is the true God and eternal life.

We have not ceased to pray for you and to ask that you may be filled with the knowledge of His will in all spiritual wisdom and understanding.—The God of our Lord Jesus Christ . . . give to you a spirit of wisdom and of revelation in the knowledge of Him. I pray that the eyes of your heart may be enlightened, so that you may know what is the hope of His calling, what are the riches of the glory of His inheritance in the saints, and what is the surpassing greatness of His power toward us who believe.

EPH 5:17. 1 Th 4:3.—Job 22:21.—Jn 17:3.—1 Jn 5:20. Col 1:9.—
Eph 1:17–19.

Draw near to God and He will draw near to you.

Enoch walked with God.—Do two men walk together unless they have made an appointment?—As for me, the nearness of God is my good.

The LORD is with you when you are with Him. And if you seek Him, He will let you find Him; but if you forsake Him, He will forsake you. In their distress they turned to the LORD God of Israel, and they sought Him, and He let them find Him.

I know the plans that I have for you, declares the LORD, plans for welfare and not for calamity to give you a future and a hope. Then you will call upon Me and come and pray to Me, and I will listen to you. And you will seek Me and find Me, when you search for Me with all your heart.

Brethren, we have confidence to enter the holy place by the blood of Jesus, by a new and living way which He inaugurated for us through the veil . . . and since we have a great priest over the house of God, let us draw near with a sincere heart in full assurance of faith.

JA 4:8. Gen 5:24.—Amos 3:3.—Ps 73:28. 2 Ch 15:2,4. Jer 29:11–13.
Heb 10:19–22.

Blameless in the day of our Lord Jesus Christ.

Although you were formerly alienated and hostile in mind, engaged in evil deeds, yet He has now reconciled you in His fleshly body through death, in order to present you before Him holy and blameless and beyond reproach—if indeed you continue in the faith firmly established and steadfast, and not moved away from the hope of the gospel.—That you may prove yourselves to be blameless and innocent, children of God above reproach in the midst of a crooked and perverse generation, among whom you appear as lights in the world.

Therefore, beloved, since you look for these things, be diligent to be found by Him in peace, spotless and blameless.—Sincere and blameless until the day of Christ.

Now to Him who is able to keep you from stumbling, and to make you stand in the presence of His glory blameless with great joy, to the only God our Savior, through Jesus Christ our Lord, be glory, majesty, dominion and authority, before all time and now and forever. Amen.

1 CO 1:8. Col 1:21–23.—Phil 2:15. 2 Pe 3:14.—Phil 1:10.
Jude 24,25.

He keeps the feet of His godly ones.

If we say that we have fellowship with Him and yet walk in the darkness, we lie and do not practice the truth; but if we walk in the light as He Himself is in the light, we have fellowship with one another, and the blood of Jesus His Son cleanses us from all sin.—He who has bathed needs only to wash his feet, but is completely clean.

I have directed you in the way of wisdom; I have led you in upright paths. When you walk, your steps will not be impeded; and if you run, you will not stumble. Do not enter the path of the wicked, and do not proceed in the way of evil men. Avoid it, do not pass by it; turn away from it and pass on. Let your eyes look directly ahead, and let your gaze be fixed straight in front of you. Watch the path of your feet, and all your ways will be established. Do not turn to the right nor to the left; turn your foot from evil.

The Lord will deliver me from every evil deed, and will bring me safely to His heavenly kingdom; to Him be the glory forever and ever. Amen.

1 SA 2:9. 1 Jn 1:6,7.—Jn 13:10. Pr 4:11,12,14,15,25–27. 2 Ti 4:18.

The LORD your God carried you, just as a man carries his son, in all the way which you have walked, until you came to this place.

I bore you on eagles' wings, and brought you to Myself.—In His love and in His mercy He redeemed them; and He lifted them and carried them all the days of old.—Like an eagle that stirs up its nest, that hovers over its young, He spread His wings and caught them, He carried them on His pinions. The LORD alone guided him.

Even to your old age, I shall be the same, and even to your graying years I shall bear you! I have done it, and I shall carry you; and I shall bear you, and I shall deliver you.—For such is God, our God forever and ever; He will guide us until death.

Cast your burden upon the LORD, and He will sustain you.— Do not be anxious for your life, as to what you shall eat, or what you shall drink; nor for your body, as to what you shall put on. . . . For your heavenly Father knows that you need all these things.

Thus far the LORD has helped us.

DEU 1:31. Ex 19:4.—Is 63:9.—Deu 32:11,12. Is 46:4.—Ps 48:14. Ps 55:22.—Mt 6:25,32. 1 Sa 7:12.

Very much of the land remains to be possessed.

Not that I have already obtained it, or have already become perfect, but I press on in order that I may lay hold of that for which also I was laid hold of by Christ Jesus.

You are to be perfect.—Applying all diligence, in your faith supply moral excellence, and in your moral excellence, knowledge; and in your knowledge, self-control, and in your self-control, perseverance, and in your perseverance, godliness; and in your godliness, brotherly kindness, and in your brotherly kindness, Christian love.

I pray, that your love may abound still more and more in real knowledge and all discernment.

Eye has not seen and ear has not heard, and which have not entered the heart of man, all that God has prepared for those who love Him. For to us God revealed them through the Spirit.

There remains . . . a rest for the people of God.—Your eyes will see the king in his beauty; they will behold a far-distant land.

JOS 13:1. Phil 3:12. Mt 5:48.—2 Pe 1:5–7. Phil 1:9. 1 Co 2:9,10. Heb 4:9.—Is 33:17.

READINGS FOR SPECIAL OCCASIONS

Birthday
Marriage
Times of Anxiety
Affliction
Sickness
Bereavement
Unwelcome News
Separation
Reunion
Recovery from Sickness
Convalescence
Disappointed Hopes
Days of Prosperity
Success
Birth of a Child
Jubilee
Long Life
Thanksgiving
End of the Journey

FOR A BIRTHDAY

The LORD bless you, and keep you.

May the LORD bless you . . . He who made heaven and earth. —God our Father.—God, who richly supplies us with all things to enjoy.

Your heavenly Father knows that you need all these things.— The Father Himself loves you.

No good thing does He withhold from those who walk uprightly.—He stores up sound wisdom for the upright; He is a shield to those who walk in integrity.—How blessed are those who observe His testimonies, who seek Him with all their heart.

He who keeps you will not slumber. Behold, He who keeps Israel will neither slumber nor sleep.—The LORD will be your confidence, and will keep your foot from being caught.—The steadfast of mind Thou wilt keep in perfect peace, because he trusts in Thee.

The Lord of peace Himself continually grant you peace in every circumstance.

NUM 6:24. Ps 134:3.—2 Th 2:16.—1 Ti 6:17. Mt 6:32.—Jn 16:27. Ps 84:11.—Pr 2:7.—Ps 119:2. Ps 121:3,4.—Pr 3:26.—Is 26:3. 2 Th 3:16.

FOR A BIRTHDAY

The LORD your God is with you wherever you go.

Every place on which the sole of your foot treads, I have given it to you. . . . no man will be able to stand before you all the days of your life. Just as I have been with Moses, I will be with you; I will not fail you or forsake you.—The land into which you are about to cross to possess it, a land of hills and valleys . . . a land for which the LORD your God cares; the eyes of the LORD your God are always on it, from the beginning even to the end of the year.—You are God's field.—Created in Christ Jesus for good works, which God prepared beforehand, that we should walk in them.

How great is Thy goodness, which Thou hast stored up for those who fear Thee. . . . Thou dost hide them in the secret place of Thy presence from the conspiracies of man; Thou dost keep them secretly in a shelter from the strife of tongues.—He who dwells in the shelter of the Most High will abide in the shadow of the Almighty.

JOS 1:9. Jos 1:3,5.—Deu 11:11,12.—1 Co 3:9.—Eph 2:10. Ps 31:19,20.—Ps 91:1.

Jesus also was invited, and His disciples, to the wedding.

Let marriage be held in honor among all.—The LORD God said, It is not good for the man to be alone.—Everything created by God is good, and nothing is to be rejected, if it is received with gratitude; for it is sanctified by means of the word of God and prayer.

It is the blessing of the LORD that makes rich, and He adds no sorrow to it.—God, who richly supplies us with all things to enjoy. —Who crowns you with lovingkindness and compassion; who satisfies your years with good things.

Christ also loved the church and gave Himself up for her.— You are not your own.

Brethren, the time has been shortened, so that . . . those who have wives should be as though they had none . . . and those who rejoice, as though they did not rejoice . . . and those who use the world, as though they did not make full use of it; for the form of this world is passing away.—Set your mind on the things above.

JN 2:2. Heb 13:4.—Gen 2:18.—1 Ti 4:4,5. Pr 10:22.—1 Ti 6:17.—
Ps 103:4,5. Eph 5:25.—1 Co 6:19. 1 Co 7:29,30,31.—Col 3:2.

I will walk within my house in the integrity of my heart.

As for me and my house, we will serve the LORD.

Seek first His kingdom and His righteousness; and all these things shall be added to you.—No servant can serve two masters . . . You cannot serve God and Mammon.

As a fellow-heir of the grace of life, so that your prayers may not be hindered.—Two are better than one . . . for if either of them falls, the one will lift up his companion.—Let us consider how to stimulate one another to love and good deeds.

Husbands, love your wives.—Encourage the young women to love their husbands.—Not provoked.—Be kind to one another, tender-hearted, forgiving each other, just as God in Christ also has forgiven you.

Our adequacy is from God.—I am the LORD your God, who upholds your right hand, who says to you, Do not fear, I will help you.

PS 101:2. Jos 24:15. Mt 6:33.—Lk 16:13. 1 Pe 3:7.—Ec 4:9,10.—
Heb 10:24. Col 3:19.—Titus 2:4.—1 Co 13:5.—Eph 4:32. 2 Co 3:5.—
Is 41:13.

FOR TIMES OF ANXIETY

Nor do we know what to do, but our eyes are on Thee.

O God, it is Thou who dost know my folly, and my wrongs are not hidden from Thee.—Teach me to do Thy will, for Thou art my God.—O LORD, lead me in Thy righteousness . . . make Thy way straight before me.—My times are in Thy hand.

If any of you lacks wisdom, let him ask of God, who gives to all men generously and without reproach, and it will be given to him. But let him ask in faith.—Who is among you that fears the LORD . . . that walks in darkness and has no light? Let him trust in . . . the LORD and rely on his God.

When my anxious thoughts multiply within me, Thy consolations delight my soul.—Why are you in despair, O my soul? And why have you become disturbed within me? Hope in God.

He (Jesus) said to them, Why are you so timid? How is it that you have no faith?—Faith is . . . the conviction of things not seen.

2 CH 20:12. Ps 69:5.—Ps 143:10.—Ps 5:8.—Ps 31:15. Ja 1:5,6.—
Is 50:10. Ps 94:19.—Ps 42:5. Mk 4:40.—Heb 11:1.

FOR TIMES OF ANXIETY

Do not fear, I will help you.

Come to Me, all who are weary and heavy laden, and I will give you rest.—For as many as may be the promises of God, in Him they are yes . . . our Amen.

He will call upon Me, and I will answer him; I will be with him in trouble.—I have done it, and I shall carry you; and I shall bear you, and I shall deliver you.—I will be with you.

Be anxious for nothing, but in everything by prayer and supplication with thanksgiving let your requests be made known to God. And the peace of God, which surpasses all comprehension, shall guard your hearts and your minds in Christ Jesus.

I will instruct you and teach you in the way which you should go; I will counsel you with My eye upon you.—I will never desert you, nor will I ever forsake you.—Lo, I am with you always, even to the end of the age.

Do not be afraid; I am the first and the last.

IS 41:13. Mt 11:28.—2 Co 1:20. Ps 91:15.—Is 46:4.—Is 43:2.
Phil 4:6,7. Ps 32:8.—Heb 13:5.—Mt 28:20. Rev 1:17.

AFFLICTION

Save me, O God, for the waters have threatened my life.

My Father, if it is possible, let this cup pass from Me; yet not as I will, but as Thou wilt.—Being in agony.—Jesus wept.

Surely our griefs He Himself bore, and our sorrows He carried.—We do not have a high priest who cannot sympathize with our weaknesses, but one who has been tempted in all things as we are, yet without sin. Let us therefore draw near with confidence to the throne of grace, that we may receive mercy and may find grace to help in time of need.

He cares for you.—I have called you by name; you are Mine! When you pass through the waters, I will be with you; and through the rivers, they will not overflow you.—I will never desert you, nor will I ever forsake you.

Though He slay me, I will hope in Him.—My flesh and my heart may fail; but God is the strength of my heart and my portion forever.

PS 69:1. Mt 26:39.—Lk 22:44.—Jn 11:35. Is 53:4.—Heb 4:15,16.
1 Pe 5:7.—Is 43:1,2.—Heb 13:5. Job 13:15.—Ps 73:26.

AFFLICTION

I, even I, am He who comforts you.

His compassions never fail. For He does not afflict willingly, or grieve the sons of men.—What I do you do not realize now; but you shall understand hereafter.—Behold, these are the fringes of His ways; and how faint a word we hear of Him!

The Lord is full of compassion and is merciful.—The Father of mercies and God of all comfort; who comforts us in all our affliction so that we may be able to comfort those who are in any affliction with the comfort with which we ourselves are comforted by God.

He has sent me to bind up the brokenhearted.—A man of sorrows, and acquainted with grief.—I will not leave you as orphans.

Another Helper . . . that is the Spirit of truth.

The eternal God is a dwelling place, and underneath are the everlasting arms.—As one whom his mother comforts, so I will comfort you.

IS 51:12. Lam 3:22,33.—Jn 13:7.—Job 26:14. Ja 5:11.—2 Co 1:3,4.
Is 61:1.—Is 53:3.—Jn 14:18. Jn 14:16,17. Deu 33:27.—Is 66:13.

FOR SICKNESS

Lord, behold, he whom You love is sick.

Surely our griefs He Himself bore, and our sorrows He carried. —He Himself took our infirmities, and carried away our diseases. —He, being compassionate.—Just as a father has compassion on his children, so the LORD has compassion on those who fear Him. For He Himself knows our frame.

Who shall separate us from the love of Christ? Shall tribulation, or distress?—Whom the Lord loves He disciplines. . . . All discipline for the moment seems not to be joyful, but sorrowful; yet to those who have been trained by it, afterwards it yields the peaceful fruit of righteousness.—We know that God causes all things to work together for good to those who love God.

He has said to me, My grace is sufficient for you, for power is perfected in weakness. Most gladly, therefore, I will rather boast about my weaknesses, that the power of Christ may dwell in me.

JN 11:3. Is 53:4.—Mt 8:17.—Ps 78:38.—Ps 103:13,14. Ro 8:35.— Heb 12:6,11.—Ro 8:28. 2 Co 12:9.

FOR SICKNESS

Be gracious to me, O LORD, for I am pining away; heal me, O LORD.

When my heart is faint; lead me to the rock that is higher than I.—He gives strength to the weary, and to him who lacks might He increases power.—The LORD is the defense of my life.

Be not far from me, for trouble is near.—Thou art near, O LORD.—Thou hast heard my voice. . . . Thou didst draw near when I called on Thee; Thou didst say, Do not fear!—A very present help in trouble.

O LORD, I am oppressed, be my security.—A battered reed He will not break off.—Even though I walk through the valley of the shadow of death, I fear no evil; for Thou art with me.—Underneath are the everlasting arms.

May our Lord Jesus Christ Himself and God our Father, who has loved us and given us eternal comfort and good hope by grace, comfort and strengthen your hearts.

PS 6:2. Ps 61:2.—Is 40:29.—Ps 27:1. Ps 22:11.—Ps 119:151.— Lam 3:56,57.—Ps 46:1. Is 38:14.—Mt 12:20.—Ps 23:4.—Deu 33:27. 2 Th 2:16,17.

Father, I desire that they also whom Thou hast given Me be with Me where I am.

He will not return again to his house, nor will his place know him any more.

While we are at home in the body we are absent from the Lord . . . Prefer rather to be absent from the body and to be at home with the Lord.—I am hard pressed . . . having the desire to depart and be with Christ, for that is very much better.—Whether we live or die, we are the Lord's.

You have for yourselves a better possession and an abiding one. —It has not appeared as yet what we shall be. We know that, when He appears, we shall be like Him, because we shall see Him just as He is.—Now we see in a mirror dimly, but then face to face.—I shall behold Thy face in righteousness; I will be satisfied with Thy likeness when I awake.

Thus we shall always be with the Lord. Therefore comfort one another with these words.

JN 17:24. Job 7:10. 2 Co 5:6,8.—Phil 1:23.—Ro 14:8. Heb 10:34.—
1 Jn 3:2.—1 Co 13:12.—Ps 17:15. 1 Th 4:17,18.

Asleep.

Fallen asleep.—Those who have fallen asleep in Jesus.—Asleep in Christ.

Our friend . . . has fallen asleep. . . . Jesus had spoken of his death.—They went on stoning Stephen. . . . he fell asleep.—He gives to His beloved even in his sleep.

Our Savior Christ Jesus, who abolished death.—That through death He might . . . deliver those who through fear of death were subject to slavery all their lives.—That by the grace of God He might taste death for every one.

Death is swallowed up in victory. O death, where is your victory? O death, where is your sting? The sting of death is sin, and the power of sin is the law; but thanks be to God, who gives us the victory through our Lord Jesus Christ. Therefore, my beloved brethren, be steadfast, immovable, always abounding in the work of the Lord, knowing that your toil is not in vain in the Lord.

1 TH 4:13. 1 Co 15:6.—1 Th 4:14.—1 Co 15:18. Jn 11:11,13.—
Ac 7:59,60.—Ps 127:2. 2 Ti 1:10.—Heb 2:14,15.—Heb 2:9.
1 Co 15:54–58.

UNWELCOME NEWS

Shall we indeed accept good from God and not accept adversity?

He will not fear evil tidings; his heart is steadfast, trusting in the LORD.—What I do you do not realize now; but you shall understand hereafter.—We know that God causes all things to work together for good to those who love God, to those who are called according to His purpose.—A messenger came to Job and said, The oxen were plowing and the donkeys feeding beside them, and the Sabeans attacked and took them. . . . Another also came and said, The fire of God fell from heaven and burned up the sheep and the servants and consumed them. . . . another also came and said, Your sons and your daughters were eating and drinking wine in their oldest brother's house, and behold, a great wind came from across the wilderness and struck the four corners of the house, and it fell on the young people and they died; and I alone have escaped to tell you.—It is the LORD; let Him do what seems good to Him.

JOB 2:10. Ps 112:7.—Jn 13:7.—Ro 8:28.—Job 1:14,15,16,18,19.—
1 Sa 3:18.

UNWELCOME NEWS

Teach Thou me what I do not see.

A messenger came to David, saying, The hearts of the men of Israel are with Absalom. And David said . . . Arise and let us flee, for otherwise none of us shall escape from Absalom.—And the king said to Zadok, Return the ark of God to the city. If I find favor in the sight of the LORD, then He will bring me back again, and show me both it and His habitation. But if He should say thus, I have no delight in you, behold, here I am, let Him do to me as seems good to Him. And David went up the ascent of the Mount of Olives, and wept as he went.—Weeping may last for the night, but a shout of joy comes in the morning.—I will make an everlasting covenant with you, according to the faithful mercies shown to David.—The LORD blessed the latter days of Job more than his beginning.—Beloved, do not be surprised at the fiery ordeal among you, which comes upon you for your testing, as though some strange thing were happening to you; but to the degree that you share the sufferings of Christ, keep on rejoicing.

JOB 34:32. 2 Sa 15:13,14.—2 Sa 15:25,26,30.—Ps 30:5.—Is 55:3.—
Job 42:12.—1 Pe 4:12,13.

SEPARATION

Mizpah.

The LORD watch between you and me when we are absent one from the other.—Pray.... And I urge you all the more to do this, that I may be restored to you the sooner.—But we, brethren, having been bereft of you for a short while—in person, not in spirit—were all the more eager with great desire to see your face. For we wanted to come to you—I, Paul, more than once—and yet Satan thwarted us.—Who shall separate us from the love of Christ? For I am convinced that neither death, nor life, nor angels, nor principalities, nor things present, nor things to come, nor powers, nor height, nor depth, nor any other created thing, shall be able to separate us from the love of God, which is in Christ Jesus our Lord.—He Himself has said, I will never desert you, nor will I ever forsake you, so that we confidently say, The Lord is my helper, I will not be afraid. What shall man do to me? —Lo, I am with you always, even to the end of the age.

GEN 31:49. Gen 31:49.—Heb 13:18,19.—1 Th 2:17,18.— Ro 8:35,38,39.—Heb 13:5,6.—Mt 28:20.

SEPARATION

I will not leave you as orphans; I will come to you.

Like cold water to a weary soul, so is good news from a distant land.—They went up from Egypt, and came to the land of Canaan to their father Jacob. And they told him, saying, Joseph is still alive, and indeed he is ruler over all the land of Egypt. But he was stunned, for he did not believe them. When they told him all the words of Joseph that he had spoken to them, and when he saw the wagons that Joseph had sent to carry him, the spirit of their father Jacob revived. Then Israel said, It is enough; my son Joseph is still alive. I will go and see him before I die.—And now, behold, I know that you all, among whom I went about preaching the kingdom, will see my face no more. And when he had said these things, he knelt down and prayed with them all. And they began to weep aloud and embraced Paul, and repeatedly kissed him, grieving especially over the word which he had spoken, that they should see his face no more. And they were accompanying him to the ship.

JN 14:18. Pr 25:25.—Gen 45:25–28.—Ac 20:25,36–38.

REUNION

I will see you again.

And Israel said to Joseph, I never expected to see your face, and behold, God has let me see your children as well.—When the LORD brought back the captive ones of Zion, we were like those who dream. Then our mouth was filled with laughter, and our tongue with joyful shouting; then they said among the nations, the LORD has done great things for them. The LORD has done great things for us; we are glad.... He who goes to and fro weeping, carrying his bag of seed, shall indeed come again with a shout of joy, bringing his sheaves with him.—When they had arrived and gathered the church together, they began to report all things that God had done with them and how He had opened a door of faith to the Gentiles.—I go to prepare a place for you. And if I go and prepare a place for you, I will come again, and receive you to Myself; that where I am, there you may be also. —For yet in a very little while, He who is coming will come, and will not delay.

JN 16:22. Gen 48:11.—Ps 126:1,2,3,6.—Ac 14:27.—Jn 14:2,3.—
Heb 10:37.

REUNION

Sorrow and sighing will flee away.

Jacob lifted his eyes and looked, and behold, Esau was coming, and four hundred men with him. . . . Then Esau ran to meet him and embraced him, and fell on his neck and kissed him, and they wept. . . . And Jacob said . . . if now I have found favor in your sight, then take my present from my hand, for I see your face as one sees the face of God, and you have received me favorably. —Joseph made himself known to his brothers. . . . And he said, I am your brother Joseph, whom you sold into Egypt. And now do not be grieved or angry with yourselves, because you sold me here; for God sent me before you to preserve life. . . . Now you must tell my father of all my splendor in Egypt . . . and you must hurry and bring my father down here.—Peter was kept in the prison, but prayer for him was being made fervently by the church to God. . . . he described to them how the Lord had led him out of the prison.

IS 35:10. Gen 33:1,4,10.—Gen 45:1,4,5,13.—Ac 12:5,17.

RECOVERY FROM SICKNESS

I, the LORD, am your healer.

I shall not die, but live, and tell of the works of the LORD. The LORD has disciplined me severely, but He has not given me over to death.—Bless the LORD, O my soul, and forget none of His benefits; who pardons all your iniquities; who heals all your diseases.—In those days Hezekiah became mortally ill. . . . Then Hezekiah . . . prayed to the LORD, and said, Remember now, O LORD, I beseech thee, how I have walked before Thee in truth and with a whole heart, and have done what is good in Thy sight. And Hezekiah wept bitterly. Then the word of the LORD came to Isaiah, saying, Go and say to Hezekiah, Thus says the LORD, the God of your father David, I have heard your prayer, I have seen your tears; behold, I will add fifteen years to your life.—A leper came to Him, and bowed down to Him, saying, Lord, if You are willing, You can make me clean. And stretching out His hand, He touched him, saying, I am willing; be cleansed. And immediately his leprosy was cleansed.

EX 15:26. Ps 118:17,18.—Ps 103:2,3.—Is 38:1–5.—Mt 8:2,3.

RECOVERY FROM SICKNESS

The prayer offered in faith will restore the one who is sick.

This sickness is not unto death, but for the glory of God.—He knows the way I take; when He has tried me, I shall come forth as gold.—I thought it necessary to send to you Epaphroditus, my brother and fellow-worker and fellow-soldier, who is also your messenger and minister to my need; because he was longing for you all and was distressed because you had heard that he was sick. For indeed he was sick to the point of death, but God had mercy on him, and not on him only but also on me, lest I should have sorrow upon sorrow. . . . Hold . . . him in high regard; because he came close to death for the work of Christ, risking his life to complete what was deficient in your service to me.—And he has said to me, My grace is sufficient for you, for power is perfected in weakness. Most gladly, therefore, I will rather boast about my weaknesses, that the power of Christ may dwell in me.

JA 5:15. Jn 11:4.—Job 23:10.—Phil 2:25,26,27,29,30.—2 Co 12:9.

CONVALESCENCE

Rest in the LORD and wait patiently for Him.

And He said to them, Come away by yourselves to a lonely place and rest a while.—Then they came to Elim where there were twelve springs of water and seventy date palms, and they camped there beside the waters.—And he lay down and slept under a juniper tree; and behold, there was an angel touching him, and he said to him, Arise, eat. Then he looked and behold, there was at his head a bread cake baked on hot stones, and a jar of water. So he ate and drank and lay down again. And the angel of the LORD came again a second time and touched him and said, Arise, eat, because the journey is too great for you. So he arose and ate and drank, and went in the strength of that food forty days and forty nights to Horeb, the mountain of God.—The LORD is my shepherd, I shall not want. He makes me lie down in green pastures; He leads me beside quiet waters. He restores my soul.

PS 37:7. Mk 6:31.—Ex 15:27.—1 Ki 19:5–8.—Ps 23:1–3.

CONVALESCENCE

The LORD is your shade on your right hand.

Do you not know? Have you not heard? The everlasting God, the LORD, the creator of the ends of the earth does not become weary or tired. His understanding is inscrutable. He gives strength to the weary, and to him who lacks might He increases power. Though youths grow weary and tired, and vigorous young men stumble badly, yet those who wait for the LORD will gain new strength; they will mount up with wings like eagles, they will run and not get tired, they will walk and not become weary.—Your youth is renewed like the eagle. Just as a father has compassion on his children, so the LORD has compassion on those who fear Him. For He Himself knows our frame; He is mindful that we are but dust.—We have this treasure in earthen vessels, that the surpassing greatness of the power may be of God and not from ourselves. . . . For momentary, light affliction is producing for us an eternal weight of glory.

PS 121:5. Is 40:28–31.—Ps 103:5,13,14.—2 Co 4:7,17.

DISAPPOINTED HOPES

In the day of adversity consider.

If you are slack in the day of distress, your strength is limited. —Behold, I have refined you, but not as silver; I have tested you in the furnace of affliction.—Through many tribulations we must enter the kingdom of God.—Though the fig tree should not blossom, and there be no fruit on the vines, though the yield of the olive should fail, and the fields produce no food, though the flock should be cut off from the fold, and there be no cattle in the stalls, yet I will exult in the LORD, I will rejoice in the God of my salvation.—Blessed be the God and Father of our Lord Jesus Christ, the Father of mercies and God of all comfort; who comforts us in all our affliction so that we may be able to comfort those who are in any affliction with the comfort with which we ourselves are comforted by God.—We also exult in our tribulations.—I have learned to be content in whatever circumstances I am.—Your sorrow will be turned to joy.

EC 7:14. Pr 24:10.—Is 48:10.—Ac 14:22.—Hab 3:17,18.—
2 Co 1:3,4.—Ro 5:3.—Phil 4:11.—Jn 16:20.

DISAPPOINTED HOPES

Tribulation brings about perseverance.

Why are you in despair, O my soul? And why have you become disturbed within me? Hope in God, for I shall again praise Him for the help of His presence.—I was envious of the arrogant, as I saw the prosperity of the wicked. . . . When I pondered to understand this, it was troublesome in my sight, until I came into the sanctuary of God; then I perceived their end.—Cast your burden upon the LORD, and He will sustain you.—At my first defense no one supported me, but all deserted me; may it not be counted against them. But the Lord stood with me, and strengthened me . . . and I was delivered out of the lion's mouth.—For it is not an enemy who reproaches me, then I could bear it . . . but it is you, a man my equal, my companion and my familiar friend. We who had sweet fellowship together, walked in the house of God in the throng.—He does not fail.

RO 5:3. Ps 42:5.—Ps 73:3,16,17.—Ps 55:22.—2 Ti 4:16,17.—
Ps 55:12,13,14.—Zep 3:5.

DAYS OF PROSPERITY

In the day of prosperity be happy.

The LORD was with Joseph, so he became a successful man.—The LORD be magnified, who delights in the prosperity of His servant.—How blessed is the man who does not walk in the counsel of the wicked, nor stand in the path of sinners, nor sit in the seat of scoffers! But his delight is in the law of the LORD, and in His law he meditates day and night. And he will be like a tree firmly planted by streams of water, which yields its fruit in its season, and its leaf does not wither; and in whatever he does, he prospers.—This book of the law shall not depart from your mouth, but you shall meditate on it day and night, so that you may be careful to do according to all that is written in it; for then you will make your way prosperous, and then you will have success.—The LORD was with him; wherever he went he prospered.—And every work which he began . . . seeking his God, he did with all his heart and prospered.

EC 7:14. Gen 39:2.—Ps 35:27.—Ps 1:1,2,3.—Jos 1:8.—2 Ki 18:7.—
2 Ch 31:21.

DAYS OF PROSPERITY

If God is for us, who is against us?

Beloved, I pray that in all respects you may prosper and be in good health, just as your soul prospers.—On the first day of every week let each one of you put aside and save, as he may prosper.—Bring the whole tithe into the storehouse, so that there may be food in My house, and test Me now in this, says the LORD of hosts, if I will not open for you the windows of heaven, and pour out for you a blessing until there is no more need.—Both riches and honor come from Thee, and Thou dost rule over all.—Solomon sat on the throne of the LORD as king instead of David his father; and he prospered.—Seek first His kingdom and His righteousness; and all these things shall be added to you.—Do not lay up for yourselves treasures upon earth, where moth and rust destroy, and where thieves break in and steal; but lay up for yourselves treasures in heaven . . . for where your treasure is, there will your heart be also.

RO 8:31. 3 Jn 2.—1 Co 16:2.—Mal 3:10.—1 Ch 29:12.—
1 Ch 29:23.—Mt 6:33.—Mt 6:19-21.

If riches increase, do not set your heart upon them.

You shall remember the Lord your God, for it is He who is giving you power to make wealth.—The blessing of the Lord that makes rich, and He adds no sorrow to it.—Let not a rich man boast of his riches; but let him who boasts boast of this, that he understands and knows Me, that I am the Lord.—Wealth certainly makes itself wings.—Instruct those who are rich in this present world not to be conceited or to fix their hope on the uncertainty of riches, but on God, who richly supplies us with all things to enjoy.—And I have also given you what you have not asked, both riches and honor, so that there will not be any . . . like you all your days.—Riches are not forever.—Give me neither poverty nor riches, feed me with the food that is my portion.—Honor the Lord from your wealth, and from the first of all your produce; so your barns will be filled with plenty, and your vats will overflow with new wine.

PS 62:10. Deu 8:18.—Pr 10:22.—Jer 9:23,24.—Pr 23:5.—1 Ti 6:17.—
1 Ki 3:13.—Pr 27:24.—Pr 30:8.—Pr 3:9,10.

Whatever He says to you, do it.

Apart from Me you can do nothing.—And when He had finished speaking, He said to Simon, Put out into the deep water and let down your nets for a catch. And Simon answered and said, Master, we worked hard all night and caught nothing, but at your bidding I will let down the nets. And when they had done this, they enclosed a great quantity of fish; and their nets began to break; and they signaled to their partners in the other boat, for them to come and help them. And they came, and filled both of the boats, so that they began to sink. But when Simon Peter saw that, he fell down at Jesus' feet, saying, Depart from me, for I am a sinful man, O Lord! For amazement had seized him and all his companions because of the catch of fish which they had taken.—Therefore, my beloved brethren, be steadfast, immovable, always abounding in the work of the Lord, knowing that your toil is not in vain in the Lord.

JN 2:5. Jn 15:5.—Lk 5:4–9.—1 Co 15:58.

THE BIRTH OF A CHILD

**For this boy I prayed, and the LORD has given me my petition
which I asked of Him.**

Behold, children are a gift of the LORD; the fruit of the womb
is a reward.—A little boy will lead them.—Train up a child in the
way he should go, even when he is old he will not depart from
it.—For I have chosen him, in order that he may command his
children and his household after him to keep the way of the
LORD by doing righteousness and justice.—Your children like
olive plants around your table.—Taking a child, He stood him in
the midst of them; and taking him in His arms, He said to them,
Whoever receives one child like this in My name is receiving Me;
and whoever receives Me is not receiving Me, but Him who sent
Me.—Jesus . . . said . . . Permit the children to come to Me; do not
hinder them; for the kingdom of God belongs to such as these.
—See that you do not despise one of these little ones, for I say
to you, that their angels in heaven continually behold the face of
My Father who is in heaven.

1 SA 1:27. Ps 127:3.—Is 11:6.—Pr 22:6.—Gen 18:19.—Ps 128:3.—
Mk 9:36,37.—Mk 10:14.—Mt 18:10.

THE BIRTH OF A CHILD

Thanks be to God for His indescribable gift!

By this the love of God was manifested in us, that God has sent
His only begotten Son into the world so that we might live
through Him.—And she gave birth to her firstborn son; and she
wrapped Him in cloths, and laid Him in a manger, because there
was no room for them in the inn. And in the same region there
were some shepherds . . . keeping watch over their flock by
night. And an angel of the Lord suddenly stood before them, and
the glory of the Lord shone around them; and they were terribly
frightened. And the angel said to them, Do not be afraid; for
behold, I bring you good news of a great joy which shall be for
all the people; for today in the city of David there has been born
for you a Savior, who is Christ the Lord. And this will be a sign
for you: you will find a baby wrapped in cloths, and lying in a
manger. And suddenly there appeared with the angel a multitude of the heavenly host praising God, and saying, Glory to God
in the highest, and on earth peace among men with whom He
is pleased.

2 CO 9:15. 1 Jn 4:9.—Lk 2:7–14.

A JUBILEE

You shall thus consecrate the fiftieth year.

And proclaim a release through the land to all its inhabitants. It shall be a jubilee for you, and each of you shall return to his own property, and each of you shall return to his family.—You shall know the truth, and the truth shall make you free. If therefore the Son shall make you free, you shall be free indeed.—You shall remember all the way which the Lord your God has led you.—He found him in a desert land, and in the howling waste of a wilderness; He encircled him, He cared for him, He guarded him as the pupil of His eye.—How blessed is he whose help is the God of Jacob, whose hope is in the Lord his God.—Who redeems your life from the pit; who crowns you with lovingkindness and compassion.—I will sing to the Lord as long as I live; I will sing praise to my God while I have my being. Let my meditation be pleasing to Him; as for me, I shall be glad in the Lord.

LEV 25:10. Lev 25:10.—Jn 8:32,36.—Deu 8:2.—Deu 32:10.—
Ps 146:5.—Ps 103:4.—Ps 104:33,34.

A JUBILEE

You shall have the fiftieth year as a jubilee.

It is a jubilee; it shall be holy to you. . . . On this year of jubilee each of you shall return to his own property. . . . The land, moreover, shall not be sold permanently, for the land is Mine.—You shall sound a horn all through your land.—Rejoice in the Lord always; again I will say, rejoice! . . . It was for freedom that Christ set us free; therefore keep standing firm and do not be subject again to a yoke of slavery.—Jesus Christ is the same yesterday and today, yes and forever.—I will extol Thee, my God, O King; and I will bless Thy name forever and ever. Every day I will bless Thee. . . . Great is the Lord, and highly to be praised; and His greatness is unsearchable. One generation shall praise Thy works to another, and shall declare Thy mighty acts. They shall eagerly utter the memory of Thine abundant goodness, and shall shout joyfully of Thy righteousness.—Praise the Lord! . . . Praise Him for His mighty deeds; praise Him according to His excellent greatness.

LEV 25:11. Lev 25:12–13,23.—Lev 25:9.—Phil 4:4.—Gal 5:1.—
Heb 13:8.—Ps 145:1,2,3,4,7.—Ps 150:1,2.

LONG LIFE

Wisdom is with aged men, with long life is understanding.

As for the days of our life, they contain seventy years, or if due to strength, eighty years, yet their pride is but labor and sorrow; for soon it is gone and we fly away. We have finished our years like a sigh.—Even to your old age, I shall be the same, and even to your graying years I shall bear you! I have done it, and I shall carry you; and I shall bear you, and I shall deliver you.—The honor of old men is their gray hair.—How blessed is the man who finds wisdom, and the man who gains understanding. For its profit is better than the profit of silver, and its gain than fine gold. She is more precious than jewels; and nothing you desire compares with her. Long life is in her right hand; in her left hand are riches and honor.—From childhood you have known the sacred writings which are able to give you the wisdom that leads to salvation through faith which is in Christ Jesus.

JOB 12:12. Ps 90:10,9.—Is 46:4.—Pr 20:29.—Pr 3:13–16.—2 Ti 3:15.

LONG LIFE

They will still yield fruit in old age.

He who dwells in the shelter of the Most High will abide in the shadow of the Almighty. . . . With a long life I will satisfy him, and let him behold My salvation.—Honor your father and your mother, that your days may be prolonged in the land which the LORD your God gives you.—You shall rise up before the gray-headed, and honor the aged, and you shall revere your God; I am the LORD.—By loving the LORD your God, by obeying His voice, and by holding fast to Him; for this is your life and the length of your days.—You shall have a full and just weight; you shall have a full and just measure, that your days may be prolonged in the land.—Trust in the LORD with all your heart, and do not lean on your own understanding. In all your ways acknowledge Him, and He will make your paths straight.—The path of the righteous is like the light of dawn, that shines brighter and brighter until the full day.

PS 92:14. Ps 91:1,16.—Ex 20:12.—Lev 19:32.—Deu 30:20.—
Deu 25:15.—Pr 3:5,6.—Pr 4:18.

THANKSGIVING

They cried out to the L<small>ORD</small> in their trouble; He saved them out of their distresses. Let them give thanks to the L<small>ORD</small> for His lovingkindness, and for His wonders to the sons of men!

Were there not ten cleansed? But the nine—where are they? —Forget none of His benefits.—God, who answered me in the day of my distress.

I sought the L<small>ORD</small>, and He answered me, and delivered me from all my fears.—I love the L<small>ORD</small>, because He hears my voice and my supplications. Because He has inclined His ear to me, therefore I shall call upon Him as long as I live.—My heart trusts in Him, and I am helped; therefore my heart exults, and with my song I shall thank Him.

Call upon Me in the day of trouble; I shall rescue you, and you will honor Me. He who offers a sacrifice of thanksgiving honors Me.

Always giving thanks for all things in the name of our Lord Jesus Christ.

PS 107:19,21. Lk 17:17.—Ps 103:2.—Gen 35:3. Ps 34:4.— Ps 116:1,2.—Ps 28:7. Ps 50:15,23. Eph 5:20.

THANKSGIVING

Those who hopefully wait for Me will not be put to shame.

Did I not say to you, if you believe, you will see the glory of God?

Daniel, servant of the living God, has your God, whom you constantly serve, been able to deliver you? . . . No injury whatever was found on him, because he had trusted in his God.

I prayed, and the L<small>ORD</small> has given me my petition which I asked of Him. My heart exults in the L<small>ORD</small>.—Come and hear, all who fear God, and I will tell of what He has done for my soul. Blessed be God, who has not turned away my prayer, nor His lovingkindness from me.—To Thee, O God of my fathers, I give thanks and praise, for Thou hast given me wisdom and power.

Thou dost rule the swelling of the sea; when its waves rise.— He caused the storm to be still, so that the waves of the sea were hushed . . . So he guided them to their desired haven. Let them give thanks to the L<small>ORD</small> for His lovingkindness, and for His wonders to the sons of men!—How blessed is the man who takes refuge in Him!

Is 49:23. Jn 11:40. Dan 6:20,23. 1 Sa 1:27; 2:1.—Ps 66:16,20.— Dan 2:23. Ps 89:9.—Ps 107:29-31.—Ps 34:8.

THE END OF THE JOURNEY

With Thy counsel Thou wilt guide me, and afterward receive me to glory.

In Thy lovingkindness Thou hast led the people whom Thou hast redeemed; in Thy strength Thou hast guided them to Thy holy habitation. . . . Thou wilt bring them and plant them in the mountain of Thine inheritance, the place, O LORD, which Thou hast made for Thy dwelling, the sanctuary, O LORD, which Thy hands have established.—Not one word of all the good words which the LORD your God spoke concerning you has failed; all have been fulfilled for you, not one of them has failed.—The God who has been my shepherd all my life to this day.—In Thy presence is fulness of joy; in Thy right hand there are pleasures forever.—Surely goodness and lovingkindness will follow me all the days of my life, and I will dwell in the house of the LORD forever.—Now Lord, Thou dost let Thy bond-servant depart in peace, according to Thy word; for my eyes have seen Thy salvation.

PS 73:24. Ex 15:13,17.—Jos 23:14.—Gen 48:15.—Ps 16:11.—
Ps 23:6.—Lk 2:29,30.

THE END OF THE JOURNEY

In My Father's house are many dwelling places.

So teach us to number our days, that we may present to Thee a heart of wisdom.—For in this way the entrance into the eternal kingdom of our Lord and Savior Jesus Christ will be abundantly supplied to you.—In Him we have redemption through His blood, the forgiveness of our trespasses, according to the riches of His grace.—For we know in part, and we prophesy in part; but when the perfect comes, the partial will be done away. . . . For now we see in a mirror dimly, but then face to face; now I know in part, but then I shall know fully just as I also have been fully known.—He shall wipe away every tear from their eyes; and there shall no longer be any death; there shall no longer be any mourning, or crying, or pain; the first things have passed away. —Your eyes will see the king in his beauty.—Behold, I tell you a mystery; we shall not all sleep, but we shall all be changed.— We shall be like Him, because we shall see Him just as He is.

JN 14:2. Ps 90:12.—2 Pe 1:11.—Eph 1:7.—1 Co 13:9,10,12.—
Rev 21:4.—Is 33:17.—1 Co 15:51.—1 Jn 3:2.

LIST OF DAILY TEXTS
ARRANGED IN BIBLE ORDER

MORNING READINGS

GENESIS
13:10,11	Mar. 22
15:6	Mar. 24
16:13	Jan. 29
21:1	Apr. 24
22:14	Mar. 10
24:63	Mar. 30
28:16	May 2
32:26	Apr. 5
32:28	May 31
39:3	June 8
41:52	Mar. 2

EXODUS
2:9	June 20
3:7	Aug. 24
12:11	June 2
12:43	July 2
13:7	Sept. 3
19:6	July 16
25:21,22	June 18
28:12	May 23
28:36	Aug. 26
30:23,25	Nov. 5
33:14	July 12
34:29	Oct. 4

LEVITICUS
1:3,4	Apr. 22
1:4	Mar. 17
4:12	Feb. 17
16:22	Oct. 2
17:11	May 29
20:8	Feb. 21

NUMBERS
6:24	Mar. 11
6:25,26	Mar. 12
6:27	Sept. 28
10:33	June 24
23:19	Aug. 20
31:23	June 12
33:55	Jan. 31

DEUTERONOMY
1:31	Dec. 31
3:24	Aug. 18
8:10	Feb. 7
12:9	Jan. 4
13:17	Apr. 20
17:16	Feb. 4
18:18	Apr. 18
29:29	June 15
32:4	Sept. 26
33:25	Jan. 28

JOSHUA
1:18	Mar. 28

RUTH
3:18	Sept. 4

1 SAMUEL
7:3	Apr. 2
12:24	Apr. 29

1 CHRONICLES
4:10	Feb. 2
4:10	June 26
22:5	Aug. 16

EZRA
9:9	Sept. 23

NEHEMIAH
5:19	Jan. 7
8:10	Aug. 14
9:17	Oct. 9

ESTHER
5:2	Aug. 30

JOB
5:8	Dec. 3
19:25	June 28
23:10	Sept. 30
28:12	Dec. 4

PSALMS
9:10	Jan. 8
18:18	Apr. 23
22:11	Oct. 11
25:9	Oct. 7
25:12	Feb. 22
27:14	Sept. 2
31:19	May 25
31:22	Apr. 16
40:17	Nov. 14
48:14	Jan. 22
50:15	Oct. 5
50:23	Apr. 17
51:2	May 19
59:9	Oct. 15
60:4	Jan. 9
63:5,6	Apr. 14
65:1	Jan. 11
65:4	Nov. 29
66:2	Dec. 14
73:28	Sept. 24
78:53	Nov. 11
80:18	Dec. 17
85:10	May 6
89:16	Oct. 17
89:19	Nov. 9
90:17	Jan. 6
92:5	Nov. 17
99:1	Oct. 26
104:34	Sept. 22
107:7	Jan. 3
107:8	Nov. 7
108:1	Oct. 22
112:4	Dec. 19
119:18	Sept. 18
119:25	Jan. 15
119:57	Aug. 21
119:71	Dec. 5
119:105	Aug. 27
119:130	Mar. 20

PROVERBS
1:33	Nov. 23
2:6	Feb. 19
2:8	Mar. 6
3:5,6	Mar. 3
3:9	Apr. 13
3:12	Aug. 6
3:13	Sept. 20
3:26	Oct. 19
4:18	Aug. 8
8:34	Nov. 1
10:19	Apr. 11
11:18	Mar. 27
16:20	Aug. 29
20:9	Feb. 15
21:2	Sept. 16

SONG
1:3	Feb. 16
1:5	Apr. 10
2:6	Apr. 26
4:7	Aug. 9
5:16	Oct. 29
7:10	July 13

ISAIAH
9:6	Jan. 20
26:3	Jan. 13
27:5	Dec. 23
27:8	Nov. 18
32:2	Dec. 1
38:14	Mar. 5
38:14	Mar. 18
38:17	Mar. 8
38:17	Jan. 17
42:10	Jan. 2
43:1	Apr. 9
51:1	Aug. 25
51:12	Sept. 14
53:10	May 8
53:11	Feb. 20
54:5	Mar. 7
57:18	Sept. 12
59:1	May 4
59:16	Oct. 28
60:20	Dec. 21
62:4	Nov. 26
64:1	July 29

JEREMIAH
15:20	July 11
17:17	Feb. 18
31:3	Aug. 23
32:39	Sept. 10
60:34	Apr. 15

LAMENTATIONS
3:26	Oct. 30
3:31,32	Aug. 12
3:40	Feb. 26
3:41	Sept. 6

EZEKIEL
1:26	Feb. 13
20:19	May 17
36:37	Feb. 24

DANIEL
5:27	Sept. 8
10:12	Oct. 13

HOSEA
14:9	Nov. 3

JONAH
2:4	Oct. 24
4:2	July 17

MICAH
7:8	Nov. 20

NAHUM
1:7	May 27

ZEPHANIAH
3:15	Dec. 12
3:17	June 6

HAGGAI
2:4	Feb. 3
2:9	June 4

ZECHARIAH
3:4	July 9
4:6	Oct. 31

MALACHI
3:16	Feb. 11
3:17	Feb. 12

MATTHEW
1:21	Apr. 25
3:15	Feb. 14
4:1	July 7
5:48	May 3
6:10	July 15
6:31,32	May 5
7:20	Nov. 19
8:17	Oct. 27
10:24	July 10
12:20	Sept. 17
12:34	July 14
24:6	May 7
25:13	June 3
25:14,15	Mar. 26
25:34	Mar. 29
28:20	Oct. 25

MARK
2:5	Dec. 28

LUKE
1:49	July 19
1:50	Aug. 3
1:53	Sept. 9
8:21	Nov. 24
11:34	Feb. 10
12:15	Oct. 23
15:13	June 10
15:20	June 11
16:25	Feb. 9
17:10	June 5
18:1	June 7

JOHN
1:16	Oct. 21
1:29	Apr. 28
3:16	Feb. 28
5:26	May 18
6:37	Nov. 21
7:37	Sept. 13
7:46	June 9
10:3	July 18
10:7	Apr. 19
10:10	Feb. 5
10:29	Dec. 10
13:1	Dec. 16
13:23	July 4
14:16,17	June 23
14:26	Aug. 7
14:27	May 22
14:28	Jan. 14
15:2	Jan. 21
15:4	June 13
15:15	Feb. 8
17:15	Aug. 10
17:16	July 20
17:17	Nov. 16
17:22	Nov. 27

NEHEMIAH (cont.)
21:3	Dec. 9
27:1	Feb. 29

MORNING READINGS

19:30	Aug. 4	4:4	July 27	3:3	June 22	**JAMES**	
19:34	Oct. 18	4:18	Dec. 27	3:4	Nov. 6	1:4	Sept. 25
		5:19	Oct. 12	4:6	July 6	2:26	Nov. 28
ACTS		5:21	Dec. 7			4:7	Feb. 25
3:26	Mar. 19	6:10	Apr. 7	**1 THESSALONIANS**		4:14	Mar. 16
20:19	Jan. 19	7:10	Nov. 12	1:3	Dec. 22	5:16	Aug. 17
				5:8	Nov. 8		
ROMANS		**GALATIANS**		5:15	Nov. 2	**1 PETER**	
1:1	May 16	5:13	Dec. 8	5:23	Jan. 10	1:6	Nov. 4
3:1	July 21	5:22	Mar. 1			1:8	Feb. 1
3:22	Jan. 25	5:22	Apr. 1	**2 THESSALONIANS**		1:15	Aug. 19
5:5	Jan. 23	5:22	May 1	3:16	Nov. 30	2:21	June 21
5:14	Jan. 18	5:22	June 1			5:6	Sept. 27
5:16	Aug. 31	5:22	July 1	**1 TIMOTHY**		5:10	Sept. 19
6:4	Aug. 5	5:22	Aug. 1	1:14	Feb. 6		
6:10	July 22	5:22	Sept. 1	2:5	Mar. 13	**2 PETER**	
6:11	Feb. 27	5:22	Oct. 1	2:8	May 13	3:8,9	Apr. 3
6:14	Sept. 15	6:2	Dec. 15	4:16	May 20		
6:18	Nov. 25			6:17	Mar. 9	**1 JOHN**	
7:22	Oct. 20	**EPHESIANS**				1:9	July 8
8:3	Apr. 12	1:4	Dec. 20	**2 TIMOTHY**		2:5	Apr. 30
8:13	Dec. 24	3:15	Oct. 10	2:1	Dec. 13	2:20	Dec. 2
8:17	July 3	4:30	May 24	2:3	July 31	3:2	June 25
8:28	Sept. 21	5:2	July 28			3:5	Jan. 27
12:2	Sept. 11	5:15,16	June 16	**TITUS**		3:8	May 10
12:11	Oct. 16	5:17	Dec. 29	2:10	Mar. 14	3:14	July 25
12:12	July 24	5:25,26	Nov. 13	3:4	Dec. 25	3:16	Sept. 29
12:12	Sept. 7	6:10	May 21			4:7	May 12
14:7	Aug. 22			**HEBREWS**		4:16	July 5
14:9	Oct. 14	**PHILIPPIANS**		2:10	Mar. 15	5:3	June 29
14:16	Dec. 11	2:13	Dec. 6	2:14	Aug. 11		
		3:10	May 14	4:3	Jan. 5	**JUDE**	
1 CORINTHIANS		3:13,14	Jan. 1	4:11	May 30	20	Nov. 22
1:5	Apr. 8	3:20	May 28	4:16	Dec. 18	25	Jan. 12
1:8	Dec. 30	4:1	Apr. 21	7:25	Apr. 6		
1:9	Nov. 15	4:5	Jan. 24	11:1	May 9	**REVELATION**	
7:29	Apr. 27	4:6	June 17	11:8	July 26	1:5	Oct. 3
12:12	Sept. 5	4:19	Mar. 31	11:16	Aug. 13	1:17	Apr. 4
15:24	July 23			12:1,2	Jan. 30	3:2	Mar. 21
15:34	May 11	**COLOSSIANS**		12:14	June 19	3:19	June 30
15:58	Dec. 26	1:10	Nov. 10	12:24	Feb. 23	4:8	Mar. 23
		1:19	Jan. 16	13:5	Mar. 25	6:17	June 27
2 CORINTHIANS		3:1	July 30	13:6	Oct. 8	12:10	Aug. 28
1:5	June 14	3:2	Mar. 4	13:13,14	Jan. 26	13:8	Aug. 2
				13:20	May 26	19:6	Oct. 6
				13:20,21	Aug. 15	21:4	May 15

EVENING READINGS

Moody Press, a ministry of the Moody Bible Institute, is designed for education, evangelization and edification. If we may assist you in knowing more about Christ and the Christian life, please write us without obligation to:

Moody Press, c/o MLM, Chicago, Illinois 60610.